# THE
# BURMA
# ROAD

# THE
# BURMA
# ROAD

The Epic Story of One of World War II's

Most Remarkable Endeavours

## DONOVAN WEBSTER

MACMILLAN

First published 2003 by Farrar, Straus and Giroux, New York

First published in Great Britain 2004 by Macmillan
an imprint of Pan Macmillan Ltd
Pan Macmillan, 20 New Wharf Road, London N1 9RR
Basingstoke and Oxford
Associated companies throughout the world
www.panmacmillan.com

ISBN 1 4050 4146 3

1 3 5 7 9 8 6 4 2

A CIP catalogue record for this book is available from
the British Library.

Printed and bound in Great Britain by
Mackays of Chatham plc, Chatham, Kent

*For my parents*

Grateful acknowledgment is made to the following for permission to reprint images: to the Hoover Library, Stanford University, for the U.S. Army Signal Corps images of General Joseph W. Stilwell at his desk, of Stilwell pinning the Legion of Merit medal on Generalissimo Chiang Kai-shek, and of Stilwell in Burma, 1944; to the National Archives, for the U.S. Army Signal Corps images of General Claire Lee Chennault and Staff Sergeant Howard M. Artnegard, of the Lisu tribal woman, of the guard with the Flying Tiger P-40 aircraft, of Gordon S. Seagrave and his nurses, of Staff Sergeant Roy A. Matsumoto, of Corporal James Fletcher and the Kachin V-Force, of Sergeant John J. Busaites, of the airfield at Myitkyina, of the C-47 transport plane, and of the first convoy along the Ledo-Burma Road; and to the National Archives, also, for the Office of War Information images of Major N'Hpan Naw, and of the bulldozer rescuing a supply truck; and to the Imperial War Museum, London, for the images of General William Slim and Major General Orde C. Wingate, of Generals Wingate and Slim together, of Admiral Lord Mountbatten and Stilwell, and of Mountbatten addressing the troops.

# THE
# BURMA
# ROAD

# Prologue

WHEN I MEET THEM at their reunions and in their homes, the Old Soldiers warn me not even to go looking.

To a man, every one of them believes the road they hacked across India's steep Himalayan passes and down through the steaming jungles of Burma into China during World War II has disappeared, destroyed by time. They say the route itself exists only as a memory, that the road's two stringy lanes—now more than sixty years old—certainly have been devoured by landslides and rain and swampy jungle vegetation.

But now, step after step—and in the cool of a mid-January morning—my feet are moving up the same gravel pike the Old Soldiers have cautioned me about. I'm walking between walls of jungle that rise from the roadside like green tapestries a hundred feet tall; setting off for the places where the Old Soldiers' friends died, their own sweat fell, and—perhaps more than anything—where the nightmares that still find them were seared into place so firmly that, when they're jolted awake in their beds at night, they can still taste the acrid gunpowder smoke and feel the jungle's leeches beneath their damp cotton uniforms.

In the morning light, the pavement ahead crooks hard right, twisting back on itself and disappearing over the brow of the next forested hill. Here, near the road's beginning, just a few miles northeast of the crowded Indian ghetto of Ledo, the road's original gravel and asphalt is pitted and

3

broken. Its shoulders disintegrate at the forest's edges, and in some places potholes stretch across the pavement's width, leaving it striped with breaks.

Still—contrary to what the Old Soldiers believe—the road exists. Thirty feet wide and snaking ahead beneath mature trees dripping with vines, it bends uphill toward green-draped mountains. It slides past barracks for Indian army border patrols and the jungle huts of tribal natives, its course run by motorbikes, buses full of coalfield workers, and trucks hauling illegal harvests of teakwood, despite such cutting having been outlawed years ago. This place is so far at the world's edge, it seems, nobody cares what goes on here.

FRIDAY MORNING, ten o'clock. Above me, inside a cloudless sky, the sun is clearing the treetops, its yellow footfall dapples the roadbed. The air is moist and sixty-five degrees. Jungle mists spill from the forest, their faint fog softening the sunlight around me. Through the surrounding trees, gray parakeets dart among branches. An oxcart creaks past, carrying sections of a teak trunk lashed to its bed. One of India's sacred bulls wanders the road just ahead: it's white furred—with one of its horns painted glossy green, the other yellow—and it seems supremely unconcerned by the vehicles that swerve to avoid it.

I stretch my back, having spent last night on a plywood bed in the Hotel Raj, a toilet-and-cold-shower-down-the-hall cell off a cobblestone bazaar in Ledo's crowded downtown. All night the locals came out to stare at the hotel's second-floor balcony from the plaza below, shouting greetings to me, the visitor.

"Hello, American!" they'd yell. Then they'd stand on the cobblestones and gaze upward, expecting me to step onto the narrow balcony and wave. Across the alley, in a small and dingy restaurant, a fire flickered in the mud oven, heating curries and illuminating the restaurant's soot-blackened walls. A handful of kids shouted to me as they played netless badminton in the alley. For a half-hour, my only response to the welcome squad below curled from the air vents of my room, as smoke from burning mosquito coils drifted into the night sky.

Finally, realizing I couldn't ignore them and expect much peace, I went downstairs and played badminton with a twelve-year-old girl named

Djela. She was four feet tall and skinny, her shiny black hair cropped at her jaw. She had dark skin and deep black eyes, and she was all smiles and "Where you come from?"

Djela and her family were also new to town, she said. Six months earlier, they'd moved into a room up the street from Bangladesh. Djela's father, she said, had relocated to Ledo to be a laborer in the town's coal mine. Then she handed me one of the two broken-stringed badminton racquets she was carrying, and we began to smack a little plastic shuttlecock up and down the alley over an imaginary net.

After a few minutes, I thanked Djela for the game. Then I walked through the spice shop that was the Hotel Raj's ground floor—watched like a zoo animal the whole time—and returned to my second-floor room.

"Hello, American" continued to ring in the alley for hours after I'd slid tight the bolt on my door, climbed beneath my mosquito net, and blown out the candle that was my room's only light.


NOW, IN THE MORNING, I stare up the road, then lift my pack to continue on. Wooden telephone and electric poles from World War II—glass insulators still in place—hopscotch the pavement, their webs of wires long gone. Back in late 1942, when this road was first being laid by American engineer battalions, no Allied commander or soldier would have believed that, over the coming twenty-seven months, as they chiseled this track over mountains and slapped it across swamps at a mile per day, the Japanese would devil them for most every foot. Before the road was complete, Japanese snipers and artillery shells (and disease and accidents) would kill more than one American soldier for each of the road's eleven hundred miles.

Back at the road's beginnings in 1942 and '43, they also wouldn't have believed that for every Allied combat casualty in the war's China-Burma-India theater of operations, fourteen more soldiers would be evacuated sick or dead from malaria, dysentery, cholera, infections, jungle rot, and a previously unknown infection called brush typhus. They wouldn't have believed that, before the road's journey was over, the theater's beloved but irascible commander—the American General "Vinegar Joe" Stilwell— would be removed; that their eccentric and death-defying special-forces leader—Lt. General Orde Wingate of the British army—would be killed in a shocking accident; and that, perhaps worst of all, the road they fought for and died to build would be deemed obsolete even as it was being finished. Before he was done there, Stilwell could do little more than lean on the scrap of dog-Latin he'd made famous as his motto: *Illegitimati non Carborundum.* He translated it as "Don't let the bastards grind you down."

I CROSS A STREAM CULVERT: its concrete is painted a humidity-stained brown; the creek beneath braids off through the vines. This road goes by many names—the Ledo Road, the Stilwell Road, Pick's Pike, the Man-a-Mile Road, the Uncle Sam Highway—but most often it is called, simply, the Burma Road. And while historians may anoint it as one of the great engineering feats of World War II, the Old Soldiers have asserted—again and again—that it stands among the most forgotten routes in modern history. And more than anything, they believe it should remain that way.

Just ahead, the road passes from India's state of Assam and into one called Arunachal Pradesh at the little border town of Jairanpur. After that, it turns back on itself and climbs between the two four-thousand-foot ridges of the Patkai Range, entering into Myanmar—the former Burma—at the second peak's summit on Pangsau Pass.

I crest one last hill, and ahead—spilling across the jungle valley—squat the low shelters of Jairanpur. Goats and cats mill around. People walk from hut to hut. There are perhaps twenty structures. At the town's center, where a steel, World War II–era Bailey bridge crosses the muddy Namchik River, sits Jairanpur's checkpoint. Just before the bridge, on the road's right shoulder, waits the security office: a weathered house of dark teakwood with an encircling porch. Sentries wearing khaki uniforms and blue berets doze in chairs, their machine guns leaned against porch railings.

One of the soldiers, a heavyset guy about six feet tall and wearing mirrored aviator sunglasses, stands when he sees me walking toward him. A whorl of white-feathered chickens and chicks scatters across the pavement. Directly across from the checkpoint, on the road's left shoulder and set back a few feet, is an open-walled gatehouse, complete with a machine gun on a tripod swivel behind a wall of sandbags. A strip of bullets has been fed into the gun's breech from a steel bin on the ground. As I approach, a machine gunner, who'd been dozing on a wooden table in the gatehouse's shade, moves behind his weapon. He reaches for the gun-arming lever on the rifle's right side, and—pulling the handle back with a mechanical *cha-ching*—cocks it.

Between the two houses sits the gate itself: a long pole of bamboo, painted alternating stripes of red and white. It has been lowered to block the road like a lever; a large stone has been lashed inside a nest of wires on the pole's end nearest the gatehouse, to act as a counterweight.

"Hello," I say to the sentry in sunglasses. I smile.

He does not smile back. "Hello," he says. "Your papers please?"

I hand over my passport and visa. He smiles now, then disappears inside the house. I can hear him hailing someone on the radio. Frequencies hum and whine. There's static. "Yes," he's saying. "That's correct. He's American."

MUCH OF NORTHEAST INDIA is still off-limits to foreigners. Portions of it have been restricted from visitation since the British colonized India in the early nineteenth century. Now, fifty-six years after the end of World War II and fifty-four years after India's independence from Britain, the northeast is slowly opening to outsiders for the first time in modern memory. Unlike the majority of India, the northeast is still largely tribal. Across the area's isolated valleys, at least 105 different languages are spoken, and for decades a few of the larger tribes have been warring with India's central government for their own freedom. Consequently—and citing my personal safety as their rationale—I have not been granted the Restricted Area Permit (or RAP) I need to travel these last eighteen miles of the Burma Road inside India.

I watch the chickens and run my hand over the paint of the gate pole. I point at the muddy, twenty-foot-wide river. "Any fish in there?" I ask another of the sentries. He's a young guy, who remains tilted back in his chair, his black-booted feet on the porch rail, his assault rifle now resting across his belly. He's smaller than the sunglasses guy, maybe twenty-five years old, and skinny inside his khakis.

"Sure," he says. "Once in a while, we see a big one." He lifts his hands, holds them eighteen inches apart, and considers the air between his palms.

Sunglasses reemerges. He smiles. "Happy birthday, Mr. Webster," he says.

I'd forgotten. Today is my birthday. Sunglasses must have gotten that off my passport.

"Mr. Webster . . ." he waits a long beat. "What are you doing here?"

FOR THE NEXT TEN MINUTES, I explain to Sunglasses that I'm attempting to travel the eleven-hundred-mile length of the Ledo-Burma Road. In India, I hope to reach the India-Myanmar border just eighteen miles up the road, at the mountaintop called Pangsau Pass. After that, I'll fly to Rangoon and travel to the other side of Pangsau's border from inside Myanmar. I understand that I can't cross into Myanmar from India today—since the India-Myanmar border ranks among the most tightly controlled boundaries on earth—but one of my aims at Pangsau is to inform both sets of sentries at the border that I'll be returning from the other side, so no one will be upset when they see me next month.

Ultimately, I tell Sunglasses, my trip along the Burma Road will stretch from India's rain forests and Himalayan foothills, down through the steamy lowland jungles inside Myanmar, and ending after a climb up onto the Tibetan Plateau in southwest China at the city of Kunming. I'll be walking, hitching rides, and hiring cars where I need to, but mostly I'll be looking for people who were here during the war, to help flesh out the epic—and now largely forgotten—story of World War II's longest active battlefront. The trip should take about three months.

Sunglasses smiles again. He removes his shades with theatrical slowness. Though his hair is dark and his skin a typically Indian mocha color, his eyes are a startling pale gray. They're disconcerting.

"I only want to *see* the Pangsau Pass," I tell him. "So I can say I've been there."

I lift my backpack and lug it onto the planked floor of the porch—leaning it against a wall. The porch is shady, and I realize the sun has already grown hot this morning. "I'll leave my things here," I say. "This will be the insurance I'll return."

I reach into one of the cargo pockets on my trouser leg and the younger sentry jumps in alarm: he swings around in his chair, planting his feet on the planked porch floor and pointing his rifle at me.

"Just getting cigarettes," I say. "Anyone smoke?"

I extract an unopened pack of Marlboros, placing the box on the porch rail as a not-so-subtle bribe. This has worked in the past.

Sunglasses shakes his head. "No thank you," he says. He smiles again.

"You understand," he continues, "that the state of Arunachal Pradesh is an area restricted to tourist movement?"

I nod. "Yes."

"You understand that you do not have a Restricted Area Permit attached to your visa?"

I nod.

"Well," he says, "then you see the problem. To travel inside Arunachal Pradesh—to transit the Ledo Road to Pangsau Pass—you need the RAP. If you don't have one, there is nothing I can do. I cannot issue one. I cannot turn a blind eye. I must send you back."

I tell the soldier about my contacts at the Indian Embassy in Washington, about the six months required for each RAP's approval investigation; about how I was told by embassy officials that—even with this six-months wait—my reapplication would likely be declined since I work as a journalist. I tell him that officials inside the embassy even suggested I come to this border post and try my luck with the guards. Especially since I'll only be going inside Arunachal Pradesh for—what?—half a day; traveling roughly eighteen miles of road that transect about six miles of jungle as the crow flies.

"I'd be happy to spend time in Jairanpur, to show I'm serious," I say. I point at my bag. "I've got provisions for a week. Fresh coffee. Rice and beans. A bottle of Scotch. I could hang my hammock over there—" I point across the road, toward a pair of trees near the gatehouse, where the machine gunner is still waiting, hard-eyed, behind his weapon.

Sunglasses smiles again. "Mr. Webster, you are welcome to stay on this side of the border," he says. "But the laws are clear. You cannot enter Arunachal Pradesh. You cannot go to Pangsau without an RAP. My orders, in fact, are to shoot anyone who breaks this law. Shoot them first, then investigate why they were illegally crossing the border after they are immobilized. This is very serious. Do you understand?"

I nod and turn to look at the river. I have come halfway around the world to get here; traveled six days inside India in crowded, backbreaking vehicles, slept on plywood beds and lived on soupy lentils while the locals stared at me like a circus act, and now—just a few jungled miles short of Pangsau Pass—an instantly erectable fence of flying bullets is keeping me from my destination.

"Of course," Sunglasses says, "you could go back to Delhi and reapply for an RAP. As you say, the prospects are not good. It could take weeks or months for approval, but you could try. I am sorry I cannot be of more help."

"You could escort me to Pangsau yourself," I suggest, trying to smile breezily while pleading. "After you finish today's shift. I would be happy to pay for your time. I have come such a long way. And to be frustrated so close to my goal . . ."

"No," he says. "The laws are very clear. As I say, I am sorry."

NEXT TO THE CHECKPOINT sits a small, shed-roofed plywood building, a combination restaurant and grocery that likely evolved through symbiosis with the guards. Sunglasses shouts toward the building. He goes to the edge of the porch, cranes his neck around, and looks inside to where a small man is sitting on a log stool. In a native language, Sunglasses says something and the man stands and begins to walk behind the shop's counter. An old woman of the local Naga tribe, her face tattooed with a faint blue line running from her hairline down between her eyes and between the small black buttons emplanted in the fleshy lobe of each nostril, peers out the shop's door. I wave to her; she ducks back inside.

Sunglasses turns to me. "Please understand, Mr. Webster, these rules cannot be bent," he says. "There is a lot of smuggling here. There are rebels. These rules exist for very good reasons. I would not enjoy giving the order to shoot you, but that is the law." He smiles again.

"Now," he continues, "I have ordered us some tea. Do you take yours with milk, sugar, or both?"

"Both," I say.

Sunglasses shouts to the man inside the grocery again, and I crane my neck out the other side of the porch, trying to see past the town and up the valley toward Pangsau Pass. I find only jungle and mountains; even the road disappears after its first bend. Eighteen lousy miles.

The tea arrives. We find chairs on the porch, then make small talk, which only increases my frustration. Moments ago, this man was telling me—in extremely unambiguous terms—that he would shoot me if I didn't act as he wanted. Now he's giving me tea and pale yellow disks of sugar cookies while I show him snapshots of my wife and children.

Maybe the old soldiers are right. Maybe I shouldn't have come looking

for this road. After all, the situation in front of me has grown solidly surreal, its civility barely veiling Sunglasses's threat just beneath. Sipping my
tea, I understand that, were I to take off running toward Pangsau Pass, they
would gun me down in the street on my birthday. Bullets or friendship?
Impediment or assistance? My forward progress has been stopped, but I
am reluctant to retreat. Argument is impossible—and anyway, further av-
enues for negotiating are now blocked by this show of frontier manners.

And then, sitting in the shade of this dusty porch, frustrated near my
limit in the morning's rising heat, I break into a smile. I realize that, more
than anyone, Stilwell would understand.

# Chapter 1

THE JUNGLE WAS EVERYWHERE. Its vines grabbed their ankles as they walked. Its steamy heat sapped their strength. And every time they reached the summit of yet another six-thousand-foot mountain, they could only stare across the quilted green rain forest below and let their gazes lift slowly toward the horizon. Ahead of them, looming in the distance, they could finally see the next hogback ridge between them and safety. They would, of course, have to climb over that one, too.

They were a ragged line of 114 tired and hungry people—Americans, British, Indians, and Burmese; civilians and soldiers alike—and they were now on the run from several thousand Japanese troops that were clawing through the jungle after them, only fifteen or twenty miles behind.

The year was 1942. It was May, always the steamiest month in south Asia's nation of Burma, where—in the late spring—daily temperatures surpass one hundred degrees and the humidity hovers near 100 percent, day and night.

And yet, each morning at dawn, they awoke, packed their few possessions, and pushed on along a network of trails heading roughly to the northwest toward India. At the column's front—leading the way—was a short, spindly, nearly blind man of fifty-nine years. He wore canvas puttees laced around his ankles, and a battered, flat-brimmed World War I campaign hat crimped on his head, covering his thatch of scrubby gray hair.

Ahead of him, he carried a stumpy, black-steel Thompson submachine gun at the ready. With each step—despite his somewhat feeble appearance—the man's movements were quick and nimble. And despite being a three-star general in the U.S. Army and the commanding American officer in World War II's China theater of operations, he wore no insignias or badges of rank on his government-issue khakis.

His name was Lt. General Joseph W. Stilwell—though he was better known to his troops as "Vinegar Joe"—and at the moment he was in full retreat from Burma, hurrying overland toward free India as two divisions of imperial Japanese soldiers pounded after him in pursuit. Although Stilwell was a career soldier, Burma was his first combat command—and he'd had the job for just three months. During that time, since his arrival in late February 1942, he had watched the situation around him skid from delicate to disastrous.

Earlier that very week, Stilwell and his closest aides and officers had stayed behind in central Burma after a roomy C-47 transport aircraft had arrived to whisk them away to safety in India. Believing he would be abandoning members of his staff—plus several divisions of Nationalist Chinese troops under his command in Burma—were he flown to India in retreat, Stilwell, with characteristic resolve, loaded the transport with as many officers and headquarters personnel as it could hold, then flatly declined the assistance for himself, informing the pilots that he "preferred to walk."

As the flight departed—leaving behind Stilwell, a hard corps of advisers, and those without authority to board—the general described his plan. He and those who remained would travel north, where they would join thousands of Chinese troops under his command in the safety of northern Burma. But even as Stilwell was laying out his strategy, fast-invading tendrils of the Japanese infantry were encircling him and his group from the south, the east, and the northeast. In a matter of days, these enemy forces—plus a string of vehicle breakdowns caused by Burma's rutted, dry-mud roads—left Stilwell and his group cut off from the Chinese and without transportation of any kind. Stilwell and his crew were on their own. The only way out, Stilwell understood, was to walk. He and his group would have to hack their way to safety in India across 140 miles of mountains and jungles, with the Japanese chasing them all the way.

————

ON THE EVENING of May 6, 1942, Stilwell sent one last radio message to headquarters in India:

> Heading for Homalin and Imphal with party of one hundred. Includes H.Q. Group, Seagrave's Surgical Unit and strays.
>
> We are armed, have food and map, and are now on foot fifty miles west of Indaw.
>
> No occasion for worry. Chinese troops coming to India on this general route.
>
> Control has entirely passed to small units in this area. Hopeless to try to handle the mob. Will endeavor to carry radio farther, but believe this is probably last message for a while.
>
> Cheerio,
>
> Stilwell.

After his dispatch (and another one requesting airborne food drops made by Stilwell's aide, Frank Dorn), Stilwell ordered the bulky, two-hundred-pound radio smashed—its files and codes burned—so communications wouldn't fall into enemy hands. Then, at dawn on the morning of May 7, with the Japanese only miles to his south and pushing north with fretful speed, Stilwell labored to defeat the impression that his command had collapsed by walking out of Burma, all the while planning for his return.

Vinegar Joe had, in truth, already laid groundwork for Burma's reconquest using existing British and Indian Army troops, plus his American forces (once they arrived), and one hundred thousand Chinese soldiers already granted to him by China's nationalist leader, Chiang Kai-shek. But before he could reinvade Burma and drive the Japanese out, Stilwell knew the job at hand was to hike to safety in India.

Traveling with Stilwell was Gordon Seagrave, a chain-smoking missionary and humanitarian surgeon known to the Burmese—who often had trouble with Anglo names—as "Dr. Cigarette." Behind were nineteen of Seagrave's seemingly delicate Burmese nurses; a favored news correspondent, Jack Belden; nineteen of Stilwell's officers; five enlisted men carrying carbines and tommy guns; twelve British commandos left behind after their army's withdrawal; seven from Seagrave's ambulance team; thirteen members of the Chinese military; and a train of twenty mules whose use Stilwell had rented the evening before from the opium and jade smuggler who owned them.

At sunrise on May 7, once the mules were packed, Stilwell stood in a jungle clearing and addressed the group. He advised them that, due to limited supplies of food, a minimum of fourteen miles per day had to be traveled. He then reminded everyone that only personal discipline would ensure their survival, and—as he had the evening before—offered that anyone believing that he couldn't follow orders should speak up, so he could be issued a week's rations to find safety on his own. No one lifted a hand. "By the time we get out of here," Stilwell concluded, "many of you will hate my guts. But I'll tell you one thing: You'll get out."

Then, while the sky was still pink, Stilwell turned and started walking; moving through the jungle at the army's prescribed marching pace of 105 steps per minute. Within hours, they came upon a small river, the Chaung Gyi, and the faint trail Stilwell had been following disappeared completely. Not missing a step, Stilwell strode into the water and kept going, picking up the path again on the river's far bank and slightly downstream.

That morning, Stilwell's column crossed and recrossed the river nine times, and by 10 a.m. several members of the group were beginning to lag. One Burmese woman, a nurse of Dr. Seagrave's named Than Shwe, was so weakened by tuberculosis she soon was being dragged up the trail and across the Chaung Gyi on an inflated air mattress. Another group member, Stilwell's own aide—Major Frank Merrill—collapsed in the late morning. He, too, had to be dragged up the trail and across the water on an air mattress. To stay cooler in the jungle's heat, several members of the column cut the arms and legs from their clothes, only to discover their mistake: they'd given the mosquitoes and grayish-green jungle leeches easier access to their skin, forcing them to slap and pluck off vermin nonstop as they walked. By 1 p.m., only a few miles into the 140-mile trip, the line following Stilwell through the jungle was stretched so chaotically behind him that he was forced to concede a ten-minute rest per hour just to keep everyone together.

Ahead lay two weeks and 140 miles of impenetrable bamboo thickets, demoralizing switchbacks, steep and jungled mountainsides, biting ants, bloodthirsty bugs and leeches, dehydration, hunger, brakes of thorny vines, muddy bivouacs, itchy sand flies, broken packs, deserting porters, withering sun, wild elephants, ingrown toenails, blistered heels, devastating bouts of food poisoning, and several cases of malaria. And yet, even on this first morning, Stilwell kept his larger objective fixed unwaveringly in his mind. Once he'd guided his group safely to India, he would turn around, go back into Burma, and complete his real job: running the Japanese off the Asian mainland and into the sea.

Despite a military career already characterized by tenacious victory over lousy odds and shifty fortune, May 7, 1942, must have been the darkest and most frustrating day Vinegar Joe Stilwell had ever endured.

HE WAS BORN on his father's Florida pine plantation in 1883. Raised in a mansion overlooking the Hudson River at Yonkers, New York, Joseph Warren Stilwell was a blue-blood Yankee, West Point graduate, and redoubtable human ramrod of a man. At 5 feet, 7 ¾ inches, he was storied to be technically a quarter-inch too short to have been admitted to the U.S. Military Academy. At seventeen, the whip-smart cadet had graduated a year early with honors from Yonkers High School, and—according to Stilwell's biographer and the recollections of a neighbor—he spent the week before his West Point physical in bed, hoping a lack of vertical gravity might "stretch" him. This story, however, is untrue, as the minimum height requirement for seventeen-year-olds at West Point in 1900 was five three— a threshold Stilwell easily cleared—making a week's stay in bed pointless. (Still, the story handsomely illustrates how legends attached themselves to Stilwell's force of personality, even as a young man.) In 1900 the academy allowed Stilwell to take entrance exams after his father appealed to President McKinley for a cadet's appointment through a mutual friend.

At West Point, Stilwell placed near the top of his class with languages, also showing gifts for cartography, and gunnery. Already cultivating a fiercely unique stripe of competitiveness, he captained the cross-country team, lettered in varsity football, introduced intercollegiate basketball to the school, and, for two consecutive years, served as a social director, or "hop manager." By his third year, Stilwell had thrown off his privileged background and had taken up talking, thinking, and writing in the semaphoric, brass-tacks style of the era's President Theodore Roosevelt. ("Oh Hell!" had become Stilwell's favorite catchall.) And while family members had always called him by his middle name, Warren, Stilwell suddenly took to answering only to Joe, since all West Point cadets were known by their given first name, and Joseph had seemed too formal. In 1904, after four years at West Point, Joe Stilwell graduated thirty-second in a class of one hundred twenty-four.

He didn't rank high enough academically to get a posting with the Army Corps of Engineers, so—as he'd always disliked the "oat blowers" of the cavalry, whom he believed were imperious—Stilwell petitioned to join the infantry. Right away, he said, he wanted to fight. For his first assignment, he chose service in the Philippines, participating in a police-style action against native Moro insurgents there as part of what would eventually be called "Plan Orange," an American strategic policy to contain the archipelago and block the equally imperialistic Japanese from taking it themselves. For the now-commissioned Second Lieutenant Stilwell, though, the post was less about politics than about experience. At the time, the Philippines was the only place on earth where America was engaged in combat.

Unfortunately, there was little real warring to be done there or anywhere else. And for the next eleven years—through the Philippine insurgencies and a series of American interventions in the Caribbean—Stilwell bounced around inside the army, mostly spending his time behind a desk or a lecturn. In terms of battlefield glory, the high point of this period came against his own army in a 1905 war-game in the Philippines. To settle a bet with a peer cavalry lieutenant, Stilwell outfitted his infantrymen with bedsheets, then had them hide in slit trenches. As the cavalry charged, the infantry exploded from belowground—sheets flapping—startling the horses into chaos. The infantry took the mock battle without a fight.

After fourteen months in the Philippines, Stilwell was directed back to West Point to teach and study languages, a post that took him on temporary duty to Spain, and on assignments to Mexico and Guatemala. While back in New York, he met and married a friend of his younger sister's, Winifred Smith—whom he usually referred to as "Win"—and the two started a family. During this period, their love of travel and new cultures flourished, and in 1911 they traveled together for a two-year posting in the Philippines, taking a pleasure tour of Japan while en route.

Eventually, in 1917, Stilwell got another shot at war, gaining first a post as a liaison with the Allied armies in France and later as a G2 (or intelligence) officer. Unfortunately, both positions seemed to require typing and language skills as much as fighting mettle. And while Stilwell did spend six weeks at the siege of Verdun, making a few VIP tours at the battle front—

where he characterized a walk among severed heads and body parts as a "very interesting day"—he remained frustrated, spending most of the war as "a damned waffle-tail clerk in a bloody office . . . surrounded by desks and typewriters." As the war ended, and despite being busy in his new post as G1 (or personnel) officer, Stilwell grew bored while awaiting his next assignment. Unfortunately, for a man constantly craving action and adventure, much of Stilwell's World War I experience could be summed up by a note sent to Win from France just after the armistice: "Sitting, just sitting."

FATE WOULD NOW enter Joe Stilwell's life. After the war—and searching for a career inside a bloated, postwar army alongside thousands of other officers attempting the same—Stilwell grabbed at a new position inside the army's Intelligence Division as the Army's first "language" officer in China. It was a chance to deepen his very basic understanding of China, and it would require in-depth language and cultural training, exotic travel, and the opportunity to break fresh ground in a country just opening to the West. On the heels of citizen rebellion against its dynastic rulers, the Chinese were emerging from five thousand years of inward-looking monarchy to become a democratic nation led by the expatriate physician and progressive politician, Sun Yat-sen.

For an action-minded man entering middle age, the rise of this new China held almost unspeakable appeal. And in the years between the two world wars, Stilwell would occupy three different posts in China, coming to know the country's language, culture, habits, and eventually its leaders with a depth few other Americans could claim. He and Win would ultimately have five children who, during periods of their father's postings in China, would be raised there. Stilwell oversaw the Chinese creation of a highway, commanded a battalion of the U.S. Fifteenth Infantry (where he became acquainted with the American officer George Marshall, who would shortly have enormous impact in his life), and (from 1935 to 1939) served as American military attaché and ranking colonel, where—after Dr. Sun's death—he came to know Sun's political successor, Chiang Kai-shek.

When not in China, Stilwell continued moving upward inside the army, teaching courses at America's most forward-thinking post, Fort Benning, Georgia. It was during a 1930s stint at Benning, in fact, that the acid-tongued Stilwell got his "Vinegar Joe" handle. By then he completely in-habited the unvarnished, antiprivilege pose he'd first tossed on at West Point. And if known to be funny and candid in private (and still capable of the aristocratic manners of his youth), the mature Stilwell—perhaps frus-trated by a slowly advancing military career without much actual fight-ing—sometimes fell prone to moodiness, misanthropy, and occasional doggerel peppered with creative and scatological cursing.

He also taught with a vengeance. At Benning, Stilwell left classroom du-ties largely to others and spent his days overseeing war games in the forests and fields of Georgia, training a generation of officers in quick, battlefield-solution tactics instead of classical studies of ancient theories. He proved an enthusiastic coach and critic, and after one ferocious battlefield dress-ing down, where he peeled the paint from some student explanation of a reconnaissance problem gone bad—it had put troops at risk—a young of-ficer with an artistic bent drew Stilwell in caricature: his head rising from a vinegar bottle, a sour grimace on his narrow, patrician face. When the por-trait was pinned to a school bulletin board, Stilwell took a liking to it, asked the artist if he could reproduce it, and sent it to friends.

But time was passing and Colonel Stilwell—who spent much of his for-ties and fifties either in China or devoted to teaching and tactics in the United States—was considering retirement from the army to the house he and Win had built near the sea in Carmel, California. In one self-appraisal, he reckoned that, "There will never be a single work of history with me in it."

Fortunately his superior, General George Marshall, assistant comman-dant at Benning, had other beliefs. In performance reviews, Marshall called Stilwell "qualified for any command in peace or war," and stated that Stilwell was "a genius for instruction." In the following year, he de-scribed Stilwell as "High principles. Too hard working." He finished that year's review by noting Stilwell was "Ahead of his period in tactics and techniques."

In war games and training maneuvers, Stilwell eventually stood victori-ous without peer. The armies he commanded were uniformly the best de-ployed and integrated, and Stilwell loved nothing better than to gin-up "screwball" tactics that confused and then destroyed his opposition.

During one war-game episode in Louisiana in 1940, Stilwell led a thirty-thousand-man invasion army against a forty-thousand-troop defensive force, winning a planned two-week battle on the opening day. By starting their invasion with a series of wide-flanking maneuvers at 3 a.m. instead of making a straightforward attack at sunrise—as his opponent had expected—Stilwell's forces streaked seventy miles inside Louisiana before 7 a.m., winning the battle by capturing the city of Alexandria on the engagement's first night. Carrying on his long-held animosity with horses, Stilwell took special pride in capturing the headquarters of the First Cavalry, commanded by Jonathan Wainwright, a leader who would suffer mightily against the Japanese in the Philippines just a few years later.

Stilwell's professional prospects had also skyrocketed when, in June 1939 (and over the heads of thirty-four senior officers), George Marshall was promoted to full general and made acting chief of staff for the War Department, to be permanently effective starting September 1 of that year. Marshall's mandate—coming straight from President Franklin Roosevelt—was to restructure the army, equip it for what appeared to be a coming war in Europe, and infuse in it the snappy decision-making style that Stilwell had virtually invented. To assist in this task, topping the first batch of names Marshall sent up for promotion to brigadier general was Joseph W. Stilwell's.

Marshall saw a big future for his former colleague from Benning. He'd already decided Stilwell would plan and command all American troops and operations in North Africa—the Allied stepping-stone to doing battle in Europe—bestowing upon Vinegar Joe the most powerful field generalship in U.S. history. World War II was soon to envelope the globe, and Joe Stilwell had been selected as the man to navigate the U.S. Army's treacherous European path through it.

Once again, however, fate would enter Stilwell's life.


BY THE TIME Joseph Stilwell was promoted to brigadier general in 1939, the U.S. Army was at a physical and spiritual low. Due to funding shortages on the heels of the Great Depression, the army consisted of only 175,000 men, making it the nineteenth largest land force on earth and ranking it in size between Portugal, at eighteen, and Bulgaria at twenty. There were also limited supplies of weapons, artillery, and ammunition, and there existed no mechanized forces to move soldiers around. Manpower, equipment, and funding were spread so thin that, across the 1930s, full-scale war-game ground maneuvers were held for only two weeks every four years.

During much of this same decade, the conflagration that would become

World War II had been simmering in Europe, North Africa, and Asia. In Europe, Adolf Hitler's Germany had already seized Austria and parts of Czechoslovakia, and, by September 1939, it would take violent possession of Poland, officially setting World War II into motion. Italy had added Ethiopia (then called Abyssinia) to its North African colonies in 1936 and had invaded Albania—quickly entrenching itself there—in April 1939. By May 1939, sensing Hitler's momentum, Italian dictator Benito Mussolini forged a "Pact of Steel" with the German führer, establishing a Berlin-Rome axis that stood poised to threaten much of the Western world.

Halfway around the earth in China, a civil war had also been roiling for years. Since 1926, following Dr. Sun Yat-sen's death, a battle for modern China's soul had unraveled China's still-young republic until it had become a vast land ruled as much by regional warlords as by the notion of Chinese democracy. While Chiang Kai-shek still directed the Nationalist Kuomintang Party and remained China's commander-in-chief, his power was slipping away. Though Chiang still controlled much of the country and its military, his army was increasingly falling under the command of individual generals in the outlands, who were using the soldiers as personal armies to police citizens and, when needed, collect taxes that went into the pockets of the generals themselves.

Opposing both the Kuomintang and the military warlords stood one more figure in China: the resourceful Communist upstart Mao Tse-tung, who was destabilizing the country alongside the warlords through rent strikes, worker uprisings, and anti-landlord rallies. By the early 1930s, in fact, Chiang's extermination campaigns against Communists had swelled forces inside Mao's Red Army by several times and inspired more peasant uprisings and strikes.

China's internal problems had also allowed an external menace to enter and threaten it almost without notice. In 1931, capitalizing on China's distractions, Japan invaded and occupied Manchuria, a large and virtually undefended area on northeastern China's mainland. As a pretext for their invasion, the Japanese claimed Chinese nationalists had blown up a Japanese-owned railroad in the Manchurian city of Mukden, prompting Japan to guard its interests more closely.

For Japan, a crowded island short on space and natural resources, the Manchurian invasion was the visible edge in a campaign to protect the nation through imperialism. For a time, the Japanese aggressions were rationalized as the exportation of Japan's supposedly superior culture to

China in exchange for land and goods. And before long, the Japanese were denouncing any and all Western commerce with Asia, cobbling together an "Asia for Asians" campaign that Japan predictably nominated itself to lead.

Still, China and its largest trade partner, the United States, weren't having it. When both nations (along with Britain) complained about the Manchurian occupation to the League of Nations, Japan responded by withdrawing from the League. Adding a semantic twist to the discussion, the Japanese continued to deny they were making war on the Chinese, referring to their invasion as an "incident" instead of an official act of war. The League did little to object.

Over the next six years—and employing similarly flimsy rationales—Japan gobbled up many of China's major cities and seaports, moving one million Japanese citizens and three hundred thousand soldiers into Japanese-occupied China. By 1937, Peking, Tientsin, and the seaports of Tsingtao, Amoy, and Swatow were under Japanese control, as was much of central China's "Iron Ricebowl," as its fertile Yellow River Valley is known. While the Chinese army began fighting back more forcefully at each successive "incident," Chiang Kai-shek continued to trade space for time, fearing that if he loosed his armies, his generals might turn on him.

In October 1937, when a Japanese naval force sailed into the harbor at Shanghai—China's biggest city for commerce and banking and its last free seaport—the Chinese army finally struck preemptively, firing upon the Japanese ships. In retaliation for this aggression, the Japanese responded by shredding the city with dive bombers and naval guns in a battle that lasted three months. Before the mauling of Shanghai was over, one of the most memorable photos of World War II would be published worldwide, finally awakening the planet to the aggressions of the imperial Japanese in China. The photo was brutally simple and self-explanatory: it showed a filthy and burned baby, sitting on rail tracks in the midst of an abandoned and blasted-apart street in the wake of a bombing. Still, if the world could finally witness the naked horror of Japan's aggressions in China, it seemed too late to slow the Japanese momentum. Shanghai's harbor—the last free port in China—was soon under Japanese control. And with Shanghai's harbor finally closed to outside commerce, the most populous nation on earth was being strangled. No new goods could flow in or out of the country by sea. All of China's international trade was now forced to enter the country overland.

Chief among these supply routes was the Burma Road. A 715-mile, two-

lane track that ran between the southwest Chinese city of Kunming
and the railhead city of Lashio in Burma, the road was a major conduit
for goods headed for China. Though an awkward means to keep China
alive, the road had been created by two hundred thousand Chinese laborers in 1937 and early '38, few of whom ever saw pay for their labors.
Paved by cobbles into a winding, patchy thoroughfare, the Burma Road
traced steep mountain valleys tiered by ancient rice paddies and crossed
bridges spanning the raging Mekong and Salween Rivers. The road
was tenuous, but it also stood among China's last hopes for fresh stores of
supplies.

The Burma Road, Chiang Kai-shek could also have feared, might soon
become his escape route. After Shanghai fell to Japanese control, Japan
turned its interests farther up the Yangtze River toward Chiang's Nationalist Chinese capital of Nanking: an ornate city of tree-lined stone paths,
bright-red Buddhist temples, and tall, octagonal bell towers made of wood
and stone. As the Japanese pushed inland up the Yangtze from Shanghai,
Chiang was forced to relocate from Nanking to the interior city of
Chungking, only a short hop from the Burma Road's Chinese terminus in
Kunming. Having finally viewed Japan's naked intentions in Shanghai's
rubble, Chiang was growing jumpy about the depths of Japan's hunger for
Chinese soil. To stop the Japanese from perhaps taking all of China, he
was now seriously considering a recent Japanese offer to "adjust" the two
nations' relationship, provided China turned over to Japan much of the
Chinese land the Japanese were already occupying.

But as Chiang delayed agreeing to this proposal, in hopes that international pressure would halt Japanese aggression, the Japanese arrived in
Nanking, and the city—without air cover or radio communications between army units—fell quickly on December 12, 1937, with Chinese troops
in sloppy retreat. The month that followed, from mid-December to January 1938, is now referred to as the "Rape of Nanking" and stands as one of
the most horrific wartime atrocities ever. In four weeks, fifty thousand
Japanese soldiers tortured and murdered a million-person city, a handful
of Chinese peasants at a time. Young girls and elderly women were gang-
raped, then were mutilated and left to die. Men were often encircled by
Japanese soldiers and used for bayonet practice. When this game grew tiresome, the soldiers would end festivities by bayoneting the "dummy" in the
heart or the throat. Other days, groups of Chinese men would be marched

out to the city boundary and machine-gunned. On one such day, twenty thousand men were shot and buried in a mass grave.

In a city whose grace and beauties were thought by the Chinese to be evidence of their culture's civility and achievement, the blood of China now congealed in the gutters. Over the month, an estimated three hundred thousand Chinese would lose their lives to the Japanese torturers, while Nanking's houses, government offices, stores, and buildings were burned to the ground. By the end of January, the Yangtze River was awash in a human logjam, with turtles and fish gorging themselves on rotting corpses.

After seven long years of lame rationalizations and increasingly belligerent "incidents," the Japanese had finally exposed their teeth. Between the German-Italian Axis and the ascendant Japanese war machine, world war was spreading across the earth like wildfire. And few of the nations soon to come under attack were prepared.

BY DECEMBER 1941 most of Europe had fallen to the Germans. Using waves of dive-bomber's and mechanized blitzkriegs followed by mop-up invasion forces, Hitler's Third Reich had kicked down the doors of Holland, Belgium, Norway, Yugoslavia, Greece, and most of France. In northern France in May and June of 1940, 337,000 French and British defensive forces were literally driven into the sea at Dunkirk, where they were ferried to England by a fleet of 655 civilian boats—from cruise ships to fishing dories—having abandoned their heavy weapons to the enemy. The Germans and Italians were now moving across North Africa. And though German attack continued to be repulsed off Britain, Germany had also turned its appetites east and invaded Russia.

During this same time, in the east, Japan had invaded and occupied an area twice the size of Germany's wartime holdings. Using an unpredictably swirling series of offensives, and thanks to its growing navy, Japan overran several oil-rich island chains in the South China Sea, then invaded and took control of northern Indochina (today called Vietnam), cutting off the only other major land route of goods into China. Then, in an effort to isolate China completely, the Japanese began negotiating with the British, Burma's colonial rulers, to close the Burma Road.

In Tokyo, there was talk of *hakko ichiu* ("bringing the world under one roof"). Japan's political and military leader, General Hideki Tojo, was convinced that he would soon control all of Southeast Asia, the Philippines, the Dutch East Indies, and the islands of Oceania. To soften nations soon to come under attack, the Japanese had spent the last decade dispatching ranking army officers disguised as journalists to capitals in the region, where they made contacts and funded Japan-friendly insurgency forces inside national armies. Encouraged by the German victories across Europe, in September 1940 the Japanese even signed a Tripartite Pact with the Axis, carving the world into eastern and western spheres of influence.

Viewed from American and British shores, the rise of Germany and Japan frightened both nations into activity. As the Germans invaded the Channel Islands off the British Coast and began flying bombing missions over London and central England with devastating results, the British continued gamely defending their skies, repulsing the airborne attackers in what came to be called the Battle of Britain. Yet despite a military force that would eventually number 4.6 million, the British and their colonial armies were underequipped and stretched across the globe as far east as Burma and Singapore. In the United States, President Roosevelt responded to Britain's emergency by transferring fifty American destroyer warships to the British navy in exchange for use of colonial British bases in the Caribbean.

For the Americans, despite a new five-billion-dollar "total defense" package that had been rolled out in August 1941 (providing for an army of 1.2 million, plus an equally sized air force and a two-ocean navy), in reality the U.S. Army still had only 275,000 troops. To buy time for building forces, the Americans entered into "lend-lease" agreements with nations fighting the Germans and the Japanese. Through these commitments, the Americans agreed to provide weapons, ammunition, and goods for undersupplied countries already at war, but no new American forces would be distributed for the indeterminate future.

Then the "back-burner" war in the Pacific leapt to equal prominence with the war in Europe. On December 7, 1941, Japan unsheathed its most ambitious attacks yet. It lashed eastward, and in a single morning decimated the U.S. naval fleet at Pearl Harbor. Eighteen ships, including eight battleships, were sunk, capsized, or badly damaged. In the same attack, the army and the navy lost nearly four hundred aircraft, and almost four thousand soldiers and sailors were killed or wounded. Then just hours later,

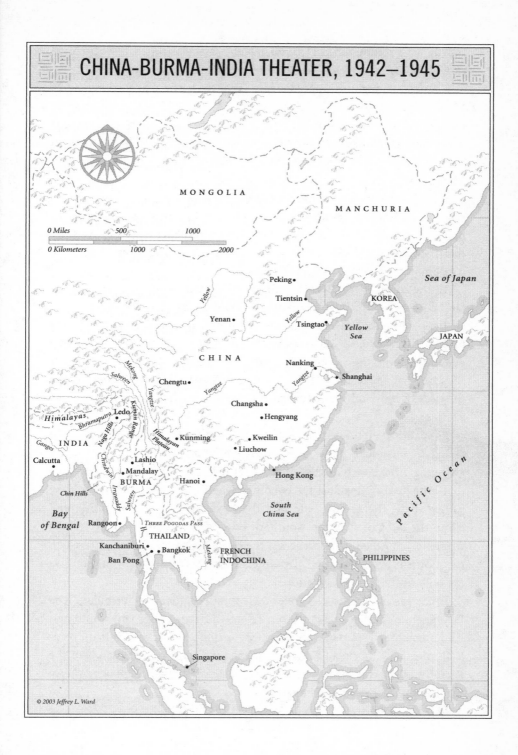

# CHINA-BURMA-INDIA THEATER, 1942–1945

MONGOLIA

MANCHURIA

0 Miles 500 1000
0 Kilometers 1000 2000

Peking •
Tientsin •
Yenan •
Tsingtao •

KOREA

*Sea of Japan*

*Yellow Sea*

JAPAN

CHINA

Nanking •
Shanghai

Chengtu •

Changsha •
Hengyang •

*Himalayas*
Ledo •

Kunming •
Kweilin •
Liuchow •

*Ganges*
INDIA

Calcutta •

Lashio •
Mandalay •
Hanoi •

Hong Kong •

BURMA

*Chin Hills*

*Bay of Bengal*
Rangoon •
*THREE POGODAS PASS*

*South China Sea*

THAILAND
Kanchanaburi •
Ban Pong •
Bangkok •

FRENCH INDOCHINA

PHILIPPINES

*Pacific Ocean*

Singapore •

© 2003 Jeffrey L. Ward

shortly after midnight on December 8, the Japanese began their preinvasion bombing of British-held Malaya (today called Malaysia).

The frightening and unpredictable Japanese battle plan had spread to all zones of the Pacific. Like Germany, Japan appeared to possess limitless numbers of soldiers and weapons, and they were using them to full potential. American paranoia about Japan ran so deep that, just days after Pearl Harbor, Japanese warships were falsely rumored to be poised off the California coast.

With Japan's attack on the United States, America was dragged into a two-front conflict it remained underequipped to join. And the British—hunkered down defensively at home—were now being forced to consider that their Asian colonies of Singapore, Burma, and India might soon be consumed by Japanese invasion as well.

To the Allies, world events were out of control. And their attackers so far had been invincible: Japan had brutally crushed every opponent it took on, and the Germans, while frustrated by Britain's defense, had pushed deep inside Russia—slaughtering tens of thousands of Russian peasants along the way—and were now within striking distance of Moscow. For the leaders of Britain, China, Russia, and the United States, the issue of how and where to begin clawing back left as many questions as answers.

As 1941 hurtled toward '42, Allied leaders and emissaries met constantly, trying to formulate plans in a global environment that was constantly changing. After much discussion, they settled on a "Europe First" program that initially drove against the enemy in North Africa. If control could be gained there, the Allies would hop the Mediterranean from Tunisia and climb the boot of Italy into southern Europe. This thrust would be buttressed by an Allied invasion across the English Channel into France when the moment presented itself. Troops executing these strokes would receive the bulk of the Allies' early support.

In the east, a "Pacific War" plan was far more difficult to formulate. The Japanese now occupied an area *three times* the size of Germany's holdings. And much of what Japan controlled was open ocean—a very difficult place to hunt down, attack, and destroy an enemy—while on the islands of the Pacific and the continents that edged that ocean, the Japanese were showing no sign of curbing their aggressions.

Like the Americans, Japan recognized that the Philippines stood as a

tactical pivot for the entire Eastern Hemisphere. And on December 10—
which, owing to the International Date Line, meant *only hours* after they'd
attacked the United States at Pearl Harbor—the first of six waves of Japanese soldiers came ashore on Luzon Island in the Philippines, taking up a
pincer-style attack on American and Filipino divisions there from north
and south of Manila. By the time Japan's initial assault was over in the
Philippines, the Japanese air force had destroyed half of all American aircraft there as they sat unused on the ground. Within weeks, the area's commanding general, the American Douglas MacArthur, would order the
evacuation of his forces from Manila.

On December 23, the island of Guam fell to Japan. Two days later, on
Christmas Day, after more than a century of British colonial rule, Hong
Kong also became a Japanese possession. The imperial Japanese war machine seemed both unbeatable and insatiable. And in early January 1942, as
Japan's forces began to invade Borneo and Thailand, the Allies hastily
created a U.S. task force for a newly formed China theater, which, in mid-
1942, would expand to become the China-Burma-India theater of operations (or CBI). The entire point of the China theater and, later, CBI was to
protect what remained of Asia for Britain, China, and the United States.
Initially, however, its sole objective was to keep China in the war and India
under colonial British rule, since both nations functioned as the gateway
not only to Central Asia, but as the obvious path for a land-based link between Japan and Germany.

The task of defending these two gigantic nations was daunting; the way
to do it undefined. It was, in General George Marshall's estimation, "the
most-impossible job of the war." Whoever oversaw the region would stand
last in line for Allied supplies and manpower. The Allied commander in
China could also expect little assistance from British forces and generals in
India and Burma, since Britain was concentrating its defenses against
a German threat at home and would be keeping most of its soldiers,
weapons, and focus on the homeland.

So there it was. In China—and soon after, the CBI—there would be
little in the way of support or reinforcement. Keeping together the disparate and undersupplied Chinese, Indian, Nepalese Gurkha, British, and
American forces in CBI would require a leader of vision, stamina, and
determination—not to mention deep stores of tactical creativity. The job
also demanded someone who could manage Chiang Kai-shek (a leader

more interested in American lend-lease goods than American partner-
ship), who could speak and understand several Chinese dialects, and,
perhaps most important, who would put the reserved and courtly Chiang
at ease.

At first, to fill this estimable job, the Allies offered the American General
Hugh Drum as commander, but Chiang—who'd recently accepted the role
of Allied supreme commander in China—responded even more cooly
than usual; a lucky break, since by then Secretary of War Henry Stimson
and General Marshall had reconsidered. Next for China's top spot, Stimson and Marshall discussed the Generals Joyce, Richardson, and Eichel-
berger, but none seemed to fit the sprawling demands of the job.

Then Stimson played an ace he'd been holding for months. He
suggested to Marshall that Joe Stilwell would be right for the China
command. Though the job requirements remained impossible, Stilwell
managed to fill every category of need. He'd also had a lifetime of practical
experience in China. When Stimson and Marshall recommended Stilwell
to Chiang's lieutenants, the proposal met with instant approval.

On January 23, 1942, George Marshall called Stilwell to his office at the
War Department. There—with a view of the broad Capital Mall outside
his windows—Marshall informed his old friend that, instead of leading the
Allied charge into North Africa and (eventually) Europe, Stilwell needed to
be "it" over in China.

In an instant, Vinegar Joe Stilwell watched the most-desired field generalship in American history evaporate. (The position eventually was filled
by Dwight D. Eisenhower.) In his promised job's stead, Stilwell was being
offered an impossible command in the wettest, muddiest, most-unknown,
most-disorganized, lowest-priority corner of World War II.

"Will you go?" Marshall asked.

"I'll go where I'm sent," Stilwell said.


ON FEBRUARY 11, Joe Stilwell left for India to take command of the na-
scent CBI. After a lifetime of waiting, he finally had ground command of
armies, with his plans overseen only by China's generalissimo and by his
own most ardent supporter, George Marshall. During the fourteen-day
trip from Washington to India along the only air route of the day (from
Miami to Brazil to North Africa to Persia to Delhi), Stilwell drew up a

list of his official positions and functions. When his toting-up was finished, Stilwell discovered—to his horror—that he was responsible for eight different full-time jobs.

His designations included commanding general of the U.S. Army in CBI, chief of staff to China's supreme commander, supervisor of CBI lend-lease programs in China, and U.S. representative on any war council in the theater. He was also charged with maintaining the Burma Road, Allied-style training for two million Chinese troops, setting up and overseeing the lend-lease air supply of China across the treacherous Himalayan "Hump" from India, and planning and building a land-based supply route from India to connect with the Burma Road—to be called the Ledo Road.

Yet Stilwell had more immediate problems. In the four months since the Japanese had bombed Pearl Harbor, imperial forces had overrun the Philippines, attacked Australia and New Guinea, and now outright occupied Borneo, Thailand, Singapore, Malaya, Indochina, and the oil fields of the Dutch East Indies. Now they were pouring over the Thai border into Burma, the last unoccupied nation in Southeast Asia and the sole buffer between India and Japanese assault, not to mention the source of China's last artery of outside supply, the Burma Road.

On February 23—as Stilwell flew the trip's leg from Cairo to Baghdad—two divisions of the Japanese Fifteenth Army had worked some one hundred miles inside Burma's southeastern border and now controlled all of the countryside on the eastern shore of Burma's broad Sittang River. As dawn came, the Japanese were readying to attack three Indian and Burmese brigades arrayed along the lower Sittang, all of whom were under British command. The Japanese target was a car and train bridge spanning the river. If the Japanese could gain control of the bridge—the only one crossing the river for hundreds of miles—they could bound over the last physical obstacle between themselves and Burma's commercial capital and largest seaport, Rangoon. Knowing the bridge was obviously the next Japanese prize, Indian demolition experts had spent several days wiring its 1,650-foot length with explosives—even as Japanese snipers *ping*ed bullets off the bridge's steel girders—and their orders were crystal clear. If control of the bridge could not be kept, the entire span was to be blown.

During the previous several days, while the Indian sappers worked, soldiers defending the bridge had spent their afternoons scrunched behind sandbags, being shot at and watching as terrorized Burmese farmers tried to escape the Japanese by swimming the Sittang's five-hundred-yard width. With each new swimmer, a hail of Japanese bullets would rip from the forest or reedy riverbank and spatter across the escaping man or woman in the river, sending each to the bottom in a swirl of blood.

Now, in the morning's rising light, more than one thousand Japanese troops were crouched in the underbrush just across a two-lane road from the bridgehead, and they were prepared to rush the bridge's defenders. As the morning's false dawn arrived, it became obvious that, when the moment of attack finally came, the bridge could not be successfully defended. It was also decided that, once the attack began, the bridge could not be destroyed with certainty. There was only one course of action: the bridge had to be blown in advance.

Just before dawn a directive went out for Burmese and Indian troops defending the area to withdraw, but few manning the machine guns and sandbags at the bridgehead heard it. Then, just a few minutes before dawn, the soldier responsible for destroying the bridge, Lieutenant Ahmed Bashir Khan, began executing his orders: lighting the backup safety fuse that led to the explosive charges wired into the bridge's steel bracings. Then Lieutenant Khan pressed himself tighter against some protective sandbags, and opened the top of an electrical switch box, which was also wired to the explosives. Turning a key inside the box, he switched on the electricity, and, with a flick of the wrist, flipped the charge's main circuit.

In a blinding flash—followed by a breath of shrivelingly hot air and a deafening BOOOOOM—the bridge exploded in the morning's pale light, sending shards of steaming metal raining into the river and across the swampy mud of the rice paddies that lined each bank.

For a long minute, the scene hung in stunned silence. As the smoke cleared, soldiers from both sides continued staring at the bridge in amazement. Despite the enormous blast, the thousands of pounds of explosives, and a still-drizzling rain of metal and debris across the area, just one of the bridge's six spans had been shattered enough to fall into the river. The bridge remained overwhelmingly intact, and it could be opened again to traffic in no time. It had been damaged only enough, in fact, to keep the few hundred Indian and Burmese soldiers still trapped on the Sittang's near bank from escaping.

As the situation became clear, with the bridge's defenders now realizing their plight, a new noise began to rise on the morning's breeze: the chatters

and jeers of the Japanese. A few of the Burmese and Indian soldiers sur-
rendered. Many more reconciled themselves to their only other choice:
swimming across the Sittang toward safety. By the middle of that day, just
as the Yangtze had grown choked with the bodies of Chinese peasants during the Rape of Nanking, the Sittang grew awash with the bodies of bullet-
riddled dead, each of whom wore the khaki uniforms and military
insignias of India and Burma.

In yet another disastrous turn of events for CBI, the way to Rangoon
remained open to the Japanese. After four days of repairing and securing
the bridge, the Japanese once again began their march on Burma's largest
city and seaport.

Burma was poised to fall.

HAVING ARRIVED in Burma just in time to watch it collapse, Stilwell
made an initial visit to Chiang Kai-shek in Chungking on March 4. While,
on paper, Chiang commanded more than four million men—giving him
the largest army on earth—the reality was far more fragmented and disor-
derly. The majority of China's troops had no training or weapons (most
didn't even have boots), and their rations consisted of rice for all meals
and one blanket for every five soldiers. Of the Chinese army's 346 divisions, many were commanded by generals who continued to consider
themselves autonomous warlords, men who believed these personal
armies would execute their wishes over those of the generalissimo.

Chiang, for his part, clearly understood the situation, including his
army's fighting abilities. So as not to equip enemies beneath his own flag,
he continued to withhold weapons and matériel from all but his most
trusted subordinates. And four days into Stilwell's visit, after dinner that
night, the generalissimo finally responded to Stilwell's constant requests
for a planning session. But instead of working with Stilwell, Chiang
launched into a wide-ranging, two-hour lecture on his chosen stripe military tactics. Before it was over, Chiang had instructed Stilwell to allow the
Japanese to continue their invasion and never to concentrate the Chinese
forces in large groups—as they would run a higher risk of being destroyed
by a single Japanese attack.

"What a directive," Stilwell wrote in his diary that night. "What a
mess . . . Maybe the Japs will go after us and solve it for us."

Stilwell was in trouble up to his ears. By March 7, Rangoon had fallen, with the defending British, Indian, and Burmese forces not even notifying Allied command as they abandoned the city. Refugees streamed north by whatever means they had. With the city's streets and bazaars emptied, roaming bands of convicts and the mentally ill—who also had been released under evacuation orders—torched buildings and looted shops. Gunfire could be heard day and night, and many of those who stayed to sack the city lay drunk in the streets anytime they weren't creating mayhem.

The silk market on Rangoon's Dalhousie Street was in ruins; the city's main commercial center, Phayre Street, was barred and shuttered. Left behind in Rangoon's Allied lend-lease warehouses on the harborside were, among other things, twelve hundred trucks in various stages of assembly, thousands of rubber tires, food and rice for ten thousand to twenty thousand, wooden cases filled with cigarettes, hundreds of cases of whiskey, more than 150 cases of champagne, fifty thousand blankets, and electrical and industrial equipment including large and valuable electric motors and generators. In the wealthy suburbs surrounding the city, Rangoon's finest houses were ransacked and burned to the ground.

Replacing the stately order of colonial Rangoon rose a pirate city. Criminals sold looted goods from curbside stands, and those Burmese remaining in Rangoon exercised their longtime hatred of Indians by shooting any they encountered then using the two-foot knives they carried on their waists, called *dahs*, to hack at the dead. With the passage of only a few days, one of the most tranquil cities in South Asia had been transformed into a fiery hell. One night, a *Life* magazine photographer named George Rodger disregarded the military curfew and, carrying a pistol in one hand and his camera in the other, set off to record the city with its howling dogs, smoky rubble, twitchy psychopaths, and blazing mansions. In one spot, outside a Buddhist temple whose outer wall had collapsed, Rodger viewed an image that seemed to sum up once-dignified Rangoon's fall. It was a row of twenty gilded Buddhas, each of them twelve feet tall, their gold skins now glowing red with the reflected light of the city in flames.

By air transport, Stilwell hurried from Chungking to Burma's Allied headquarters just north of Mandalay, in central Burma. There—on "unlucky" Friday March 13—Stilwell encountered the commander in charge of the deserting troops from Rangoon: Lt. General Sir Harold Alexander, the same British general who, before arriving in Burma, had directed the Allied evacuation at Dunkirk under German attack in 1940. Alexander, on the defensive, was cold and distant, allowing Stilwell the ammunition to be his usual cranky self. When Alexander learned that Stilwell was in command of one hundred thousand Chinese troops in Burma on loan from Chiang, he responded with only "Extrawdinery!" Then Alexander stared at the American, in Stilwell's assessment, "as if I had just crawled out from under a rock." It was an exchange that sent Stilwell spinning for days.

As the Japanese continued their northward invasion of Burma from Rangoon and points farther south, two other realities became obvious to Stilwell and the Allies. First, under their invented slogan "Asia for Asians," the Japanese had succeeded in turning portions of the Burmese army away from the British. Instead, the Burmese had joined the new Burmese Independence Army, made up of expatriates led by General Aung San. And with this change of associations, the old Burmese military was providing devastatingly accurate intelligence and guidance to the invading Japanese. Second, having battled across much of Southeast Asia in the last half-decade, Imperial Japanese troops were intimately familiar with jungle fighting, while the British and Indian armies were not. The Japanese would often cut trails through the jungle along roadsides, traveling invisibly around the British and Indians. They would then proceed north, ahead of the evacuating armies and, employing roadblocks, cut them off with devastating results.

To stop the Allied losses, Stilwell and Alexander agreed to a defense of Burma at its narrow waist, about 150 miles north of Rangoon. There, where the nation's three north-south river valleys run close to one another—the different waterways separated by tall spurs of the Himalayas—Alexander's British and Indian forces would defend the country's western flank, along the broad Irrawaddy River near the city of Prome. Stilwell and the Chinese (the arrival of American forces was still months away) would defend Burma's eastern side along the Sittang and Salween Rivers. Thankfully for Stilwell, the British were to be commanded on the ground by Lt. General William J. Slim, a tall, unaffected, straight-talking leader for whom Stilwell quickly developed admiration.

Almost immediately, however, practical problems arose. With supply lines from Rangoon cut, the British were living on dried beef and hard biscuits infested with weevils—or "vitamin W," as the soldiers were calling the insects. Slim's British and Indian forces had also been forced to withdraw from the humid seacoast to Burma's "dry belt": a dusty, cactus-studded plateau situated at the nation's center.

"The country," wrote William Slim, "instead of being green and thickly covered, was brown and bare with occasional patches of parched jungle. The water courses, worn through the low undulating hills were dry, and the general effect was of heat and dust."

The dry belt was more akin to a desert than a tropical jungle, and within days the British forces were beginning to weaken from thirst. To get moisture, Slim's troops away from the river were forced to urinate on their hands, then touch their fingers to their mouths. Beneath a relentless sun, their skin and lips began to crack and bleed.

And the Japanese kept coming, racking up increasingly heavy British casualties in daily ambushes. When they took British prisoners alive, the Japanese were known to strip them, tie them to trees, and use them for bayonet practice. Other times, they would hurry ahead of British forces and lash still-living British or Indian prisoners to roadblocks; then they'd shoot from behind the blockades as the British approached.

Tired, thirsty, and battling an opponent they rarely saw until they were engaged in a firefight, Slim's army was soon in retreat again. On April 15, Stilwell learned that, on orders from Slim, British soldiers had destroyed all five thousand oil derricks at Yengyaung, two hundred miles north of Rangoon, the sole source of the Allies' gasoline and oil in Burma. Then he learned the British were withdrawing from the oil fields, which exposed Stilwell's Chinese army on its western flank. Despite the lack of support, Stilwell gave orders for the Chinese to stand firm. Instead, they took to the hills. One of his armies, the thousand-man Chinese Fifty-fifth Division, vanished so completely under Japanese attack they were never reconstituted again.

"There's no trace of it," Stilwell told Jack Belden of *Life* magazine as the two went in search of the Chinese Fifty-fifth. "It's the God-damnedest thing I ever saw. Last night I had a division. Today, there isn't any."


IN HIS FIRST COMBAT COMMAND, under the scrutiny of the world's leaders, Vinegar Joe Stilwell was naked in the spotlight. "What a sucker I'll look like if the Japs run me out of Burma," he noted in his diary on April 1, 1942, in an entry that began "Am I the April fool?"

In the midst of the Burma front's collapse, Generalissimo Chiang Kai-shek further complicated matters by continually sending Stilwell memos reversing approvals on where, when, and which Chinese armies could be used. Then the "Gi-mo" (as Stilwell was now calling him) began making impractical, impossible-seeming demands for the welfare of his troops. One directive to Stilwell ordered the bodies of all Chinese casualties to be shipped home in pine coffins, so they could be buried near ancestors. Another demanded one watermelon be issued to every four Chinese soldiers in Burma.

By April 20, the Japanese had pushed to Burma's border with China, threatening the Burma Road. On the twenty-fifth, British General Alexander informed Stilwell that, on orders from British command, his troops were making a tactical retreat from Burma to India. During this meeting, which took place in the interior courtyard of a house in the town of Kyaukse, a Japanese air raid sent both command teams scrambling for cover, with only the two generals not moving: Alexander stood defiantly in the open garden looking upward as the bombs fell, while Stilwell quietly smoked a cigarette and leaned against a porch rail.

Stilwell was now on his own, and the news reaching him was getting no better. On April 29, he learned the Japanese had taken Lashio, severing the Burma Road. With that single event, Vinegar Joe knew, for the moment, that he was finished in Burma. The British, Indian, Burmese, and Gurkha forces were already gone, retreating to India across a land whose civilian population was now awash in rape, arson, and roadside robbery by Burmese *dacoits*, or highwaymen. Chinese and Indian forces, fearful of a people they'd been policing and didn't truly understand, began shooting the Burmese on sight, even if they posed no threat. Driven out ahead of the  invading Japanese, an estimated nine hundred thousand Burmese civilians, most inadequately provisioned, also began making their way north. For months they would wander old trade or hunters' routes or stumble through trackless jungles or over the impossibly tall Himalayas, ending up—if they were lucky—in India, Tibet, or China. If they were less fortunate, they would die alone in the jungles of disease or mishap. In the remote towns of northern Burma, tattered, bone-tired, and starving clutches of refugees often huddled together.

One British officer, Geoffrey Tyson, while making a sweep for Indian army stragglers on his own way out of Burma, described one of these camps: "The clearing was littered with tumble-down huts, where often whole families stayed and died together. I found the bodies of a mother and child locked in each other's arms. In another hut, were the remains of another mother who had died in childbirth, with the child only half-born. In the one jhum [clearing] more than fifty people had died. Sometimes pious Christians placed little wooden crucifixes in the ground before they died. Others had figures of the Virgin Mary still clutched in their skeleton hands. A soldier had expired wearing his side cap, all his cotton clothing had rotted away, but the woolen cap sat smartly on his grinning skull. Already the ever-destroying jungle had overgrown some of the older huts, covering up the skeletons and reducing them to dust and mould."

Everything about the grandeur of Burma—from its gold-domed temples to its quiet, British-Colonial order—was now dying. And no place or tribe or tradition in Burma, no matter how ancient or beautiful, would be left intact. Even the imperial glory of Mandalay's palaces and gardens, which had housed Burma's kings and queens before the British had colonized the country, was destroyed. Its ancient palaces and pagodas were shattered and burned beyond recognition by Japanese shelling that lasted a full twenty-seven days and nights. In its place, in the tranquil moats that still surrounded the city's razed palace, decomposing corpses floated amid the lotus blossoms and leaves. Destruction and decay had become Burma's new rulers.


AS STILWELL ARRANGED for his and the Chinese army's evacuation of Burma—north by rail to airfields in the city of Myitkyina (said Mitch-chee-na), then out to India by air—events continued conspiring against him. When he woke on May 1, he learned that a Chinese general named Lo Cho-ying had commandeered a freight train for overnight troop carriage of his men to Myitkyina, and had crashed the train into an unscheduled locomotive heading south on the same track, completely blocking the line. "Unfortunately," Stilwell wrote in his diary, "he [Lo Cho-ying] was not killed."

That same morning, Stilwell made a list of which of his staff should be flown out and which should remain with him, then he radioed out the evacuation orders. Late that afternoon, air transport Colonels Caleb Haynes and Robert Scott flew from India to Stilwell's headquarters at Shwebo with orders to "Effect evacuation: Stilwell and staff, most urgent."

Arriving at the tea planter's house Stilwell was using as his offices, the fliers found Stilwell at a desk, writing. When Haynes informed Stilwell of their orders to evacuate him, Stilwell squinted at the pilot through his thick eyeglasses—then he declined the lift. Stilwell's staff members were ordered to get on the plane and zoom for India, but the general was staying. He planned to travel by whatever means possible to Myitkyina and regroup with the Chinese.

On May 3, using a string of vehicles in an attempt to reach Myitkyina, a group of roughly eighty of Stilwell's handpicked staff plus stragglers began their trip north, with the Japanese only twenty miles to their south. Right away, however, their cars and trucks fell prey to the rutted ox trails of Burma's dry-mud roads.

First to go was their scout car. "Burn the damn thing . . . Keep moving," Stilwell ordered.

When a transport vehicle's axle snapped, Stilwell instructed the crew to "Burn the son-of-a-bitch."

Another transport blew its crankcase. "Burn it," Stilwell commanded.

When a supply truck's engine caught fire, Stilwell ordered the vehicle flipped to put out the fire; then several members of the group were told to scavenge it for provisions before torching the remains.

Within two days, all of the motorcade's trucks and jeeps had been abandoned, and any transit toward Myitkyina was now impossible, since Japanese invasion forces had inserted themselves between Stilwell and his goal, cutting off the trip to Myitkyina. On the morning of May 7, after a last radio message the night before had informed command of his change of course for India, Stilwell set off on foot, leading a column of people and mules northwest through the jungle as birds and monkeys chattered in the trees. For three days, they crossed and recrossed rivers and small streams, slept in the mud or in rudimentary shelters, and were living on half-rations of porridge, rice, corned beef, and tea. As they walked, Seagrave's Burmese nurses sang hymns, especially an exceedingly long-winded version of "Onward Christian Soldiers." Then on the morning of May 9, as if to underscore the remoteness of their location, the group encountered an enormous bull elephant cutting its own swath through the underbrush.

Stilwell and a few of his officers "ganged up on it," their weapons ready, and a more violent confrontation was luckily avoided.

Another morning, Stilwell discovered a far-larger-than-average bedroll packed on one of the mules. He removed it, learned it belonged to a junior officer, and grew furious as he inspected the contents: sheets, pillows, an air mattress, extra clothing, and squirreled-away food.

As the sun rose, Stilwell assembled the full group to regard the cache. "I had you all line up here," he said, "so you could see how little one member of this party cares about the rest of you—so long as he has his own comforts. I'm not mentioning his name because you might hurt him, and that would slow up the column . . . I'll take care of this matter after we get to India. When we take off in a few minutes, the owner will leave these things here. I hope he feels properly ashamed."

As Stilwell stalked off, one member of the group drew laughs when he gestured at the way the general's flat-brimmed World War I hat was tipped forward, then whispered aloud: "Jeez! Even his old *hat* looks mad."

After three days of hard walking, as Stilwell's column reached the broad and shallow Uyu River, malaria and dysentery had joined the trip as full-fledged members, and many in the party were growing weak. On the Uyu's shore, however, bamboo rafts awaited, as Stilwell had sent Burmese runners ahead to construct and ready them for a trip downstream toward India, still one hundred miles to the west. As the rafts were being loaded, Seagrave's nurses created roofs for the rafts by weaving grasses and vines together, then laying them over frameworks of bent bamboo. And then, after an hour of hard work, the group began poling its armada downstream, with everyone going overboard anytime the boats ran aground on shoals too shallow for passage. They navigated all night, and the next morning they found the sunrise obscured by heavy clouds that soon became a rainstorm. It was the beginning few drops of Burma's annual, three-month monsoon.

Later that day, as the clouds cleared, a twin-engine aircraft made its way over the river, then circled back around. In unison, the group cowered—waiting for a machine-gun or bombing attack—then they noted the red-and-blue insignia of the Royal Air Force. As they began waving and cheering, the plane opened its bomb-bay doors and, in three low sweeps, dropped provisions on a beach just downriver. Stilwell, Seagrave, and several officers jumped overboard to collect the bags in a race against some jungle people who'd emerged from the bush and were hurrying toward the provisions themselves. Stilwell let the natives take a few bags; then, for the first time in days, the group ate its fill, devouring several cans of beef whose containers had been damaged by the drop.

The plane's arrival energized column members: at least they'd not been forgotten. In a second stroke of morale-building luck, the air-drop also contained medical supplies. With the medicines (quinine for malaria and drugs for dysentery), the sick grew stronger, and for two more days they poled and pushed the rafts downstream before finally arriving in the town of Homalin, where the Uyu met the mighty Chindwin River near the border with India. There they were met by their string of mules, which had taken a shorter but more demanding land route while the larger group had negotiated the Uyu. In Homalin, Seagrave's portion of the column cajoled a local merchant into opening his shop, where they bought new shoes, new flashlight batteries, and "a lot of cigarettes." The group's mood turned happier; India waited just past the Chindwin's far bank.

The following morning, May 13, following a crossing by the mules, the column navigated the Chindwin's several-hundred-yard width using three dugout canoes. Just beyond the far shore, the general exchanged his Burmese porters for tribal Naga ones more knowledgeable about the area and more used to its mountainous demands. Stilwell immediately took to the Naga's mix of easy manners and ferocious looks: many wore bearskin clothes and had crests of hair running down the middle of otherwise-shaved heads. The Naga shared rice beer with the outsiders and were pleased to shoulder fifty pounds of supplies on wooden racks that they carried like backpacks.

They continued on. And the next morning, after Stilwell removed a leech—"Big, bright green sucker, about eight inches long," he noted in his diary—the group humped three thousand vertical feet into the Naga Hills beneath a monsoonal downpour. As the party approached a small cluster of huts (actually the town of Kawlum, along the Burma-India border), they were met by a grinning British district official named Tim Sharpe. On orders from High Command, he had been dispatched to meet and supply Stilwell's group with four hundred porters, live pigs for a roast dinner, a doctor with medicines, fresh pack animals, food, cigarettes, and whiskey.

While the group was now safe from the Japanese, the trip to Imphal—

the British corps headquarters in India—still required six more days of trudging up and down the Naga Hills. And with the advent of Sharpe's understanding of the terrain and ample pack animals to carry the invalids, the party even made twenty-one miles one day. Finally, on May 19, a British officer in a  government station far outside the town of Imphal looked up from his desk to see Stilwell's muddy column emerging from the jungle in the rain. Stilwell, still dressed in his flat-brimmed campaign hat and canvas puttees, was leading the procession. Even the tubercular Than Shwe and Major Frank Merrill (who now appeared to have a heart condition) were with them.

The British officer wanted to know: How many men had been lost on the march out of Burma?

Standing in the afternoon's rain, Stilwell looked over the group, a broad smile creasing his narrow face. "Not a one," he told the officer. "Not a single one."

THREE DAYS LATER, Stilwell was aboard an Allied air-transport headed for Delhi. On this trip, he was accompanied by, among others, the British General Alexander, who'd abandoned both Stilwell and Burma just three weeks—and a seeming lifetime—earlier.

In the intervening days, Stilwell had learned from Generals Alexander and Slim that, while Stilwell's column had escaped Burma unmolested, for the British, Gurkhas, and Indians the withdrawal ranked among the most deadly in a century. Low on water and rations, dogged by Japanese snipers and "jitter parties," and working their way north on oxcart roads not found on most maps, the British-supervised forces, like the Americans, had been required to abandon much of their mechanized transport and heavy equipment due to the impassability of the roads.

After four days of retreat, Slim's troops made it to the Chindwin, discovering that they could use six river-crossing ferries just north of the town of Kalewa. But the ferry landing there—a horseshoe-shaped depression bounded by two-hundred-foot cliffs—was a natural spot for ambush. The next morning, as Slim was being motored across the river on the first ferrying trip, the Japanese attacked; red tracer bullets slashed just above the general's head.

Before long, the Brits, Gurkhas, and Indians were taking heavy casual-

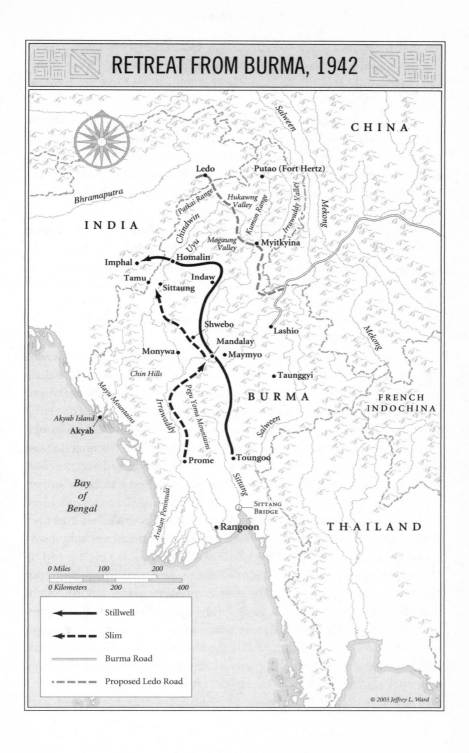

# RETREAT FROM BURMA, 1942

CHINA

Bhramaputra

Ledo

Putao (Fort Hertz)

INDIA

Patkai Range

Hukawng Valley

Kumon Range

Chindwin

Uyu

Mogaung Valley

Irrawaddy Valley

Mekong

Myitkyina

Imphal

Homalin

Tamu

Indaw

Sittaung

Shwebo

Lashio

Mandalay

Monywa

Maymyo

Chin Hills

Taunggyi

Mayu Mountains

Irrawaddy

Pegu Yoma Mountains

BURMA

FRENCH INDOCHINA

Akyab Island

Akyab

Salween

Mekong

Bay of Bengal

Arakan Peninsula

Prome

Toungoo

Sittang

SITTANG BRIDGE

Rangoon

THAILAND

0 Miles    100    200

0 Kilometers    200    400

→ Stillwell

- → Slim

Burma Road

Proposed Ledo Road

© 2003 Jeffrey L. Ward

ties and firing back with everything they had. A Bofors antiaircraft gun was turned from sky to earth, pounding Japanese terrestrial targets virtually point-blank. Meanwhile, Japanese rifle fire whistled past from seemingly every angle.

Just before the final barge started across the river, Slim ordered that all shells, mortar rounds, and matériel left behind be destroyed, and—taking heavy fire as they worked—British sappers wired the gigantic cache of artillery shells with explosives. Then, as the last barge made it to safety in India, Slim gave the order and the left-behind weapons and ammunition went up in an enormous blast.

The Japanese chose not to follow, and instead began to inspect their spoils. Left behind at the ferry landing were twelve hundred British, Indian, and Burmese dead, more than two thousand vehicles, 110 tanks, and forty artillery field pieces. But if the threat of the Japanese was now behind the withdrawing British forces, that didn't mean Slim's problems were over. Ahead lay ninety miles on foot through the swamps and jungles of the malarial Kabaw Valley.

In testimony to the trip's hardships and pressures, the brown-haired General Slim, now carrying few personal effects, even abandoned his daily shave. The following morning, Slim discovered his usually dark beard had started growing in *white*. To spare his troops the shock of his speedy aging, Slim shaved each day afterward with "a relic of a blade" hunted up by one of his aides. And six muddy and sweat-soaked days later, the British made it to safety at Imphal. For Slim and the British, the losses had been terrible: twelve thousand men survived, but thirteen thousand had been lost on the trip.

Now, on an airplane headed for Delhi, Stilwell and his "walk out" of Burma were famous. Stilwell's iron-willed withdrawal had made him (incomprehensible as it was to him) a hero. And accompanied on this trip by General Alexander—the "hero" of Britain's cross-channel withdrawal against the Germans at Dunkirk—the association likely rankled. When Stilwell's plane touched down in Delhi, he found hundreds of reporters waiting and quickly called a press conference. After an hour of polite question-and-answer about CBI and the chances of the Allies versus the Japanese, Stilwell showed the correspondents—and the world—exactly what they should expect from him in the future.

Just before ending the meeting, Stilwell took a long moment to stare across the crowd of reporters. "No military commander in history ever made a voluntary retreat," he told the press. "All retreats are ignominious as *hell*. I claim we got a *hell* of a beating. We got run out of Burma—and it is humiliating as *hell*. I think we ought to find out what caused it, go back, and retake it."

# Chapter 2

SHORTLY AFTER THE FALL of Rangoon, as forces under Stilwell, Alexander, and Slim—not to mention an estimated nine hundred thousand Burmese refugees—hurried north to evade the Japanese, troop ships filled with Imperial Japanese Army soldiers began pulling into Rangoon's still-smoldering waterfront.

The trip from Japan to Burma had been a long one. Working down the coast of China and around the Indochinese peninsula, stopping for longer layovers at the Japanese-occupied ports of Kaoshung on Formosa and at Saigon in Indochina, each ship's journey from Japan to Rangoon had taken almost three months.

Now, finally in Burma, Japanese occupation forces came ashore to find Rangoon nearly deserted. One of these soldiers, a trim twenty-three-year-old private named Atsumi Oda, was surprised to learn that, while he was a member of the Fifty-fourth Transport Corps and had been trained to operate any vehicle in the Imperial Army, in Burma he would command only a cart and its horse—an animal with which he'd had no prior experience. For Oda, it was his first intimation that Japan, in its rapacious "Asia for Asians" quest, had spread its resources dangerously thin. Still—being a good soldier who believed in the superiority of the Japanese culture and its military—Oda did his duty, proudly taking control of his charges.

Like many of Japan's educated class of soldiers, Oda believed in Japan's strict Bushido tradition: never questioning his orders, never admitting fear, and perhaps most of all, never crumbling to the enemy. According to the Bushido code, a warrior was to commit suicide rather than become a prisoner of war. But at the moment in Rangoon, what Bushido called for was the care and feeding of a beast with which Oda had no understanding. At his home university in Okayama, Oda had been educated as an electrical engineer, and upon graduation he had worked at a radio-engineering job in Tokyo. Then, at twenty-three, he had been drafted and sent for six months of military training. Now, not knowing what else to do, he endeavored to care for his horse and cart the way he'd been trained to treat any car or truck. Though frightened by the horse's size and skittishness, Oda persevered, hand-feeding his "vehicle" and hand-washing the entire animal—including its hooves—daily.

Finally, after two weeks of feeding and washing and waiting on Rangoon's waterfront, Private Oda's orders came through. He was to load his horse and cart with issues of rice, guns, ammunition, and camping provisions, and proceed north toward the city of Taungoo, in the rich Sittang River Valley, roughly 120 miles north of Rangoon. Once there, he was to assist the infantry in occupying and securing Burma in a series of staged jumps farther north. For Oda and thousands more Imperial Army troops, these first steps inside Burma were the beginning of a long, hard, grotesque purgatory in what would be the most demanding forward area of World War II.

ACROSS THE VARIED LANDSCAPE of Burma, nearly fifty thousand Japanese troops began fanning northward from Rangoon, spreading overland to meet Japanese invasion forces that had entered the country overland from the east in the weeks and months before.

As this occupying force oozed northward, they navigated the country's wild rivers and mountains, and began to set up garrisons in cities and remote jungles, where invasion troops awaited the fresh provisions they carried. But just as the defense of Burma had been a nightmare for the Allies, the landscape would be equally difficult for Japan to occupy.

Shaped like a gigantic archway keystone that connects the Malay Peninsula to the Indian subcontinent, Burma possesses the most varied terrain of any nation in South Asia. And the Japanese immediately met problems with Burma's topography and climate. In the south, along the lowland seacoast, the earth is soggy and marshy, with its thick, hot air (not to mention the malaria it brought) taking a constant toll on energy and morale. Farther inland, the landscape rises across several steep mountain ranges and lifts toward the country's "dry belt" central plateau: the broad, arid, sunbleached tableland around Mandalay where the British forces, only a few months earlier, had met initial hardship as they ran out of water. North of Mandalay, the steep and sometimes snowcapped spines of several mountain ranges—the foothills of the Himalayas—begin to rise from Burma's forested lowlands.

Given this variety of terrain, the task of clearing the country of enemy holdouts was arduous. There were pockets of Burmese, Chinese, and Indian soldiers still hiding and fighting sporadically in the jungles. And while the friendly Burma Independence Army (led by the expatriate General Aung San and his imperial counterpart, the Japanese Colonel Keiji Suzuki) seemed to quell some natives, the Burmese soon discovered the Japanese weren't honoring their "Asia for Asians" propaganda any more in Burma than they had in China. Soon word spread that the Japanese occupiers were treating Burma's citizens much as they had the Chinese at Nanking. As arbitrary bayonetings, executions, and gang-rapes became commonplace, with the dead often left lying in the street or hanging from streetlamps for all to see, even General Aung San was forced to question his fealties.

For the Japanese, as they drove deeper north into the mountainous jungles of Burma, malaria and parasites were soon grinding at their resolve. And compounding their troubles and worries, they were encountering two new and equally horrifying predators.

The first found Private Oda's detachment one midnight as he and the dozen members of his transport platoon camped deep in the jungle. As they slept in a small clearing, the group's hobbled and haltered livestock began to panic, whinnying and bucking to get free. Then, out of the darkness, an eight-foot tiger slashed from the underbrush and, attacking from behind, crushed the head and neck of a sentry named Private Sasazawa as he knelt to tend a fire at the clearing's edge. With a snarl from the tiger and a quick scream, Sasazawa was gone, carried off into the jungle. For the rest of the night, those remaining made a bonfire at the clearing's center, then they sat in a circle with their backs to the flames and their guns loaded and ready.

With the coming of full daylight, the group followed a trail of Sasazawa's blood for more than two miles. Finally, they came upon a large pool of blood on the earth beneath a tall and spreading banyan tree. Looking up, they found Sasazawa's gnawed bones draped across a wide branch fifteen feet off the ground.

A tiger was now stalking them.

A few days later, when the tiger killed a Burmese native in the jungle outside a nearby village, the Japanese took what remained of the native man's body down from another banyan, and—leaving it on the ground near the tree's trunk as bait—they built a watch platform high in the safety of the tree's branches, eighteen feet off the ground. That night, as they scanned the darkness for evidence of the tiger, they heard only the gentle soughing and chirping of a nighttime jungle. The hour grew late. At two or three o'clock in the morning, and with only a feral snarl to warn them, the tiger shot from some underbrush near the tree and bounded, in a single leap, onto the tree's watch platform.

The animal's speed and strength—and its shiny, almost-glowing eyes— were so startling that the soldiers were shocked awake. They fumbled with the safety switches on their rifles. As the tiger slapped an enormous forepaw across a soldier to Private Oda's right, the men watched in terror as it began to open its jaws to crush the head and neck of its next victim.

Stunned and flustered, the men began to beat the tiger with their fists and rifle butts. Finally, after an eternal-seeming half-minute of punching and shouting and snarling, the tiger leaped down from the platform and loped into the jungle, chased by sprays of bullets. Over the next three years, as two hundred different men cycled through Oda's transport unit, several would be hunted, killed, and eaten by different tigers. Throughout the war, however, no soldier in Oda's outfit would ever kill one of these predators.

Yet if being hunted by tigers weren't unsettling enough, in the more northern areas of Japanese occupation, word of even more gruesome events began to filter back to rearguard support units. Japanese soldiers were routinely being found stretched out on the jungle floor as if sleeping peacefully. Closer examination, however, revealed that their throats had been cut and their ears had been bloodily removed. Other times, Japanese soldiers would be traveling along a road or trail and find fellow troops laid out dead, their bodies licked by the sprays of irregular puncture wounds, their ears sliced cleanly from each side of their skulls with almost-surgical precision.

The Japanese had entered the land of the Kachins.

FROM ITS ANCIENT PAST to Britain's colonial era to today's fractious nation of Myanmar (as it's now called), Burma has always existed as an agglomeration of tribes more than as a unified country. While the majority of Burma's people are Tibetan in origin, ethnologists have identified 135 different linguistic groups inside Burma's borders. The modern government officially recognizes sixty-seven different languages and eight individual races inside Myanmar.

While the majority of these tribes are placid Buddhists, a few of the most isolated groups—particularly the Mons, Nagas, Karens, and Kachins—are religious animists that have remained fiercely independent for centuries. During British colonial times, in fact, the Crown had so little use for these most combative of Burma's natives that they usually left them alone, placing their tribal areas off-limits to anything beyond the extraction of Burma's rich resources of rubies, opium, sapphires, heroin, jade, and teak.

By July 1942, Japan's Imperial Army had pushed far enough north— about two-thirds up Burma's keystone shape—that they began to encounter the Kachins. By most accounts, early exchanges between Kachins and the Japanese were one-sided and bloody, with the Japanese— confronting yet another Burmese culture and language they didn't understand—slaughtering whole villages that resisted them, then topping off the butchery by torching the settlement until nothing remained but a charred clearing on a hilltop.

With the tone set, the Kachins wisely chose not to engage the Japanese directly, and the first true, guerrilla fighting of World War II emerged. At first, the fate befalling the Japanese arrived in the form of booby traps: pointed bamboo scantlings called *panji* sticks that were honed to razor-edged tapers then hardened by flames, their sharpened ends finally coated with a layer of human feces. Stuck into the ground—and angled to impale people diving for cover along paths through the underbrush—rows of *panjis* were placed at constrictions in narrow jungle trails or along road-sides, then covered with a layer of vegetative camouflage.

Their trap set, the Kachins would hide in ambush a safe distance away. When a Japanese soldier or column came up the trail or road, the Kachins would fire a shot from one of their few flintlock shotguns. At the gun's re-port, the Japanese would generally dive for cover in the trailside under-brush, impaling themselves on *panjis* that would either bleed them to death or leave a deadly jungle infection from the now-rotted feces.

To warn of Japanese troop movements, the Kachins also fashioned early-warning systems. They would fell bamboo, then split the stalks halfway up their lengths. With the bamboo cut and split, they'd then jam foot-long sticks between the opened halves of the bamboo, and attach a trip wire to the smaller, "trigger" stick. Then they'd stretch the other end of these wires across trails and roads and peg it to the earth. When a Japanese soldier's footfall would jerk the trip wire, the short stick would be ripped from the opened bamboo, sending the bamboo halves together with a *clack* that could be heard for half a mile through the jungle.

Finally, while the Japanese continued their practice of cutting new paths through the jungle instead of following established roads, the Kachins did their enemies one better. A seminomadic people who derive much of their food from hunting, the Kachins rarely used trails or roads at all, preferring to cruise the thick jungle in the bush. To the Japanese, the Kachins became a ghostlike force that passed around forts and encampments in haunting silence. Oda and his compatriots never knew where the Kachins were. "They were everywhere and nowhere. It was very frightening."

In response to the Kachins' brutal shadow war, the Japanese halted their drive into northern Burma, and—for the Allies—the first foothold in their long drive back to Rangoon became evident. By August 1942, with the Japanese having stopped their northward advance at the city of Myitkyina—two-thirds up Burma's seven-hundred-mile, north-to-south length—British aircraft began swooping low over Kachin villages and rice paddies, dropping leaflets written in both English and the Kachins' main language, called Jingpaw. Printed on these messages was an announcement that, in the autumn and after the rice harvest, British forces would return. Together, the leaflets boasted, the British and Kachins would "drive the Japs back to Bangkok."

A few weeks later, in late August, a light aircraft bearing Royal Air Force insignia made a low pass over the airfield at Fort Hertz—a rutted dirt landing strip whose radio beacon lent the place its name—in the wide Putao Valley in extreme northern Burma. In an entrance consistent with CBI practice thus far, the aircraft disintegrated upon landing at Fort Hertz's rough airstrip, and, luckily, the soldiers inside emerged fazed but unhurt. As the dust cleared, it became apparent to the Kachins and straggling refugees at Fort Hertz that the British "force" coming to fight the Japanese with the Kachins consisted of just two men: a Lieutenant-Colonel Gamble and a Captain Leach.

Gamble, a bearlike and boot-tough Australian, had spent some time in British colonial northern Burma and could speak snatches of Jingpaw. Inside an hour's time, he'd recruited more than twenty Kachins as the nucleus of an organized fighting force.

At first, all Gamble and Leach could offer the Kachins were regular rations of rice, beans, and dried meat, which were sometimes dropped daily by sorties from the Allied airfields of northeast India. As there were no Allied weapons in India to spare—since CBI remained last on everyone's provisions list—Gamble and Leach were forced to make do with the Kachins' own arsenal, which consisted mostly of spears, a few muzzle-loading shotguns that fired loads of pebbles, and the sharp steel blades of their long *dahs*. Over time, as the paucity of weapons became clearer to their superiors in India, the Northern Kachin Levies (or NKL)—as the force was now called—began to receive airdrops of firearms: mostly double-barreled shotguns that had been purchased or borrowed from British colonial sportsmen on tea plantations of eastern India.

BY NOVEMBER 1942, the Northern Katchin Levies were five hundred men strong, with more hungry applicants waiting to join. They were also beginning to push back in a more orderly manner against the Japanese. British army headquarters in India—which commanded Gamble and Leach— cautioned the NKL not to ambush the Japanese too regularly or fiercely, since the aggressions might touch off a full-scale attack and overwhelm the Levies' relatively small regiment. Still, skirmishes were coming with increasing regularity, and the Japanese were now taking the worst of it. When the Kachins chose to fight—Gamble and Leach had taught them to engage the Japanese only when victory was assured—the Japanese would often be run off "like scalded cats," in the estimation of the British NKL officer Ian Fellowes-Gordon. Then the platoon would return to camp, and "hand over a dozen ears on a string as proof of its success."

One of the Levies, a fourteen-year-old conscript with the tribal name of Ah-Gu-Di, came to work with Gamble. Ah-Gu-Di—like many of the younger Kachin Levies—was used most often for spying. Gamble would send him on intelligence-gathering trips, always dressed in native costume, to areas where the Burmese and Japanese coexisted. "We were told never to shoot, never to carry our guns into the towns; those were the instructions," Ah-Gu-Di said. "On the spying trips, we had orders not to kill unless we ourselves were about to be killed . . . or unless we could kill the Japanese without arousing suspicion. Still, we killed the Japanese whenever we could. I will not say we took pleasure in killing, but after the way the Japanese were treating the native people of Burma, we felt we were doing a patriotic duty."

In the war's first year, Ah-Gu-Di did not do much killing. "That came later," he said, "after we began to engage them with more British and American support."

One time early in the war, however, as he bushwhacked through the jungle at dawn, having spent the night in a Japanese controlled outpost, he did some patriotic duty. As he headed back into the Kachin lands, he came upon three Japanese sentries sleeping in the jungle. "They looked up, surprised," he said. "And they were all shot dead in seconds. *Bang! Bang! Bang!* A bullet in each of their heads. Then I hurried back to headquarters. I did not even pause to take their ears. I was worried my gunfire would bring more Japanese."

As the months passed and the Kachins grew armed with more skills and weapons to make war, the NKL began refining their guerrilla tactics. While the *panji*-pointed ambushes continued, the Kachins also grew adept at making booby traps of trip wires attached to hollowed-out bamboo cups, beneath which they placed instantaneously fused hand grenades that had been pegged tightly to the earth. When the trip wire was pulled and the cup yanked free by an enemy footfall, the grenade's spring-loaded firing lever would pop upward, setting off the explosive and taking more casualties.

To keep track of the numbers of enemy dead, the Kachins also continued their simple if brutal bookkeeping. What the Kachins didn't know was that—by removing the ears of their kills—they had inadvertently stumbled onto the single most terrifying psychological warfare tool employed against Japan in all of World War II. The Japanese in the 1940s were largely Buddhists and Shintoists, people who believe each human body is a temple that must go to heaven undefiled. Further, both religions also trust that the soul of every dead person is pulled to heaven by the ears. Consequently, the mutilation of these soldiers was nothing short of abomination. As images of earless souls unable to be lifted to heaven lodged in the mind of each Japanese soldier—especially those in the forward areas—Imperial Army fighting morale was soon compromised. And owing to infiltrations of Kachin spies and the mobility of the NKL forces through the jungle, anytime the Japanese formulated a counterpunch to their native tormentors, they would find the Kachins had already emplaced countermeasures.

For Private Oda, the fear of dying was soon being overshadowed by his understanding that, were he killed in the borderlands between the Japanese and the Kachins, he would be mutilated after death and rendered unable to ascend to heaven. Though he bravely soldiered on, the thought of losing his ears disturbed him, as it did most any Japanese solider on Kachin lands.

With the number of Japanese dead in northern Burma rising through the hundreds and into the thousands, the Japanese would eventually strike back. Still, it took until March 1944 before they felt confident enough to push up the road north out of Myitkyina along the Irrawaddy River. And within sixty miles, they engaged with the Kachins in a scrap for the village of Sumprabum—"The Grassy Hill"—halfway between Myitkyina and Fort Hertz. Initially, at Sumprabum, the Japanese and Kachins fought almost surgically, taking individual houses and knocking out sentries and small fighting groups. Then, when the Japanese realized the Kachins were holding fast, they called in a ferocious air attack followed by a full-frontal ground assault, and the naive Kachins learned for the first time that, "The more Japanese you kill, the more there are."

Despite the airborne punishment, the Kachins inflicted their own damage in the battle for Sumprabum, and after being driven out of Sumprabum's village they set up a strong defensive line along the banks of a feeder stream to the Irrawaddy called Hpunchan Hka—"The Smaller

River"—just north of town. When advance parties of Japanese scouts arrived at Hpunchan Hka, the Kachins put up an assault with seemingly every weapon they had, halting the Japanese. It would be the farthest north an organized Japanese force ever reached into Burma.

By then, however, reports of the Kachins and their guerrilla-style successes had long since reached command in CBI. A favorite tale making the rounds among soldiers in India concerned a now-forgotten NKL fighter who, to protect himself from tigers, spent one backcountry night sleeping high in a tree. As he began to doze off, a patrol of six Japanese soldiers wandered through the jungle and, stopping for the night, made camp beneath the same large tree where the Kachin was resting. In the darkness, as the Japanese slept with their backs against the tree's trunk, the Kachin climbed down from his perch and, one by one, slit each soldier's throat with his *dah*. When the bloodletting was over, the Kachin had added twelve Japanese ears to his collection.

As the exploits of the NKL filtered out of north Burma, even General Stilwell—always a skeptic of nonconventional soldiers—grew amazed by the skills, knowledge, and resources said to be displayed by the Kachins. Yet for all their successes, Stilwell steadfastly refused to believe the casualty figures that the NKL command of just eight British officers continued to claim. After little more than six months, the NKL asserted thousands of Japanese dead by their own hands. To satisfy himself, Stilwell eventually had an American-commanded Kachin brought to him for a meeting. After congratulating the Kachin on his battlefield performance, Stilwell asked how they maintained such precise counts of Japanese dead. "How can you know so exactly?" Stilwell wanted to know. "How can you be so sure?"

Without missing a beat, the Kachin unhooked a bamboo tube that had been hanging on his belt. Then he pulled a stopper from the tube's top, and—turning the tube upside down—he dumped a pile of small, blackish lumps onto the tabletop between himself and the general. The blackened lumps resembled bits of dried fruit: apricots perhaps, or peaches.

"What are those?" Stilwell asked.

"Japanese ears," the soldier answered. "Divide all of these by two and you know exactly how many Japs I've killed."

Stilwell was flabbergasted. He dismissed the Kachin and quickly sent out a general order to all Allied officers in command of Kachin Levies, demanding that they curb the practice of "ear taking." Attached to the order, Stilwell included the appropriate paragraphs from the articles of war prohibiting mutilation of enemy dead.

He also never questioned the Kachins' casualty counts again.

# Chapter 3

IN THE U.S. ARMY'S OFFICIAL HISTORY of World War II, historians Charles F. Romanus and Riley Sutherland point out that, "Normally, planning precedes logistical preparation, and logistical preparation [in turn precedes] fighting. One of the noteworthy aspects of The North Burma Campaign . . . is that the logistical preparations, the planning, and the fighting proceeded simultaneously."

Because of this bedrock disorganization, Stilwell would have to wait a full eighteen months—from mid-June 1942 to November of 1943—before he and his theater of war could reenter Burma. During this time, as he dangled last on the Allies' list of tactical or supply importance, Stilwell advised Allied Command of a half-dozen different plans to fight his way back inside Burma. Each blueprint had an aggressive-sounding code name— some of the names were Toreador, Buccaneer, Tarzan, and Gripfast—but his superiors' distractions and a profound lack of supply thwarted every one of Stilwell's planned offensives from getting under way.

Even as the first American troops began to arrive in India—coming to Calcutta and Bombay after long ocean voyages from San Francisco— Stilwell couldn't get Allied Command to budge on any of his requests or proposals. In fact, Stilwell's messages often weren't even answered, prompting the general to spend precious days and weeks flying from his newly formed China-Burma-India theater headquarters near Chiang Kai-shek's new residence in Chungking to CBI's British Headquarters in Delhi, then on to Washington or London in what Stilwell came to call "sleeve tugging."

In another of his capacities, he had started planning construction of the Ledo Road, defined as "a 478-mile, all-weather track of gravel, thirty feet wide and four inches thick." Once the Burma Road was reopened, the Ledo Road would eventually connect the railheads and airfields in India with it, leading all the way from India to China and Kunming. It was not until Stilwell and his engineers began to assess the situation, however, that they understood the scale of the undertaking facing them.

THE PROPOSED LEDO SUPPLY ROAD out of India, through northern Burma, and connecting with the Burma Road near the Chinese border, needed to twist across sometimes vertical rain forests, where as much as 150 inches of rain fell during the three summer months. At the India-Burma border, the mountains rose as high as thirty-eight hundred feet above the valleys. The landscape, deadpanned army engineer scouts, was "mountainous terrain, canyon sections, with narrow terraces along torrential streams. This area is unsettled and relatively unexplored. Existing maps were found to be highly inaccurate in their portrayal of ground conditions under the 150 feet of vegetation cover. . . . The soil is largely clay over a weak sedimentary rock structure broken by innumerable fault planes and subject to frequent earth tremors. . . . [observed] rainfall intensity reached fourteen inches in twenty-four hours."

Beyond the mountains, the jungles, and the rain, though, the road also had to hopscotch down three river valleys—the Hukawng, the Mogaung, and the Irrawaddy—each of which flooded every August and grew bone-dry by the following February. Completing the road would require seven hundred bridges, seven to thirteen rain culverts per mile, and as many as seventeen thousand American Engineer troops overseeing an estimated fifty thousand to eighty thousand laborers. It would also demand the movement of billions of pounds of soil, vegetation, and rock, with engineers and laborers working twenty-four hours a day in the wet season and dry. And—rain, terrain, and labor problems aside—it needed to be completed in a most timely manner because China was already starving.

Compounding the problem, in August 1943 at the Allied planning conference called Quadrant in Quebec, it was decided that four (and eventually *six*) oil and gas pipelines needed to follow the roadbed as well. They, too, were to start from five hundred feet of elevation in northeast India, track across the mountains into the valleys of swampy Burma, then climb up over the ten-thousand-foot passes on the Himalayan plateau before ending in Kunming. When completed, these conduits for gasoline and aviation fuel would form the longest pipeline on earth.

Then there was the small obstacle of the Imperial Japanese Army that was still occupying Burma and fortifying its positions there by the day. Practically speaking, building the road demanded overwhelming battlefield success, since construction could only progress from India into occupied Burma after Allied advances had driven back the Japanese. After the recent show in Burma, leading to Stilwell's and Slim's walks out, the job of clearing the landscape ahead of the road by construction crews seemed dubious at best. Upon considering the Ledo Road plan, Winston Churchill dismissed it as "an immense, laborious task, unlikely to be finished before the need for it had passed."

Churchill wasn't alone in dour prediction. In the estimation of the American Colonel Charles Gleim, commander of America's 330th Engineers in Ledo, the Ledo Road would stand as "the toughest engineering job on the planet." And Gleim was in a position to know; he'd been a project supervisor for construction of New York's Holland Tunnel, Lincoln Tunnel, and George Washington Bridge.

IN SPITE OF ALL of these head-swimming impediments, the combined Ledo Road was approved for construction in early February 1942. Because, behind all the problems, the road's creation and existence was to be tangible proof that the Allies could succeed with their one simple, yet endlessly complex, task. In the Allies' view, the Ledo-Burma Road's entire objective was to keep China supplied and in the war; in other words, to keep it out of Japanese hands.

To the Allied war planners, especially the Americans, an overland route toward Japan across China had to remain open, no matter the costs. That way, when and if the time came for attack on Japan, the Allies could use northern China and the Korean peninsula as leaping-off points for the imperial homeland across the Sea of Japan. How the Allies would gain this offensive position in northern China, given the Japanese occupation there already, remained beyond the Allied planners' immediate knowledge. But the Allies had to start building a plan of attack on Japan, and—with the exception of a few critics—the combined Ledo-Burma Roads seemed a step—or more than a few steps—in the right direction.

Churchill, however, kept intensely and vocally hurling brickbats at the Ledo Road offensive, likening the taking of north Burma to munching a porcupine, quill by quill. In his estimation, the Allies "could not choose a worse place to fight the Japanese." He also continued railing against the proposed road, recognizing that no matter what he said, the road was a foregone conclusion. "We argued that the enormous expenditure of man-power and material would not be worthwhile," he wrote. "But we never succeeded in deflecting the Americans from their purpose. Their national psychology is such that the bigger the Idea, the more wholeheartedly and obstinately do they throw themselves into making it a success. It is an ad-mirable characteristic, provided the Idea is good."

No matter what Churchill said, though, the road was going through. And, as it came under the rubric of Allied lend-lease to China, responsibil-ity for it and its completion fell to none other than Joseph W. Stilwell.

# Chapter 4

DURING THE EIGHTEEN MONTHS of delays and abortive plans following the Allied retreat from Burma, one of the few bright spots in CBI appeared overhead. As the Japanese continued to fortify themselves—and the Allies dithered over their next move—Claire Lee Chennault's American Volunteer Group was laying waste the Japanese air force.

Chennault—a hard, tenaciously charming Louisiana Cajun with a solid jaw and sun-scarred face—had been advising Chiang and his Chinese air force since 1937. A distant relative of the American Civil War General Robert E. Lee, Chennault had a love of military airpower matched only by his boyhood ardor for hunting, fishing, and trapping across the bayous near his childhood home in Waterproof, Louisiana. Never a good student, he'd been a southeast Texas schoolteacher before, at age twenty-eight, joining the Army Air Corps in 1917. In the closing year of World War I, he'd discovered military applications for airplanes and had learned to fly.

By the early 1920s, Chennault was one of the world's best aerobatic pilots. Inside the American Army Air Corps, he railed at superiors to increase the numbers of pursuit squadrons, despite the army's overwhelming belief that groups of fast, large, and heavily fortified bomber aircraft—like the Martin B-10—were a more lethal tip for the

American spear. As Chennault unsuccessfully pressed his fighter-based approach inside the army, he also captained a three-man squadron of aerobatic planes that gave breathtaking performances around the United States. He capped their shows by linking the three aircraft together with twenty-foot lengths of rope, then going aloft to fly precision loops.

The army, however, didn't shift its thinking—it stuck with a bomber-based air attack—and Chennault's constant badgering earned him no friends. It did, however, get him noticed. When Captain Chennault was retired from military service in 1937 for medical reasons—he was partially deaf and had chronic bronchitis (though many believed the army merely wanted him gone)—Chiang Kai-shek contacted the forty-seven-year-old firebrand to advise the Chinese air force.

If, on paper in 1937, the Chinese boasted five hundred planes in their war with Japan, in real terms it possessed less than one hundred flyable aircraft. And few of China's pilots were skilled: one morning in January 1939, in perfect flying weather, Chennault watched as Chinese pilots destroyed six aircraft on takeoffs and landings.

Chennault went to Chiang. He requested that American instructors come to China and join him, but the generalissimo and even the U.S. government resisted—fearing it might appear the Americans were entering the war. Instead, the Russian air force stepped forward to help, and the Chinese air force's skills began to improve.

Still, by late 1940, Japan's deepening attacks on China were taking a toll. As the Japanese continued their virtually unmolested air raids—hammering Shanghai, Nanking, Chungking, Kunming, and the Burma Road with five-hundred-pound incendiary bombs—Chiang Kai-shek finally agreed that a new strategy had to be found, and fast. So in January 1941—with both Chiang's and President Roosevelt's approval—Chennault began seeking out American fighter pilots between the ages of twenty-three and twenty-eight who had to retire their military commissions to join his American Volunteer Group (or AVG).

The AVG's financial benefits were alluring: a salary of $600 to $750 a month—almost twice what they made in the army—plus a $500 bonus for every Japanese aircraft shot down. Only a dozen qualified pilots bit at the opportunity, however, and soon Chennault was forced to approve four-engine bomber pilots and the pilots of two-engined submarine-chasers into his program, few of whom had ever flown pursuit aircraft and several of whom were in their forties.

For equipment, Chennault purchased a fleet of aging P-40 fighters from the Americans after British lend-lease officials deemed them obsolete. And in late summer 1941, Chennault's AVG mercenaries were sent to Burma and China—disguised as aeronautics engineers—for fighter training. During the trip to Burma, and inspired by shark-tooth markings he'd seen painted on a British squadron's aircraft in Africa, an AVG pilot named Allen "Crix" Christman painted a toothy, sharklike sneer on his P-40's snout after he arrived in Burma. Soon all the AVG pilots were asking Cristman, who'd been an illustrator for the Associated Press before the war, to paint similar tiger sharks on their planes, and the AVG soon owned what would become the most distinctive insignia of World War II.

The AVG's fighter-pilot training proved quick, and after only a few months, Chennault's for-hire flyboys were ready to enter the fray. On December 20, 1941, as Japanese ground forces invaded Malaya in the first step toward Rangoon, a report of ten Japanese Mitsubishi bombers departing Hanoi and headed for Kunming filtered through Chennault's ground-station network to AVG Command. And for the first time, a "scramble" call went out to the AVG. Twenty minutes later, just thirty miles east of Kunming, the flight of Japanese bombers was met by four darting fighter aircraft, each plane's nose painted like a freakish, hungry predator.

On the open radio frequency—for the first time over China—the voices of American fighter pilots rose to fill the crackling static.

"There they are."

"No, no, they can't be Japs."

"Look at those red balls."

"Let's get 'em."

The Japanese, who had been flying unescorted, jettisoned their bombs early and turned for home. As the bombers ran, ten more fighters appeared; all of them had their two wing cannons and four .30-caliber guns blazing. In the 130-mile running fight that followed, the AVG pilots had themselves an orgy of unorthodox flying and aerial marksmanship. Diving, slashing, and barrel-rolling while firing their weapons wide open, the AVG pursuit team chased the slow and ungainly bombers like sharks on bloodied prey. One by one, twin-engined Mitsubishis began spiraling to the earth in flames. Fritz Wolf of Shawano, Wisconsin, knocked down two "Mitsus" single-handedly, then cursed his weapons crew over the radio, informing them that his guns had jammed. Only after landing would Wolf learn he'd emptied his full load of 1,465 rounds of ammunition in minutes. The air had been so full of bullets and wildly flying P-40s that Chennault later expressed amazement that his pilots had neither collided nor shot each other down.

With the bombers on the run for Hanoi, the AVG pilots broke off the engagement with reports of three certain kills. Later, the AVG would learn that by the time the Japanese returned to their base in Hanoi, only one bomber was still crawling through the sky. In China, it was a rare moment of victory, and as the AVG pilots made their base outside Kunming, each member steered his aircraft through a series of slow, aerobatic rolls over the airfield in triumph. Only one AVG pilot, Ed Recter, was missing: He'd run out of gas and crash-landed east of Kunming. Claire Lee Chennault's "Flying Tigers" had made their debut.

Though they only existed for seven months before being absorbed into CBI, the 113 pilots and 55 planes of the American Volunteer Group would not only shoot down 299 Japanese aircraft (with 153 more "probable kills"); they would lose just four pilots in combat. More important, however, they filled an enormous psychological void for the Allies, providing the first tangible evidence that, in China, the Japanese could be soundly defeated. Only five days after the Tigers' first active engagement—on Christmas Day 1941—the Flying Tiger Edward O. McComas earned international fame by becoming the war's first "One Day Ace," gunning down four Japanese bombers and an escort fighter in a single battle.

Initially deployed in three squadrons—with bases in Kunming, Taungoo in central Burma, and Rangoon—the Flying Tigers were as formidable on the ground as in the air. Equal parts relentless pursuit pilots and rakish, comic-book heroes, the men of the AVG exuded two-fisted energy—and a formidable lack of discipline. As mercenaries outside the restrictions of the army, they flew in cowboy boots and rumpled, oil-stained khakis, dressing in full uniform only for funerals. At night in Rangoon, they scandalized British officers by wearing loud Hawaiian-print shirts and drinking hard with local girls at the tony Silver Lake Grill. Other times, after a few dozen drinks, AVG pilots might be seen riding domesticated water buffalo down the streets of Rangoon shouting "Ya-hooo!" In Kunming and Taungoo, they killed time drinking bootleg whiskey and Carew's Gin and, if no worthy opponents could be found, playing baseball, basketball, and fistfighting among themselves.

One booze-soaked evening in Rangoon, several AVG pilots convinced the captain of an American C-47 cargo plane to make an unscheduled bombing run on Hanoi. Loading the ungainly aircraft with discarded French, Russian, and Chinese ordinance (and plenty of liquor), they proceeded over their target in darkness, kicking bombs from the plane's passenger door between swigs of drink.

After Rangoon fell and all three squadrons of the AVG became based in Kunming, they kept up their unruly ways with their commander's tacit approval. They'd affectionately taken to calling Chennault "Old Leatherface," and the AVG's afternoon baseball scrimmages and nightly poker games (which Chennault often won) were Kunming's social hot spot.

Meanwhile, in the air, the Tigers remained even scrappier and more resourceful than on the ground. Because they didn't have spare aircraft, Flying Tiger planes were soon heaps of scavenged parts, their pilots sometimes filling Japanese bullet holes with wads of chewing gum and adhesive tape. To deceive the enemy into thinking the AVG had countless aircraft, the Americans repainted their propellers new colors every week. And since the P-40s possessed no bomb racks, pilots crafted incendiary "gifts" for the Japanese of gasoline-filled whiskey bottles that they'd ignite and toss from their cockpits. Other times, they'd drop homemade pipe bombs onto Japanese encampments.

Before long, Radio Tokyo was calling the American pilots "unprincipled bandits," and demanding that, unless these tactics were halted, the Americans would be "treated as guerrillas"—implying execution if captured. By early 1942, the Japanese vowed to destroy "all two hundred planes" possessed by the Flying Tigers, despite the AVG having only twenty-nine aircraft in commission at the time.

This unorthodox success provided great lift for Chennault's career. And when the AVG was finally disbanded and reformed as the Twenty-third Fighter Group inside CBI's new China Air Task Force (or CATF) in July 1942, Chennault—who had been recommissioned—retained command, with the new rank of brigadier general. Back inside an army that only five years earlier had drummed him out, Chennault knew his star was on the rise. But despite his recent success, he remained subordinate to Stilwell, a condition he thought unfair, since he'd achieved international renown in a sphere beyond the Allies' narrow assignations. Chennault had delivered on his promises, and now he wanted President Roosevelt and General Marshall to grant him more power.

A showdown was coming.

# Chapter 5

DURING THE SUMMER and fall of 1942, Joseph W. Stilwell remained beset by problems and obstacles on all sides. "CBI command . . ." wrote the journalist Theodore H. White, was "a fabulous compound of logistics, personalities, Communism, despotism, corruption, imperialism, nonsense, and tragic impotence."

Adding to Stilwell's woes, he'd contracted jaundice from a tainted yellow-fever inoculation, leaving him chronically weak and tired—an affliction that seemed to perfectly mirror the condition of his theater of operations. Stilwell couldn't get Chiang or the British to agree on any plans or policies, Allied Supreme Command refused to approve any of CBI's invasion plans for Burma, Stilwell's Ledo Road was still not started, and he had few of his new Chinese or American troops ready for war. He was also increasingly having to disabuse Chiang Kai-shek of his "Let the Allies do it" thinking.

Since December 1941, Chiang and the Chinese had unswervingly believed that America's entry in World War II signaled the end of imperial Japan's war machine. Often, it seemed to Stilwell that Pearl Harbor Day in America seemed to signal Armistice Day for Chiang and China. This belief on Chiang's part was further supported by events of April 20, 1942. That morning, sixteen American B-25 bombers—led by the American Colonel James Doolittle—had taken off from the aircraft carrier USS *Hornet* in the northern Pacific and more than seven hundred miles off the Japanese coast. The trip would be a one-way affair, since the *Hornet*'s landing deck was too short to accommodate the B-25s for a return landing. Instead, each aircraft was to bomb selected targets in Japan, then make its way to free China, where Chennault's growing array of airfields waited. Weaving low across the ocean to elude the Japanese fleet, Doolittle's Raiders slipped in and successfully bombed Japanese naval yards and the cities of Osaka, Yokohama, Kobe, and Nagoya, shocking the Japanese by attacking their supposedly impervious homeland.

After the raid, however, all sixteen bombers—which were slated for CBI after the mission—were either shot down or crash-landed in Japanese-occupied China, with nine of the eighty Doolittle crewmen being taken prisoner.

In retaliation, the Japanese sent fifty-three full divisions across China's eastern Chekiang Province, killing more than 250,000 civilians, pillaging any village believed to have assisted Doolittle's American pilots, and plowing up every Chinese airfield for twenty thousand square miles. To the generalissimo, who was initially furious—having not been informed of the action—the raid and the success of Chennault's AVG were proof the Allies could mount offensives against the Japanese from the air and on their own, obviating the need for Chiang to expend troops and equipment.

BUT JAUNDICE AND Chiang's low motivation were but two of the slivers beneath Stilwell's skin. With the closing of the Burma Road, China's supply of food and lend-lease equipment had been cut. To keep goods flowing to China until the Ledo Road could be completed and the Burma Road reopened, President Roosevelt had promised Chiang and Stilwell one hundred new C-46 cargo planes to create the Air Transport Command (or ATC), a new air-freight service that was scaled to carry twelve thousand tons of goods a month over the Himalayan "Hump" to China from airfields in Assam.

The C-46s—made by American manufacturer Curtiss and promised for delivery in July 1942—were said to be more reliable, heavier fitted variations of the two-engine Douglas C-47 transports (better known by their civilian denomination, DC-3) the army had been using since the war's beginning. Capable of carrying nearly eight tons of payload (twice the amount that could be lugged by a C-47), a C-46 could also operate at altitudes higher than the twenty-four-thousand-foot maximum ceiling of a C-47—a comforting fact for the Hump pilots, who often skimmed the Himalayas on runs between Assam and Kunming.

Unfortunately, for all this promise, the C-46s were tied up in production and weren't being delivered. In their stead, Air Transport Command slurped up whatever aircraft were available: primarily the older C-47s (few of which had standardized engines and equipment, giving each plane a personality all its own), plus dozens of refitted American B-24 Liberator bombers rechristened C-87s (for cargo) and C-109s (carrying fuel).

If the lend-lease supply route to China had been tenuous while the Burma Road was open (by rail to San Francisco, boat to Rangoon, railroad to Lashio, and over the Burma Road to China), arrivals of ATC-ferried supplies were even more unreliable. The route—still departing from San Francisco by ship and arriving for rail transport in Calcutta—necessitated three different train changes inside India before reaching Assam. Then came the truly dangerous part: five hundred miles by air over the Hump.

From today's perspective (with our jet aircraft, radar, and satellite navigation systems), crossing the ten-thousand-foot Naga Hills of India and Myanmar and the twenty-thousand-foot peaks of the Himalayan Santsung Range of southwest China is a cakewalk. In 1942, the route was a nightmare. Allied maps of the area weren't reliable, and the range of even the most powerful navigational radios reached only thirty to fifty miles. Then there was the enemy: Japanese fighter aircraft out of Myitkyina and antiaircraft ground fire—which hurled up gardens of flak explosions the pilots called "black roses"—were constant threats. Monsoons poured from May to October, with freak winds to 248 miles per hour sometimes buffeting the aircraft over the highest Himalayan peaks. Other times, turbulence could literally flip an aircraft over as it skirted the Himalayan mountaintops, or gusts would sling it up or down thousands of feet in a minute.

One Hump pilot, a B-24 bomber captain named Charles F. Linamen, who flew thirty "gas hauling" missions in a C-109 during rainy periods when bombing wasn't needed, described the flights:

> The first thing you'd do when you climbed into the cockpit for a Hump run was to cinch down the leg and chest straps of your seat harness until they were so tight you could hardly breathe. Because when that aircraft would hit turbulence, you'd get bounced all over the place. The plane would meet an

updraft, and you'd be pushed down into the seat until the belts were so loose you wouldn't even know you had them on; you could easily pass your hand between your leg and the belt. Then, a minute later, you might get slammed by a downdraft and you'd be thrown against the harness belts—they were the only things keeping you in that seat. Sometimes, in an up- or downdraft, I'd look at the altimeter and it would be spinning so fast my eyes couldn't follow. You'd rise one thousand feet or fall one thousand feet in no time, the aircraft sometimes tilting over on one side or the other to ninety degrees or more: you'd look out the side windows see the ground directly below your shoulder. After especially rough flights, my shoulders and legs would be bruised from the pressure of the harness against them. And we did that every day, the way people these days get in and out of their cars.

Because of the turbulence encountered on flights, ATC crews took to calling their airlift runs over the Hump "Operation Vomit," and an average of eight ATC planes were going down a month. Before the war was over, nearly six hundred planes would crash along the route. As the airlift continued, the Hump pilots—some of whom flew the route three times daily—began to joke that they could pick their way from India to Kunming by following "The Aluminum Trail" of crashed aircraft along the ground.

BETWEEN THE SUMMER and fall of 1942, despite the ATC's promised initial "ramp-up" of five thousand tons a month to Kunming from India, only one hundred tons were being delivered. Beyond the dangers of the Hump, another part of the problem lay with infrastructure in India. Only one airfield had been completed at the ATC's Indian leaping-off point in Assam (though twelve airfields would eventually be built). The Allies were also directing lend-lease goods to other parts of the globe: to the British in North Africa and to the Russians. More ominous for CBI, bomber units from CBI's Tenth Air Force and C-47s from the China National Aviation Corporation (the precursor and American commercial brother to the ATC) were being withdrawn from India to assist the British in Egypt, infuriating Chiang Kai-shek.

Yet another problem seethed inside India itself. By 1942, the subcontinent's nationalist leader, Mohandas Gandhi, had risen to prominence as a statesman and he was calling for India to be freed from British colonialism. When Gandhi was jailed for his views, he urged followers to practice civil disobedience, hobbling the nation's efficiency as telephone and telegraph lines were cut, towns were looted, and the trains and railroads that supplied CBI were dismantled by angry mobs. In some cases, Europeans were being pulled off the halted trains and hacked to death in the streets.

Rail supply stuttered, sometimes halting altogether. At Allied bases in India and China, gasoline grew so limited that motor-pool drivers resorted to carrying a "CBI credit card": a jerry can fitted with a length of siphon hose to steal fuel from unwitting comrades. Chennault's China Air Task Force was so bereft they were using electrical wire in lieu of shoelaces. Before long, the British and Americans were inventing derisive nicknames for CBI, calling it "Confused Bastards in India" and "Confusion Beyond Imagination."

SUPPLIES WERE LITERALLY DRIBBLING into China, and Chiang Kai-shek, feeling neglected by the Allies, began to blame Stilwell. In June 1942—despite Stilwell's sympathetic view on China's privations—Chiang felt he'd been patient enough. On June 21, after grumbling for weeks, Chiang presented Stilwell with a three-point ultimatum followed by a document reiterating the requests. With each demand, the generalissimo also provided the Allies a deadline. For China to remain partnered with the Allies, Chiang wanted

- Three American divisions of troops to arrive in India between August and September with the restoration of communications between China and Burma.
- Five hundred combat airplanes to operate from China beginning in August to be maintained continuously at that strength.
- Delivery of five thousand tons a month by the ATC beginning in August.

If these three demands were not met, Chiang claimed he had no alternative but the "liquidation" of the China theater and a "readjustment" of the Chinese position relative to the Allies. Chiang was bluffing that he'd make a truce with the Japanese.

Stilwell, knowing the Allies couldn't bear losing China as a strategic foothold, forwarded the three demands to President Roosevelt along diplomatic channels. Hoping to find the time and resources to placate the generalissimo, the president responded with a letter pledging resolution soon. In the meantime, the job fell to Stilwell to keep the Gi-mo happy.

YET AS STILWELL AND Chiang wrangled—and with Chennault's China Air Task Force continuing to defend China and buoy Allied spirits— Vinegar Joe turned his energies toward cultivating another sunny prospect inside CBI. In India, the nine thousand Chinese troops that had walked out of Burma behind him were finally ready to be trained by American forces. And from the outset, the Chinese responded beautifully. If they had straggled from Burma starving and sick—carrying unusable rifles coated with rust—once billeted at an Allied training camp near the Indian city of Ramgarh, they thrived.

Treated by Seagrave's medical staff and fed three good meals a day, the Chinese soldiers had an average weight gain of twenty-one pounds during their first three months. And once issued new uniforms and equipment, they became ready warriors. Stilwell took great pride in his trainees, and he trained some of them himself, patiently lying down beside each soldier on Ramgarh's rifle ranges to coach the proper technique for sighting a rifle.

Each day, Chinese troops by the hundred poured into India on return Hump airlifts from Kunming. Unfortunately, they often arrived in pitiable condition—89 percent of one Chinese unit were rejected for poor health—and many were clothed in nothing but rags. Several Chinese soldiers actually froze to death during the three-hour Hump flights. Still, those who passed into the Allied camps were made combat ready. By December 1942, thirty-two thousand Chinese were in training at Ramgarh, and more than seventeen thousand Americans had arrived in CBI. Stilwell's program for invading and reoccupying Burma was coming together, and he was finally being accorded respect in China.

But if the Chinese army was flourishing at Ramgarh, Stilwell himself seemed to be entering some sort of personal entropy. He was still battling jaundice, and despite his energetic efforts instructing the Chinese—which British General Slim labeled "magnificent"—Stilwell appeared drawn, haggard, and even thinner than usual. Due to the lack of supplies, he had even been forced to replace the chin strap for his trusty World War I campaign hat with a shoelace; and having finally accepted short pants as part of CBI's military uniform, he now dressed constantly in shorts and open-collared shirts, even for officers' dinners.

If worn and shriveling, Stilwell remained tireless, flying from CBI's British Headquarters in Delhi to Ramgarh to Ledo to Kunming then beating it back to his own headquarters in Chungking, all the while pushing his latest plan for the invasion of Burma slated for the postmonsoon winter and code-named Anakim.

AT ITS MOST BASIC, Anakim depended on a straightforward pincer movement into Burma called the "X-Y Plan." To initiate the invasion, an "X Force" of American-trained Chinese soldiers would invade northern Burma from India, crossing a mountain notch in the Patkai Range called Pangsau Pass. As the X Force pushed into Burma—clearing out the Japanese in advance of the Ledo Road—a "Y Force" of Chinese divisions would then smash inside northern Burma from the east along the Burma Road. Coupled with a British thrust to retake Rangoon—by naval blockade of the seaport and of the Bay of Bengal—Stilwell believed that the Japanese could be strangled and driven out of Burma the way they'd come in: southeast and back into Thailand.

For once, Allied Command approved Stilwell's invasion plan. All sides—the Americans, the British (which mostly was made of Indian troops), and the Chinese—agreed that the time to retake Burma had finally arrived. But as the rainy summer of 1942 moved toward fall, hard timetables for the engagement were being avoided by both the British and the Chinese—neither of whom truly wanted Anakim to begin. By summer's end, Britain's overall commander in India, General Alexander, had been reassigned as commander in chief in the Middle East, where Hitler's armies were creating more immediate Allied problems. In India, Alexander was replaced by British General Sir Archibald Wavell, who—along with Slim—assessed pre-Anakim manpower and supply conditions in India as unacceptable for an offensive. Wavell's view was fully supported by Winston Churchill, who continued pooh-poohing the retaking of Burma at every turn.

For Anakim in China, the generalissimo (still concerned about arming future enemies beneath his own flag) also continued fretting about potential troop and equipment losses, and he was now greeting Stilwell's Anakim-related entreaties with silence. Having sent Chiang six memoranda requesting meetings on invasion timetables without reply, Stilwell grew frustrated. "This is the most dreary type of maneuvering I've ever done," he wrote home to Win, "trying to guide and influence a stubborn, ignorant, prejudiced, conceited despot who never hears the truth except from me and finds it hard to believe."

BUT STILWELL POSSESSED a powerful lever under Chiang. Since he alone administered China's lend-lease deliveries, the American subtly threatened to slow shipments into Kunming. And finally, on August 1, Chiang sent a message back to Stilwell. In it, he agreed to the invasion, contingent on full British cooperation by land and sea, and with full Allied air force support. These commitments, the generalissimo correctly assumed, would not be honored, since the defense of Britain's homeland, the support of British troops in Egypt, and the quelling of Gandhi-inspired disarray in India were keeping the British fully occupied.

Stilwell—succumbing to his darker side—took to openly bad-talking the lot, calling the British "yellow Limeys" and publicly referring to the shaven-headed Chiang by his former CBI code name: Peanut. Stilwell was now sniping at "the Peanut dictator," sometimes in front of Chiang's people, who might send word of such impudence streaking back to the generalissimo himself.

Chiang Kai-shek, in his frustrations with Stilwell's unvarnished style, began calling for the American's ouster and listening more intently to Chennault, who believed he could defeat the Japanese with pure airpower. With Chiang's approval, Chennault began ordering the creation of forward airfields across eastern China. And despite inadequate supply to these bases (Chinese laborers, in some cases, had to roll drums of fuel one hundred miles up dirt roads to reach the most forward bases), Chennault's China Air Task Force was continuing to slap back the Japanese, just as his Flying Tigers had done before.

By moving aircraft between his growing lattice of airstrips, and radioing fake communications from imaginary China Air Task Force bomber and fighter squadrons on frequencies monitored by the Japanese, Chennault and his men kept the enemy off balance with imaginary aircraft while inflicting very real damage daily. When the Japanese would strike back, bombing CATF airstrips on night raids, Chennault answered with man-power: scores of Chinese laborers at each airfield could repair the bomb craters in a few hours.

Where Stilwell was stumbling and stymied, Chennault was succeed-ing. And there was nothing Stilwell could do to change the situation. On a tour of one new Chinese airfield, Stilwell asked the strip's engineering officer, Colonel Henry Byroade: "What the hell are you building this air-field for?"

"Well," Byroade answered, "Chennault says he needs it."

"How's he going to defend it?" Stilwell countered.

Byroade never answered. The strip was completed anyway.

INSIDE CHINA Chennault and his CATF were ascendant.

By October 1942, when the failed presidential candidate Wendell Willkie was sent around the world as an emissary by a third-term President Roo-sevelt (who had vanquished Willkie two years earlier), Willkie expressed keen interest in meeting privately with Chennault, the man whose air force appeared single-handedly to be keeping China free. And Stilwell, much to everyone's surprise but his own, agreed. For the meeting, in fact, Stilwell instructed Chennault to speak his mind freely, giving him a specific order to do so.

His insistence on openness would soon cause Stilwell no end of aggra-vation. After a meeting with Chennault that lasted two hours, Willkie de-parted Kunming the following morning—October 8—carrying in his jacket pocket one of the most remarkable documents of World War II. In a letter addressed directly to President Roosevelt, Chennault claimed—in his "professional opinion"—that with 105 modern fighter aircraft, plus 30 medium and 12 heavy bombers, his China Air Task Force could "accom-plish the downfall of Japan . . . probably within six months, within one year at the outside."

Such a campaign, Chennault wrote, would spare the lives of "hundreds of thousands of American soldiers and sailors." Then Chennault person-ally guaranteed "to destroy the principal industrial centers of Japan." To execute this feat, however, he would need "freedom of fighting action"—in other words: full command and freedom from Stilwell. "This latter," Chennault also informed the president in his letter, "I know the generalissimo desires."

While Roosevelt was intrigued by Chennault's "simple" plan (that adjective was used four times in the letter), the War Department and Allied Command were of other opinions. First, Chennault's bombing of Japan would likely produce the same response as the April 1942 Jimmy Doolittle raid: bloody Japanese retribution on Chinese citizens and air bases. Second, there was no way to supply CATF forward bases in China except over the "Hump," which thus far was underperforming spectacularly.

Since June, as the first new C-46 cargo aircraft began arriving in Assam (appeasing another of Chiang's three demands), most of the new planes had been rejected for profound structural and systems problems. Flying in the monsoon, their joints leaked constantly, bubbles of vaporized gasoline blocked their poorly designed fuel lines, and faulty defrosters allowed buildups of ice to choke their engines' intake manifolds. One C-46, known as the "Leakin' Deacon," was so plagued by an inability to hold hydraulic fluid—critical to controlling any heavy aircraft in flight— that its crew chief refused to let it leave the ground with less than fifty gallons of spare "hydraulic juice" aboard, so the Deacon could be quenched en route.

Stilwell was shocked to hear that the vast majority of ATC pilots were actually *requesting* to fly the older, more eccentric, less-efficient C-47s. And there were now other problems, as well: the summer's rains had drenched CBI so severely that though several new airfields had been bulldozed across Assam in recent months, the wet season had rendered them all muddy and unusable. For the ATC to work, poured concrete airfields would be required.

CBI continued to languish as the Allies' lowest priority. To keep the leaders of CBI engaged on Anakim, Stilwell was now flying from Chungking to New Delhi constantly, "tugging sleeves" and forcing Chiang Kaishek and Wavell to honor their commitments for Anakim's winter invasion. Though Stilwell had finally licked his jaundice he'd taken to making only terse, gruff daily entries in his diary, like this loquacious one for September 6: "Office. Pushed papers around." Or this one from October 8: "Rain. Conference at War Ministry, usual crap."

With most of the Allied supplies and support still being directed to North Africa and an impending Allied amphibious landing there—to be called "Operation Torch"—Stilwell wrote to General George Marshall, requisitioning buildup provisions ahead of Anakim. Then he waited. Weeks passed. Then nearly a month. Finally on Thanksgiving Day, Stilwell received his old friend Marshall's response. Because of the continuing North African activity—plus larger matériel concerns in the European theater against Germany—Stilwell could expect little beyond the lend-lease equipment already in CBI or currently in transit to support the Anakim invasion.

That evening Stilwell wrote Win: "This is Thanksgiving Day and I received a most appropriate message right on time. You know I have a little job to do over here, so I asked for a few tools to do it with. I have tried it once without any tools at all and it didn't work, so I reminded our folks of some promises and made what I thought was a very modest request. You should have seen the answer—I believe you would have helped me bite the radiator. Peanut and I are on a raft, with one sandwich between us, and the rescue ship is heading away from the scene . . . This is proving to be as lousy a job as was ever invented. All we can do is keep on swinging."


BY LATE NOVEMBER 1942 in India and Burma, the summer rains had ceased. Winter's cooler, drier weather was on the doorstep, and a firm date for Anakim was still shimmering like a mirage beyond Joe Stilwell's grasp. Then Anakim evaporated completely.

By early December, the British (still mired with their own supply problems and continuing to deal with Gandhi's Indian uprising) informed Stilwell they lacked the naval force to control the Bay of Bengal or launch amphibious attacks on Rangoon. This admission, like a toppling domino, gave Chiang Kai-shek his out, since British control of the bay had been a condition of his own participation.

On January 8, 1943, Chiang Kai-shek formally refused to participate in the Allied invasion of Burma. Tellingly, in his declination to Roosevelt, the generalissimo peppered the letter with Chennault-like phrases ("the remarkable potentialities of an air offensive," for example) and suggested—with a brio reminiscent of Chennault—that instead of a ground battle, the Allies could mount "an air offensive, for which I guarantee results out of all proportion to the force used."

When Stilwell picked up his diary on January 8, he began the day's entry by writing: "Black Friday . . ."

The Anakim invasion was off the table.


WITH ANAKIM DEAD, however, the British—without alerting either Allied or CBI command—began their own limited invasion of Burma. Beginning in December 1942, Wavell had sent an army southwest from India's Bengal Province into Burma's Arakan division: a mountainous coastal region of Burma along the Bay of Bengal. This invading force—under General W. L. Lloyd—pushed south through the jungle valleys of the steeply severe Mayu Mountains, their objective the capture of relatively undefended Akyab Island, ninety miles south along the Burmese coast. Once secured, it was believed Akyab's sole air base would provide convenient air support for future attacks on Rangoon.

After a slow start along difficult roads, the morale-building British thrust was only fifteen miles north of their objective when, somewhat surprisingly, they encountered Japanese forces bunkered into the Mayu hillsides. Each bunker was made of heavy logs covered by several feet of earth, and each was placed halfway up the mountainside and at pressure points of the British advance, where it could provide overlapping fields of rifle and artillery fire against the invaders. Cut into the mountainsides and covered with bamboo and trees from the thick jungle, the bunkers were almost invisible. And judging from the return fire the Japanese were giving, these positions were also heavily stocked with ammunition and provisions.

For weeks, the British would charge a bunker, be driven back, and regroup to attack again. When a British or Indian army unit would penetrate close, nearby Japanese emplacements would put them under heavy artillery and rifle fire, the enemy seemingly unconcerned with the welfare of their fellow countrymen inside the threatened position. Lloyd's troops continued to pound the bunkers using tanks and artillery, which produced little effect. Then, after a week of British tank fire, the Japanese produced high-velocity, armor-penetrating antitank weapons and began systematically destroying the British heavy equipment.

The Arakan campaign was becoming a nightmare. As January crawled into February, Lloyd's division swelled to nine brigades (about six thousand men), yet they still couldn't budge the Japanese. And when Imperial

Army reinforcements began streaming into Arakan's zone of combat in late February, the Japanese began to push back. By March 1943, the Japanese had scaled the steep Mayu Range and were cutting off and attacking the British from the rear and flanks, blocking routes of supply and troop movement to and from India along valley roads between the peaks.

In the second week of March, exactly a year after British General William Slim had been called to preside over the British retreat from Burma, he was ordered to "visit" General Lloyd's command at Arakan. As Slim traveled to Arakan, Lloyd was discharged of his duties and replaced by Major General C. E. N. Lomax, who had already started to regroup the discouraged troops. After only a day's assessment, Slim pronounced things "fantastically bad." At one point during his five-day visit, Slim watched two units from the Indian army mistakenly attack one another. But if some in Arakan joked that, with the Indians firing on each other, "at least we'll win the battle," things couldn't be worse. The Japanese were now on the offensive. And were they to break through the British defense, they'd have a clear route to India. To halt them, Lomax encircled the Japanese forces, and was about to counterattack when two British and Indian battalions guarding the road toward India collapsed under fierce pressure from the Japanese. And with the Japanese now straddling the road to India, British troops were cut off from friendly territory.

When Lomax looked to Slim for tactical advice, Slim offered only one plan: another full withdrawal from Burma, once again through the jungles where necessary, and this time on the run from forces whose numbers were far smaller than his own.

"It was no use crying over spilt milk," he later wrote. "In war, you have to pay for your mistakes, and in Arakan the same mistakes had been made again and again until the troops lost heart." As Arakan ended, with the British pulling back out of Burma and into India, British resolve was shattered. More than twenty-five hundred British soldiers had been sacrificed on a mission that had been as much about good publicity as about strategy. Arakan had been a disaster.

WITH ANAKIM FORGOTTEN and the Arakan invasion in rubble, March 1943 became a time to reassess the American and British plans for CBI and World War II's entire Pacific theater.

Faced with continuing supply problems and a Chinese generalissimo reluctant to fight a ground war, President Roosevelt chose to follow his own instincts. Still enthralled by the inexpensive possibilities of Chennault's proposal to defeat Japan from the air, Roosevelt and the War Department dissolved the China Air Task Force and placed Chennault in command of a new, full-blown Fourteenth Air Force based in China. The president also presented Chennault with a fleet of more than fifty new fighter and bomber aircraft and a new rank: his second general's star. He was now a major general, though one still stranded subordinate to Stilwell.

Chennault had arrived. Now he had to make good.


FOR THE BRITISH and Indians in CBI after Anakim's stillbirth and Arakan's embarassment, General Wavell, too, understood that changes had to be made. The plans and policies for the war in Burma so far had all been either unsuccessful or simply wrong. If the Allies were ever going to drive the Japanese from Burma, they had to shift how they'd been doing things. If they didn't, their sorry record of losses and clumsiness was only likely to continue. To accomplish this leap, Wavell knew he had at least one truly unconventional weapon at his disposal. It was an idea that had been sparked by the only real Allied success in Burma so far: the British-led Northern Kachin Levies.

Wavell had finally committed to change. It was time to get behind Wingate.

# Chapter 6

BY THE TIME Orde Wingate arrived in the China-Burma-India theater, he ranked as perhaps the British army's most respected—and most distrusted—officer. And it was a reputation he largely deserved. He was also, as it happened, coming off six-months' convalescent leave following an unsuccessful suicide.

If Stilwell and Chennault were the twin pillars of American determination inside CBI, they found their British counterpart in the brilliant and blazingly eccentric Wingate. He was a complex soldier and mercurial leader whose troops—no matter where he commanded them—invariably grew to love him, even though he would beat them for insubordination and push them until they collapsed in exhaustion. To toughen up his men, Wingate made them forage for their own meals, which often included courses of frogs and insects. When they grew sick and undernourished from his training, Wingate would order his medical officers to stanch the "prevailing hypochondria" by refusing to treat any new patients.

And yet, by word and example, each of Wingate's troops knew his leader would ask nothing of him that Wingate wouldn't do himself.

A FOURTH-GENERATION military man, Orde Wingate was born in India in 1903 to fundamentalist Christian parents. Wingate's father, George, found proof of God, in fact, on the night of Orde's own birth. That night, shortly after George Wingate's wife, Ethel, had "delivered an unusually fine large baby weighing nine pounds," she began to hemorrhage. And as the blood poured from Ethel after the arrival of her first baby boy, she floated between life and death for more than an hour. The entire time, George sent an earnest and endless loop of prayer to God for her health as he sent a flurry of telegrams worldwide, asking friends and family members to pray for Ethel as well. Miraculously, Colonel George Wingate was granted the miracle he had asked for.

After his wife's survival, George Wingate underwent a change so complete and above reproach that it was never questioned. While on maneuvers to contain bands of headhunting Naga tribesmen in northeast India later that year, the elder Wingate not only ordered his troops to pray daily; he declined to march them on the Sabbath, a breach of orders for which he was never disciplined. When he retired from India in 1905—giving up both his British army commission and his position as a Plymouth Brethren Missionary in India—the family returned to England, where the five Wingate children (Orde was third) were raised in the family's cavernous country house on a diet of porridge, bread sopped with meat fat, and the "sweet milk from the Word of God."

Schooled at home for years due to his parents' fear of "corrupting influences," Orde was pushed by his father into constant tests of character, such as mercilessly long hikes and full days of reading and memorizing the Old Testament. Sundays the family dressed in black, worshiped, prayed, and spent their afternoons studying the Bible for "improvement." As a young man, Orde grew so convinced of the Old Testament's warnings he personally tucked his brothers and sisters tightly into bed each night, fearing they'd otherwise be snatched away by either angels or the devil.

As a teenager, Orde was finally allowed to attend British private schools as a day student, returning home each night to study and pray. By this time, though, he was so profoundly unsocialized that he left little impression on his schoolmates. Only his lack of normal hygiene earned him distinction. He was nicknamed "Stinker."

Following his secondary education, Wingate headed off to military college at Woolwich, in the British countryside of Kent. Because Orde was the eldest son in a four-generation military family, his religious parents had no reservations about a career in the army, and absent the pressures of home, Wingate's mix of masochistic physical determination and righteous religious fervor began to glow. If there was one episode at Woolwich that set the tone for Wingate's future, it came during a first-year hazing ritual known as "running." In this punishment, each underclass student was accused of a minor infraction, then was stripped and driven down a gauntlet of senior students who popped knotted towels across his naked body. When the end of the line was reached, the "run" was ended with the accused student being thrown into a cistern of icy water.

When it came time for Wingate's "run" (he'd kept a horse from the stable for too long, depriving a fellow student of a recreational ride), he was pulled from his bed in the night, stripped of his nightclothes in a courtyard, and faced with the line. Rather than emulate other students—who cupped their hands over their genitals and sprinted the gauntlet's length— Wingate did the opposite. Standing nude in the darkened yard, he walked to the upperclassman at the head of the line, stared him squarely in the eyes, and waited.

After the first punisher declined to strike him, Wingate stepped to the second upperclassman in line and repeated this behavior. In a few minutes, Wingate had walked the line without a towel being raised. Then, in the darkness, he climbed the side of the water tank at the line's far end, perched on its lip, and dove in. Moral authority and strict self-determination had trumped petty military custom. Orde Wingate had taken his first stride toward legend.

AFTER GRADUATION from Woolwich in 1923, Wingate spent three years on England's Salisbury Plain with a detachment of the Royal Artillery. And like Stilwell, the young officer quickly grew bored with the ease of stood-down army life. To fill his days he began reading incessantly, working to school himself in subjects from philosophy to art and music to history. To get past his career blockade, he took the advice of his famous uncle, Sir Reginald Wingate, Britain's high commissioner in Cairo—effectively the prime minister of Egypt—and left the Royal Artillery to study Arabic and Arab cultures at London University. Four years later, having graduated and read everything he could lay his hands on (and having become a skilled fox hunter in his free time), Wingate applied for an army posting in the

Mideast. Then he traveled to the Sudan where—using his uncle's political pull—he was given charge of a company of natives in the Sudan Defense Force.

The job was everything Wingate could have dreamed. He was billeted in a remote outstation near the Sudanese border with Ethopia. There he presided over 275 men and their families and concubines like a magistrate, functioning more as a regional chieftain than as a military commissar. Employing his fox-hunting skills, he took up his primary objective with zeal. Almost immediately, using feints and small, mobile groups of soldiers, he began halting Ethiopian ivory traders who were sneaking across the dry and eroded borderlands near his post. And with each success, he was storing away tactical lessons for future use.

In April 1931, though, Wingate also took another kind of lesson. That month, as Wingate and one of his patrols chased a group of nine ivory poachers across the craggy desert, one of the smugglers chose to stand and fight, firing at Wingate's troops using an antique rifle. When Wingate's team returned fire, they shot the man dead, and, for the first time in his life, the twenty-eight-year-old Wingate witnessed blood shed at his order. He approached the smuggler's corpse—an undernourished old man dressed in rags—and felt immediate revulsion. "He only possessed one thing of any value or importance," Wingate would later remember, "and that was his life. And we took it away."

While mercy and guilt aren't character hallmarks for any military officer, inside Wingate's psyche they warred with his strictly military responsibilities, and the paradoxes hardened into an anger against anyone who used force to oppress others. Not surprisingly, this "spiritual vertigo," as he called it, left him regularly beset by depressions. Other times, when his religious fervor and impressive physical and emotional armor were fully deployed, Wingate fervently believed his mix of intellect, vision, idealism, discipline, and nonconformity gave him insight into life that left him, in his own estimation, "destined for greatness."

To Wingate's superiors, his black moods and sweeping manic declarations rendered him a perplexing mix of idealist and mystic. Certainly he was as tough and resourceful as any officer in their army, but his methods in the Sudan could be unreliable. His patrols, in their ranging across the desert, sometimes overlooked the more obvious smuggling routes. And when times got tight or he was without an answer, Wingate was given to spouting snatches of the Old Testament. Still, because of his family name, Wingate was well regarded in the Sudan, and in 1933—after five years away from home—he returned to England to marry his fiancée, Lorna, and gain higher command by attending the army's Staff College.

When his application to the Staff College was suddenly declined for unspecified reasons (due probably to his erratic leadership), Wingate had a stroke of fortunate timing. The day after he'd learned of the Staff College's refusal, he came upon General Sir Cyril Deverell—chief of the imperial general staff—during a routine troop inspection. In a brazen breach of protocol, Wingate walked directly up to Deverell and confronted the general, telling him of his exploits in the Sudan and appealing to be granted Staff College entrance. While Deverell could do nothing about Wingate's appointment, the general was so impressed after verifying the brash young officer's claims that he promised Wingate the next appropriate staff position.

Days later, Wingate received orders to proceed immediately to Palestine, as a captain on the army's intelligence staff.

ALL HIS YOUNG LIFE, Orde Wingate had been looking for a cause. In Palestine, he would finally find it. Controlled by the British, Palestine in 1936 was "to become a national home for the Jewish people" by government decree. But a national and deep-rooted Arab revolt—which targeted the new Zionist settlements—left the creation of a Jewish state second to keeping peace.

At first, thanks to his history and Arab-studies training, Wingate felt sympathy for the Palestinian Arabs, who he believed were being wrongly run off their land. After only a few days, however, he grew transfixed by the vigor and bravery of the Zionist settlers, finding their kibbutz encampments marvels of agriculture and activity. Soon he'd become convinced that, as a partner to Britain, a Jewish state would be far preferable to the current Arab one. And he decided to use his practical fighting skills to redress the inequities.

Wingate learned Hebrew, became cozy with Zionist leaders, and came to be called "Hatedud" (The Friend) by them. As a British intelligence officer, his obvious preference for the Jewish cause began to earn Wingate mistrust from his colleagues. And Wingate, who had little regard for the

British administration's brittle orthodoxy or the army's "military apes" who enforced it, did little to hide his contempt.

As the Arab revolt continued, Wingate pestered his superiors until they allowed him to organize Zionist fighting units to protect Jewish settlements and keep the national oil pipeline secure against sabotage. Called the Special Night Squads (or SNS), these Wingate-trained groups soon benefited from Wingate's fox hunting of smugglers in the Sudan and Ethiopia. At first, the Night Squads made only defensive stands against raiding Arabs. Then, their confidence growing, the SNS graduated into ambushes and attacks upon Arab encampments.

Within a year, the Special Night Squads were perhaps the world's best elite-force: they marched in tight formation (often fifteen miles through the desert at night before making an attack), sheathed their bayonets in black cotton to keep them from flashing in the moonlight, used newfangled radio communication to outrun the enemy, and ran roughshod over the less well-organized Arabs. Unafraid of bullets that cracked past him during skirmishes and battles, Wingate commanded his units from the battle line, and during one encounter he was hit five times by his own troops. Even the bullet holes didn't cool his passions.

Inside British Command in Palestine, Wingate's fellow officers began to suspect he was trying to upset the British army—and perhaps was even planning an uprising against the current administrators to place himself into power. Increasingly they called to disband the Special Night Squads, and their requests were being met with growing support from the British administrators. Yet if Wingate's professional intentions were coming into question, they still took second place to his personal habits, which had become astonishingly erratic.

For months, Wingate had cultivated an unkempt beard (unheard of for a British officer), worn unwashed and wrinkled clothing, and had given up his flat-brimmed British officers' hat for a cork-lined Wolsley pith helmet like those favored by explorers in the previous century. Because he was often late for meetings, he'd taken to wearing a large alarm clock that dangled off his wrist on a string, its bell set in advance of his next appointment. By 1938, Wingate had also foresworn bathing, preferring instead to scrub himself daily with a hard-rubber brush and without soap and water. And he was eating only raw onions, which he claimed were key to good health. Perhaps strangest of all, however, was a behavior that seemed a throwback to his "running" experience at Woolwich. For meetings he thought potentially combative, Wingate would schedule the conference in his private quarters, where he'd flummox the opposition by conducting the talks naked, often while scrubbing himself with his brush.

By late 1938, the Special Night Squads were decimating Palestinian Arabs, while schooling a future generation of Israeli generals that included Moshe Dayan. Wingate's bravery and organizational elan—not to mention his famous last name—grabbed the attention of General Sir Archibald Wavell, the officer then in command of Palestine and the man who would eventually oversee British forces in CBI.

But the Special Night Squad's runaway success was also spawning aberrations. As the SNS grew powerful, they began bullying Arab combatants and prisoners. In one case, SNS soldiers halted the destruction of a section of Palestine's oil pipeline by a group of Arab rebels, then forced their captives to eat oil-soaked sand. In another episode, they executed three rebel suspects in the village of Sila el Daher without a trial.

To Palestine's administrators, the Night Squads had become Zionist vigilantes with a one-sided (and British-supplied) advantage. In May 1939—with little forewarning—the Special Night Squads were disbanded, and Wingate was recalled to England under a cloud of controversy. Back home, he was attached to an obscure, antiaircraft post that saw little action against the German Luftwaffe, which was already taking control of the skies over central and western Europe.

In Wingate's own estimation, he had been placed in a convenient drawer and forgotten by the British army. He was, in his own mythology, now officially a prophet in exile. And while he continued energetically trying to be returned to command in Palestine, none of his requests was even accorded the dignity of an answer.

IF WINGATE FOUND HIMSELF in purgatory as World War II flared across Europe and into North Africa, his exploits had not been forgotten—and they would not be limited to Palestine.

In 1935, the Italians—who already held the territories of Somaliland and Eritrea in North Africa—had also invaded and occupied Ethiopia, driving Emperor Haile Selassie from power and absorbing the nation into Italian

East Africa. Then, in June 1940, after Italy's Generalissimo Benito Mussolini linked arms with Hitler's Germany—officially entering the war—the British grew concerned that Ethiopia would be the springboard for Italian invasions into the neighboring British colonies of Kenya, Egypt, and the Sudan. And, as feared, three months later, five Italian divisions invaded Egypt from across its western border with Libya. Suddenly, the Allied fear of losing all of North Africa to the enemy became a real possibility.

With Italian-British border skirmishes intensified, General Wavell—by then promoted to commander in chief of British forces in the Mideast—suddenly remembered the Special Night Squads and their creator, Captain Wingate. To see if Wingate might be able to help in Ethiopia, he summoned the guerrilla leader from England to Khartoum at once. While British officers in the region remained cautious of Wingate—who was traveling incognito as "Mr. Smith," despite his Wolsley helmet and eccentricities giving him away—Wavell remained completely supportive, giving Wingate whatever he needed to create a Selassie-supporting revolution inside Ethiopia. For his campaign, Wingate was also promoted to the temporary rank of lieutenant colonel, and given charge of sixteen hundred Sudanese and Ethiopian troops, a tenfold leap in command size since Palestine.

Wingate, again feeling that he'd found a righteous cause—the return of Selassie to his throne—immersed himself in the task. His plan involved chesslike steps across northeast Ethiopia supported by division-sized British invasions into the country from the north and the south. Wingate (with Selassie in tow) then planned to push his sixteen-hundred-man force between the larger invasions, driving southeast into Ethiopia from his old haunts in the Sudan. Once inside the country, he believed his small, mobile unit could smack down the Italians and retake the capital of Addis Ababa.

Wingate named his army Gideon Force, for his favorite Old Testament warrior, and on January 20, 1941—as invasions were already under way to his north and south—Wingate, Selassie, and the Gideon Force started into enemy territory. Instead of vehicles, Gideon Force moved using camels and mules. But northeastern Ethiopia's thorny plains and flinty mountains proved more arduous than planned, and soon Wingate's "camel cavalry"—as it had been named by critics—was slowed by lack of water and daily animal deaths.

Wingate kept pushing, and within a week Gideon Force was harassing Italian military outposts by night, sniping down sentries and bombing machine-gun nests. Wingate split his troops into forked columns, to foster the illusion of greater scope, and the Italians—believing these raids came in advance of an even larger invasion to rival those under way in Ethiopia's north and south—dropped back in what can only be described as a surprise retreat.

Gideon Force moved quickly—attempting to encircle the withdrawing Italians—but in the vacuum of fighting, Wingate's troops also began to make tactical errors that could have ended far worse but for luck.

One Gideon attachment of three hundred, for example, took a night's rest on an exposed hill on the far side of a suspected Italian retreat road, where a bridge crossed above the Charaka River. The following morning, Wingate's troops were awakened by a full battalion of mechanized Italian forces—perhaps one thousand men—approaching the bridge. The Italians, supported by a machine-gun-equipped Savoia bomber, eventually smashed their way across the bridge after absorbing serious Gideon Force fire. The Gideons, moving quickly and remaining flexible, quickly put the Italian's armored vehicles into flame and eventually knocked the Savoia bomber out of the sky with ground fire. When the battle was over, more than 140 Italian troops had been killed and an additional two hundred were wounded. The Gideon Force had lost twenty-one men, with only another fifty requiring hospitalization.

As Wingate hoped, Gideon Force victories in northeast Ethiopia rallied area partisans, who began fighting in support of their returning emperor. The Italians (warned by their leader, General Nasi, that it was "a long way to Rome") became mired in low morale. Each night they were harassed by Wingate's unconventional forces and—while occasionally counterattacking—their general movements were usually in collapse and retreat.

For Wingate, as he drove toward Addis Ababa, he once again began manning forward positions himself, growing so occupied by fighting that he rarely communicated with command, often staying out of touch for days or weeks. By May 5, Haile Selassie was back in his imperial palace in Addis Ababa, the Italians now being run out of Ethiopia to the southwest, squeezed by British forces from every other direction. On May 23, as the Italian surrender of Ethiopia was given, more than fourteen thousand Italians were made Allied prisoners of war.

That night, however, Wingate was not even allowed to attend Selassie's victory banquet. Instead—because of his dismissive lack of communication during the campaign—Wingate was summoned to Cairo on the "next available flight." The following day, he walked into British Middle-East Headquarters a brash and victorious colonel. A few hours later, he left the same building demoted to major.

Anxious about his future, trapped in Cairo without orders, and having been reduced in rank, Wingate skidded into a bout of depression abetted by the onset of malaria. When not laid out in his Cairo hotel room— sweating and hallucinating from the parasites in his blood—he bellyached in letters home that God had abandoned him; that he had been deprived of the glory he deserved; and that his military career was damaged permanently—if not finished. Once again, the greatness he'd once been destined to achieve had eluded him.

On July 4, 1941, still in Cairo and feverish from a fresh bloom of malaria, Wingate stood in front of the bathroom mirror in his hotel room and—using a knife—tried to slit his throat. At first he plunged the dagger into the right side of his neck, but he managed to create only a flesh wound when he tensed his neck muscles at the moment of impact, halting the blade before it could prove deadly. He then stabbed his neck on the left side, this time making a deeper cut, but missing the arteries that would bleed him out.

Poleaxed by malaria, blood loss, and shock, Wingate collapsed to the floor in a gory, unshaven heap. Fortunately a Colonel Thornhill in the next room heard the *whump* of his fall and, finding Wingate's door locked, enlisted the hotel manager in rescuing him. Wingate—his eyes afire— screamed at Thornhill and the ambulance drivers. "I am *dead* and in *Hell!*" he shouted repeatedly as they carried him out of his room and down through the hotel lobby.

It would require six months of rest, physical and psychiatric treatment, and antimalarial recuperation in Egypt and England before Wingate finally returned to his old—if still singular—self.


BY FEBRUARY 1942, Wingate was again judged fit for military service. On February 7, he received his next orders: regimental duty on a Royal Artillery battery in Dorset, in the English countryside. For the flashy commander of the Special Night Squads and the Gideon Force, an artillery regiment was a slap in the face. Devastated, Wingate was convinced his enemies in the War Office had finally "fixed" him and his nonconforming ways for good.

Yet the same day—with British troops being routed in Malaya by the Japanese and Japanese forces starting to cross the Thai border into Burma—General Sir Archibald Wavell (now promoted to commander of all British forces in India) ordered Wingate to Rangoon "by the fastest route at the first opportunity."

Two weeks later, as Wingate arrived in Burma, Rangoon was collapsing under full Japanese invasion. British and Chinese forces in Burma were being driven northward, Stilwell's walkout waited three months in the future, and—in the chaos—there was little Wingate could do to organize a guerrilla counteroffensive.

After the retreat, as Stilwell sweated his command and Chennault took to the skies, Wingate drew up plans for a guerrilla force to go back inside Burma. In June 1942, the plans were approved by Wavell (without consulting Stilwell or CBI Command) and Wingate—now promoted to brigadier—was given the Seventy-seventh Indian Infantry Brigade: three thousand British, Indian, Gurkha, and Burmese soldiers, whom he began training in preparation for what he was calling a "Long-Range Penetration" invasion.

His initial plan was to train his troops to diamondlike hardness, preparing them for an on-foot attack on Burma out of India. Once inside enemy territory, they would travel light, be reprovisioned by air drop, and distract the Japanese during initial stages of Stilwell's Anakim invasion into Burma. Each day during training—as Wingate had now generated a belief that marching stopped malaria—the three thousand men of the Seventy-seventh Brigade drilled until they dropped. Wingate forbade his troops shaving (to save an extra five minutes a day), and taking a cue from the Japanese, Wingate's men were schooled to cut trails through jungles rather than use roads for transport. They were also taught to guide and care for more than one thousand mules, which would function as both their pack animals and—in times of low provision—their source of meat.

All across Wingate's school, the usual military disciplines were either tortured or abandoned. One second lieutenant, Philip Stibbe, wrote this of the training: "A constant stream of orders, pamphlets, information, en-couragement and invective showered down on us from Brigade HQ . . . Saluting was to be cut down to a minimum. Everything was to be done at the double. Everyone must eat at least one raw onion per day. Only shorts should be worn when it was raining. Swearing must stop. When marching in mass formation through the jungle, thorn bushes were to be ignored and only thick plantations of bamboo were to be looked upon as obstacles . . . "

To acclimate his men to suffering, Wingate ordered them to forage for the majority of their meals. Soon hunger was forcing them to boil up scav-enged frogs, fish, bugs, birds, and lizards alongside ground-up Indian bis-cuits, called *shakapura*, to create a vile stew that masqueraded as nutrition. At one point during the training, two men died of dysentery on the same day. At another, 70 percent of one regiment was either hospitalized or seeking hospitalization. Wingate, however, saw only mental weakness. He scolded the "prevailing hypochondria" and lectured to those still standing that there would be no soft hospital beds behind enemy lines.

"Everyone is taught to be doctor-minded," Wingate railed. "Although it is all right in normal civilian life, where ample medical facilities are avail-able, it will not apply to us in the jungle. You have to diagnose your own complaints and then cure yourselves . . . We shall not stop for you, for our very lives may be jeopardized by waiting for stragglers. If you are sick, you are of no use to us—you are an unwanted liability. We shall leave you to ef-fect your own salvation."

By now, Wingate was calling his force the Chindits, a poor translation of the Burmese word *Chinthe* (pronounced "Chin-*de*"), after the griffinlike half-lion/half-eagle statues that guard doors to Burma's Buddhist temples. Across the rainy summer of 1942, as Wingate continued pushing the men of the Seventy-seventh Brigade—whose motto became "Peace at Any Fucking Price"—the Chindits began to harden. Soon Wingate's men were being sent on three-day training maneuvers into the jungle carrying virtu-ally no rations.

But instead of resenting their leader, the men of "Wingate's Circus" warmed to their commander. Flabby bellies disappeared. Soldiers shared what little food they could scavenge or cadge. Through their close work, the Chindit army was becoming a collective organism, so tightly aligned they could virtually read each other's minds. Battle plans evolved where, if

Chindits were beginning to lose a skirmish, the officer in command would give a signal (firing a flare or ordering a specific bugle tune, for example) and the troops would slip into the jungle and meet at a prearranged spot far from the fighting. The men grew practiced in hand-to-hand combat, using street-fighting techniques like ear-biting, eye-gouging, and testicle-kicking to prepare for times when guns or other weapons might be out of reach.

Wingate's men were now calling him Tarzan—or, when he gave them a disapproving stare, "Brigadier Bela Lugosi"—and their leader constantly hounded them with the bedrock Chindit principle until it became a slo-gan. Employing a line from Ecclesiastes, Wingate kept repeating: "What-ever thy hand findeth to do, do it with thy might."

As the winter of 1942–43 arrived, Wingate's troops were in fighting form. By December, they had been moved from their training area in India at Saugor, three hundred miles southeast of Delhi in central India, to Im-phal along the India-Burma border. There they waited for the beginning of the Anakim operation, where they would finally test their skills. For twelve days, Wingate and his men waited in a pouring rain for orders. But as Stil-well's Anakim plan crumpled and evaporated with British naval—and then Chinese—extenuations, General Wavell personally went to Imphal, planning to order Wingate to cancel his Chindit thrust. When Wavell ar-rived, however, Wingate put on a two-hour harangue against the washout ("The anticlimax would be unbearable . . .") and—somewhat amazingly—Wavell relented.

As February 1943 arrived, Wingate gathered his three thousand troops together and informed them they were about to "embark on a great adven-ture." The men of Wingate's Circus were to be split into two "dispersal groups," each then further divided into equally sized brigade columns of men "big enough to deliver blows of the necessary weight but small enough to slip through the enemy's net."

To feint the Japanese into thinking a large-scale invasion was coming, a smaller, "diversionary" Southern Group—roughly 800 men and 250 mules—would invade Burma, loudly crossing the Chindwin River near the Burmese city of Tamu. With them would be a Major Jeffries, who was to wear a brigadier's uniform and loudly pretend to be Wingate in an attempt to deceive the enemy. Once across the river, Southern Group was to dawdle near the riverbank for a full twenty-four hours before breaking into their columns and moving eastward over a north-south range of mountains to Tamu's east. Once east of the mountains, the columns would work through the jungles, knock out the Japanese-held Mandalay-Myitkyna railway near the town of Kyaikthin, and continue east to the Irrawaddy River, two-thirds of the way across Burma.

Using the Southern Group's diversion, Wingate's larger Northern Group—2,200 men and 850 mules—would cross the Chindwin at Tonhe, thirty-five miles north of Tamu. Once across the river, the mission was to spread a far-wider net of destruction, blowing the Mandalay-Myitkyna railroad at several places, disrupting enemy communications, and testing the "revolt potential" of the Burmese. Wingate and his superiors were especially interested in conscripting the hill tribes who, like the Kachins, had lived beneath the brutality of the Japanese for a year and were likely soured on Japan's clubby "Asia for Asians" propaganda. The Allies—in the form of the honed and ready Chindits—were prepared to strike deep inside Burma.

FROM FEBRUARY 13 to 17, 1943, and under the code name "Operation Longcloth," the Chindits made their way inside Burma from India. They crossed the Chindwin River at their appointed places, then started into the jungles toward their targets by walking in long, single-file columns they called "snakes."

For the diversionary Southern Group, problems presented themselves almost immediately. Inside Burma, Southern Group began to move very publicly toward the rail town of Kyaikthin, with Major Jeffries—doing his best Colonel Blimp—attracting Japanese forces too effectively. On March 2, unbeknownst to Southern Group command, two trains of Japanese infantrymen arrived in Kyaikthin the same day the Chindits planned to dynamite its train station. That evening, just after eleven o'clock, as one of the Southern Group's two command columns—one overseen by a Major Emmit—walked the rail line toward the station, they were met from the front and both sides in a Japanese ambush. With bullets flying and mortar shells exploding around them, the Chindits dived to the freshly mowed ground, looking for cover and finding little. As they began to return fire, the Chindit retreat signal was given and those men still alive started to withdraw.

Less than half the group—seventy-four soldiers and officers—finally convened a safe twelve miles to the southeast, in the town of Taungaun. Their radio had also been destroyed, shot through with a Japanese soft-point bullet. As they inventoried their goods—sixty-five mules, four machine guns, and a very limited amount of ammunition—Emmit realized there was only one option. He would lead his men back to India.

There were other problems as well. Though airdrops were steadily provisioning Wingate's men, the Chindits were discovering the maps they carried were horribly inaccurate. Owing to the slash-and-burn techniques of Burmese farmers, agricultural villages were forced to move every few years, since the tropical earth is quickly exhausted of nutrients. Almost daily, Chindit columns led by Burmese guides would hack through the jungles toward the hilltop village on their map, only to find the town abandoned and the smoky plumes of village campfires visible on another hill miles in the distance.

As the Southern Group was doing its job and attracting Japanese attention, the Northern Group worked easily east across Burma's mountains and jungles on the Carstens Track, a game and logging trail left from the British colonial era. Within weeks, the Northern Group had put two mountain ranges between themselves and India. Already they were halfway across northern Burma and within striking distance of the Mandalay-Myitkyina railway. One Northern Group column (called Number Five) had already spent several nights preparing wired charges of dynamite at a number of bridges and rock overhangs inside the bottleneck of the Bon Chaung Gorge, which would disrupt north-south rail travel in Burma for weeks, if not months.

The only Northern Group snake that hadn't followed the Carstens Track—Column Number Three—was overseen by Mike Calvert. A stockily built, twenty-nine-year-old natural athlete who had just missed joining Britain's Olympic team for the 1936 Pentathlon, Calvert was Wingate's right-hand man and had been director of Britain's Bush Warfare School in Burma before Wingate's arrival. Like Wingate, he had also been born in India and possessed a long, thin nose, a heavily boned brow, and a piercing blue-eyed gaze. Though Calvert was a decade younger than his superior, he and Wingate could have been brothers, and both men recognized their remarkable similarities. In no time, the faith and trust they placed in each other's skill and judgment was unbreakable. Which is why Calvert and his Column Number Three were singled out for the Chindits' toughest assignment.

Shortly after crossing the Chindwin River with the Northern Group, Mike Calvert's Column Three bushwhacked southeast through Burma's mountainous and unmapped jungle. Within two weeks, on March 1 (the night it was agreed Calvert would radio his column's location), Brigadier Wingate grew ecstatic upon learning that Column Three was nearly at the Irrawaddy River, halfway across northern Burma. He was equally thrilled to learn that Calvert and his men were poised to strike hard into the Japanese gut in an attack choreographed to begin on March 6. Wingate's plan was coming together.

But as February turned to March, not all was good for Wingate's Northern Group. Column Four (a Gurkha group led by a Major Conron) had been out of touch and assumed lost for days. Though Column Four was moving slowly, the larger problem proved to be Conron himself: he hated the screech of his radio's charging mechanism so much he ordered the radio permanently turned off. When Wingate discovered the insubordination, he relieved Conron of command and placed Column Four in the hands of a brigade major named George Bromhead. That same day, hurrying to catch up with the other Northern Group columns, Bromhead's Chindits began bumping into Japanese patrols.

Only one day after taking command, on March 2, Bromhead's column was ambushed as they crossed a small river. The attack's timing was perfect. Slightly more than half of the column's thousand-yard snake had crossed the waterway when the jungle erupted with enemy mortar explosions and gunfire. For a time, the rearguard—still commanded by Bromhead—held off the Japanese while the forward group, already across the river and commanded by Lieutenant Stewart-Jones, spread into the forest. Because many of Bromhead's soldiers were teenage Gurkhas— strong but still untested in battle—they fell to panic, and by the time Bromhead signaled for dispersal into the jungle, half were dead. Also destroyed was Bromhead's radio, meaning he could no longer contact command or request aerial resupply. After considering his options, Bromhead, like the Southern Group, deduced that he and his fifteen or so survivors needed to turn back for India.

On the river's far side, Lieutenant Stewart-Jones and his 136 men—also without radio equipment—had to confront their own limited options. At first they worked east, then north, through the jungle, thinking of making for China, perhaps sixty miles to the east. Two days later, however, lost and disoriented, Stewart-Jones turned over command to his ranking officer, Captain Findlay, and struck out in search of other Chindit groups he believed to be in the area. Eventually, Findlay's group would struggle back to India, having stumbled hundreds of miles—first farther north, then west—through the jungles while nourishing themselves with what little plant and animal life they could find to eat. Weeks later, in the extreme northern outpost of Fort Hertz, hundreds of miles north of where he'd turned over command to Findlay, Stewart-Jones and four Gurkha riflemen emerged into safety, sick, hungry, and exhausted.

Despite the problems, Wingate refused to flinch. And on March 6, precisely on-schedule, Wingate began hearing of Chindit successes. That afternoon, Mike Calvert's Column Three celebrated the daring "Mad Mike's" thirtieth birthday by blowing up the Mandalay-Myitkyina railway at dozens of spots—and in hundred-yard intervals—near the town of Nankan. Then, still not satisfied, Column Three also dynamited two rail bridges, one of them a three-span, 120-foot monster. When three truckloads of Japanese response troops arrived to root out Column Three, Calvert's men trained three-inch mortars on the vehicles and set fire to two of the trucks with bullets and one extremely lucky mortar shot. Later that evening, Column Number Five blew the forty-foot rail bridge at Bon Chaung Gorge. Then they exploded the gorge's overhanging rock walls, dropping hundreds of tons of rubble onto the railroad bed. Farther to the south, Wingate's own Column Number One had blown yet another bridge.

In one day, Wingate's Chindits had severed the Mandalay-Myitkyina railroad in more than seventy places. Japanese lines of communications and transportation were severed, and—despite the successful Japanese ambush on the Chindits' Southern Group at Kyaikthin—the Japanese had been knocked onto their heels. Still, except for Calvert's column, which had yet to sustain a casualty, there had been losses. Because of the fast-moving nature of guerrilla warfare, several column leaders had even been forced to leave behind soldiers unfit to move with Burmese locals, where they would likely be turned over to the Japanese.

AFTER ONLY TWO WEEKS in Burma's jungles, Wingate's Chindits had made good their commander's plans. And feeling momentum was his— and that the greatness he'd so long deserved was now within his grasp—

Wingate pondered his next step. Should he order all Chindits into the northern highlands to regroup among the Northern Kachin Levies? Should he order a full Chindit withdrawal to India before the Japanese slipped between him and the Indian border to cut off his men? Or, most aggressively, should he push his men on, deeper into Japanese territory in an attempt to wreak further havoc?

The choice—one of the largest of Wingate's career—was his alone to make. For several days Wingate ordered all Chindit forces to bivouac in the forest while he considered his options over endless pots of tea. Then, on March 11, having heard nothing from the Southern Group for more than a week, Wingate received a message that, in accordance with his orders, the remaining Southern Group troops had successfully crossed the thousand-foot width of the Irrawaddy River.

It was the signal he needed. The Chindits would drive deeper inside Japanese-occupied Burma.

JUST SEVEN DAYS LATER, Wingate and his Northern Group had all reached, or crossed, the Irrawaddy. On March 18—late in the afternoon—Wingate's own column, Column One, began crossing the broadly smooth river in a flotilla of air-dropped inflatable rafts, each towed by local boatmen rowing dugouts. By dawn the following day, all of his men stood on the great river's far shore.

While Wingate's crossing had incurred no enemy fire, two other columns crossing farther south—Major Bernard Fergusson's Column Five and Mike Calvert's Column Three—had been fired upon by Japanese troops garrisoned near enough to the river to detect them. While Fergusson's men got across without direct conflict (shots fired their direction might have been only probes for a reaction), Calvert's still-casualty-free Column Three finally met death head-on.

On March 13, as they crossed the river near the Burmese town of Tigyaing, Japanese troops on the far side began firing, and Calvert and his men were forced to put ashore on a midstream island and return fire. The fight went furiously, with Calvert's men even resorting to mortar fire to slow the Japanese fusillade. Then, as the shooting subsided, Calvert discovered the Burmese boatmen who'd rowed his column halfway across the river had retreated in the heat of battle. Despite the setback, Calvert instructed his men to keep fighting as he tried to figure out a way off the is-land. For a time, the shooting came even more relentlessly than at first. Then, at another short break in the battle, a flotilla of Burmese boats drifted past in the dusk, and Calvert—using one of his Burmese soldiers as a translator—commandeered the vessels, though he had to leave some mules and equipment behind on the island for lack of cargo space.

As Mad Mike's column left the island under cover of darkness, Calvert, for the first time, felt defeat and loss. He had been forced to abandon twelve Chindit casualties, five of whom were still alive. It was, in his recol-lection, "a difficult moment," and he instantly recognized the morale-crushing blow his decision had dealt, both to the wounded being left behind on the island and to the men being ordered to leave.

To try to soften the future for those left behind, Calvert wrote a note—in English—to the local commander of the Imperial Army. In the letter, he stated that these men were his soldiers: humble warriors doing the bidding of a king, just as the Japanese troops were. Then he requested that each of his men be accorded a warrior's respect. Calvert ended the letter with: "I leave them confidently in your charge, knowing that with your well-known traditions of Bushido you will look after them as if they were your own."

The soldiers abandoned on that island by Calvert were never heard from again. Their loss haunted Mike Calvert to the day he died.

ON THE IRRAWADDY'S EASTERN SHORE, the remaining Chindit columns moved still deeper into enemy territory. And with each step farther east, the landscape itself began to change. Instead of being jungled mountains, with plenty of hiding places and ample water as had existed west of the river, once beyond the Irrawaddy's eastern shore the Chindits were march-ing into a hot, extremely dry hardwood forest during the Burmese dry sea-son. Worse yet, the Japanese were aware of the Chindit crossing and were sending streams of patrols along a network of roads and trails that forked everywhere through the forest.

While Wingate and Column One continued their Special Night Squad–style harassment of Japanese encampments near the river—creat-ing diversions in one direction, only to snipe at sentries and soldiers from another—the Chindit commander sent out orders by radio that Calvert's and Fergusson's columns should drive farther southeast to destroy a critical viaduct near the town of Gokteik. When the tall, thin, bearded, and mustachioed Fergusson checked his map for his target, he became despondent: they were to push one hundred more miles into Burma. And between them and the viaduct at Gokteik stood nothing but dry, almost desertified mountains. "The mountains between us and our goal were stinkers, nothing less," he wrote.

Feeling the Chindit presence all around, the Japanese continued stepping up patrols east of the Irrawaddy. Soon, two full Japanese divisions—nearly two thousand men—were searching for the Chindit columns. Fearing for their security, the Burmese soldiers functioning as Chindit guides began avoiding villages where, until recently, the columns could find rice and other bits of resupply. Across Wingate's invasion army, little about Burma could be trusted anymore, since any sign of Chindit presence would bring Japanese curiosity and often gunfire. Soon Fergusson was creating fake encampments to draw in the Japanese, with his Chindits then encircling the enemy in rearguard attacks. The Chindits were still taking casualties, too, with many wounded growing so weak that evacuating them was impossible. More troops were left in villages with hopes that the Burmese would not serve them up to the Japanese; others were merely left behind in the jungle with a few day's store of food and supplies.

Inside these close quarters, those Chindit units whose radios still worked were calling in the coordinates of any Japanese camps they came upon, and Royal Air Force (RAF) bombers began to pound them. On the ground, Wingate, Fergusson, and Calvert began selecting spots for ambushes where they'd least like to be ambushed themselves; then they'd lure in the Japanese. In one of these attacks, at a bend of the Nam Mit River, Calvert's Column Three destroyed a patrol of more than one hundred Japanese soldiers down to every man, with the opposition caught so off guard that Calvert later consoled himself that, at least, they "could never have known what hit them."

But after more than a month constantly on the move inside Burma, the Chindits were wearing out. Many had not bathed in weeks, and they were crawling with lice and leeches. When the leeches were pulled off, a part of the parasite's head often remained embedded in the skin, creating infected, open, oozing sores. Because there was no water, the Chindits resorted to sucking fluid from the stems of whatever green bamboo they could find.

Their mules became meals, and when these were gone the Chindits followed the example of their Burmese guides, who happily cooked up locusts, monkeys, jungle cockroaches, rats, and plants. What little rice was left was baked inside foot-long tubes of hollowed bamboo, creating hard sticks of starch that the soldiers could then suck on when their hunger grew great.

During their month in Burma, Wingate's well-conditioned men slid toward cadaverous gauntness. The majority of units no longer had radios to call in airdrops and others had progressed so far east that they couldn't be provisioned by air anymore, because though the British cargo aircraft had sufficient range to reach them, the transport's fighter-plane escorts did not.

Grasping at straws, Fergusson combed his Bible and radioed to Wingate that he should remember Psalm 22, verse 17: "I can count all my bones: they stare and gloat over me."

Not skipping a beat, Wingate radioed back a paraphrase from the Gospel of St. John: "Consider that it is expedient one man should die for the greater good of all people."

Wingate, however, recognized that he'd pushed inside Burma too far. On the evening of March 23, Calvert had driven forty more miles toward the Goktiek viaduct, and when he radioed in still more news—his column had ambushed and destroyed yet another full company of Japanese troops—Wingate ordered Calvert to cancel his approach on Goktiek and to "return to India by any route."

The following day, when a supply drop for Wingate's Column One near the town of Baw had to be scotched—a Chindit junior officer showed himself in daylight there, tipping off the Japanese and starting an open-field battle for control of the town—Wingate was furious. After withdrawing all Column One troops from Baw, Wingate had the junior officer demoted, tied to a tree, and lashed. Then Wingate got some really bad news in the form of a radio message from British Headquarters (HQ) in India. According to HQ, the RAF now believed it was too dangerous and difficult to continue supplying the Chindits, and perhaps it was time for Wingate to "consider a withdrawal."

Two days later, Wingate ordered his column commanders to return to India with all speed and to recross the Irrawaddy where they had crossed it originally, since he believed the Japanese wouldn't guard those locations as closely as other spots along the river.

AS THE CHINDITS TURNED west and headed for India, their evacuation would prove as hard—though faster—than their invasion had been five long weeks earlier.

With his orders to withdraw from Burma by any route, Mike Calvert's Column Three first attempted to escape northward, toward the Burma Road and China; the shortest way to freedom. But as they continued east, they were met at every village and river crossing by Japanese sentries. So on March 30, after one last supply drop, Calvert separated the men in his snake into five "dispersal groups," whose smaller numbers had a better chance of slipping past the Japanese. Then he gave each group leader a stout drink of rum and—with their backpacks full of food—bade all of his men good luck and good-bye.

Within days, two of Column Three's five parties had reached the Ir-rawaddy, where they paid a Burmese man with a large boat to ferry both groups (about ninety men in all) across the river. Two weeks later, on April 14, having encountered little resistance, these first two of Calvert's

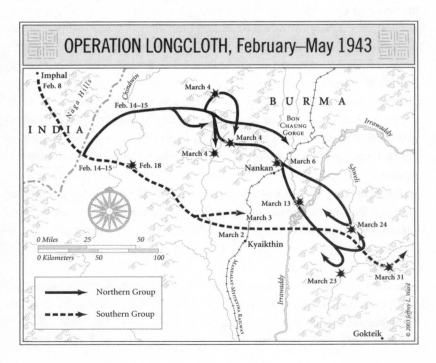

OPERATION LONGCLOTH, February–May 1943

parties crossed the Chindwin into India. By now, though, the men were literally collapsing and dying of malnutrition; some were so weak they were unable to feed themselves.

The following day, Calvert and his group staggered back into India as well, having been slowed when Calvert took a day to blow up the Mandalay-Myitkyina railway in a few more places, just for kicks.

In the weeks that followed, other stragglers from Calvert's Column Three arrived in India. And before the withdrawal was finished, 205 of Calvert's original 360 men got safely back. Ironically, upon his return to India, what Calvert most remembered was being unnerved by India's narrow doorways. And it took him several weeks to figure out why.

During his seven weeks in Burma's jungles, Calvert had led a column of 360 men, several hundred mules, one immature elephant picked up along the way, and a spotted dog through the rain forest every day. As Column Three had—more than any other Chindit unit—bushwhacked the jungle, Calvert's mule drivers had hectored him constantly to cut his trail between trees that stood wider apart than four feet, since the girth of each fully loaded mule (as well as the elephant) spanned almost that width. Knowing the value of the mules and their drivers, Calvert worked hard "every hour of every day" to honor his muleskinners' requests. Once he returned to India, however, he was able to finally lay down his burden and enjoy several weeks of R&R at a hotel in Calcutta. Yet anytime he crossed a doorway threshold narrower than four feet, he found himself reflexively pausing; then he'd become anxious and search for another approach to his goal— be it the hotel bar, restaurant, or entrance to the swimming pool. It was only after days of this obsessive avoidance that Calvert finally figured out his strange behavior: he was still leading Column Three back in Burma.

For that level of commitment and leadership, Mike Calvert would be awarded Britain's Distinguished Service Order, or DSO, for what would eventually be known as "First Wingate."

FOR ORDE WINGATE HIMSELF, the withdrawal of his Column One was less speedy and orderly than Calvert's. Harassed constantly by Japanese patrols, Wingate made it to his former crossing spot on the Irrawaddy, only to be driven back by Japanese fire from the river's far side. Moving downstream a bit, he then spent several days on the riverbank where he stalked the riverside like a second-string prophet, complete with a flowing beard, a bamboo walking staff, his now-grimy Wolsley helmet, and a blanket always wrapped around his shoulders. Eventually Wingate decided that, instead of crossing the Irrawaddy where he had before, his column would—like Column Three—break into five smaller parties, each of which could spread out along the river's length and slip more easily through enemy defenses.

Upon sending the other four parties of his men on their way, Wingate led his own detachment of forty-three soldiers into a jungle thicket near the Irrawaddy where he sat tight for a full week. Having found a good hideout, Wingate first established a camp perimeter with sentries. Then he ordered all of the remaining mules slaughtered, their throats slashed to preserve bullets and not alert the enemy, after which he treated his men to seven days of grilled-meat banquets. Across the week, Wingate also provided the camp with a nonstop monologue on anything that came into his head. He spoke eruditely of the delicate balance between Zionism and Palestine; philosophy and eighteenth-century painting; detective fiction versus novels; how symphonic music was far superior to concerti; Da Vinci; the varied possibilities of cinema; and the relative human value of the cartoon characters Popeye the Sailor Man and J. Wellington Wimpie.

For a Burmese Kachin soldier named Lieutenant Gum-Jaw-Naw—a former Northern Kachin Levie transferred to be Wingate's guide—those seven days were the height of glory. "Every day, Wingate talked the whole time . . . talk, talk, talk," Gum-Jaw-Naw recalls. "But at some time during every day, he would come to me and place his hands on my shoulders. Then he would look me in the eye. 'Good Job,' Wingate would say to me every day. 'You're doing a good job.' Wingate was a leader I would have done anything for. I would have walked into a rain of bullets for him . . . believing I would not die. He had convinced me that I could do anything. He was great."

For others, such as the affable Major John Jeffries, who was also a member of Wingate's Column One dispersal party, being secreted away in a jungle thicket and surrounded by the enemy for a week as Wingate droned on became excruciating. "In those seven days," Jeffries later recalled of Wingate, "he talked like a man possessed, rather as if he was striving to set in order the sum total of his beliefs . . ." And Jeffries, who apparently was not immune to opinion himself, regularly jazzed up afternoons in the jungle by encouraging Wingate in sometimes fierce debates as they dined on meals of grilled mule tongue and kidneys.

Finally, on April 7 Wingate gave orders to move again. He led his group south along the Irrawaddy's banks and, dodging Japanese patrols, recrossed the river not far from where Calvert's group had initially hopped it a month earlier and in the opposite direction. Unfortunately, on the last ferry trip across, a Japanese patrol arrived on the river's eastern shore just as the last members of Wingate's team were preparing to move, and the ferryman charged with skulling these last seven members of Wingate's group to safety aborted the trip and disappeared into the jungle.

Wingate waited several hours, but then abandoned these last soldiers—the Lost Seven—out of concern for the rest of his unit. Still, four of these abandoned soldiers would eventually arrive in India several days after Wingate and by roughly the same route.

FOR TWENTY-TWO DAYS after crossing the Irrawaddy, Wingate drove west through the jungles and over the mountains of central Burma, teasing and avoiding the Japanese in equal measure as increasing numbers of enemy search parties followed in pursuit. When he arrived at the banks of the Chindwin on April 29, Wingate was so concerned the Japanese might catch up he ordered his men to swim the two-hundred-yard river to India and freedom in midafternoon daylight.

Three days after Wingate and his men made it to safety, Fergusson's Column Five walked out as well: they were sick, skinny, and only six hours ahead of a Japanese patrol that had been dogging them for a week. A few days after that, on June 6, 1943, the last Chindit group out of Burma was a nine-man party from Wingate's Column One, led by British Lieutenant Dominic Neill. As they crossed the Chindwin by boat in the early afternoon, they were told that, just thirty minutes behind them, yet another Japanese patrol had been stalking them for days.

When he arrived back in civilization, Neill opened *The Times of India* to discover that—despite his own limited combat experience while soldiering with Wingate—the Chindits and their commander had apparently triumphed over the Japanese, not only shattering the Imperial Army's perceived invincibility, but dealing them a huge and deadly blow.

As often happens in wartime, reality and propaganda were now at odds. Later, despite stacks of glowing newspaper accounts, Neill said of the Chindit raids and the daring of Column One: "I killed a lot of lice. Not too many Japs. . . . In my view, only Number Three Column under Mike Calvert had achieved anything."

Neill's slightly grumpy perspective was also shared by Wingate's superior, General William Slim, who noted that of the three thousand Chindits who went into Burma, only 2,182 came out—and only six hundred of those men were ever fit for military service again. He also noted that, while damage was done to the Japanese rail and communications systems by the Chindit mission, only an estimated 205 Japanese were killed. Because of these inequitable casualty rates, not to mention the costs in airpower and equipment lost for what was ultimately only a short-term disruption to the flow of Japanese troops, information, and goods, Slim was forced to assess the Chindit raid as a failure.

General Slim did note, however, that, "Whatever the actual facts, to the troops in Burma it seemed the first ripple showing the turning of the tide . . . and by every means in our power we exploited its propaganda value to the fullest."

STILL, HAVING SEEPED into Burma, smashed a spoke of Japan's defensive wheel, and emerged to tell about it, Orde Wingate and his Chindits—no matter what the reality—were heroes worldwide. In Britain, Prime Minister Churchill first read of the Chindits' daring in the news, then scoured Wingate's field report to learn more about the unorthodox invasion. After finishing Wingate's report, Churchill summoned Wingate to England immediately to meet him, forging an instant friendship. Like the supportive alliance between President Roosevelt and Claire Chennault in the United States, the British prime minister saw Wingate as a leader of flashy innovation, whose plans for CBI's future offered a fast and reasonably inexpensive way to destabilize the Japanese in Burma.

Until the Chindits' success, Churchill felt his generals had spent too much time and energy bickering among themselves for status and power instead of driving for victory. Having found Wingate, Churchill began entertaining the idea of promoting the Chindit leader to direct all British and Indian troops and tactics in India. Though Churchill's senior commanders ultimately discouraged the prime minister from such a drastic shift in philosophy and leadership, they also did little to slow Churchill's fascination with Wingate's theory of Long-Range Penetration.

In the midst of their first meeting in London—over drinks and dinner—Wingate presented his plans for a network of larger, more heavily manned and more permanent Long-Range Penetration (or LRP) bases inside Burma. Churchill was enthralled (as was Churchill's daughter, Mary, who very favorably assessed Wingate as "a tiger of a man").

As the meal progressed—and feeling the rush of support from Churchill—Wingate began to argue that LRP-style forces should be considered the main instrument of attack against the Japanese in Burma, instead of leaving them as the second-tier, supplemental force they currently occupied. Thinking on his feet, Wingate began to invoke his vision of air-supported Chindit outposts deep inside enemy territory: fortifications dug in heavily enough that Japanese assaults couldn't drive them out, and from which needles of still deeper penetration could be driven into the occupying army. Churchill grew so excited by these prospects that he invited Wingate to the next Allied planning session, called the Quadrant Conference, held at the historic Château Frontenac in Quebec City. There was only one hitch: Churchill was departing in an hour.

Wingate—who had only telephoned his wife since landing in England, and who had yet to change clothes since arriving from Cairo—agreed to Churchill's travel offer. Then, with one order, Churchill instructed his aides to have Lorna Wingate brought to meet them at the *Queen Mary* for the five-day ocean voyage to Canada.

By the time Churchill's entourage arrived at the Quadrant Conference, Wingate—who'd now had a week to comb out his theories—proposed his Long-Range Penetration program to the combined Allied Supreme Command. According to Wingate's plan, eight full brigades of select LRP troops (about eight thousand men) would be inserted into Burma during the coming winter's dry season. From there, like a spreading infection, they could further disperse and move in small groups across the landscape, slowly exhausting the Japanese. While the British generals attempted to shout down Wingate's proposal—arguing the commitment in men and resources was far too great—Churchill and his staff remained encouraged by the idea. The Americans were also impressed, so much so that George Marshall offered U.S. troops as one of the combat units, the first American battlefield forces in CBI.

Hearing the news, Stilwell responded predictably. "After a long struggle," he wrote in his diary, "we get a handful of U.S. troops and by God they tell us they are going to operate under WINGATE! . . . That is enough to *discourage Christ!*"

But Churchill still wasn't finished with his upgrades at Quadrant. Because it was understood that America wouldn't commit troops to assist Britain in reacquiring her former colonies, Churchill proposed a new super-structure for the Allies in South Asia, one that would widen Britain's authority, granting it a more equitable alliance with the Americans. He suggested calling it Southeast Asia Command (SEAC) and offered up the dashing, forty-three-year-old Vice Admiral Lord Louis Mountbatten to run it. Mountbatten was a cousin to King George IV and a successful naval commander. He was also a recent veteran of the Allies' daringly successful, multinational raid against the Germans in the French port of Dieppe, where he had proved he could unite soldiers of many flags to one cause. Mountbatten also loved aggressive battle plans and—perhaps most important—he possessed enough stores of charm to calm the escalating tensions between Stilwell and Chiang Kai-shek.

To keep footing even between the British and the Americans, Churchill suggested that Stilwell be named deputy supreme commander of SEAC, adding yet another job to Stilwell's already knee-buckling portfolio of tasks. Aside from his other problems, Vinegar Joe would now be answerable to three sets of command: to Mountbatten and the Allied Combined Chiefs; to George Marshall and the American Joint Chiefs; and to the generalissimo in China.

Stilwell's reservations aside, the suggestion was approved, and as Quadrant ended—with Mountbatten headed for India to take control of SEAC—it finally appeared that the China-Burma-India theater of operations would get the recognition it had long needed.

At the Quadrant Conference, a plan to retake Burma was also finally laid out and agreed upon, with final approval to come when the Allied chiefs met next in Cairo in November. Starting in February 1943, after Burma's monsoon-swollen rivers had receded, Burma would be invaded in steps out of the north, with the conquest of northern Burma and the reopening of the Burma Road taking priority. Stilwell's India-based Chinese battalions would drive into the northern Burmese lands of the Naga and Kachin tribes—a world of swamps, jungles, and villages with unpronounceable names—out of India, advancing just ahead of the Ledo Road.

The new roadbed would begin in Ledo, cross the rugged Patkai Mountains into Burma via the old commercial foot trail at 3,727-foot Pangsau Pass. Once inside north Burma, the X Force would drive south down the broad Hukawng River valley, followed closely behind by the road engineers. The X Force would drive the Japanese back wherever they found them, pushing farther south into Burma through the villages of Shingbwiyang ("the place of the bamboo shoots" in Kachin), Walawbum ("the big hill"), and Shaduzup ("Shadu's village, where the rivers come together"). With the upper Hukawng Valley cleared, the X Force would then turn slightly east, entering the smaller Mogaung River valley—which opens into the Hukawng—and snake its way east to attack the Japanese at the airfield-served city of Myitkyina ("by the big river," the Irrawaddy), roughly 290 miles southeast of Ledo.

When the X Force was finally attacking Myitkyina, Wingate's Chindits would then be dropped by glider into Burma southwest of Myitkyina: their mission to cut enemy communications and drive out rearguard units that might be skirmishing with Stilwell's troops. Then, conditions permitting, Stilwell's armies would meet with the Chinese Y Forces pushing out of China along the Burma Road and across the Burmese border. Together, the combined X and Y Forces would push the Japanese south of Lashio, reopening the Burma Road.

Finally, the British Fourteenth Army under General Slim would cross into Burma along another road—this one built by the British—between their headquarters in Imphal and the India-Burma border town of Tiddum. From there, the Fourteenth Army Corps would provide the "body punches" to the Japanese forces. They would advance down the Arakan Peninsula again toward Akyab Island and Rangoon's seaport beyond, reopening Allied supply by sea and allowing goods to be transported by rail to the Burma Road's starting point in Lashio. China would soon be back in overland supply.

After sixteen months of waiting—and with the winter dry season fast approaching—the Allied invasion of Japanese-occupied Burma was set to begin. As Stilwell returned from the Cairo planning conference in mid-December, he summarized all of his concerns with a typically succinct, yet strangely timid, entry into his diary for December 20, 1943: "Off for Burma again. Under better auspices than last time. CAN WE PUT IT OVER?"

# Chapter 7

IN MARCH 1942, just as it had been for the British and Americans before them, Japan's only reliable path for moving new occupation troops and goods into Burma was by sea. But due to Chennault's Flying Tiger air patrols over the South China Sea, the Japanese supply routes to Rangoon had grown more perilous by the day. Despite acquiring eight hundred thousand tons of Allied goods and weapons abandoned on the wharves of Rangoon as the city collapsed, Japanese occupation forces in Burma were constantly in danger of running out of food and supplies. By May 1942, as the invasion and occupation of Burma was being completed, Japan lost 67 ships, plus 314 tons of goods, sunk while en route to Rangoon. Like the Chinese being deprived of their sea trade under Japanese occupation, the Japanese occupiers of Burma were soon being throttled by the American ship hunters.

To circumvent this stranglehold, the Japanese—who were only gaining a handle on the breadth of Asia they'd snatched in the past year—decided a more secure land route for soldiers and supplies was needed immediately. So in March 1942, Imperial Japanese Command rescinded its initial eighteen-month plan for a single, meter-gauge railroad to connect all nations inside its new Greater East Asian Co-Prosperity Sphere, and instead ordered the railroad completed in a single year (a feat they would not, in the end, be able to accomplish). Fortunately for the Japanese, the job was already almost finished. Largely due to the colonial British enchantment with rolling stock, serviceable rail networks already stretched across much of the region before Japan began its invasions.

There was, in fact, only one gap in the entire system: a 260-mile zone though the jungles and mountains of west-central Siam (increasingly called Thailand since 1936) and into a similarly trackless maze of eastern Burma. Once this stretch of wilderness was fitted with rails, trains could run the breadth of south Asia: from Japanese-held regions of eastern China south to Hanoi in Indochina's deepest south and west to Bangkok, Singapore, and distant Rangoon. All that remained, the Japanese understood, was the task of slapping a pair of tracks across 260 miles of tall mountains, narrow valleys, and thick jungles.

Within weeks, Japanese surveyors were pacing out their newest project. And as they mapped and planned, they also began to understand the audacity in their mission. The mountains and jungles were virtually impenetrable (there was good reason the British had never put rails there) with only one path between the two cities seeming even a realistic possibility. The line would have to stretch northwest from the railroad's current end west of Bangkok—near Ban Pong, Thailand—and past the farm village of Kanchanaburi. From there, a three-hundred-yard bridge had to be constructed across a river called the Kwae Yai (or Big Kwae), before the rails could be laid northwest through the rain forests and between two steep and parallel mountain ranges—the Dwana and the Tanen—for about one hundred miles. Eventually the rails would have to climb a grade to nearly seven thousand feet, then they would cross the natural summit at Three Pagodas Pass on the Thai-Burmese border, take a harder turn to the west, and thread through several more forested valleys before finally dropping onto Burma's coastal flatlands to meet with existing rails for the final stretch to the seaport at Moulmein, Burma.

But it wasn't only the route and its topography that presented obstacles to the Japanese. Beyond the mountains, the jungles, and the hundreds of inches of rain that fell on the landscape each summer, two other problems confronted them. First, there was virtually nothing in the way of new supplies—bridging materials, rail fittings, or running rail—anywhere inside the Greater East Asian Co-Prosperity Sphere. (Most of the railroad steel in south Asia, it turned out, had come by boat from Great Britain.) And second, they had none of the machinery usually employed for construction of a modern railroad.

To overcome these problems, the Japanese had to get creative. First, to acquire materials, they ordered the ripping up of several rail spurs in Thailand and Burma, including 170 miles of redundant double track between Rangoon and the city of Tongoo in east-central Burma. Then they began cannibalizing less crucial lines in Java, Singapore, and Malaya. Instead of heavy construction equipment, they reverted to old-style building techniques: stone-weighted pile drivers that would employ elephants, ropes, and pulleys to do the truly heavy lifting. For day-to-day work, the Japanese would use their most disposable store of human muscle-power: the prisoners they had taken in recent months. They would put their POWs to work.

When it came to constructing railroads, Japan had long relied on outside engineering prowess. Japan's first rail line, an eighteen-mile stretch between Tokyo and Yokohama, had been built in 1872 under the direction of European engineers. The Japanese, though, had proven quick studies. By the turn of the century, they'd developed an impressive detail of expert rail designers, who had since designed and laid track all across their nation.

Now in south Asia—with the British and other Westerners as their captives—they had an opportunity not only to show off their railroad engineering flash, but to pound their professed cultural superiority into people they felt saw them as inferiors. To underscore their campaign, Imperial Japanese Command issued a pamphlet to every officer and soldier occupying the southern region of Japan's Asian holdings. Among other things, the flier claimed that Westerners had treated the Japanese as "an inferior race" for a century, and stressed that Japanese troops "must, at the very least, here in Asia, beat these Westerners into submission, that they may change their arrogant and ill-mannered attitude."

It was an order the Imperial Japanese Army would take deeply to heart.

THESE DAYS, what most people know of the Burma-Siam Railway and its famous span across the Kwae Yai has one foot firmly planted in the manipulations of fiction. In 1952, Pierre Boulle, a French-born engineer, author, and British Special Forces resistance fighter in China, Burma, and Indochina during World War II, published his second novel. Titled *The Bridge on the River Kwai*, it was based loosely on events at one Allied POW Camp near Kanchanaburi during the war.

In the course of the novel, British prisoners are forced by a brutal

Japanese commander to build a wooden rail bridge across the river, only to watch it be blown by their own countrymen upon completion. In a novelist's trick, however, the pitiable conditions and backbreaking work done by the POWs become vehicles for the prisoners to rediscover their self-respect in the face of Japanese humiliations. In real life, of course, as men died and others sweated and struggled to live another day—while working at the slowest pace possible under the Japanese—the broad strokes of heroism Boulle described were far less showy and far more lethal. According to historians, when the railroad was completed seventeen months later, in October 1943, more than sixteen thousand Allied prisoners—a city's worth of men—would perish, as would as many as 150,000 Thai, Burmese, Indonesian, and Malaysian conscript laborers, people barely mentioned in Boulle's book.

Still, *The Bridge on the River Kwai* became an international best-seller and a critical smash: it even won the prestigious French literary honor, the Prix St. Beuve in 1952. But bigger accolades for Boulle's story still waited five years in the future, when the movie director Sir David Lean released Boulle's fiction as a hit film starring, among others, Alec Guinness and William Holden. The screen adaptation, which was nominated for eight Academy Awards, took even more liberties with the facts than did Boulle's novel. And due to the film's enormous popularity, the fiction of the bridge on the river Kwae—with its tortures, horrors, tiny moral victories, and that famous last-breath destruction of the bridge by Alec Guinness's mortally wounded Colonel Nicholson—will probably overshadow the truth forever.

Which is tragic, since the reality of what happened along what the POWs came to call "The Death Railway" is just as heartbreaking.

WITH THE HEAT of spring presaging the rains of summer, few Allied POWs in Japanese-controlled South Asia could understand why suddenly, after months of neglect, their Japanese captors began distributing questionnaires inquiring about each prisoner's education and professional history. Then, ominously, the POWs were made to sign contracts in which they agreed not to attempt escape.

Shortly after the forms had been completed and returned—with most of the POWs explaining to the captors that before the war they had been dedicated professional "beer tasters," "centenary bell ringers," and "brothel inspectors"—yet another inexplicable event occurred. Inside prison camp wires across south Asia, from Java and Sumatra to the thick walls of the stifling Changi Prison in Singapore, the Japanese announced that all able POWs would soon be moved to "rest camps" in the mountains of Thailand and Burma. Once there, housed in the cooler altitude and jungle shade, the POWs were told they would receive improved food and medical care, allowing those who'd been left sick and exhausted by their captivity to stand better odds of recovery.

By late October 1943, as the summer monsoons came to a drizzly end, the Japanese had also finally amassed enough rail and fittings to begin, and they turned their interests from setting up a few jungle base camps along the proposed rail line to actually constructing a railroad. By early November, trucks and trains began carrying the first of an eventual sixty thousand POW laborers (mainly from Singapore, China, and the Dutch East Indies) into the highlands between Burma and Thailand. But even before the demanding task of railroad building began, any POW's journey to the work site was universally inhumane.

One soldier, a British second lieutenant named Geoffrey Pharoah Adams, began his trip at Changi Prison in Singapore. Adams, a butcher in Bournemouth, England, before joining the Royal Army Service Corps, had arrived in Singapore on February 6, 1942, just fifty hours before the overwhelming Japanese invasion crumbled British defenses, leading to the island's surrender nine days later.

Now Adams and his fellow prisoners were being marched in groups of roughly three hundred from Changi to Singapore's rail station. As each group left the prison, they would strike into the chorus of "It's a Long Way to Tipperary," a song that came to infuriate the Japanese guards so much they would beat the POWs with clubs in attempts to quiet them. At the rail station, the prisoners were separated into groups of thirty and driven onto boxcars forty feet long by eight feet wide. After each train's ten cars were filled, the whole snaking, clanking carrier would begin a long, puffing trip north, bumping along the rails, each steel car baking like an oven beneath the day's sun.

For four days and five nights—with only two stops in any twenty-four hours for bowls of rice—Adams and his fellow captives continued north on the sluggish train. "There was no room for thirty people to lie, or even sit down," Adams later recalled. "So we took it in turns to rest." The only relief came each afternoon: as the cars heated up beneath the sun, the Japanese guards would allow the POWs to ride with the boxcar's sliding doors open. Still, Adams remembered, though the captives were weak and sick with dysentery, malnutrition, and thirst, the heavily armed Japanese guards were quick to remind the prisoners that they could not run: "We had, after all, signed those 'No Escape' forms!"

Finally, after one thousand miles of cramped travel—during which the men inside the cars had traded spots regularly to be near the doors to defecate or vomit from the heat—the train pulled into the city of Ban Pong, current end of the existing rails in Thailand. The POWs were then assembled on the rail platform, to be counted and recounted (and counted again) beneath a crushing sun. After hours of this torment—which was repeated so often it came to be called "sun treatment"—the POWs were marched to the fenced and fetid Ban Pong Camp at the edge of town: a patch of mud a few acres across, with falling-down and bug-infested barracks. The camp's trench-style latrines were so filled they ran over and flooded the ground, filling the air with a smell so nauseating prisoners were forced to breathe through their mouths so they wouldn't begin to heave. Housed in "decrepit huts made of bamboo" whose muddy floors were slippery as porridge in the wake of the monsoon season, the POWs were met by a number of sick men, all of whom appeared to be waiting for death. "There was nothing to do," said Adams, "but join them."

After two days at Ban Pong, where Adams and his crew learned from their captors that they were going to help the Japanese in their "conquest of India," the POWs were once again loaded up and transported. This time they were put onto trucks and driven farther north along muddy roads to the tiny village of Tamarkan on the west bank of the Kwae Yai, just a mile north of Kanchanaburi. As the men exited the trucks, the reality of their situation—and the Japanese duplicity they'd all feared for weeks—was finally made clear. Around them was only jungle. There was no rest camp. There were no dispensaries or hospitals. There were no mess tents or latrines. Instead, there stood only a few stacks of rails and ties, a handful of storage sheds, and an open-sided barracks hundreds of yards long and made from bamboo and woven palm fronds, a style of building known as *atap*. Encircling all of this, as almost a mockery of a boundary, stood a thin fence of bamboo.

Adams and his fellow POWs were met by a British captain named

David Boyle, who described himself as "Camp Adjutant" and whose men had already started building a rudimentary rail bridge of timbers across the river. After a few minutes of greetings, the inmates were assembled in the camp's yard and introduced to its director, Sergeant Major Saito. Saito then introduced his chief engineer, Lieutenant Fuji, and the camp manager, Kokuba. Then he issued orders. All prisoners were to sleep on one of the two raised platforms of bamboo that ran the length of the barracks Captain Boyle's men had tossed together. Each man was allowed twenty-nine inches of the platform's width, just enough room to lie on his back at night and sleep. Every morning at roll call, or *tenko*, all POWs who could stand upright were to fall in for their day's instructions. The laborers would then be divided into smaller work details of twenty to thirty POWs, called *kumis*, which were overseen by Allied officers, usually lieutenants, that the Japanese called *kumichos*. When two or more *kumis* were to work on the same task, they were said to form a work party or *han*. To keep the *hans* in line, they would be presided over by an Allied officer—usually with the rank of captain or above—whom the Japanese called a *hancho*.

The POWs' first task was to finish construction of the three-hundred-yard wooden bridge over the wide but shallow Kwae Yai, just above where it was joined by the Kwae Noi (the Little Kwae). This job was to take no more than two months. When the bridge was nearing completion, Saito said, members of the work parties no longer useful for construction would be sent to camps deeper in the jungle along the proposed rail line. There they would deforest and level the earth for the coming rail bed, set down the rail ties and rails, and continue this process to the northwest, where they would eventually link with parties of POWs laying rail southeast from Burma. In a year, the two rail lines were to meet at roughly the halfway point, near the town of Kon Kuta, Thailand. Eventually, Saito said, the wooden bridge above the Kwae Yai would be replaced by a sixteen-span steel bridge being disassembled and transported to the site from its old location in Malaya. All of this—the completion of 260 miles of rail, including almost seven miles of large and small bridges—was to be completed, as the Japanese ordered, in double-time, or "Speedo."

Finally, Saito pointed out the flimsy boundary fences around the camp and reminded the POWS that the surrounding mountains and jungles made each outpost an island. Should any prisoner attempt escape, tigers and poisonous snakes awaited, as did one thousand miles of suspicious lo-

cals not used to seeing white faces and blue eyes. To encourage area natives
to cooperate with the return of POWs, Saito said, the Japanese had announced to surrounding populations that anyone delivering an escaped
prisoner to authorities would be issued a cash reward and a year's extra
ration of rice.

FROM THE FIRST MORNING, railroad construction was a living, sweating,
grunting hell. With every new dawn, the prisoners faced illness, exhaustion, jungle leeches, exasperating mosquitoes, thirst, hunger, and humid,
stinking heat. On occasions when jobs were almost completed, a workday
could stretch to twenty hours. And then, with the next morning's sunrise,
Lieutenant Fuji would select the day's tasks and inform Saito of the number of laborers needed.

To assure enough POWs were present each morning, Japanese officers
would rely on the POWs' own commanding officer, or "head *hancho*," to
produce the required number of workers. If the head *hancho* couldn't deliver a large enough force of healthy men, Japanese and Korean guards
would raid the barracks (and eventually the camp hospital), digging up the
fittest of the ailing—the "light sick"—over protestations from camp medics, usually members of various Allied medical corps.

The *hanchos* were in a delicate position. Acting as both Allied commanding officers and labor organizers for the Japanese, they had to bridge
the subtle gap between outright disregard for Japanese authority and com-
plicity with it. To survive, they followed the only viable course: keep contact with the Japanese to a minimum and be the human buffer between
Japanese brutality and the prisoners themselves. Some mornings, when illness or exhaustion sapped a camp, the head *hancho* would refuse to field a
sufficient number of workers, for which he would be personally beaten—
often punched or hit with a rifle butt—in front of his men. Other days, the
head *hancho* might gather enough laborers, but might then order a collective "go slow," for which he might be tied to a stake at the camp's center
and publicly beaten. Still other times, everyday relations would grow so
tense that blows would be struck on the *hanchos* just to inspire fear.

One day a *kumicho* named Lieutenant Bridge struck a Japanese noncommissioned officer who had been overseeing the POW work detail.
Upon the return to camp that night, Kokuba gave Lieutenant Bridge such

a ferocious beating with fists and clubs that only the protestations of a
*hancho* named Lieutanent Colonel Toosey (the Alec Guinness character
in the movie based on Boulle's book) and Camp Adjutant Boyle spared
his life.

Each morning at dawn, Adams and his fellow POWs fell in for *tenko*
and were directed to work on different components of the bridge. Using axes and two-man saws fitted with wooden handles, teak trees in the
area were felled to make bridge pilings. It was punishing work, especially
since the Japanese ordered the prisoners to use their saws in the slower,
traditional-Japanese manner: pulling them across the trees instead of
pushing them. Then, once a tree's trunk had been severed, it often still
stood upright, since it was secured to its neighbors through the jungle
canopy's mass of vines and tangled branches. When a cut tree would remain standing, elephants would be employed to push it over. If no elephants were available, bridge workers with ropes would be brought in to
pull the tree down. Sometimes, because of the unpredictable way the en-
snared trees would fall, men were crushed. Still, a dozen or so trees were
being dropped and prepared each day. And the bridge—despite the primi-
tive conditions, the dysentery and malaria, and the inefficient tools—had
stretched from the hillside rail bed and out across the Kwae in a matter of
weeks.

After each new piling was made ready for the river—by slashing away
its branches—several *kumis* assisted by elephants would enter the river
(employing boats where necessary) and, using hands, ropes, and the
strength of the elephants, position the piling vertically on the floor of the
Kwae Yai. Then, with the timber in place, "rope detachments" of hundreds
of men each would use the camp's six pulleys to lift a boulder fitted with a
metal sleeve that fit over the top of the raised piling. Finally, a Japanese
noncommissioned officer charged with that day's overseeing would begin
a rhythmic count of, "*Ichi ni no sai yo—no sai* yoh ("One two and three
four—and three *four*"). In time with the count, each rope detachment
would strain to lift the boulder into the air and, on the last word in the
chant, let it drop onto the piling, hammering the pillar a half-inch deeper
into the river's bed.

The work was hot, monotonous, and grueling. Men sick with dysentery
and cholera were releasing their guts along the riverbank or into the water,
which spread the disease further. Undernourished and riddled with ma-

laria, soon the POWs were dying, sometimes at a rate of a dozen per day.
Often Adams would wake in the first light of dawn and find men nearby
had expired overnight, their skin cool as wax. Other times, men would keel
over dead as they worked, feeding vultures that spent every day sitting,
waiting, on a sandy island just upstream of the bridge.

Men too chronically ill to work were trucked back to the rotting camp
at Ban Pong, so as not to "infect" the others with their laziness. Once at
Ban Pong's "sick camp," they often deteriorated and died. Those hearty
enough to push on worked seven days a week, from shortly after sunup
until dark, with only thirty minutes of rest at lunch. Before the war was
over, twenty-seven of every one hundred Allied soldiers held prisoner by
the Japanese in south Asia would be dead, compared with four of every
hundred held by the Germans and the Italians.

To keep pace with the losses of laborers, the Japanese were now trucking
hundreds of POW and Thai conscript reinforcements to Tamarkan every
day, and soon the camp had a population of more than two thousand.
Most of the new POW laborers were British, with companies from East
Surrey, Leicester, Gordon, the Coast and Searchlight Gunners, and the
jungle-trained Argyll and Sutherland Highlanders. They, too, were forced
to make their own meals, which largely consisted of low-quality rice the
Japanese provided. The rice was infested by weevils and worms, which
could be picked out at midday, but not during breakfast or dinner, since
those meals were eaten in darkness. Because there was no tea, the men
drank either water or a burned-tasting "coffee" brewed from blackened
kernels of rice.

As autumn 1942 progressed, so did the bridge. By the end of that year,
the bridge's superstructure extended nearly halfway across the river, and
the Japanese—now feeling a flush of success even as the POWs and Asian
conscripts were dying all around—ordered the workers to the opposite
bank, where they were to begin building the bridge's other half. To cross
the river each morning, the soldiers took long, narrow boats they began
calling "pom-poms" for the puttering noise their small engines made.
Within weeks, the river's far bank, too, had sprouted pilings and trestles.

Then one night toward the end of 1942, as the soldiers lay on the hard
wood planks of their *atap* (barracks) sleeping platform, an unseasonable
deluge poured several inches of rain into the Kwae valley upriver. The following morning, as the sun rose, the POWs and Japanese guards and engi-

neers looked to the river and discovered that it had not only risen several feet, but that hundreds of trees had been uprooted in the storm and had floated downstream on the torrent, smashing at the bridge's pilings like battering rams and taking all unbraced timbers downstream with them. After months of constructing the bridge, only to see it washed out, Adams and the other POWs at Tamarkan were broken. They would have to start over.


DISHEARTENED AND FORCED to redo hard labor they'd already completed once, the POWs firmed up their resolve and began again. Some prisoners, however, couldn't absorb the disappointment and began to more openly oppose the Japanese, setting into motion an increasingly devious and painful hierarchy of punishments. In response to a "go slow," the Japanese would withdraw smoking or bathing privileges. If the "go slow" continued—or if the Japanese felt the prisoners had done "bad work" that day—POWs from the offending unit would be lined up facing one another and, on counts of *ichi . . . ni* (one . . . two) be made to slap each other across the face for extended periods of time. For slightly larger acts of disobedience, POWs would be ordered to stand at full attention in front of Saito's office for the day—despite rain or blistering sun—waiting for the commander's dismissal. Other times, Saito or one of his commanders would order a POW to stand in place and hold a heavy log above his head. If the log was lowered or dropped, meaning the order had been disregarded, the soldier was beaten.

For still more serious offenses, such as a *hancho*'s disregard of an order or the illegal possession of a shortwave radio smuggled in from the outside, the Japanese fashioned "isolation boxes"—cells of galvanized tin barely large enough for a man to stand inside—which heated up beneath each day's tropical sun like a sauna. If a POW were to strike a Japanese soldier, as Lieutenant Bridge had done, he was generally stripped and lashed at the ankles, elbows, and wrists, with his back to a thick bamboo stake near the camp's center. Then he would be beaten with clubs, fists, knotted ropes, and, to finish the job, rifle butts. When the flogging ended, the prisoner would be left there, hanging on the stake, bleeding, swollen, and often unconscious as a public reminder of the price for insolence.

Still, worst of all, for repeat violent offenders, there waited the "bucket torture." In this, the offending POW was stripped and lashed at the ankles, elbows, and wrists to one of the camp's "beating stakes." Then, over the prisoner's head, the Japanese would hang a large five- or six-gallon bucket, its narrow string or wire handle tight across the nape of the prisoner's neck. The bucket would then be filled with water or, if the offense was deemed truly excessive, rocks and stones. After that, the prisoner was to be left alone in excruciating pain for days—as the sun baked down, the cool night's fog chilled him, and the bucket's handle cut away at his neck and shoulder muscles.

Faced with these prospects, some POWs began considering their chances of escape through the jungle. One night, Adams was introduced to a group of prisoners who were planning a breakout. Because the camp was not lit, the group knew that any POW who went "over the wall" shortly after the evening's roll call had a healthy twelve-hour lead on any search party chasing him. While Adams declined to join the breakout crew, he watched with fascination as, shortly after a day's end, six men pushed through the flimsy bamboo fence and lit into the dark forest.

By dawn the following day, four of the six had been captured and summarily executed. Only two—a Brit nicknamed "Pom" and a British artillery captain, both of whom Adams helped provision—were still on the run. For three weeks, the two traveled only at night, walking road edges in darkness and sleeping in the jungle during the days. In the hearts of Adams and the other POWs at Tamarkan, pride began to swell as they felt Pom and the artillery captain had negotiated their way to freedom.

As it turned out, with the passage of time and miles, the two escapees began to relax. To speed their trip along, they decided to travel in daylight. That same afternoon they were caught by Thai militiamen and trucked back to Tamarkan trussed "tight as chickens." To make an example of them, Saito sentenced both men to death. But first, in front of the entire assembled camp, the two were beaten by guards. Then, when nearly dead, they were untied, hurled into the back of a truck, and driven into the deep jungle. That night, they were forced to dig their own graves and were bayoneted to death by their captors.

With so little hope of emerging from the jungle alive, other POWs began to make daily mental escapes, detaching their thoughts from each day's mindless labor and feeding on the fat of their pasts. These daydreams were often so involved that a prisoner might relive old conversations aloud or remark on the beauty of Britain's countryside as if he was standing on a terrace inside it. Unfortunately, once snapped out of these happy recollections and reminded of the privations at Tamarkan, a number of men grew so broken they completely gave up. They would stop eating, communicating, and working—despite Japanese beatings to inspire them back to their labors. Eventually, in a phenomenon reported by the British medical officer A. A. Apthorpe, these men would spend their days lying on the bamboo slats of their sleeping platforms, staring catatonically at the hut's roof; even visits to the "isolation box" would do nothing to bring these men back. In every case of "*atap* staring" that Apthorpe witnessed or heard of, the sufferer eventually died.

BUT IF THE JAPANESE were hard on their prison labor force, under their own Bushido code, they could be equally brutal to their own soldiers. In his early days at Tamarkan, Adams recalled one episode that left him stunned. After a month or so of bridge building, the POWs had managed to befriend one of the few Korean guards who would engage them in conversation and barter. Named Kaneshiro (and nicknamed "The Undertaker" for his job as Tamarkan's coffin maker), he often traveled to Kanchanaburi for supplies, and he could be trusted to smuggle in small goods like cigarettes and jars of tea that he'd trade with the prisoners.

One night, possibly in retaliation for his fraternizing, Kaneshiro was discovered by a Japanese sentry asleep with his legs hanging beyond the end of his platform. It was, Adams surmised, an infraction of some kind. As Adams watched from the darkness of his bed, the guard swung his rifle butt down hard on Kaneshiro's legs, cracking it across the Undertaker's shins. Startled awake and in excruciating pain, Kaneshiro was then made to kneel and kiss the guard's boots. And as Adams watched, each time Kaneshiro bent to attempt a kiss, the sentry would kick him in the face, knocking his head violently backward. After several minutes of this—now bloody, nearly senseless, and unable to walk on still-traumatized legs—the Undertaker was dragged off to the camp guardroom and further beaten in private.

Other times, just to keep the POWs off balance, the Japanese guards could be puzzlingly open and friendly. One of them, a Hawaiian-born, American-educated, Korean guard named Okamoto, appeared to have been designated as a "good guard" by Saito himself. He would often tell Adams and his compatriots news from the outside world, and would share food and cigarettes with them, sometimes in plain sight.

One night, Adams recalled, he was on his way to the latrine when he saw the shadowy shape of a Japanese or Korean guard just ahead. He stopped short and bowed. "For Chris' sake," came Okamoto's voice through the darkness, "cut out that crap. Come over and talk. Have a cigarette." By Japanese design, the twin monarchs of Tamarkan were paranoia and fear, with just enough relief on hand to keep the camp working.

EACH DAY, over the cries of the Japanese guards to "*Speedo*" and "*Hurree-Uppu*," the bridge continued to grow. Soom Adams became part of a crew that no longer worked on the bridge, but began building the columns and footings for the larger steel bridge whose different sections had started to arrive from Malaya. POW divers—using brass, deep-sea helmets on pressurized air supply hoses—cleared the riverbed of rocks and silt to eight feet deep, and wooden coffer dams made onshore and floated out into the current were positioned around the holes on the river's floor. Then, once the structure was firmly in place on the riverbed, the coffer dam's interior would be emptied by soldiers with hand pumps.

As the dams were dug, Adams and hundreds of other men were pulled off their bridge-building assignments to form a human chain. From sunrise until dark each day, they passed baskets of river stones and pebbles from the Kwae's floor and up the bank to a row of motorized concrete mixers. When enough concrete had been made to create a new footing inside a coffer dam, the human chain would begin passing buckets of concrete in the opposite direction, from the mixers to the river.

One afternoon in early 1943, worn out by the nonstop work, Adams sat for moment on the gunwale of a small barge that had been beached on the riverbank. As he sat, his friend and fellow POW Jim Taylor stepped over and the two began to chat. Tired and slightly dazed with the exertion and the afternoon's heat, neither man noticed that, approaching up the shoreline was the great man himself: Lieutenant Fuji, chief of the engineers. From the belt of his baggy officer's jodhpurs, Fuji was extracting his samurai sword. In another few seconds, Fuji strode to the barge's edge, slapped Adams across the face, and, speaking in English, ordered him out of the barge. Then, as Adams stood and began back to work, Fuji lifted his sword and began to swing it toward Adams's neck.

"Christ, look out!" Taylor shouted, alarming the work crew and providing a gallery of witnesses.

That warning may have saved Adams's life. The engineer had, however, made his point and sheathed his sword, and, in good English—with a palpable tone of threat—asked for Adams's name and rank.

"I shall not forget you, lieutenant," Fuji said. "Next time, I kill you."

A few days later, Fuji got his opportunity. As Adams and another acquaintance, a Sergeant Davies, were trading for cigarettes and hard-boiled eggs with some Thai merchants who'd stepped to the riverbank from the jungle, Adams grew perplexed when the merchants suddenly scattered.

He turned and, once again, saw Fuji. Again Fuji's sword was drawn and he was screaming. He punched and slapped Adams, then began beating Davies. Luckily, Fuji didn't seem to remember Adams and his promise from just a few days earlier. Instead of killing Adams and Davies, Fuji only sentenced the two to "sun treatment" on a nearby hillside for the rest of the day.

FOR ANOTHER FEW MONTHS, the bridge building continued, with fresh brigades of Dutch, Australian, and British soldiers—not to mention thousands of civilian conscripts—moving through Tamarkan on their way to camps still being created deeper inside the forest.

Unfortunately, these newest soldiers brought with them only unhappy news of the war: the Japanese tide of victory had yet to be contested and the Allies—who were only starting to bomb Burma's now-Japanese-held ports of Rangoon and Moulmein out of India—were nowhere near fielding an infantry to reinvade south Asia. The only hopeful moments Adams and his fellow POWs were able to string together were ones they concocted in the hell of Tamarkan. Early in the new year of 1943, the Japanese allowed a portable phonograph to be used by the prisoners, and each night the men would listen to what few records they possessed or could trade for. Long after the war was over, Adams still was able to bring back the rich smells and exhausted sense of the camp in vivid detail anytime he heard Bring Crosby singing "El Rancho Grande," "Poor Old Rover," or "Marcheta."

Then, one afternoon in February 1943, the first train from the Ban Pong rail yards suddenly puffed into view, paused at the beginning of the wooden rail bridge over the Kwae Yai and rolled slowly above the river. It churned off to the northwest over the new railroad, carrying steel and supplies deeper into the jungle. The Japanese were so elated that they threw up a loud—and very nonimperial—cheer. Acknowledging the success of their mission, Saito and Fuji gave the POWs the remainder of the day off.

But just because constructing the bridge had been achieved, that didn't mean the work and deaths and beatings would stop. For the next eleven months, the POWs would keep hacking at the jungle and laying rail ties and rails. The malaria would continue, as would the malnutrition, which grew so severe it began to leave many POWs wholly or partially blind. In the coming months, a cholera epidemic would break out at Tamarkan and all along the rail line, killing thousands of POWs, closing two of the "rest camps" forever, and forcing Saito and all Japanese camp commanders to outlaw bathing. To free themselves of the hell of the jungles, hundreds of prisoners would attempt escape; all but a handful were recaptured.

But on that one February afternoon, as that first train crossed the Kwai Yai, Adams and his fellow captives could feel both fulfilled and a little smug. Now that the bridge was complete, each of them knew, the Allied air forces had a new and psychologically valuable target for bombing.

# Chapter 8

THROUGHOUT THE RAINY SUMMER of 1943, the aircraft filling the skies above Thailand and Burma were far more likely to be C-46 and C-47 cargo planes (or "Dakotas," as the British called them) than the B-24 liberator bombers that would eventually destroy the Kwae bridges.

The cargo aircraft were being flown by dozens of American units in support of the Allied "Hump Airlift" to China, and literally hundreds of the planes were making the six-hundred-mile crossing daily—sometimes as often as *three times* a day. Flying runs were Air Transport Command squadrons and troop carrier wings. Extra cargo flights to China were also being picked up by American bomber pilots, who were "borrowed" during the rainy season from the American Tenth and Fourteenth Air Forces and were ordered to fly B-24s converted to carry solid or liquid cargoes. Perhaps most remarkably, 150 civilian fliers making laps over the Himalayas had been personally requisitioned by President Roosevelt from American Airlines, for a unit called Project 7-A.

While deliveries of goods and material to China remained substandard, the warehouses for Chennault and China were slowly beginning to fill, and aircraft creased the skies twenty-four hours a day. By June 1943, three thousand tons a month were moving to Kunming by air—up from just 106 tons the previous June.

Ray Dahl was one of the Hump pilots. A flight officer from Silverton, Oregon, who piloted a C-47 for the army troop carriers, he would eventually fly more than eighty missions over the Hump, which, at the height of the airlift, was chaos. "Sometimes we'd be taking off in heavy weather in India—thick clouds and zero visibility—and then we'd get above the ceiling and break out into open sky, and I'd see dozens of aircraft all around us. Sometimes, just as we broke out into clear air, we'd pop from the clouds and see a C-46 flying straight at us: twelve o'clock and coming fast. We had no real air-traffic control, no radar, and our radios only worked for about a thirty-mile radius. Cargo aircraft sometimes collided in midair. It was crazy."

But for all the airborne insanity, the Hump pilots and their crews were having "a wonderful time." Most of the flight crews were American boys off farms and from small towns, and the location's romance, as well as the trip over, had been life-broadening. In Brazil, they'd all bought wristwatches and green-canvas jungle boots. In Cairo, the belly dancers far outshone the Pyramids and the Sphinx. In Delhi, life was made livable by the India Coffee House, a café on the shady side of the street just off the colonnaded shopping district called Connaught Circle. In Calcutta, the dollar steaks and martinis and beer at Firpo's—where, like a Rockefeller, you got aspic or Becty à L'Anglaise as an appetizer—made everyone feel like a high-roller. They were worldly, they were pilots, and inside each of their footlockers was taped a picture of Marilyn Maxwell or Jinx Falkenburg or Betty Grable and her glorious gams.

And all of this experience was important, because once the flight crews got to Assam in northeast India (or Chittagong or Calcutta in India's south), they would be met only by hardship, since supplying the needs of China—through the "three demands" of Chiang Kai-shek—stood paramount to their own standard of living. At the Air Transport Command bases in India, troops were living on gruel, Spam, and rice, while those close to Hump deliveries in China grew fat on American-bought pork, chicken, and beef. The fast and somewhat sloppy influx of goods into China also created a huge black market in Kunming and beyond, where the cost of any saleable item—from shoe polish to gas-powered generators—sent inflation skyrocketing. "Coolies go around with $50 bills," Stilwell wrote of Kunming in his diary. And he, like many, was appalled when he learned that, in order to keep up with the plummeting value of their currency, the Chinese treasury was paying to have money printed in other countries—due to their own lack of paper—which was also being flown to Kunming by the planeload.

In India, the inequities and privations were beginning to affect morale. As the American print and radio correspondent Eric Sevareid put it:

> When I saw the American establishment at Chabua, where hundreds of Americans and thousands of natives slaved in scorching sun or dismal rain to get supplies into China, I could not help feeling a certain resentment of the Chinese resentment over the inadequacy of these supplies. Our men were killing themselves and being killed every day in the effort. Save for a few officers who could enjoy the comfort of tea-garden bungalows, they were living in shocking conditions. There were at this time absolutely no amenities of life—no lounging places, no Red Cross girls, nothing cool and refreshing to eat and drink, no nearby rest resort to visit on leave. It was a dread and dismal place. . . . They were trying to do too much with far too little. Pilots were overworked, and when they had made the perilous flight to China and back the same day, having fought storm and fog and ice, they simply fell into their cots as they were, unshaved and unwashed, to catch a few hours of unrefreshing sleep before repeating the venture the next day.

The Hump pilots, however, played gamely along. Each day they awoke in the humid air of jungle India, then carried shearling jackets and overtrousers to their aircraft in preparation for cockpit temperatures that would dip to forty below zero as they crossed the highest Hump peaks. They made unit pets of live leopards and baboons, and their motto became "Living like dogs, flying like fiends." Sartorially, they cultivated a rumpled but specific style, in which they wore their officer's hats with the crowns crushed flat, and always kept their .45-caliber pistols shoulder holstered beneath their left armpits. In India, different Hump transport units began vying to see who could carry the most goods per week or month. They formed elaborate betting pools and handicapped different bases, tracking the daily tonnage reports the way they followed baseball standings and racing forms back home.

Stilwell also saw the inequities and they infuriated him. As the rainy summer of 1943 passed, he started making unheralded inspections of the bases in Assam in an effort to keep the Indian detachments of his ATC troops equitably supplied. During one stop at the Polo Ground Mess in Chabua, Vinegar Joe—now increasingly being called "Uncle Joe" by the troops—went through the mess line with his GIs and found the food so inedible he took it upon himself to incite a riot. With only a moment's notice, sitting aside his men on a mess table bench, he announced, "All right boys, let 'em have it," and the mess hall erupted with flying food, tin plates and cups, and overturned tables. As the melee ended, Stilwell called in the mess commander to view the destruction, advising him, "There's your mess." Stilwell then gave an order that unless decent conditions were found during his next unscheduled visit, the commander would be relieved and shipped home.

FOR MORE THAN A YEAR—since June 1942—the airborne supply of China over the Hump remained Stilwell's and the Allies' number-one priority in Asia. And as the airlift continued, its less-than-organized efforts had become a bad joke in olive drab. Insane situations—sometimes involving lunatic cargoes—were the rule. Planeloads of chili powder and laxatives flew the Hump, as did cargo trucks that had to be cut in two for weight reasons (they were welded back together in Kunming), as did a grand piano for Madame Chiang that "unfortunately" had to be pushed out of the aircraft after the plane developed "engine trouble" somewhere over the Hump.

"I remember the coolies, who maintained the airfields in China, they'd run in front of our aircraft's spinning propellers," said Ray Dahl. "They believed the propellers would chase away any evil spirits following them. It sounds crazy, but our aircraft used to hit the Chinese all the time. You'd be throttling up engines for your takeoff, and—*BANG!*—there'd be this strange thud and the radioman would say: 'Uh, we got one.' "

Dahl saw his share of improbable loads. "This one guy was sent to China from Assam with eight thousand trash can lids. Nobody ever knew what they were using them for. Another time, this was later in the war, when we had troops in Burma again, we were dropping loads of live pigs to soldiers on the ground. Somebody fashioned up parachute harnesses for individual animals, and we'd fly in over the troops, drop our airspeed to 120 or 125 miles per hour, and when we got down to two hundred feet altitude or so . . . out went the pork through the cargo door. We used to say that if the chute didn't open, the troops on the ground had instant tender-ization for the pig."

But the task of flying over Japanese-occupied Burma wasn't all so com-ically strange. Each morning at takeoff—as pilots taxied out onto runways in India and China, ran up their engines, then hurtled down the still-dark runways whose edges were bordered by burning smudge pots—each crew-man aboard would check the pocket of his flight jacket to make sure it held a blue-cardboard envelope. Inside the envelope was what each crew-man called his "blood chit," which contained a detailed map of China and Burma plus pieces of paper printed with messages in several languages and dialects stating: "I am a downed American flier. Please return me to Allied troops and a reward will be given."

Fortunately, for Ray Dahl, his blood chit never got used. The whole time he was in CBI, "it just rode back and forth to China inside the pocket of my A-2 flight jacket."

Not everyone was so lucky. As the months passed, Hump fliers and their aircraft disappeared every few days. By the time the Allied airlift to Kun-ming was over in 1945, more than a thousand Hump fliers were listed as ei-ther crashed and dead or missing in action.

ON AUGUST 2, 1943, print and CBS Radio correspondent Eric Sevareid was one of seventeen passengers who stepped aboard a new Allied C-46 at Chabua for a trip to Kunming. Taking his place on the portside row of aluminum seats that faced each other across the aircraft's cabin, the tall, thin, wavy-haired Sevareid couldn't help but notice the last thing tossed aboard the plane—just before its hatch was shut—was a load of heavy canvas bags, each of which looked like a backpack with extra straps. They were, Sevareid surmised, parachutes. Then he was handed one of the bags and, imitating the rest of the plane's passengers, he began fitting the bag's straps to his body, leaving the actual parachute folded under him to create a soft cushion. As he returned to his seat, however, Sevareid felt the leg straps were too constricting, and he decided to leave them un-buckled.

Then, in the sunrise, he heard the plane's twin engines rumble to life, revving several times, and the C-46 began its taxi to the far end of the run-way and made its trip up the airstrip. The takeoff was smooth; in a few minutes the C-46 had risen out of the morning's ground mists, entering that strange spherelike world of dense green below and crystalline blue above, with only a morning fog veining the river valleys and adding to the morning's palette of saturated color. Aboard the C-46, Sevareid recognized John Davies of the State Department (who was functioning as an adviser to Stilwell) and Duncan Lee, a bright and boyish operative for the Office of Strategic Services, a new arm of the executive branch now charged with intelligence gathering in every theater of war.

The aircraft's cabin was loud. With the roar of the engines, it was so noisy that conversation at anything lower than a shout was impossible. So as Lee—familiar with the boredom of a Hump crossing—opened a book and settled back, Sevareid stared out the windows, then busied himself by making notes for a dispatch he was working on.

Over time, Sevareid realized that his flight was following the longer southern track across the Himalayas' foothills. This route would add roughly two hours to the trip, but was far less perilous than a more direct northern trip, dodging the snow-covered peaks of the Himalayas in China. As he stared out the window across the rolling green mountains below, Sevareid's only concern was that the unescorted C-46 would soon cross over the Chindwin River and enter Burma, whose airspace was controlled by Japan.

About an hour into the flight, lost in his thoughts and enjoying the view, Sevareid looked up when someone bumped against his legs. It was a young corporal he'd noticed when the aircraft had been boarding, Stanley Waterbury, of Blue Hill, Nebraska. The corporal leaned close to his ear. "Know what?" the young soldier shouted. "The left engine has gone out."

Sevareid stretched his neck to look out the window and saw the plane's portside propeller turning freely in the wind. This was one of those new C-46s, he thought, and its engine had likely fallen prone to the vapor locks that were still plaguing the design. As he began to ponder the implications of flying to China on one still-functioning engine, he noticed the sun was now blazing into the airplane through his window—in a way it hadn't a minute ago. The C-46 had made a turn; perhaps they were headed back to India.

Sevareid now began to lament the loss of a day in his trip across CBI— he doubted he could catch another flight to Kunming until tomorrow— and as he began slipping into a moment of self-pity, he was jarred from his thoughts by a blast of light and a deafening noise. The crew chief, a sergeant of about forty, had popped the plane's exit door open and was now hurling out all the suitcases and baggage stowed near the door.

"All passenger baggage out!" the sergeant screamed, and soon a line had been formed, with barracks bags, boxes, and suitcases being passed toward the airplane's opened door. Sevareid penned three last sentences into his notebook: "Nine fifteen a.m. Baggage out. Left engine not working." He placed the notebook in his briefcase, snapped the bag's latches tight, and handed it along to be tossed from the airplane in the same manner he'd just watched his suitcase go. Inside his already-jettisoned suitcase, Sevareid was only now realizing, were all of the clothes and toiletry items he'd brought from the United States. Somewhere over Burma, with one engine on his plane out, he now possessed only what he wore on his back or carried in his pockets.

Sevareid grew even more uneasy as he watched members of the flight crew—the pilot and copilot included—scrambling to strap themselves into parachutes that had, until just moments ago, been piled casually next to the radioman's desk. "This can't happen to me," Sevareid began thinking. "Not to *me*!"

Yet even as he was trying to rationalize the scene away—reminding himself that the C-46 remained in level flight with the pilot and copilot, now fully strapped into their parachutes, busy back at the controls—the chaos was disorienting. Over the roar of the engines, Sevareid heard a fragment of Duncan Lee's voice. Then he looked over and saw Lee gesturing his way. "I want to jump near you!" Lee was screaming.

Sevareid watched Lee in stunned disbelief. As he was helping to throw the last of the baggage from the airplane, Lee was also now clutching a pistol. Sevareid then noticed John Davies, his parachute tight to his back, crouched next to the door and staring off into the void below with a tight, strange smile on his face. Sevareid watched, awestruck, as Davies leaned out the aircraft's door and jumped "froglike" into space.

To rid himself of the shock of watching Davies jump, Sevareid glanced back at the flight crew—"We're still flying level!" he reconciled himself— then he returned his gaze to the cabin, only to realize that Duncan Lee was now gone as well. People were jumping, saving themselves, and Sevareid began thinking that, well, perhaps this parachuting approach was something to *consider*. As he glanced around the aircraft cabin, pondering what to do next, he discovered only two or three passengers still inside the plane.

It was then that Sevareid remembered he hadn't buckled himself completely into his parachute. Tightening and fighting with the parachute's leg harnesses as he stumbled across the passenger area, he was further shocked when, from the corner of his eye, he saw the plane's black-haired pilot run past him—his mouth wide open—and leap into space through the open door.

His mind swimming to make sense of the scene, Sevareid finally got to the C-46's doorway, still believing the airplane—which was *still flying level!*—would somehow manage to land perfectly in the thick jungle. The passengers behind him were now pushing him toward the door, and as he willed himself into the doorway's opening, leaning into space from what still seemed the safety of the C-46's cabin, he looked down and found that, at that moment, even jumping had become impossible. A mountain peak was moving directly beneath the plane—so close that Sevareid could make out individual branches on the trees. Were he to leap at that moment, his parachute wouldn't have time to open.

For a seeming eternity, Sevareid stood in the doorway and waited, feeling as if he were standing atop some impossibly tall cliff. People were pushing out the door past him, and he remained frozen and amazed. Then, quite unexpectedly, the C-46 bucked hard to the left. With the plane's lurch, Sevareid's knees buckled and as he began to right himself, he realized he'd been tipped out the open door as the aircraft began to pitch into a dive.

In the next second—since he was already falling through the opened doorway—Eric Sevareid threw himself headfirst into space, waited a long second to pull his parachute's rip cord, and closed his eyes. A titanic blow struck his body, and when he reopened his eyes, he was drifting gently toward the green jungle below in what had now become a "crushing silence." Ahead of him, green mountains appeared to be rising into the sky. Then a ball of oily orange flame erupted from the foot of a jungled peak ahead of him. The C-46 had crashed.

Drifting gently to earth, Sevareid took a mental accounting of the area: a muddy river slipped between two mountains, neither of which appeared to have any roads or trails, though a small village of grass huts did sit a few miles to the west, on the side of another mountain. Below him, a few other parachutes were drifting into the jungle's treetops.

In another minute, Sevareid could once again make out the individual branches of trees below him, then individual leaves, and in the next instant he was twisted around, his world having gone dark as branches and thick leaves slashed and ripped at him. Then he was rolling head-over-heels downhill through thick jungle. When he finally came to a stop, Sevareid again opened his eyes. He was on his back and above him—seen through a scrim of leaves—was blue sky. He was down.

He had survived the C-46's crash. Now, was he alone? And where was he, anyway?

ON THE GROUND in thick jungle, Sevareid began to gather his faculties. He didn't have any food, spare clothing, razors, toothbrushes, or any pens or papers . . . and blood was seeping through his pant leg from somewhere. He thought of his wife and two small boys back home in New York, an image that brought with it both a feeling of warmth and a sense of despair. Were he to die in this jungle or, equally bad, in some Japanese POW camp, he had not provided well enough for his family's future.

Then, as he unbuckled his parachute harness and stood up, he heard a noise coming through the forest. It was human . . . and it was speaking English. Stumbling through the underbrush, Sevareid began walking toward the noise, and where the jungle cleared a little, he found the sergeant crew chief—Ned Miller, of Ottumwa, Iowa—and the younger, almost white-haired Sergeant Francis Signor of Dobbs Ferry, New York. Their faces were bleeding, but they, too, were smiling in relief. Then they all sat down without saying a word and waited to see what would happen next.

After a few minutes of sitting, they heard yet another noise through the jungle: a weak-sounding cry of "Hellllp!" It was coming from near where the burning C-46 was sending a column of black smoke into the sky. The group stood, then hacked and fought through the jungle toward the plane. In another minute, they saw a white parachute tangled high in a scrubby tree and beneath it, sitting on the ground and staring at one of his feet, was the radio operator, Walter Oswalt from Ansonia, Ohio. He had stayed with the plane until the last minute, calling off their position to headquarters in India. He'd barely made it out before the C-46 crashed.

They got the radioman out of his parachute harness and, again, they sat wordlessly. They examined the radioman's damaged ankle, which was red and swollen. It was likely broken. As they began to consider their future options, they heard a noise and, looking up, saw the black-haired pilot and flight officer—Harry Neveu of Coleman, Wisconsin—crawling through the jungle's low plants and holding a hand pressed against his chest.

Neveu looked sheepish. "I sure am sorry," was all he could say, over and over. Then, after a full minute of apologies, the pilot informed the group he'd broken a rib.

Leaving the injured radioman beneath the tree, the survivors scrambled to the aircraft and checked its still-smoldering hulk for casualties; thankfully, there didn't appear to be anyone aboard. Following a quick conference, each man went back to his landing site, gathered his parachute, and began to hunt for the "survival pouch" said to be attached to each parachute's harness. Inside the pouch was supposed to be a jungle kit filled with tools and medicines, which would aid them in their efforts to stay alive. But in another example of the supply problems in CBI, the knives, rations, mosquito nets, and first-aid boxes that were to be inside each of these pouches were missing.

Lost in the jungle with no food or shelter, the group launched into another, deeper round of worry. Then, over the sound of their conversation, there came a noise: the familiar drone of a twin-engine Douglas transport plane—and it appeared to be coming closer. In another minute, the aircraft cleared the ridge ahead of them, dipped a wing, and began to circle the plume of smoke that rose from the crash site. As the plane kept circling, the group noticed its doorway had been opened, and a wrapped bale of some kind had been pushed into it. Those able to stand and move jumped to their feet, ran toward a grassy area nearby, and began to wave their arms. On the plane's next circuit over the grassy spot, the bale slid from the plane and—*poof*—above it an orange parachute opened against the blue sky.

As the bale slowly drifted to earth, the plane flew over one more time. On this pass, a small gray sack attached to a cloth streamer hurtled earthward from the cargo door, hitting the grassy area's ground with a *whump*. Inside the bag, the group found a typewritten note:

"Remain at wreckage until rescue party reaches you. You are safe from enemy action there. Give some sign of life to searching aircraft by building a fire or displaying unusual signs by parachute panels. Further provisions coming by air tomorrow, including a radio. Your location: 26° 25' north latitude to 95° 20' east longitude."

The bale of survival goods had now landed as well. After dragging it to the clearing, they tore into it and found an axe, some jungle knives, two blankets, canned rations, mosquito netting, cigarettes, and two Springfield rifles (one of which had a broken stock). More minutes passed. And, from over the ridge, Sevareid and his group again heard a twin-engined airplane. This time, after clearing the mountain, the cargo plane banked, and from its open door fell two more parcels, each slowed on its descent by an orange parachute. The first bale landed squarely in the grassy area, the other drifted off-course and disappeared into the jungle a few hundred yards away.

As they broke open the new bale and inventoried its contents—mostly it held a radio set—Sevareid and the group began to hear yet another noise. This one appeared to be human in origin: it was a "rhythmic singsong," and whatever words were being chanted did not appear to be in English. As the group stared in the direction of the approaching chants, they grabbed any weapon they could find and readied for what they feared might be a fight for their lives. Then, with their hearts in their throats, they watched as fifteen or twenty squat, coffee-brown native men emerged from the underbrush and onto the grassy area.

THE NATIVES WERE fantastic-looking. Each was small in stature, but had a broad chest and thick, muscular legs. They also had narrow thatches of black hair running the length of their skulls, black waistcloths around their hips, and faded blue tattoos on their arms and bared chests. Each of them was carrying a long spear in one hand, and several had long, metal *dahs* in the other. Sevareid and his group were face-to-face with the Nagas.

While the Nagas had been accommodating to Stilwell's group during their walk out of Burma in May 1942, the tribe had long been recognized by British colonists to be headhunters. Word on the CBI air bases in India was that, were you to crash land along the Burma-India border, you were to be wary of the Nagas and avoid contact at virtually any cost. Now, not knowing what to expect, the two groups stared at each other. Still more Nagas from the back of the line pushed forward to create a semicircle in the grassy area. Sevareid raised his open hand in a gesture of peace and the

Nagas—almost in unison—drove their spear points into the earth and slid their long *dahs* back into wooden sheaths on their waistcloths. Then both sides, the Americans and the Nagas, broke into smiles.

In minutes, several of the Nagas were sharing gourds of strong alcohol with Sevareid and his crew, while a second group of tribesmen streaked off into the jungle and returned with the lost bale from the most recent airplane. Almost as an afterthought, the plane's black-haired captain, Harry Neveu, reached inside his jacket, pulled out his blood chit, and found in it a cardboard sheet titled: "Useful Phrases in Kachin and Burmese." Neveu and Sevareid attempted a number of different words and phrases on the natives. None worked.

As they stood at an impasse, sipping the peace-offering drink and trying to find a common language, the Nagas—in a sudden, startled moment— lifted their spears again. Another native was running through the jungle from behind the downed party, loping toward them through thick forest. As the runner approached, the air became thick with nervous fear. Then, at a barely safe distance, the runner stopped and flashed a piece of paper. It was a handwritten note: "Those who bailed out this morning should join the rest of the party at the village. The bearer will lead you. This means you, too, Eric.—John & Duncan"

Davies, Lee, and several other passengers now appeared to be OK. Things were looking up. Finding a blank page from a booklet of correspondents' passes he had in a pocket, Sevareid borrowed a pen from another member of the crew and scrawled a message back: "Dear John. Eleven men here—two have bad legs—supplies dropped here, plane will return here—rescue party on way—please come here—we about one mile south of wreck. Eric."

Sevareid then ripped off a swatch of the orange parachute, draped it across the runner's shoulders, handed him a half-dollar (the only bright thing he had in his pocket), and handed the runner his note. The messenger turned and was gone.

FOR THE REST of the afternoon, the Nagas helped the downed crew back to their village, which sat downhill through the valley and across a wooden footbridge of felled trees. Over the next few hours, as the Nagas made their guests comfortable and Sevareid waited on Davies and Lee, other survivors of the bailout were being led into the settlement as well. This village, a cleared hillside barnicled by huts and surrounded by small plots of millet, was in constant activity, with men, women, and children—and what appeared to be an endless number of small black pigs—moving incessantly along its footpaths.

Sevareid's group was then shown to a long *atap* hut that apparently was to be their new home. As the group was cleaning their cuts and scrapes using air-dropped first-aid kits, some of them began accepting food from the Nagas, including rice and bits of roast pig. With the coming of twilight, still more survivors were led into the village. And, from overhead, three medics—led by Lt. Colonel Don Flickinger, a surgeon—parachuted in. Flickinger quickly assessed the radioman's ankle, and, as feared, pronounced it broken.

As evening arrived, Flickinger set and splinted the radioman's foot while the Nagas built fires and roasted more pig for their guests. The village began to quiet for the night and Sevareid went to sit in his hut when a cold rain began to fall. Still, he kept a wary eye on the darkness outside, fearing a sneak attack by the headhunters. After several hours, he noticed fiery torches approaching through the dripping jungle. The torches wended inside the village's rough fence of woven sticks, then paused at several houses, before resuming their way toward him. Soon, in the cool rain and darkness, the torches were coming too close for comfort, and Sevareid pulled back a bit into the darkness of his hut. Then, the torch fires were dancing just outside the doorway of his hut, and from the darkness, a voice reached inside.

"Dr. Sevareid, I presume?"

It was Davies, doing his best Stanley and Livingstone.

Davies, Duncan Lee, and three others stepped into the grimy, damp shelter. Now almost fully reunited, the group talked through the night, trading stories of the crash and their rescues. At one point, Flickinger remembered he had a passenger list that had been given to him at the last second while back at Chabua's airfield. He made a roll call, and the group learned that only two from the plane—the copilot, Charles Felix, and Corporal Basil Lemmon—were missing. More hours passed as tale after tale, parachute landing after landing, was recounted. Midnight came and went, and everyone discussed the possible whereabouts of Felix and Lemmon. Finally, a few hours before dawn and with the fire burned low, each member of the group felt relaxed enough to lie down on the hut's soggy matting and drop instantly to sleep.

OVER THE NEXT TWELVE DAYS, as Sevareid and his group awaited the rescue party rumored to be coming for them, American rescue-supply planes out of Chabua rained goods and food upon the jungle. Soon the group had blankets, rations, new clothing, guns, boots, and even reading material from the sky. Command had even air-dropped maps to the group, showing that, yes, they were in the tribal lands of the Naga, on the Burma-India border and about eighty miles from British-controlled territory. One message informed them they were about eighty-five ground miles—or about sixty air miles—from the British garrison at the town of Mokokchung, which sat to the southwest across the mountains in India. Other messages reassured the group, now being commanded by its senior officer, Flickinger, that help was on the way.

All there was to do was wait. On the third day, as the Nagas investigated the now-cold wreckage of the C-46, they found the mutilated body of flight officer Felix, which was still strapped into his copilot seat in the cockpit. After the Nagas had carried Felix's remains to the village, the group buried him in a jungle grave: a ceremony the Nagas honored by momentarily stopping their ceaseless activity in a long moment of silent respect.

Two days after the burial, a still-alive corporal Lemmon was carried into the village by two tribesmen from another village, his clothing in rags. Between sips of coffee, Lemmon informed Flickinger that, fearing enemy search parties, he had lain still in the jungle for four days, enduring the nightly freezing downpours without any cover or shelter. After four nights of this, realizing he would die if he didn't help himself, he'd crawled to a native hut at the edge of a neighboring village, made his presence known, and was carried to the rest of his group by the natives.

A week passed. Soon the Nagas and their new friends from the sky were trading: native knives and spears were exchanged for can openers and spoons, which the Nagas quickly fashioned into necklaces and earrings. Flickinger opened a clinic and began tending to the Naga sick as well as the GIs and civilians wounded in the crash. On August 13, a supply plane dropped, among other things, a three-day-old copy of the Calcutta *States-*

*man*, so the group could read about their crash on the front page. The newspaper's arrival made Davies furious, since his name stood among the list of those lost or stranded. As a high-level government official and known adviser to General Stilwell, Davies feared Japanese spies in Calcutta might now know that he was present in the Naga village—hiding in plain sight—and they would come looking for him, endangering the whole group.

Thankfully, the Japanese never searched. Instead, on the evening of August 14, a tall, slim young Englishman named Philip Adams—blond-haired and dressed in a blue polo shirt, blue shorts, and low walking shoes—emerged from the jungle trailed by two rough-looking Americans and sixty Naga porters. Adams was the sahib of Mokokchung, which meant he functioned as the main government official on the India side of the border, and—aside from his striking resemblance to the actor Leslie Howard—the group grew astonished when Adams spoke to the Nagas in *their* language. As night fell, he further flabbergasted the group with the depth of his understanding about the region, its people, and events surrounding their crash.

The C-46, Adams said, had crashed in the Patkai Range, a row of long mountainous ridges that separates India from Burma. He also told them that these ranges were controlled by neither the Allies nor Japan, but were instead the home of active headhunter villages, one of which—Ponyo, where Corporal Lemmon was rescued—had taken 106 skulls from neighboring villages in 1942. The reason Adams himself had hurried eighty-five miles overland in five days to assist the downed group, he said, was because word had leaked to him that several villages in the area, including Ponyo, were beginning to call for skull-taking raids on the foreigners and Adams hoped to slow them down or buy them off with bribes.

On August 17, following a few days' rest for Adams, the group began preparations to leave. The following morning, after an evening of fond farewells (one tribesmen, Mongsen, whose child Flickinger had saved with medicines, gave the doctor an ornate wooden crossbow with ivory inlays), the group set off on foot for India.

The trip would last nearly a week, with every day's up-and-down slogging, leech bites, and alternating sunburn and torrential drenchings bringing them closer to safety. All the while, transport planes continued to parachute food and equipment on them as they walked. Soon the group was so well supplied that they even had umbrellas to use against the sun and rains. One afternoon, August 21, when yet another twin-engine supply plane came overhead, it dropped a message that rations of fried chicken and ice cream were forthcoming.

Six days after they'd set off—and twenty-two days after the plane crash—tired and sunburned but otherwise OK, the group walked up the long path to the bungalow of Philip Adams, sahib of Mokokchung, complete with a lawn and hedgerows out of the English countryside. Over a huge dinner of all the curry and meat Mokokchung had to offer, the group drank wine and brandy and listened to Frank Sinatra records, reveling in the civility as if this were their graduation from some jungle-survival course. Then, after a few days' rest, Adams led the crash survivors to Mokokchung's airstrip, where they were picked up and returned by transport plane to Chabua.

A week after that, having gathered up new clothes and equipment—and having filed the story of his ordeal with CBS radio—Sevareid again climbed aboard a transport plane in Chabua, this time for an uneventful flight to Kunming.

By now Sevareid's fellow correspondents were ribbing him about his newfound international fame, since stories of his "bailout group" and their ordeal filled the airwaves and newspapers. Still, as he left India and flew above the cool green folds of the Naga Hills toward China, he couldn't help but wonder what events were taking place in the string of native villages that he could see beneath the aircraft. And, like everyone in India, Burma, and China in the early autumn of 1943, he had no idea of the blood that was soon to be shed on the slopes of that same jungled terrain.

# Chapter 9

AS THE SUMMER OF 1943 turned to autumn, it began to appear—for the first time since World War II's beginnings—that Allied armies in some corners of the earth were gaining traction.

In Europe, though a cross-channel invasion of occupied France was still ten months off, the Allies came ashore on the Italian mainland on September 3, forcing the Germans and the Italians into a defensive posture on their own turf for the first time. In Russia, the Red Army, after repelling Hitler's Wehrmacht forces from outside Moscow and Stalingrad, had gone on the offensive and engaged for a long fight in the German-occupied Russian city of Smolensk.

In the Pacific war, American warplanes—assisted by American and New Zealand warships—sank the Japanese submarines I-25 and I-182 off the island of Espiritu Santo in the island nation of New Hebrides (today called Vanuatu). But beyond that, the war against Japan remained bloody and undecided. In New Guinea and the Solomon Islands, Allied and Japanese ground troops were still engaged in fierce fighting for control of both islands. Farther north on the strategically critical island of Tarawa, an Allied firebombing campaign was being undertaken to deprive the Japanese of any land structures in advance of the Allied invasion there.

In the China-Burma-India theater (CBI) and the Southeast Asia Command (SEAC), however, the situation remained confused and stalled. With the Quadrant planning conference in Quebec now in the past, and the "go-ahead" orders for the North Burma Campaign awaiting approval at the next inter-Allied meetings—code named Sextant—in Cairo and Tehran in November, Vinegar Joe Stilwell remained engrossed in Chinese Army training. And as he looked around the Allied Command "in this mess of a war," he began the long process of trying to identify whom he could rely on.

As Stilwell surveyed the landscape, he understood that Chiang Kai-shek was clearly off his "trusted friend" list. Chiang was now siding openly with Chennault, another commander Stilwell was leery of, and the generalissimo was now sending an almost constant stream of requests to President Roosevelt for Stilwell's recall. Whether Chennault admitted it or not, he wanted Stilwell's job, and he'd found a sponsor he felt could help him get it. Escalating matters, Stilwell had taken to continually pestering Chiang for a solid timetable regarding the North Burma Campaign, especially for a start date for his China-based Y Force.

On the British side of CBI, in September 1943, changes in command were continuous. Stilwell's British counterpart, General Wavell—with whom Stilwell had finally forged a trustful bond—was suddenly gone, having earned the dubious honor of being promoted to viceroy of India. And stranded in Delhi with all of India to govern, Wavell now had a bigger job. He was charged with placating a nation increasingly following the anti-colonial beliefs of Mohandas Gandhi, who—despite remaining in prison—was continuing to incite revolt against the British.

In Wavell's place came General Sir Claude Auchinleck, former British commander of the Middle East. "The Auk," as he was called, was both charming and steel-willed. And though Stilwell's British confidante and co–field commander, General Slim, said the Auk could be relied upon, Stilwell's distrust of the British meant Auchinleck's words and actions were to be constantly watched and weighed by Vinegar Joe. Regarding Lord Louis Mountbatten, Stilwell hoped to trust him, too. Labeling Mountbatten "a good egg" in his diary, Stilwell had another reason to find relief in the arrival of the new SEAC commander: Mountbatten had already started deflecting bits of Chiang's animosity toward the American.

Back in Washington, George Marshall and President Roosevelt remained supportive, but Chiang's constant calls about Stilwell's "unacceptability" were growing louder and more regular, prompting Marshall to order Stilwell to "Stop the wisecracks" toward Peanut. By the end of September, Chiang's foreign minister (and brother-in-law), T. V. Soong—a man always resplendent in black circular eyeglasses, a black suit, a black bowler hat, and walking cane—would once again arrive in Washington to present Roosevelt with China's request for the recall of Joseph W. Stilwell.

Worn down with Chiang's steady torrent of demands, Roosevelt distanced himself from the situation and turned the matter over entirely to General Marshall, adding only this cover note to this most recent of China's ouster requests: "Dear George, will you talk to Dr. Soong about this? FDR."

In Washington, Marshall and Secretary of War Henry Stimson—the men who'd decided Stilwell was "it" for American command in China back in January 1942—now wondered if it wasn't time to withdraw Vinegar Joe from his post and, as Stimson would later write, find him "some less impossible task." But throughout September, despite the call for Stilwell to step down, Marshall kept his old friend in place.

Without Stilwell as CBI's institutional memory and whip, Marshall believed that the problems of the Hump, the training of the Chinese troops, the dribbling Ledo supply lines, and the national leadership problems presented in both China and India were intractable. He felt that only Stilwell's intelligence and no-nonsense drive had any chance of keeping the theater in shape.

ON OCTOBER 15, and with the sole mission of introducing Mountbatten to Chiang Kai-shek, Stilwell traveled to Chungking from India. When he arrived at his headquarters, he was shocked to learn that, once again, the generalissimo had that very day made yet another explicit demand for his recall, claiming that Stilwell had now "lost the confidence of the troops." At the generalissimo's residence in Chungking, Chiang and T. V. Soong had reported to General James Somerville, commander of the British Far Eastern Fleet, that President Roosevelt had finally assented and that Stilwell would soon be going home.

Stilwell knew the real reason for Chiang's recall order: frustration with the Americans' controlling use of lend-lease goods to goad Chiang into action, coupled with his unrelentingly hard-eyed view of China's military situation. "I have told him the truth," Stilwell wrote in his diary. "I have brought all deficiencies to his notice. I have warned him about the condition of his army. I have demonstrated to him how these things can be corrected. All of this he ignores and shuts his eyes to the deplorable condition of his army, which is a terrible indictment of him, his War Ministry and his General Staff."

Later that day, on the afternoon of October 15, 1943—and having arrived in Chungking to present his credentials to Chiang—Mountbatten also heard of Stilwell's recall and he was determined to fix the problem. So before visiting Chiang's residence, Mountbatten decided to first stop by and see Stilwell. As he walked into the general's headquarters, Stilwell warned Mountbatten: "You should not be seen shaking hands with me. It will be bad for you."

Yet fearing the removal of the theater's primary architect and second-in-command on the new leader's first day in SEAC, Mountbatten told Stilwell he had other ideas. "If you want your job back," he told the general, "I'll get it for you."

Stilwell responded that, in fact, he did want the job. And—charmingly and surefootedly as ever—Mountbatten sent advance word to the residence before making his appearance there. The message, which was sent directly to Chiang, stated that Mountbatten could not proceed with plans to use Chinese forces if their American commander of the past two years was withdrawn. With the diplomatic skill of a master, Mountbatten had found and taken control of Chiang's greatest weakness.

The subtext of Mountbatten's message was simple: to have Chiang's Nationalist Chinese forces go unused would imperil all flow of lend-lease goods. And that, to the generalissimo, would prove unacceptable.

To lay an extra push on Chiang and his advisers, when Mountbatten arrived at the residence he was carrying a makeup compact for Madame Chiang, the one person, Stilwell had suggested, who could always sway the Gi-mo. The compact had been made specially as a diplomatic gift by the French jeweler Cartier. On the case's cover, set in diamonds, were Madame Chiang's initials. And after the introductions, gift-giving, and some friendly conversation, Mountbatten moved directly to his objective. He remarked to Chiang that he was inexperienced at such a high position of command and that he needed to "lean on [Stilwell's] vast experience for help and advice."

As always, the Chinese generalissimo smiled and nodded, saying nothing. In another part of the residence, however, Madame Chiang was admiring her new Cartier case, and together Mountbatten's veiled lend-lease threat and the generous gift turned the trick. Two days later official word was issued from Chiang: General Joseph W. Stilwell was to retain his positions inside CBI and SEAC.

BUT THOUGH SUPPORT of the U.S. War Department remained flimsily affixed to Stilwell, the Allies were also beginning to lose faith in the larger mission of CBI and SEAC: meaning the destruction of Japan from the Chinese mainland. The British, busy with the defense of England against the Germans—and with Gandhi's disruptions in India—weren't fully engaged in the offensives for Burma and occupied China. And while Stilwell and his able Chinese commanders—the Virginia Military Institute–educated General Sun Li-jen, and General Liao Yao-shiang—had succeeded in upgrading the Chinese X Force in India, the Y Force in Kunming was still horribly inadequate: they had outmoded weapons, tattered uniforms, and were underfed, sick, and arrayed in such a broad sweep of southwest China that they couldn't be mobilized. As it had been since the 1930s, Chiang wouldn't move them, wouldn't train them, and wouldn't arm them out of fear of strengthening Chinese commanders beneath him.

Compounding the problems inside China, the Japanese had revived their overland assaults. After a year of spectacularly daring air raids on Japanese ships and on railroads, Chennault's Fourteenth Air Force had started coming under increasing Japanese air pressure in July of 1943. By October, Japanese troops were driving south by west, deeper inside the middle third of China and toward the city of Changteh, with smaller units now nearing Chennault's undefended forward bases in China. The Japanese intention was obvious: they were going to shut down the Fourteenth Air Force.

Chennault, remembering his promise to President Roosevelt to defeat Japan in China, began sending pleas to Roosevelt and his emissary Harry Hopkins for more aircraft. But since these requests had to be approved by Stilwell before being sent to Washington, and Stilwell felt the resources were better employed elsewhere, they were being "pocketed" and permanently halted somewhere inside China or India by Vinegar Joe.

Stilwell, snared in the dark and vituperative side of his personality—especially when it came to Chennault—further let it be known to the War Department and the Fourteenth Air Force that he was disinclined to divert any extra fighter or pursuit aircraft to Chennault, since Stilwell's Tenth Air Force out of India were busy protecting the equally important Hump airlift route. Chennault, an opportunist who Stilwell recognized was after his job, would get no sympathy from Vinegar Joe. "He has been screaming for help. 'The Japs are going to run us out of China!' " Stilwell wrote in his diary. "It is to laugh. Six months ago he was going to run *them* out."

In Washington, however, talk of the Pacific War had grown far larger than the petty allocations of aircraft. Around the Capital Mall, military and political leaders were starting to favor a completely new approach to the war against Japan. The China-Burma-India theater—and the land route to Japan—was proving far too slow in coalescing, while the island-hopping approach across the Pacific was proceeding quickly—if at great human cost to the Americans. To government and military analysts above the fray, the expense of keeping China in the war was too extravagant for the potential it—and CBI—had shown so far. By the end of October 1943, a position paper entitled "Re-Analysis of Our Strategic Policy in Asia" was making its way through the War Department and the Executive Branch. The paper's thesis was concrete: expend as little money (and goods) as possible to keep China in the war, abandon the reconquest of Burma, and remove all excess troops from CBI for use in other theaters, particularly the more successful Pacific Island one.

Stilwell remained undaunted by dark messages from Washington. Instead, he kept attacking the situation inside CBI and SEAC with characteristic and energetic crustiness: driving the Hump airlift harder and planning for a new—and soon-to-be stillborn—campaign on north Burma, called *Saucy*. As acting deputy commander for SEAC, he was now answerable to both Mountbatten and Chiang, and he fully understood he occupied the secondary role. Frustrated by having to answer to another new superior in the theater, he'd started referring to himself as "The Deckhand."

Then there was Stilwell's other job: field general for China's thirty-three thousand-man X Force in India, a rank that also placed him even farther down the CBI command chain, under General George Giffard, commander in chief of all British and Indian forces in India. Stilwell, however, didn't respect Giffard and refused to serve under him. As a compromise, Stilwell asked that, as lowly X Force chief, he be allowed to serve under William Slim, who had recently been given command of the entire British Fourteenth Army in east India. When Joe Stilwell the lowly Chinese troop commander's request was granted by Mountbatten and, laughably, by General Stilwell of SEAC, Vinegar Joe took the opportunity to turn SEAC command meetings into comic opera, a farce that Slim, more than most, appreciated. As one meeting came to a close, Stilwell is said to have saluted Slim asking: "Sir, as Fourteenth Army commander, do you have any orders for me?"

"No sir," Slim said. "And as deputy supreme commander, do you have any orders for me?"

Stilwell was now grinning from ear to ear. "Not on your life," he said.

THEN, SOMEHOW, the remarkable began to happen inside CBI and SEAC. Despite the theater's thicket of rumor and mistrust, the operational snarls and obstacles in India and China were being combed out. After a year of sputtering airborne deliveries across the Hump, more than the promised five thousand tons of lend-lease equipment a month were now streaming into China from India; in December of 1943, 13,450 tons arrived in China from India, up more than nine thousand tons since July. Using the new supplies, Stilwell's China-based Y Force was starting to catch up in skills and training with his X Force at Ramgarh, as well as with General Slim's Fourteenth Army billeted in and around the Indian city of Imphal, fifty miles west of the Burmese border.

At Ledo, the road and the fuel pipelines alongside it inched out of town in November and crossed into North Burma at Pangsau Pass, where forward units erected a large plywood sign reading: WELCOME TO BURMA! THIS WAY TO TOKYO! Then in six more weeks, with laborers felling timber like a giant and cutting through muddy hillsides and over mountains, the road suddenly had been extended seventy miles southeast into Burma, to the village of Shingbwiyang ("the place of the bamboo shoots"), 109 miles from Ledo.

Directed by American General Lewis Pick, designer of the Missouri River Dam System, the road's Engineer Battalions (including the soon-to-arrive 858th Aviation Engineers, the only African-American unit in the Pacific War) and fifty thousand Indian and tribal laborers were laying new roadbed—complete with as many as thirteen rain culverts per mile—at a rate of three-quarters of a mile per day. Spirits on the construction crew were high. Pick's engineers had taken to calling the road "Pick's Pike," and by March of 1944, the roadbed was staged to plumb the length of Burma's wide, flat Hukawng River valley. Once there, the construction pace would increase even more, thanks to an existing oxen trail of mud, which crossed the valley to the south as straight as a taut string headed for Myitkyina, and, two hundred miles beyond that, its meeting with the Burma Road out of China.

A second, British-built road—leading from Imphal to the Indian city of Kohima and toward the India-Burma border at Tiddum—was also in construction under Auchenlick and Slim. Their road, called the Tiddum Road, had encountered its own set of logistical problems: any way a roadbed was laid through the steep valley of India's Manipur River, the track degenerated into a slippery mire with the slightest rain. For one seven-mile stretch of road, in fact, where forty hairpin curves changed elevation four thousand feet, the British took to calling the switchbacks "the Chocolate Staircase" for the color and consistency of the impassible thoroughfare anytime the landscape was less than bone dry. To fix the problem, Auchenlick and Slim requisitioned hundreds of Indian brick artisans, who quickly built mud—and, later, brick—kilns along the road every few miles, paving the most problematic sections with millions of new bricks.

All that remained was for the wet season's rivers to drop so the Allied invasion of Burma—the first step in an overland march toward Japan—could begin. Stilwell's invasion program for the winter of 1943–44, code named Capital, had been modified since Arakan the year before. Now he was placing far more emphasis on his competent and battle-ready X Force in India and leaving the British to worry about their drive on Rangoon to the south. All Stilwell's energies would be concentrated on his North Burma Campaign. His X Force would advance along the Ledo Road to its current end just beyond Shingbwiyang, then it would begin driving the Japanese south down the wide Hukawng River Valley.

When the Hukawng Valley was cleared, with forward airstrips cut into soil along the advancing Ledo Road, Stilwell's and General Sun Li-jen's Chinese army would slip through a low pass that connected the Hukawng Valley with the valley of the Mogaung River, about sixty miles inside

Japanese territory. Once the X Force moved though the Mogaung opening, Stilwell would have Wingate's Chindits air-dropped in to the south—behind any Japanese opposition the X Force might encounter—to support the larger army with their trademark guerrilla attacks on Japanese communications and supply. By hook and crook (and strategic hold-backs of lend-lease equipment), Stilwell had also finally gotten Chiang to commit one-third of his Y Force to invade northern Burma from China beginning on January 1, 1944.

With the X and Y Forces pushing south into Burma, Stilwell now believed they could capture the critical northern Burmese cities of Mogaung and, ultimately, Myitkyina before the monsoons of mid-1944 began. By sticking with these supported stages of invasion into Burma, Stilwell was convinced the Japanese would be forced into full evacuation of Burma's north, allowing the Ledo Road to be quickly laid down and the Burma Road to China reopened, which would allow the infusion of still more X and Y Forces into northern Burma, ultimately securing the region.

When northern Burma was reopened to the Allies, Stilwell also felt that General Slim's Fourteenth Army could invade Burma out of India, slamming into the occupying imperial armies via the Tiddum Road, providing the roundhouse punch that would ultimately drive the Japanese back toward Thailand.

STILWELL COULDN'T WAIT. Secretly, as October 1943 came to its end—and six weeks before Capital had been finally approved by the Allied Chiefs at the Cairo Conference—the Chinese Thirty-eighth Division, commanded by General Sun Li-jen, began marching up the Ledo Road, crossing into Burma from India under orders from Stilwell. Vinegar Joe's battle plan for the recapture of northern Burma was succinct: "We have to go in through a rat hole and dig the hole as we go." He was not thrilled with the prospects for what they might have to do along the way, but Stilwell remained overjoyed to be on the move. After a year and a half of waiting, his Chinese X Force was under way.

Moving south along the same trails they'd followed north during the retreat from Burma in 1942, the Chinese began encountering reminders of the withdrawal: around water holes and in now-deserted encampments, the bones and skulls of thousands of refugees who'd become too weak or sick to complete their trips moldered on the leafy ground. Along the road-sides, abandoned cars and trucks sat, rusting.

As recalled by Colonel Nevin Wetzel—an American engineer accompa-nying the initial X Force from Ledo—the remains were both shocking and macabre. At one point along the road in Burma, he saw:

> Jeep YBR 102, resting off to one side of the road, apparently in good shape, except for the tires, and with a skeleton sitting behind the steering wheel. . . . The skeletons were everywhere. . . . But the worst part of the walk to our destination five days up the road were the leeches. Now, because of all the dead, the leeches were thick along the trail and on the leaves of bushes lining the trail, it appeared the bushes were being touched by a slight breeze, until you noticed that the leaves did not move—only the leeches.

Yet it wasn't just the dead or the leeches that made the Allied soldiers entering Burma jumpy. It was the jungle's other wildlife, too. One day, early in the advance, Wetzel was to meet with an assistant, Lieutenant John Jouett, at a rendezvous point along the road—"which at that time was barely a jeep trail"—halfway between two Chinese bivouac camps. "He had been about two hours late, and when he did arrive, he looked lost and shaken. He said he had become surrounded by some big male monkeys on his way to our meeting, and had had to shoot to frighten them off."

Another time, as Wetzel himself walked a jungle trail, he was confronted by an aggressive elephant, which had probably been abandoned during the withdrawal in April 1942:

> I came around a turn in the narrow trail, striding along without a care in the world, and found an elephant looking right at me with his little beady eyes. A broken hobble was on his ankle, which convinced me he was tame—but had he just come unfastened or was he a rogue? He completely filled the trail—jungle on either side. We stood looking at each other for about a minute. Should I try to slide past him? I took a step forward. He raised his trunk and snorted. I moved into that jungle as if it were a wheat field, being cautious to find the contour of a hill. An elephant can move up a hill or down a hill, but due to its weight, it cannot move level across a hill. Finally, a wide circle through the jungle brought me back on the trail—with no fur-ther encounters with the elephant.

Every day, the Chinese divisions pushed deeper into northern Burma. Then, just a few miles north of their goal at Shingbwiyang, five days along the road, they began encountering enemy troops and fire. Though intelligence reports had indicated the Japanese were not occupying northern Burma, shortly before the Allies had started their invasion, imperial army forces had started moving up the Hukawng Valley in advance of *their* planned winter invasion of eastern India. Confronted by machine-gun and mortar fire, and directed in battle by Stilwell's deputy, Brigadier General Hayden L. Boatner (Stilwell was still in Cairo with the Allied Chiefs) and General Sun, the Chinese slowly beat back the Japanese defenders at the village of Sharaw Ga.

Allied progress remained slow. Despite overwhelming Chinese forces, Sharaw Ga fell in three long, blood-soaked days, with one Chinese unit taking a week in "preparation" before a supposedly simple flanking maneuver. Still, in their first test of battlefield will, the Chinese had defeated Japanese jungle fighters from the Imperial Army's heretofore invincible Eighteenth Division, which had been pushing north across Malaya and Burma since taking Singapore almost two years earlier.

Yet by late December, as Stilwell caught up with the X Force from Cairo, Allied progress down in the Hukawng Valley had degenerated into a standoff. At the town of Yupbang Ga, the next village to the south of Sharaw Ga, the Chinese were now pressing against at least one full battalion from the battle-tested Japanese Eighteenth. Though frustrated by the X Force's slow progress, Stilwell was returning to Burma ecstatic about a change in his fortunes with Chiang. Miraculously—and having been cajoled into the decision by Mountbatten—Chiang had given Stilwell complete command and control of the X Force ("without strings" Stilwell noted in his diary on December 19). Now, with the X Force under his full control, Stilwell believed that if the Chinese could just win a few decisive battles, the tide of the invasion would turn. He quickly installed himself at the front, establishing a field headquarters in Shingbwiyang, then he set about to take Yupbang Ga from the enemy.

On December 23, two days after his arrival in India—and having spent the dawn hour watching live pigs being air-dropped for a Christmas feast—Stilwell made a speech in fluent Chinese to his troops a few miles outside the grid of dirt streets and *atap* huts that made up Yupbang Ga. He told his men that the following morning's attack was "important and must go." And at 6 a.m. the next morning—December 24, 1943—after a spectacularly accurate artillery barrage on the Japanese lines, the Chinese attacked with Stilwell standing beside them, shoulder to shoulder. He had exchanged his flat-brimmed World War I hat for a steel infantry helmet, but after all the time spent waiting, Stilwell wasn't going to be some shrinking, rearguard commander. (His insistence on being at the battle line terrified the Thirty-eighth Division's Chinese commander, General Sun Li-jen, who feared the general would be killed or wounded and that Sun himself would be held responsible.)

Within hours, the majority of the Japanese had been driven out of Yupbang Ga, with isolated units, snipers, and machine-gun dugouts holding tight. For the X Force and their American advisers, it was their first taste of just how tenacious the Japanese could be, and clearing and securing the village would require almost a week—with the trapped and entrenched Japanese often killing themselves with their own rifles and grenades rather than become prisoners. In the fight for Yupbang Ga, the Chinese suffered as well, sustaining 315 casualties. Still, in the end, the victory went to Stilwell, General Sun Li-jen, and the Chinese Thirty-eighth Division.

After twenty months of planning and training, the Chinese had gone into battle against the forward forces of a supposedly invincible opponent and had bashed them to destruction. The X Force's confidence was soaring. Over the coming days, as they worked south into the Hukawng Valley, the Chinese Thirty-eighth Division—buttressed by fresh X Force troops from elements of the Chinese Twenty-second Division—pushed the Japanese farther south through the hilly jungle, driving the enemy back any time they encountered resistance.

Supplied from behind by the Ledo Road, and disregarding radioed demands for his presence in Chungking and Delhi, Stilwell stayed near the front, sleeping on a cot, bathing out of his helmet, cleaning his own weapon, and hiking miles a day through the jungle to check on his forward troops as they fought for, and took, the next village south: Ngajatzup. Stilwell was finally soldiering again, and Vinegar Joe was in heaven, lavishing parsimonious yet Stilwell-style compliments on the X Force in his diary for December 29: "Good work by the Chinese: aggressive attack, good fire control, quick action."

———

YET FOR ALL the X Force success, the Hukawng Valley invasion was taking a visible toll on Stilwell. Already gaunt from his bout with jaundice the year before, he looked terrible. He was drawn and ashen, his face was deeply lined; his clothes hung on him, and he was taking very little food. At base camp in Shingbwiyang, his personal cook, Sergeant Jules Raynaud—better known as "Gus" and a chef at the venerable Stork Club in New York City before the war—complained that Stilwell was eating "like the birds." For dinners, Stilwell often ate only a few buttered slices of the raisin bread that Gus baked every day.

Despite his body wasting away, Stilwell's spirit, like that of his Chinese troops, was stratospheric. His son, Joe Jr., was now at his side as a G-2 adviser, and his two sons-in-law, Colonel Ernest Easterbook and Major Ellis Cox, were also on board as his military executive and deputy G-2 officer. As the urgent "Z-Z-Z-Z" messages from headquarters in India and China piled up at Shingbwiyang, Stilwell referred each to his second-in-command in Delhi, Major General Dan Sultan.

As the X Force drove into north Burma, set to retake a string of towns and villages with unpronounceable names, Stilwell had made his choice. With the exception of one day, December 31 (when he flew to Delhi for meetings), Stilwell would stay at the front with the soldiers he'd trained. In his diary, he noted that the Chinese were "full of beans and tickled to death at beating the Japs." And in a high-spirited letter to Winifred from Shingbwiyang, he recounted: "Progress is slow; the jungle is everywhere and very nearly impenetrable. Yesterday, on a cut trail I took 3 ½ hours to do three miles, tripping and cursing at every step. I expect to see Tarzan any day now."

By January 1944, Joe Stilwell was personally leading the push deeper into Burma, with the weight and breadth of his invasion forces now driving the Japanese farther south—sometimes without shots even being fired. As would happen for all the North Burma Campaign, provisions were dropped from cargo planes, with the rice hurtling to earth in double burlap sacks and all other food—canned meat and vegetables, coffee and tea, and dried beef—drifting through the air on parachutes. Ammunition, explosives, and detonators were also parachute-dropped, always by cargo planes bearing flashing red lights, which warned of the nature of the items floating to earth and allowing those in the area to take cover in case an explosion occurred on impact with the ground.

With success piled on success, the X Force kept pushing south. Though British command had taken to sniping that Stilwell had become "the best three-star company commander in the U.S. Army," and members of Chennault's Fourteenth Air Force were openly belittling "Walking Joe" to any and all members of the press, Stilwell, Sun Li-jen, and the Chinese troops were making astounding progress.

By early February, the X Force—with the Ledo Road tagging closely behind—had shoved the bulk of the Imperial Japanese Army nearly seventy-five miles to the south. The Chinese and their cantankerous American commander had cleared out the northern half of the Hukawng Valley, though Stilwell knew that his biggest challenge still lay ahead. Another sixty miles to the south, and spread across the broad Taro Plain, the rear headquarters of the Japanese Eighteenth Division was waiting—dug in and ready—at the occupied town of Maingkwan. Still, he remained ebullient. "We are chewing them up in bunches," he wrote home to Win on February 8. "And the boys opposite are tough eggs."

Stilwell understood that February and March 1944 would be the North Burma Campaign's defining months. And having already used up much of February pushing the X Force down the upper Hukawng Valley, Stilwell and his army were now approaching Maingkwan—hemmed in by the six-thousand-foot ridgeline of Jambu Bum to its west and the Kumon Range to the east, the mountains that separated the Hukawng and Mogaung Valleys.

Beginning the second week of February, Stilwell and the Chinese tried to encircle the Maingkwan at a distance, pounding on the Japanese Eighteenth Division with light artillery fire and attempting flanking maneuvers across both the Taro Plain and the mountainsides of Jambu Bum. But led by the equally wily and seasoned Lieutenant General Shinichi Tanaka, the Japanese kept staving off their encirclement. Frustrated by the slowness of his troops' movements, on February 17, Stilwell set off on foot into the jungle to the southeast, working his way up Jambu Bum in search of the Chinese Sixty-sixth Regiment, a unit charged with plugging the final hole in his envelopment of the Japanese—and which hadn't been heard from for a week. When he found the Chinese Sixty-sixth, camped in the jungle and "way off course," Stilwell listened to its commander's explanation and decided the excuse was unacceptable.

Whether it was incompetence or a back-channel set of orders from

General Sun (who himself might have been getting secret orders from Chiang), the Chinese Sixty-sixth Regiment had let down the effort, and Stilwell believed that most of Tanaka's forces had already slipped away. Furious, he relieved the Sixty-sixth's commanding officer, gave new orders to his successor, then dragged his scrawny, almost used-up body off to sleep in a dirt dugout.

Stilwell was tired and discouraged. He had hoped to crush the Japanese Eighteenth Division completely at Maingkwan, and now that victory would have to be put on ice. But he also understood he had an advantage. As he contemplated how to overrun Maingkwan, he knew the Japanese were off-balance and in a full defensive posture, expecting the full brunt of his X Force to lay its weight upon them across a wide front. Because this was such an expected attack, Stilwell began to contemplate keeping the brute strength of his Chinese forces in reserve and unseating the Japanese another way.

It was time to deploy a few of the "screwball ideas" that had made Joe Stilwell America's most successful war-game commander in the years before World War II. The time for unconventional American warfare had arrived.

# Chapter 10

SEVENTEEN MONTHS BEFORE Stilwell began his battle for Maingkwan—back on a mid-August afternoon in 1942—a U.S. Army major named Carl Eifler had barged unannounced into Stilwell's headquarters in Chungking. The major informed Stilwell's staff that he'd just flown in from India, and though Eifler believed he'd been scheduled for a meeting with the general, Stilwell knew nothing of it. Eifler had been in CBI since mid-July, and despite several formal requests, he still hadn't received the promised support from Stilwell he needed to begin his mission.

Stilwell had known Eifler since before the war. A smart, ferocious, and physically imposing man of about forty—schooled in judo and boxing, riflery and piloting aircraft—Eifler had, before the war, been a U.S. customs agent along the Mexican border and an army reservist under Stilwell in the 1930s, and Eifler's competence in any matter had impressed Stilwell greatly. But Eifler was on a different mission now, one that Stilwell wanted to avoid but that he'd set into motion himself. Major Eifler directed Detachment 101.

Invented by a Brooklyn newspaperman turned government adviser named Millard P. Goodfellow—and called Detachment 101 because it implied an organization larger than did Detachment 1—the unit was overseen by the Office of Special Services, or OSS. Shortly after Stilwell's walkout from Burma in 1942—long before the arrival of Wingate's Chindits—a still-angry Vinegar Joe had gone to Washington and convened with General William "Wild Bill" Donovan, director of the OSS, to discuss ways of reinfiltrating Burma to fight a guerrilla war there. Donovan had encouraged Goodfellow to share his Detachment 101 plan with Stilwell. In it, guerrilla cells would be air-dropped behind enemy lines, then would set up small base camps, rescue downed pilots and passengers (such as Sevareid and his group), and conscript natives to the Allied cause while disrupting the enemy's communications and supply. Because of their proximity to the Japanese, Detachment 101 would also be charged with gathering and radioing out intelligence reports. Stilwell, having listened to the proposal—and understanding the job would require a leader of independence, across-the-board skills, and a fluency in the ways of stalking and smuggling—signed on for Goodfellow's idea, provided Eifler could run it.

Now, just two months after Stilwell's initial approval, Eifler was standing in Stilwell's office in China. He had trained twenty-one American and Anglo-Burmese operatives (men picked so they wouldn't arouse suspicion in Burma) plus a few Kachin and Naga tribesmen to function as guides, and Detachment 101's troops were now fit and ready. They had even spent some weeks training with the formidable Northern Kachin Levies in northern Burma.

What Eifler needed now, he said, was Stilwell's go-ahead.

After a typically prickly Stilwell greeting—"I didn't send for you and I don't want you"—Eifler began briefing the general on his status and his plans. Eifler and his unit had made their headquarters at an Indian tea plantation in Nazira, just south of Ledo on the Burma border, and they had spent the past month refining their skills on extended training trips through the jungles, where they masqueraded as malaria researchers.

Eifler was excited with the prospects for covert operations against the Japanese. His Kachin instructors had already shared several techniques for assassinating the enemy. They had shown Eifler's men, for instance, how to booby-trap trails with trip wires and crossbows, passively hunting both backcountry game and hapless enemies. They had shown the Americans how to make *panjis* and deploy them to impale the Japanese, and together the Kachins and the Americans had invented another type of small spike, which was inserted deep into the soil and was topped with a .30-caliber ri-

fle cartridge on a pressure detonator. When stepped on, the bullet fired
straight up through a soldier's foot and body.

Stilwell listened politely. He was a busy man, not to mention a soldier
more interested in conventional war than the "games" of espionage, but he
let Eifler finish. Then, wanting to get back to his plans for CBI and the retaking of Burma by regular forces, he sent Eifler away with a single directive: "I don't want to see you again until I hear a boom from Burma."


THE BOOMS BEGAN four months later, when, on January 27, 1943—a
month ahead of Wingate's first Chindit invasion—twelve men from Detachment 101 parachuted into Burma about one hundred miles south of
Myitkyina, roughly two-thirds up the country's north-south length. The
unit, called "A Group," was led by an Anglo-Burmese captain named Jack
Barnard. Each man in the unit carried his own food, several weapons (a
carbine rifle, a pistol, hand grenades, and whatever personal devices he
favored), a potassium cyanide capsule (called an "L-pill") to be eaten if
they were captured, supplies of blasting caps and waterproof fuses, and
a forty-pound block of Composition C, a light and malleable plastic
explosive.

Moving relentlessly for two days and nights, A Group hiked fifty miles
to the northwest along the Kaukkwe River, then broke into working pairs
and spread out along the Mandalay-Myitkyna rail line and a spur off of
it to the town of Katha. Every few miles along the track, the teams set
delayed-explosive charges of Composition C, then slipped away. Before the
night of January 29 was finished, five miles of track were destroyed. A few
days later, A Group used more Composition C to blow one large railroad
bridge—dropping it into a river below—and two smaller ones. Then they
began attracting and organizing Kachin guerrilla forces south of Myitkyina.

Using word of mouth they called the "jungle grapevine," A Group sent
word from village to village that the Americans would pay silver rupees for
all returned American pilots and air crews—probably the reason Sevareid's
bailout crew received such a warm welcome by the Nagas—and that they
would also pay for useful information about the Japanese. Then they began radioing intelligence back to Nazira.

Before long, Stilwell's ground troops and the Tenth Air Force out of India were relying heavily on Detachment 101's reports, with the air force making bombing runs on hidden targets like underground aircraft hangars and weapons magazines. Owing to one report alone, the air force bombed the Burmese town of Moda, which had never been visibly reconnoitered by the Allies, destroying both a fuel dump and an ammunition depot and causing more than two hundred Japanese casualties.

NOT EVERY DETACHMENT 101 MISSION was a success, however. In early March 1943, a Detachment 101 team—a six-man unit called "O Group"—was flown out of Kunming and parachuted into the Lawksawk Valley, about seventy-five miles southeast of Mandalay, to rescue a downed Hump pilot and his crew.

The drop area was two miles from the nearest village—a group of huts outlying the larger city of Lawksawk—and even as O Group men began their mission by leaping from the C-87 transport to began drifting to the ground, disaster was already crowding them. Their mission commander, the American Captain Ray Peers, who remained in the C-87 as an observer, noted that, as the 101 operatives drifted to earth, "we could see a discomforting sight: villagers streaming out from every direction, heading toward the drop zone. I had an aching feeling that their lines looked hostile. I couldn't get it out of my head that they were out to kill . . ."

The men of O Group were never heard from again, though several days later Radio Tokyo reported to the Americans that, "We got your men." The radio announcer was happy to inform the Americans that the infiltrators were dead.

But soon, despite the setbacks, American operatives all across Burma were being escorted by Kachins and Nagas to a network of twenty-nine different Detachment 101 field stations behind enemy lines. In one story, 101's Kachin members even saved the life of an airman about to be executed by his own crew. After parachuting from their burning C-87, one of the crew, a sergeant, had been perilously entangled in the spreading upper limbs of a mahogany tree, breaking both his arms and opening a deep gash on his forehead. Because there was no way to get the sergeant down, his fellow crewmen had decided to shoot him and end his suffering. As the Americans drew straws to see who would provide the unpleasant mercy, a team of OSS Kachins stepped from the jungle, assessed the situation, felled a smaller tree against the larger one, and climbed one hundred feet up the "ladder tree" to rescue the injured sergeant.

By late December 1943—as Stilwell's X Force began invading down the Hukawng Valley—Eifler had ramped up his program. His Detachment 101ers conscripted hundreds of Kachins who hadn't joined the British Northern Kachin Levies, and a handful of units from Detachment 101 joined in the push into northern Burma from several angles. Working with village leaders north of Myitkyina, a mostly Kachin unit of the 101—led by Captain William C. Wilkinson—had even turned garrisons of General Aung San's Burma Independence Army away from Japanese control, holding them steady around the town of Sumprabum (the famed "Grassy Hill") until the time for a full-on revolt was at hand. Other units made intelligence-gathering missions down the Hukawng Valley ahead of Stilwell's X Force and construction of the Ledo Road. Still others had been delivered to the airstrip and radio beacon at Fort Hertz in northern Burma, where they began edging south toward Myitkyina alongside the Northern Kachin Levies, who continued fighting and taking Japanese casualties with ear-lopping ferocity. Still more Detachment 101ers were parachuted into the valleys of central and eastern Burma between Mandalay and Myitkyina, where they spread across the landscape and set up indigenous training sites.

As the ranks of the Detachment 101's Kachin Rangers continued to grow, the most promising of them were sent to Nazira for training, where their fearlessness, far-ranging surveillance skills, and fluency in the jungle impressed CBI command. Soon, as much as 85 percent of the intelligence going to Stilwell for his X Force was coming from Detachment 101. At each jump south in the X Force invasion, Stilwell instructed Eifler to increase the 101's activities. Soon they were blowing bridges at an increasing clip (ultimately fifty-seven would be destroyed), derailing trains (nine in total), recovering Allied fliers (more than four hundred), taking Japanese casualties (more than fifty-four hundred), and destroying more than fifteen thousand tons of Japanese supplies and equipment.

By the end of 1943, Detachment 101's successes were coming with such swift emphasis that Stilwell was using Eifler's nickname—Buffalo Bill—and was providing him with weapons and cargo aircraft to move his men. After only a year of operations—and despite never having had more than 120 Americans at any time—Detachment 101's Kachin guerrilla conscripts now numbered in the thousands. At one point, Captain Wilkinson had more than seven hundred Kachins in his unit alone, while another 101 commander, Lieutenant Vincent Curl, had united with Zhing Htaw Naw—a Kachin leader fighting his own war against the Japanese in the Hukawng Valley—and created a guerrilla force of nearly five hundred. Eifler began implementing schemes to unhinge Japanese confidence as quickly as he could think them up.

One of Eifler's most famous "psychological warfare plans," as Detachment 101 labeled these projects, was to dye the Irrawaddy River bright yellow to agitate the Japanese along its banks. Eifler's operatives wanted to use the same antishark dye the air force's transocean pilots carried to show rescuers their location and keep away predators; only Eifler's men were going to introduce hundreds of gallons of the liquid to the Irrawaddy. Unfortunately, as they discovered during a preplanning run in a hotel bathtub in Calcutta, the dye had been manufactured to float on heavier saltwater—it sank in fresh water—and the plan had to be scrapped.

Unfortunately, as 1944 beckoned, Eifler, too, had started to sink. Having fallen and struck his head on a boulder while personally making an amphibious pilot retrieval along the seacoast in southern Burma, Eifler was suffering constant and pounding headaches. Always a hearty friend of alcohol, Eifler took to treating his headaches with ever-larger infusions of bourbon. And as a man already prone to risky behavior, the arrival of the headaches (which would plague him the rest of his life) and his chosen treatment of them left Eifler unsuited to command Detachment 101. When Eifler's boss, General "Wild Bill" Donovan, arrived in Nazira for an inspection in late December 1943, he felt compelled to replace Eifler after witnessing several cases of poor judgment. Detachment 101's operations officer, Colonel William R. "Ray" Peers, would succeed him. Buffalo Bill was to return to Washington forthwith for briefings at headquarters.

A day later, the man who had created Detachment 101 was gone.

AS THE X FORCE KEPT hacking its way south into Burma, Stilwell grew so impressed by Detachment 101—especially in the wake of sweeping Allied favor for Wingate's Chindits—that he'd started further emulating both guerilla units. Through his field officer, General Hayden Boatner, Stilwell ordered a select group of his toughest American ground troops into jungle training for a unit called the "Kachin V Force." With the coming of the spring dry season's finest weather, in January, the V Force was to act as a regular army version of Detachment 101, supporting the X Force invasion and providing diversions and intelligence. In December 1943, Boatner issued these orders: 1) "Following breakfast this morning, the following named individuals will not eat any more meals except those which they prepare themselves." A list of names was attached (including that of Corporal James S. Fletcher, who would eventually write a book on the subject). Boatner's second order was the first order's insurance: 2) "There will be no evasions of this order . . ." To ready them for their mission, the men of the V Force were only to take lessons from a unit of Detachment 101's now-famous Kachins.

Though Stilwell continued to command the Chinese army, he was realizing that Wingate had been right: a well-trained guerrilla force that augments a larger and more traditional army was a useful tool in Burma—and perhaps beyond. And as the X Force continued beating its broad path south down the Hukawng River Valley, Stilwell decided it was time to unsheath his most ambitious irregular force yet.

And he had high expectations for them.


BEYOND THE RISE of Eifler's Detachment 101, Wingate's Chindits, the Northern Kachin Levies, and the Kachin V Force, early 1944 had seen the arrival of yet one more unconventional force inside CBI. Back on August 31, 1943, in the United States—and throughout the entire U.S. Army—a call from President Roosevelt himself had gone out. The request was for 2,830 army officers and troops to volunteer for "a dangerous and hazardous mission." Of this group, all members must be both "jungle trained" and "of a high state of physical ruggedness." Within days, three thousand men had been selected and divided into three one-thousand-man battalions (each of which held two full combat teams), whose characteristics were based on Wingate's Long-Range Penetration groups. Called the 5307th Composite Unit (Provisional)—but better known by the code name "Galahad"—they were the troops George Marshall had promised Wingate upon hearing his Long-Range Penetration plan in Quebec.

By January 1944, the Americans of Galahad had not only been transported to India; they had trained for nearly three months under Wingate. But desiring to use them for his own purposes, Stilwell had fussed at Marshall so relentlessly for Galahad's control that in December 1943, Marshall granted Stilwell's request and the command of Galahad was switched. Hearing of Galahad's new orders, Wingate flew into a blue rage. He had trained these men (depriving them of food and water and marching them until they collapsed). And eventually, once he'd calmed enough to speak, he agreed to the transfer with only this rare, non-biblical proclamation: "You can tell General Stilwell that he can take his Americans and stick 'em."

The Galahad force was as unconventional as irregular armies get. Some of the 5307th hailed from American jungle-training camps in Trinidad and Panama. Others volunteered, having already honed their combat skills in battles on islands across the South Pacific. Still others had been "encouraged" to volunteer as escape passes from army jails and psychiatric hospitals. And with this motley group came yet another component: each battalion contained two Japanese-American Nisei soldiers, whose Japanese language skills might prove a prime asset in close-quarters fighting with imperial troops.

As testimony to the near sociopathy of some Galahad members, the unit's late-January departure from Wingate's Deogarh training camp to Ledo was slowed for three days by an attempted multiple homicide. Three Indian servants had been shot by two privates from Galahad's third battalion. The reason for the shootings, it was uncovered, was that the *dhobis* had refused to give the soldiers rum. When all three battalions finally moved out (leaving the two guilty privates behind and incarcerated), Galahad was anointed by James Shepley of *Time* and *Life* with a nickname that would both stick and make them world famous. Shepley, and all the members of the press corps, were now referring to the Galahad force as Merrill's Marauders, for their leader, Brigadier General Frank Merrill: a Japanese-language scholar, West Point graduate, and one of Stilwell's most trusted aides. Unfortunately, Merrill was also the soldier who'd developed heart problems during Stilwell's walk out of Burma in 1942. It was a malady that would soon create more problems.

On the evening of February 7, 1944, following Stilwell's orders and marching only at night to avoid detection, the Marauders and hundreds of loaded pack mules set off down the finished portion of Ledo Road toward

Japanese-occupied Burma. They marched silently, an endless line of American faces, each one chalky white beneath the iridescent moon. Even as they walked toward the Burmese border, no matter how excited they were to be going into battle—or how much they worried about the torments of the jungle and the Japanese that awaited them—there was no way they could be prepared for the horrible reality that was coming.

But as they left Ledo, every member of the Marauders was walking proud. They were all wearing new uniforms and carrying new kits, each of which had been issued just before the mission's start. The uniforms were "jungle clothing," said Fred Lyons. "Not the splotched camouflage uniforms of the New Guinea boys [the South Pacific troops], but solid dark outfits that offered even more complete concealment in the bush. Our fatigue blouses and our pants, our undershirts and drawers, even our handkerchiefs and matches were green." Disconcertingly, however, each soldier had been issued only one set of clothes. Perhaps, they all wondered, they'd be air-dropped new clothing as the trip went on?

As the only American military outfit officially fighting on Asian soil, the Marauders felt a deep sense of national pride. They also knew their orders, which were pared down to Stilwell-simple. By employing assistance from Vincent Curl's Kachins in the Hukawng Valley, the three thousand Marauders were to hike together to the Ledo Road's current end, near Stilwell's forward base at the village of Shingbwiyang. Then they were to split into their thousand-man battalions (each containing their two, color-denoted combat teams) and work south through the jungle, sweeping wide around Maingkwan to the east and flanking the Japanese. When the moment was right, the Marauders were to hit the Japanese garrison at the town of Walawbum, about twelve miles south and east of Maingkwan, giving the Japanese the impression they were surrounded. With this softening attack diverting the Japanese, Stilwell's X Force would then sweep down over Maingkwan from the north and overrun the village frontally.

LEAVING THE SECURITY of India behind, the Marauders passed through the Hellgate (a bridge just inside India's border with Burma) and—like a bobbing river of green combat helmets and backpacks—they began over Pangsau Pass and into Burma, their marching disrupted only by the six-wheeled GMC cargo trucks transporting goods and ammunition up the dusty road to the X Force. All night, they followed the road's muddy and steeply graded twists and turns. During the daytime, from their jungle bivouacs, the Marauders gazed to their north, amazed at the eastern escarpment of the Himalayan Range, which rose so high and snowy it looked more like cloud stratum than mountain tops. "The Himalayas were a backdrop I never grew tired of looking at," said Marauder sergeant and unit leader Joseph Ganlin. "I could stare at those mountains all day. They were like a wall rising up out of the jungle. And, I'll tell you, there was nothing like that where I came from in Massachusetts. I was amazed just to be standing there in this jungle, halfway around the world from my home, and staring. Remembering it now, plus the nervousness we all felt about going into Burma, I recall it as clearly as if I were still there today."

Nine days and 109 sweat-stained miles later, Galahad finally reached the end of the Ledo Road near Shingbwiyang, making camp in an array of clearings near a river south of Stilwell's field headquarters. By now, their uniforms had become sweat-stained and muddy, and the Marauders were already joking that they had "a new uniform for every day, and the one I'll be wearing tomorrow is even more stained and ripped than the one I've got on now."

On February 19, as the last of the Marauders caught up in Shingbwiyang, they were addressed by the general himself. Speaking calmly and slowly, Stilwell informed his troops of the North Burma Campaign's two most promising developments. The Chinese, it turned out, were even more disciplined and aggressive than Stilwell had hoped. And now, accompanied by the Marauder's own "hard-hitting American unit," it was time to "get things done. You're going to find it rough going, but I'm sure you won't let me down."

With his short speech ended, Stilwell, Merrill, and their staffs repaired to the general's hut to discuss a written directive. But after only a few minutes, as the discussion bogged down over a map table, Stilwell stood up and interjected to Merrill and the room: "Aw to *hell* with this. Come on outside, Frank, and let's get this thing settled." The two grabbed the campaign map off the hut's planning table, walked outside, laid it on the dirt of Burma beneath a tree, and squatted on their heels in the shade to hash out the details for Galahad's first mission in Burma.

In two weeks, on March 3, the Marauders were to swing wide through the mountainside jungles to the east to attack the Japanese at Walawbum. This flanking would create a second line of fire that would free the X Force to frontally overrun all imperial troops still holding Maingkwan. Between then and now, however, they were to stay hidden in the jungle and avoid Japanese contact whenever possible. And four days later, on February 24, the Marauders split into their battalion units—creatively named First, Second, and Third—and entered the network of two-foot-wide game trails over the foothills of the six-thousand-foot Kumon Range, which rose to form the imposing eastern boundary of the Hukawng Valley. Because of the mission's secrecy, the Marauders maintained strict orders to be silent, and—beyond footfalls and the clopping of their pack mules—the only noise heard were whispers of trail features that each man would pass over his shoulder to the soldier following behind. "Tree roots," he might say as he scrambled across the tangle at the base of a banyan. Or, "Big rock."

Because they were in the jungle and off the Ledo Road, all three Marauder battalions were now free to move during daylight, which added sun-scorched heat to the mission's already punishing catalogue of demands. "I remember, as we'd walked along the last of the Ledo Road and into the jungle," said Joseph Ganlin of Second Battalion, "I saw all these colorful, really beautiful veins of minerals sticking from the mountainsides at road-cuts. At first, I thought I'd carry some of the rocks with me, to take home as souvenirs. Then we began walking up and down mountains in the jungle—Lord, it was hot—I began to think better of hauling extra rocks in my pack. So I threw 'em out. Glad I did, too. If I'd known what was coming, I'd have never picked them up to begin with."

For several days, all Ganlin did was stumble up and down mountains, while simultaneously hacking at thick jungle. "We just kept humping it up and down, day after day. And the mules were already giving us trouble. With the mules, you just never knew how they were going to react, day to day, mountain to mountain. When we came on wild tigers and elephants, or even the recent tracks of elephants, the mules would smell them and go crazy. The thing was, we needed them to carry the heavier equipment, like our radio sets. And we knew we'd need the mules later to butcher for meat."

There were also leeches. "Anywhere you went, anytime you stepped off the trail and into the jungle, when you checked yourself later, you have leeches all over you," Ganlin said. "And you wouldn't even notice them on your skin at first. You wouldn't even feel them attaching their little blood-sucking mouths to your skin. Eventually, though, they'd become these big, gray, engorged strings hanging off of you. Kind of like half-size sausages. Some of the guys would get upset and quickly rip them off. That was the wrong thing to do, since pulling them snapped off their heads beneath your skin. The heads would fester and rot, which created ulcers and infections that wouldn't close or heal. Eventually the infection would eat all the way through your skin to the bone. We took to calling them Naga sores, since we'd first seen them on natives. And, boy, those sores were ugly."

After much trial and error Ganlin and the other Marauders figured out that if they took a lit cigarette and touched the leech, it would drop off. "That way we didn't get those infections as much. Still, though, once in a while you'd still pull one off by mistake—it was always a shock to find one of them on you—and the sore would start."


THE MARAUDERS KEPT WALKING, each battalion following one of three parallel trails south toward Walawbum. Now enveloped by jungle, First Battalion pushed nervously farthest east, toward the village of Tanja Ga, which American intelligence claimed, erroneously, was held by a Japanese platoon. Second Battalion, however, was not so fortunate. On February 25, on the trail outside the village of Lanem Ga, a few miles west of Tanja Ga, a Marauder scout and Pacific-war veteran, Private Robert Landis, was killed by machine-gun fire, making him the first Marauder casualty.

That same day, a few miles still farther west, near the village of Nzang Ga, Third Battalion's lead scout, Corporal Warner Katz—who'd already fought on Guadalcanal—came upon an Asian soldier motioning him closer. Thinking it was a Chinese ally, Katz stepped into a clearing, then spotted a Nambu machine gun pointed his way. Katz fired at the leader, hitting him in the forehead. Then, as he dove for a trailside depression, the Nambu opened up. Miraculously, the only bullet that struck Katz hit his wristwatch, ricocheted away, and creased his nose. Merrill's Marauders had sustained and drawn first blood.

Each day's march began to melt into the next. There came more days of hot sun and sweat, more mountain bivouacs, and more trudging along ridges. Smaller skirmishes with Japanese outland platoons became regular occurrences. And slowed by the terrain, all three battalions of the 5307th didn't arrive near Walawbum until the day they were to attack—March 4.

Then they prepared for their offensive, massing in the villages of Wesu Ga and Lagang Ga along the Numpyek River just north of Walawbum.

Unfortunately, by March 1, the skirmishes had alerted the Japanese Eighteenth Division's resourceful leader, General Shinichi Tanaka, to the Marauder's constant movements. And with the American flanking forces now giving him more pressure than the Chinese division holding to the north of Maingkwan, Tanaka decided to adjust his troop deployments. He left only a small rear guard to defend against Stilwell and the Chinese, and in only a few days had repositioned the majority of his soldiers twelve miles to the south in Walawbum.

The Marauders had, in fact, been noticing retreating Japanese on the jungle trails for days. And as the sun rose on March 4, 1944, with the Marauders spreading out to ready for attack, units from the Japanese Eighteenth Division fixed bayonets and began pushing back, making fifty-man patrols into the jungles near Marauder positions north and east of town. The time for collision between Merrill's and Tanaka's forces had arrived. On that first morning, an Intelligence and Reconnaissance Platoon had hiked south of Walawbum, waded across the shallow Numpyek River, and set up a perimeter along the dirt road leading south from the town. As they were reinforcing their perimeters, the Japanese snuck close and began to make successive waves of Japanese "banzai" charges that edged closer and closer to the Marauder positions. With Japanese grenade launcher fire raining down, the Americans, who were firing nonstop, became showered in tides of flying mud.

As the day ground on—with each Japanese charge bringing the defenders closer to Third Battalion's positions—the I&R platoon began to form into a small, updated version of the British Square: a combined offensive and defensive formation like a three-pointed star, using troops at each point around a central core of soldiers. With impressive calm, one of the I&R Platoon's Nisei interpreters, Henry "Horizontal Hank" Gosho, then worked close enough to the Japanese on his belly to overhear their voices, translating back to command what the Japanese orders were.

The Japanese kept coming. Soon the well-defended Marauders began to run low on ammunition and the Japanese—sensing that they could overrun the pinned-down Americans—redoubled their rifle fire and grenade assaults. Under pressure, the I&R Platoon requested assistance, and the

Third Battalion on the river's far side began to fire rounds from their big, 81-millimeter mortars across the river. As the American explosions marched through the jungle toward the Japanese, the banzai attacks were slowed just long enough for the platoon to melt back across the Numpyek toward the relative safety of the far bank.

At 5:45 p.m., General Merrill radioed the day's events to General Stilwell from his headquarters at Wesu Ga. One Marauder from Third Battalion had been killed, seven more had been wounded, but, by the intelligence reports coming in from the field, the Japanese had lost twenty-five times as many men in their charges on the I&R Platoon positions.

Stilwell was ecstatic: "*FRANK MERRILL IS IN WALAWBUM*," he penned in big italics in his diary. His X Force drive toward Maingkwan could now go forward.

Unfortunately, he would have to hold back the X Force attack for at least another day, since SEAC "Supremo" Lord Mountbatten was scheduled to arrive at the battlefront the next morning by aircraft. Stilwell, however, was keyed-up and ready to go. And once Mountbatten arrived, he was going to take the village as a show of what his capable X Force could do. He was desperate to show Mountbatten—and by extension Chiang—just how battle-hard his Chinese troops had become.


AROUND WALAWBUM, though, the Japanese were not going to fold. The next morning, March 5, as Mountbatten flew in to visit Stilwell, it was the Marauder Second Battalion that began to feel General Tanaka's wrath at Walawbum. At dawn, as the Americans set up along the two-track road running north a mile out of Walawbum—using some unoccupied Japanese foxholes as cover—they peered through the sunrise and saw a long line of Japanese soldiers marching up the road from town. The Japanese were obviously going to retake the foxhole positions they'd abandoned the night before—the ones the Marauders were *now occupying*. As they watched the Japanese approach, the Americans began to jitter nervously.

"I could feel the muscles trying to cross in cramps and the blood pounding in my face," Fred Lyons said. And in the dawn, at Lyons's signal, a burst of American machine guns felled a file of seven Japanese with a single tattoo.

"Then," Lyons recalled, "the firing began in earnest. More Japs ran into view, so close you could see the bronze star shining dully on their bouncing little hats."

The firefight set off a day complete with six different banzai charges, and in between waves of Japanese troops, the Japanese shelled the Americans with mortars and field artillery. As each charge would come, the Americans began to counter the Japanese screams of "Banzai!" with their own war cries of "*Fuuuck youuuu!*" accompanied by rifle fire through the flying mud.

"The Japanese artillerymen were amazing," says Joseph Ganlin of the Second Battalion. "Especially the guys firing the mortars. They had us fixed just right, and as we hunched down in the foxholes, they were putting mortar rounds in our pockets. There was mud flying. That's what I remember most about that day. Clods of mud going everywhere, and bits of exploded grass and vegetation flitting on the wind."

The Americans stood tough. Across a day of constant explosions and weapons fire, they took only six casualties—only one of whom died—and another of whom, after having his belly ripped open by machine-gun fire that left his intestines hanging open in the air, was cleaned up, sutured shut, and evacuated back to Wesu Ga. With a section of the road secured by the Americans, a sharp-eyed technician tapped the Japanese communication line that ran through the treetops between the command post at Walawbum and the forward command center in Maingkwan. Then a Second Battalion Nisei interpreter Sergeant Roy A. Matsumoto, started listening in. At Walawbum, the Japanese Eighteenth Division had become spread far too thin: there were only three men with machine guns guarding the town's ammunition depot, and the Japanese commander was begging for Takana's "help and advice."

Through the afternoon of March 5, dodging bullets from snipers as he stood on a tree limb above the ground and monitored Japanese communications, Matsumoto began intercepting desperate calls from Imperial Army troop commanders all across the battlefield. "Listening in to those radio transmissions," Matsumoto said, "I felt like I was floating high above the battlefield and watching everything unfold. The snipers kept shooting at me, and once in a while the trunk of the tree I was standing in would splinter from a bullet and I'd move around to the other side of the tree to get a little cover. But I was a small target—I'm a little guy, five feet two inches—and what I was hearing was just so, so important to the events of the battle. So I kept standing there in the tree, all through the afternoon, listening."

What Matsumoto was hearing and passing to his superiors was some of the most dramatic news of the invasion so far. Under pressure from the Chinese and the Americans, it seemed that the Japanese at both Maing-kwan and Walawbum were crumbling simultaneously.

From Walawbum, the call went out: "Casualties very large, we cannot protect river crossing . . ."

From Maingkwan, the response: "Every man in the next few days must fight hard. Enemy is very strong and we must destroy him at all costs . . ."

From Walawbum: "Cannot hold much longer, if help does not come . . ."

From Maingkwan: "No help available, fight to the end."


FINALLY, LATE IN THE DAY, Matsumoto heard the transmission that he, Merrill, and ultimately Stilwell had been waiting for. It was from Tanaka's headquarters and it was ordering the entire Eighteenth Division to with-draw to the west and south from both Maingkwan and Walawbum. By dawn on March 6, the Japanese had pulled back from their engagement with Second Battalion, and the Marauders abandoned the foxhole posi-tions they'd held for nearly thirty-six hours without food and with little water. Their initial contact with the Japanese had been a success, and they waded back across the Numpyek River and rejoined the other Marauders at Second and Third Battalion headquarters in Lagang Ga.

Once safely away from the line of conflict, the Marauders Second Bat-talion rejoined the Orange Combat Team from Third Battalion in nervy consideration: would the Japanese be coming for them or retreating? And as they waited for a rations supply drop from India, all the Marauders knew for certain was that they'd soon learn General Tanaka's plans.


IN THE JUNGLES east of Walawbum, after two days of hard fighting, the morning scene of March 6 was oddly pastoral. In the rice paddy that made up Second and Third Battalion headquarters, a bamboo and thatch "basha" hut sat at the northern edge of the open field. Thirty yards from it, the corpses of several Japanese soldiers lay fly-covered where they'd been shot the day before, after blundering into the open field by mistake. And some of the Marauders, hungry and not waiting for the air drop, had started husking rice from the paddy in the sun, using their steel helmets to mash the hard kernels. Then, overhead, they heard a sort of "tobaggan-slide rustle."

A moment later, seventy-five yards behind the paddy, the jungle exploded with a gigantic *BOOM*! In another minute, Japanese artillery shells of every size and order—from 50-millimeter "knee mortars" to 81-millimeter mortar rounds to 70-, 75-, and 150-millimeter Howitzer shells—were exploding across the paddy, and the Marauder battalions began frantically digging foxholes and trenches. All day, every seven minutes, another barrage of Japanese artillery shells would fall, hitting all around the rice field and the network of newly dug trenches. Apparently the Japanese had decided not to evacuate after all.

Then things got *really* threatening. Above the head of Joseph Ganlin and the other Marauders, "The Japanese started doing something we called 'tree bursts.' They'd fire big 81-millimeter mortar rounds into the trees above us at the back of the rice paddy, and the explosions would shatter the trees, sending hunks of log, bits of bark, and limbs and branches down on us. It was fearsome. We were covered in mud and chunks of exploded wood. There was smoke everywhere, and I'd be lying if I said that all of us weren't scared to see what was coming next."

The day of shelling continued. Through the morning and afternoon, new waves of explosion would fall and shatter the explosion-pocked earth every seven minutes. Then, shortly after 5 p.m.—with the sun beginning to set—the Japanese fire became even more intense, with artillery and mortar rounds falling constantly. And with the sun at the Japanese army's back and directly in the eyes of the Marauders, the men of the Third Battalion's Orange Combat Team began to make out a frightful scene. Just across the river, a line of Imperial Japanese soldiers was advancing behind the smoky pops from their grenade launchers. The Japanese were coming and the far riverbank was suddenly full of running, crouching enemy soldiers. Japanese officers were waving their swords—flashing them in the sunset—and shouting "Banzaiiii!" above the explosions.

The Marauders opened fire, their Browning automatic rifles and two heavy machine guns sweeping across the attacking Japanese, killing them in waves. In the recollection of Marauder Charlton Ogburn, "The first rank of the Japanese went down like stricken figures in a ballet . . . The persistence of the Japanese was horrifying. When a machine-gun crew fell dead with its weapon, another would rush forward, grab up the heavy mechanism, and carry it a few steps and then go down in its turn, only to be replaced by another crew. The Browning automatic riflemen and machine gunners on the east bank, hardly slackening in the deadly business, worked a slaughter."

Though the 250 men of Orange Combat Team were facing 5,000 attackers, the riverbank opposite Orange Team was soon stacked with Japanese dead, and the Browning rifles and machine guns kept roaring. One machine gun—operated by corporals Joseph Diorio and Clayton E. Hall—was hit by rifle fire, its water-cooled encasement punctured. For the rest of the evening, Diorio and Hall called for assistance, as soldiers poured the contents of their canteens on the weapon's barrel to keep it somewhat chilled while Hall's hands—operating the red-hot machine gun—grew burned and scorched. Still, they managed to fire another four thousand rounds of ammunition. The Japanese kept coming, and the Americans goaded them on. As the artillery shells and mortar rounds burst around them, the Marauders began shouting at the Japanese through hands cupped at the sides of their mouths: "Come and get some more of it, you yellow sons of bitches," they taunted. "Get those bastards! Get the bastards!" In English and Japanese, the Marauders started yelling, "Tojo eats shit!" To which the Japanese were responding: "Eleanor eats powdered eggs!" in an attempt to humiliate Mrs. Roosevelt.

Finally, with dusk, the Japanese waves of attack slowed. By 8 p.m., as a mule train with more ammunition arrived from Wesu Ga, the last of the banzai charges had passed, though Japanese artillery continued to fall. Eventually the men of Third Battalion felt secure enough to send a few platoons of scouts toward the riverbank, where they tallied the dead: 350 Japanese lay on both sides of the river. Back in the foxholes, the Marauders began to assess their own losses. Compared with the huge casualties of the enemy, Galahad had sustained only seven wounded and no dead.

The next morning, as the Marauders again began arraying themselves out around Walawbum, Japanese artillery pieces began to pitch waves of explosives upon them once again. But as scout platoons pushed forward, it

appeared the morning's new barrages were warnings to keep away; the reconnaissance teams found no new troops preparing to charge. The Japanese and General Tanaka were withdrawing from Walawbum, and the
Marauder advance parties began to probe the edges of the village, where
they found only piles of dead Japanese troops.

The following day, March 9, as the Marauders continued to secure the
village, they began to hear the clatter of motorized vehicles and friendly
sounding cheers from the road north out of town. At first, Merrill's men
thought they might be confronting the bulk of Tanaka's army. Instead, as
the approaching army came around a last bend in the jungle road and into
full sight, the troops turned out to be a portion of the X Force. The Chinese army was rolling into town.

As the relieved Marauders began to mix among the Chinese, the scene
was one of comedy and relief. The shaven-faced and crop-haired Chinese
marched toward the bearded and tattered Marauders, embracing them in
bear hugs. To Marauder signalman Charlton Ogburn, Jr., what he liked
best about the Chinese troops were their mess porters, who carried "a ver-
itable kitchen divided into two loads slung on either end of a pole . . . it
was time to rest and catch up on our eating before moving out again for
the next mission."

In five days at Walawbum, the Marauders had killed eight hundred of
the enemy. Only eight of their own had died, and thirty-seven were
wounded. In a grim foreshadowing of events to come, however, more Marauders had been disabled by the jungle than by their most recent encounter with the Japanese. Since leaving Ledo, "miscellaneous sickness"
had cost the Marauders 109 men, with malaria taking 19, jungle fevers 8,
and psychoneurosis 10.

As March 9 fell on Walawbum, the combined Chinese X Force and
5037th Composite Unit had cleared the upper Hukawng Valley of Shinichi
Tanaka's formidable Eighteenth Division, vanquisher of Singapore,
Malaya, and Burma. And as the Marauders listened, English-speaking
members of the X Force recounted how they'd pounded into the underde-
fended village of Maingkwan, killing whatever Japanese rearguard remained. Then, after the Chinese had secured the village, Generals Stilwell,
Sun, and Boatner had ordered them, as advance infantry forces, on with all
speed to Walawbum.

The final battle for Maingkwan and the upper Hukawng Valley had been so quick and decisive that Stilwell barely mentioned it in his diary. For March 7, 1944, perhaps the best day in Joseph W. Stilwell's past two years, this was his full diary entry: "Up at 5:30 and in to Maingkwan and south a mile or so to ambush location. Plenty of dead Japs, horses, and junk. Louis much impressed. Doesn't like corpses. Left at 9:00."

# Chapter 11

AFTER ALMOST TWO YEARS of war in Burma, the Imperial Japanese Army transportation Private Atsumi Oda was promoted to lieutenant in March 1944. But the elevation in rank and the endless hours now spent on the muddy plains and humid mountainsides of Burma had done little to raise his spirits, or those of the entire Japanese occupational force.

As was becoming more obvious by the day, Japanese provisions in both the forward and the rear areas of Burma were virtually nonexistent. And the Japanese stores of ammunition were being depleted even more quickly, now that the X Force had invaded out of India. Even if Lieutenant Oda now had a truck at his disposal instead of the horse and wagon he'd been assigned in Rangoon in 1942, he recognized that—as much as fighting the Allies—feeding himself had become a near-impossible mission: "We got rice and sometimes tea from the local people, because we had nothing else. Two years before, we had viewed the Burmese people as no more than docile animals. Now they were feeding *us*. We were starving. And after almost two years of belittling the Allies as weak and cowardly, as they began to press upon us we were *shocked*. Absolutely *shocked* at both their power and their numbers."

The Allied war at home, especially as it was being fought in the retooled factories of the United States, was, by late 1943 and early 1944, going full-tilt. In the United States, the monies allocated to armaments spending *alone* had risen almost tenfold since the start of the war: from $40.5 billion in emergency spending in 1941 to a steady flow of $378 billion in 1944. Britain, which had seen a large portion of its manufacturing and production facilities destroyed by German bombings, still managed to double its armaments spending during the same time frame: from $50 billion in 1941 to $100 billion. In the Pacific Theater, by the start of 1944, four tons of supplies and weaponry were available to every Allied soldier deployed, while his Japanese opponent could muster just two pounds of guns, ammunition, and food.

The Japanese undersupply that Private Oda had pondered back on Rangoon's docks in April 1942 had arrived, and now it was undercutting Imperial Army strength.

IF ANYONE INSIDE SEAC and CBI understood this shift in fortunes and morale, it was Vinegar Joe Stilwell. And by early March 1944, despite the logistical threats posed by the coming rainy season, Stilwell was set to take advantage of the growing Japanese weakness. On March 12, he ordered the Marauders on to their second mission. They were to push south from Walawbum, disappearing back into the jungled hills of the Kumon Range on the east side of the Hukawng Valley. Their goal was now to gain control of the Mogaung Valley town of Shaduzup ("Shadu's Village, where the rivers join"), which sits just above where the Mogaung River Valley enters the Hukawng at an angle. Once they could control the entrance to the Mogaung Valley, they had a clear shot down it toward Stilwell's ultimate goal: the Japanese transport and supply hub in the city of Myitkyina, on the mighty Irrawaddy River.

To Stilwell, control of the Mogaung River Valley was perhaps the most critical piece of the entire North Burma Campaign. Because it connected the forward units of the Japanese Eighteenth Division in the Hukawng Valley and the Japanese Eighteenth's supply and troop headquarters at Myitkyina in the Irrawaddy Valley, the Mogaung Valley was the transport artery between the two centers of Japanese activity. To block it and take control of the Kamaing Road—a dirt track that ran between the two valleys and connected them with the village of Kamaing—would deprive the Japanese in the Hukawng Valley of new troops and rations.

By Stilwell's own orders—and against the advice of Merrill and Hunter—the Marauders were again to break into their three battalions. First Battalion would go shallowly into the Kumon Range, to more closely follow the Kamaing Road south from Walawbum, while Second and Third Battalions were to fan out in an arcing line against the taller Kumon Range peaks to the east, swinging wide around the Japanese-controlled town of Shaduzup and emerging along the Kamaing Road south of Shaduzup at a village called Inkangahtawng. Once south of Shaduzup, they could close off the entrance to the Mogaung Valley and shut off the Japanese Eighteenth's overland supply.

Like it or not, it was time for the Marauders to head back into the jungle. But as they hacked their way back into the overgrown forests of northern Burma, instead of finding an enemy ready to fight, they were seeing signs of a weak and retreating opposition. By the end of the first day, all three battalions were encountering signs of Japanese withdrawal everywhere. Wherever they looked in the mud, they saw the southbound imprints of Japanese hobnail boots or the cloven-hoof marks left by the rubber soles of Japanese jungle boots, whose soles were split to allow the big toe of each foot freer movement. For three days, as the Marauders followed the constantly freshening boot-prints south, they met with only occasional skirmishes put up by rearguard Japanese sentries.

But while the Japanese were in retreat, the Americans—who'd been living and sweating and fighting in the jungle now for more than a month—were also showing signs of fatigue. As they worked into the ridges of the Kumon Range, the hillsides grew steep, sometimes too steep for the heavily laden mules, necessitating regular stops to break up pack loads. Each battalion commander also had the unholy job of hacking through thick forests of bamboo, whose older, thicker stalks resisted the blades of their machetes. For twelve hours a day, the Marauders chopped and slashed to make new trails, carrying packs on their backs whose straps were now cutting into the skin of their shoulders. Due to the unclean cooking and living conditions of the past six weeks, dysentery had also arrived in force, becoming the scourge of all three battalions. Many of the Marauders' tattered uniforms were stiff and discolored from sweat, blood from minor wounds and leech bites, and diarrhea. Worse yet, in the mountains, each evening's radio call for fresh supplies couldn't be heard by Stilwell or his headquarters, and the Marauders were running out of food. As Charlton Ogburn put it: "We had two conditions—one in which we felt unfed, the other in which we *were* unfed."

Every fourth or fifth day, when the radio calls got through and K rations were parachuted in, low murmurs of barter would fill the air of Marauder camps as men broke open their boxes and tried to trade for their favorite items. Each ration box generally held two hard biscuits and two soft ones; canned protein in the form of chicken or pork and egg yolks; a bar of cheese; bouillon cubes; some Nabisco crackers or cookies; a few date-and-prune fruit bars; a packet of lemonade for the canteen; packets of ground coffee and sugar; a chocolate bar; a pack of cigarettes, and a pack of Wrigley's Spearmint gum or an unchewably waxy substitute from the Walla Walla Company of Nashville, Tennessee.

"Pack of Cavaliers for two lumps of sugar, anyone?" a Marauder might suggest.

"Pork-and-egg-yolk for a cheese component?"

"Coffee for a fruit bar?"

"What am I offered for a D ration?" ("D rations," or "dysentery rations," were chocolate bars, so nicknamed because they were the only food soldiers with dysentery could stomach.)

A week into their second mission, halfway to Shaduzup, First Battalion encountered their first patrol of Kachin Rangers, led by OSS Lieutenant James L. Tilley. After reconnoitering their location, the combined Marauders and Kachins began searching out any still-held enemy positions that might prevent First Battalion's successful roadblock of the Kamaing Road near Shaduzup. In spots where too many Japanese troops existed to fight, the Marauders would disappear back into the jungle, moving around the Japanese, secure in the knowledge that, once the X Force pushed south from Walawbum, the imperial troops would be caught between the X Force hammer and the Marauder anvil that was now sliding through the jungle to block their evacuation.

On March 19, as First Battalion and the Kachins wandered down the small Chengun River to where it entered the larger Mogaung River, they discovered they were only a few miles south of Shaduzup, and at a spot that Colonel Osborne thought would be good for a roadblock and attack. After giving a general bivouac order, First Battalion commander Lt. Colonel William Osborne began laying out his initial plan to take possession of the Kamaing Road south from town. Osborne, Merrill, and Stilwell all believed the Japanese expected the next Marauder attack to come not from the Kumon Range, but from Hukawng Valley farther north. To support that suspicion, Osborne ordered a First Battalion platoon to make some noisy movements northwest of the village in a feint. Then, just south of Shaduzup, where the Kamaing Road's dirt ran close to the river, Osborne sent a few scouts across the broad, waist-deep, and muddy Mogaung River on reconnaissance.

Just as Osborne thought, there were roughly three hundred Japanese troops in Shaduzup proper, with the remainder of the Eighteenth Division somewhere north of them and coming south along the road. After dark, Osborne called together his officers and gave his orders. Before dawn, the Marauders were to cross the river, secure the Kamaing Road, and then push north into Shaduzup in stages—with two platoons going in first, with unloaded rifles and fixed bayonets, followed by a third. They were to strike at dawn, and once the element of surprise was lost they were to start shooting—and keep shooting, no matter what—supported by mortar fire from the far side of the river.

At 4:30 a.m., the Marauder platoons were across the river and moving slowly upstream toward the Japanese encampment area, which was fully visible in the darkness, lit by dozens of small fires. But as they were getting into position, a burst of unexpected machine-gun fire ripped through an area to the south, where some Japanese latrines had been dug and where an imperial soldier had spotted a platoon of Marauders who had been sweeping wide of the road. Ready or not, the battle for the Kamaing Road and Shaduzup was on.

In the darkness, the muzzle flashes of Japanese rifle fire began to light the village at dawn. As the Japanese spread across the landscape to defend themselves, the Marauders shouted for backup. Some of the Marauders had been caught without cover, and were now crying in pain from bullet wounds; others kept shooting and pushing closer, crawling on their bellies and running from tree to tree in what they'd come to call "the National Guard crouch." One hundred yards behind the Marauder front, medics were following and watching for casualties, which they dragged down the river's steeply cut bank to get away from the fighting. As the Japanese composed themselves and began a counteroffensive, the Americans were caught out. They were exposed on the road, hemmed in on one side by the river and on the other side by several platoons of Japanese soldiers who were now flanking them. There was only one thing to do: the Marauders had to dig in, take cover, and hold their ground.

At 9 a.m., after two hours of sporadic shooting, the forward platoons of First Battalion radioed across the river to Osborne that mortar fire might throw the Japanese off guard. Within minutes, American mortar rounds began to fall on the Japanese, just as Japanese mortar rounds began to boom near the two-man Marauder positions arrayed along the road. As a full company of Japanese reinforcements moved in from the north to secure Shaduzup's encampment, several teams of First Battalion machine gunners—who'd worked upstream along the river's steep and vegetated banks—popped up from the undercut riverbank and sprayed the line of solders with bullets. In a single burst, more than sixty Japanese soldiers were killed.

By early afternoon, U.S. Air Force bombers began hammering the Japanese positions at Shaduzup, turning some fire away from the Marauders, who kept edging closer to the village up the now explosion-pocked, bullet-strewn dirt of the Kamaing Road. But as evening approached, with the aerial bombing over for the day, the Japanese again turned their concentration on the Marauder ground fighters. They began to shoot randomly down the road, making probing volleys to see where the Marauder positions were. Then they began to pound the riverbank with mortar rounds. Along the Kamaing Road, First Battalion of Merrill's 5307th Composite Unit was being slowly surrounded. And as the barrages kept falling, and the muzzle flashes of Japanese rifle fire grew closer with every minute, the forward Marauders began to worry that they'd soon be overrun. They began to radio back across the river, where Colonel Osborne ordered them to stay put.

Things looked bad, and in the twilight, a voice rose up in a slack moment between rifle bursts and explosions. "Where the *hell* are the other 5,306 composite units?" it asked. Along the riverbank, with fear of an overwhelming banzai attack bursting constantly in their minds, some of the Marauders managed a chuckle—but the fear was icy, immediate, and real.

Then, minutes later, from somewhere north of Shaduzup's village, the Marauders heard a series of four large explosions. A few minutes passed and the explosions came again—and again. Soon, every minute or two there would be new eruptions, and the huts and buildings of Shaduzup were engulfed in smoke. At first the Marauder forward platoons couldn't understand it. But as even larger artillery rounds began landing all around the Japanese encampment, the Marauders were spared by another of Stilwell's screwball ideas. And this one came in right on time.

Shortly after the Marauders were off from Walawbum on their second mission, Stilwell had ordered a light-artillery unit from the X Force, the Chinese 113th, to begin tracking the First Battalion through the jungle, carrying their disassembled cannons on mule backs. At the first sign of full battle for Shaduzup, they were to support the Marauders with screens of artillery fire. The 113th's Howitzers had now been reassembled and they were raining blasts upon the Japanese. In minutes, the imperial forces were not only having to defend the Kamaing Road from the south; they were being simultaneously shelled from the north, and they began to collapse in the chaos. As the Chinese explosions walked farther south and the Marauders held their ground, the Japanese, almost in unison, began to evacuate Shaduzup, disappearing into the jungle to the west.

In the several hours of mop-up that followed, the Marauders learned that the battle for Shaduzup had cost Japan three hundred dead, with a great loss of supplies. Of the Marauders' First Battalion, eight men had been killed and thirty-five were injured. While a surgical unit, put together by Dr. Gordon Seagrave—now a lieutenant colonel under Stilwell's command—began to patch up the wounded, the Marauders were relieved, platoon by platoon, as the Chinese secured and occupied the town. Then, with the battle for Shaduzup won, they waded back across the Mogaung River and celebrated their victory by downing cool cups of water beneath an arriving drizzle. Even in their illness and fatigue, the Marauders of the First Battalion were ecstatic. They sang and laughed. They joked and ate what rations were available. In the night, they recounted the day's successful battle, indulging in the joy gained after overcoming a life-or-death situation. Despite the hardships of the past six weeks, every Marauder in First Battalion felt the same way: it was good to be alive.

The day had gone dark when Colonel Osborne wandered back into camp from his nightly radio call to Stilwell's headquarters. And with his return, Osborne carried some truly staggering news. Two hundred miles to the south and east of Shaduzup, Japan had invaded India.

# Chapter 12

IF THE ALLIES WERE STUNNED by the bold Japanese strike into India—blocking the Tiddum Road into Burma and attacking British encampments in the towns of Imphal and Kohima—Joseph Stilwell had little time to help. "This about ruins everything," he wrote in his diary for March 16, 1944. Despite calls from General Slim for an X Force counterattack on the Japanese from inside Burma (plus a second set of requests from Chiang to halt his advance for the rainy season), Stilwell kept pushing the X Force south down the Hukawng Valley. Flying to Chungking for a rare day away from the battlefront, Vinegar Joe convinced Chiang and T. V. Soong that the Chinese armies were doing a splendid job, and that—thanks in largest part to the fighting will of Chinese troops—all of north Burma would soon be in Allied hands. Chiang and Soong, too, were thrilled with the results, and after a quick conference the Chinese agreed with Stilwell's plan to keep going. Regardless of the coming rainy season, the drive for Myitkyina would continue.

Back at the front and heading south down the almost emptied Hukawng Valley, Stilwell's X Force pushed the last of the Japanese stragglers from the mountainsides of Jambu Bum to the Hukawng Valley's west. The next goal was the transport hub city of Myitkyina, with its giant airfield and its wharves on the broad Irrawaddy River. Once "Mitch" had been taken, the Ledo Road could be attached to China by two alternating routes:

one directly across the Irrawaddy River and into China from Myitkyina (along an old trade spur called the Marco Polo Trail, as it led to the ancient trading town of Tengchung, which Polo was said to have visited), and the other continuing south from Myitkyina through the town of Bhamo, where it would later link with the true Burma Road at the Burma-China border in the town of Wanding.

To augment the invasion's momentum, Stilwell had also deployed other irregular troops into north Burma. He'd given the signal to drop Wingate's men behind the Japanese forces south of Myitkyina, while the Marauders were now spreading farther out through the jungle to continue their counter-punches to the Japanese. Stilwell had also given instructions to the Northern Kachin Levies and Detachment 101's Kachin Rangers to prepare for a drive south down the Irrawaddy River valley toward Myitkyina from their current battle line at Sumprabum.

Stilwell had also finally extracted—much to his pleasure—a hard promise from Chiang to loose the Y Force into north Burma out of China starting in mid-April. After clearing the Japanese from a few key cities along the Burma Road in southwest China, Chiang's Y Force would be free to meet with the X Force in the Irrawaddy River Valley and push south. Once these two Chinese forces were linked, Stilwell believed, there was no way the Japanese could hold north Burma.

BUT AGAINST THE SUCCESS of the invasion, there were problems. And the one taking first priority was getting all twelve thousand Chindits inserted into Burma. Inside Wingate's Circus, the problems began with Wingate himself. Several months earlier—during a witheringly hot stop in Castel Benito, Libya, while on his trip back from the Quadrant Conference—Wingate had grown impatient while waiting for the airfield's canteen to open. In a lapse of judgment that was characteristically Wingate, the newly promoted major general had thrown some flowers out of a vase and consumed the container's water. A few weeks later, safely back in India, he was hospitalized with a life-threatening case of typhoid. By early May, while back on his feet, Wingate's strength, stamina, and ability to command with his usual enthusiasm were profoundly compromised. He was skinny and weak. He was tired. And his eyes, which always burned blue from beneath his prominent brow, were now so lifeless

General Joseph W. Stilwell, in a rare moment behind a desk during World War II

General Stilwell pins the Legion of Merit medal on Generalissimo Chiang Kai-shek, July 7, 1943.

(*below*) A member of Chiang Kai-shek's Kuomintang Chinese Army, guarding a Flying Tiger P-40 aircraft at Kunming, 1942

General Claire Lee Chennault, center, Commander of the Fourteenth Air Force in China, displays the new emblem of his force. With Chennault is the designer of the insignia, Staff Sergeant Howard M. Arnegard (left).

Gordon S. Seagrave, the famed Burma Surgeon, shown here with three of his capable Burmese nurses

General William Slim,
commander of the
British Fourteenth Army

A Lisu tribal woman working as a laborer along the Ledo-Burma Road
near the border of Burma and China

(*above*) A detachment of Kachin V-Force, led by Corporal James Fletcher, wade a narrow river, or *chaung*, in north Burma, 1943.

(*above*) Major N'Hpan Naw, the most famous of the Kachin Levies. N'Hpan Naw participated in more than forty ambushes against Japanese forces, in which several hundred Japanese troops were killed. In one jungle engagement, he fought nonstop for seven days without food.

Staff Sergeant Roy A. Matsumoto, 1944

Major-General Orde C. Wingate, 1944

British Generals Wingate (left) and Slim

(*below*) The airfield at Myitkyina, with pack animals carrying food, ammunition, and weapons to Allied Infantry fighting nearby

A U.S.-built bulldozer to the rescue of a lead truck in a supply convoy, somewhere along the Ledo Road, 1944

American Sergeant John J. Busaites takes a break during the five-month siege of Myitkyina.

(*above*) SEAC Supreme Commander
Admiral Lord Louis Mountbatten with
Deputy Commander Stilwell (left), likely
at Taipha, near Walawbum, during the
Hukawng Valley Campaign, March 6, 1944

(*right*) Just another ground soldier:
Stilwell somewhere in Burma, 1944

On a rare non-rainy
day during the battle
for Mytikyina, a C-47
transport plane parachutes
supplies and ammunition
to American and Chinese
forces, dropping the sup-
plies less than fifteen
hundred feet from the
battle front.

Admiral Mountbatten addresses the troops with "spontaneous vitality."

First Convoy along the Ledo-Burma Road. Lieutenant General Lewis A. Pick rides the first Jeep of the Convoy from Burma across the border into China, at Wanding, China, January 28, 1945.

and sunken that they appeared to be nothing more than black holes in his head.

Still, his health wasn't Wingate's biggest problem. On the evening of March 5, 1944, just as the Third Indian Division—twelve thousand Chindits and, remarkably, their three thousand mules—were to begin their invasion by glider insertion to two large jungle clearings (code named "Piccadilly" and "Broadway") inside Burma, reconnaissance photos showed that Piccadilly had, incomprehensibly, been strewn with felled trees, rendering it unusable. Frustrated by this eleventh-hour turn of events, Wingate exploded when he discovered that, despite his specific instructions for all Allied aircraft to stay away from the landing zones, photos of both sites had appeared in a recent issue of an American magazine. Had Japanese spies seen the photos and covered the field with trees?

When he finally calmed down—the tree-felling culprits turned out to be Burmese loggers—Wingate pulled his newly promoted Brigadier "Mad Mike" Calvert aside to reconsider options. After a few minutes' discussion, it was decided that all Chindit gliders would be diverted to the forward airfield at Broadway, a complication that would slow the invasion, since many of the Chindit targets lay closer to Piccadilly.

They would press on. Calvert and Wingate quickly rebriefed the glider units, and after being bid good luck by Wingate and Slim, the Chindits and Mike Calvert went to work. Leading the first group, and under the cover of moonlit darkness, Calvert took off with the first flight of wood-and-canvas gliders, each one towed by a C-47. One of the gliders was even piloted by the former Hollywood child actor Jackie Coogan, who had special status across all of CBI for once having been married to World War II's pinup queen, Betty Grable. Through the darkness, Calvert and his men flew across the Naga Hills and over the Chindwin River toward central Burma. Gazing down at the dark mountains below, which were lit by the moon and the stars, Calvert was delighted to be traveling by air over a landscape that had proved so difficult to walk across just a year before. They passed above the tree-strewn Piccadilly—ghostly in the moonlight—and when the C-47 tow planes began to turn in circles, Calvert looked down and saw the opening of Broadway in the jungle below. The glider pilot, another American named Lees, pulled a lever that released the tow-plane's cable, and the glider popped free in a "sudden, tremendous silence."

The plane banked down steeply and moments later, it slammed hard to earth, then bounced fifty feet into the air again, before crashing to a stop with a huge, tumbling, horrifying series of booming crunches. During the landing, a support stanchion on the plane's interior slammed into Calvert's back, giving him a deep bruise. Another soldier aboard, a Sergeant McDermott, had his hand smashed and bloodily flattened between two other collapsing stanchions. Still, in the jungle darkness, they were down and alive. They were at Broadway.

After freeing McDermott's hand from where it had been crushed, Calvert and his team deplaned and discovered the reason for their bumpy landing. Another of the gliders, the one that had landed directly in front of them, had hit a ditch and sheared off its undercarriage. Flight Officer Lees, responding quickly to the moonlight crash unfolding in front of him, had gotten airborne just enough to hop his glider *over* the crashed glider, bringing his aircraft to a safe, if ungainly, stop.

Now on the ground, Calvert set up his headquarters as more gliders landed safely or crashed down in Broadway's darkness. One of the gliders—which was carrying a small bulldozer intended to cut a smooth runway on the site—had landed barely at the edge of the field and then hurtled off into the jungle, losing its wings before colliding head-on with a tree. In the wreck, the bulldozer had torn free of its moorings, and at the moment of collision with the tree, several tons of bulldozer had smashed forward—crashing into the cockpit and stopping only when it hit the tree itself. Miraculously, the soldiers inside escaped unhurt, having swung out of the way of the dozer at the moment of impact. Within minutes, in fact, soldiers had gotten the crashed bulldozer running, and as they drove it belching onto Broadway from the jungle, the Chindits cheered. In minutes, it began carving a smooth runway into Broadway's soil.

Still, in the darkness, the scene was dispiriting. Crashed gliders littered the landing zone, and as Calvert raced to determine whether the first night of Chindit invasion was a success or a failure, he kept receiving conflicting information: More aircraft were coming in. Many aircraft had crashed and no more were coming. The Japanese had Broadway surrounded. There was no sign of the Japanese. As Calvert weighed the reports, he knew the time for his radio transmission—2:30 a.m.—had arrived and he had to make a report: was the first night of the Chindit invasion a success or a failure? Finally, as more information flowed to him, the fate of the initial Chindit glider party seemed to tilt toward failure, and the time for his radio call was at hand. If the landings had gone poorly, Calvert had orders to radio Wingate and headquarters with the code words "Soya Link," the British name for inadequate, soy-based sausages that the British and Indian soldiers were often given to eat in India. If the night's maneuver had gone well, Calvert was to radio a code of "Link Sausage" back to headquarters.

At 2:30 a.m. on March 6—the morning of Calvert's thirty-first birthday—Mad Mike had no choice but to radio off a "Soya Link." Then, shortly after the transmission to India, the situation began to improve. As dawn arrived, and with the addition of burning smudge pots to delineate the relatively flat runway now bulldozed on the site, successive waves of gliders began landing in safety. By sunrise, thirty-seven gliders were on the ground at Broadway; eighteen had either crashed in Burma or force-landed back in India. Calvert had 350 men with him, plus two bulldozers and a jeep. He was now pleased to radio in a revision to his earlier message. The scene at Broadway had been upgraded to "Link Sausage."

Over the next five nights, nearly twelve thousand men, three thousand mules, multiple tons of equipment—including antiaircraft guns and artillery—and ample supplies of food glided to the earth at Broadway and at a second strip, code named "Chowringghee" (after Calcutta's central thoroughfare), which waited roughly sixty miles farther southeast. With just a few more precious days of preparation, the Chindits would be ready to join in with the Chinese and the Americans for the drive on "Mitch."

BUT AS THE CHINDITS readied for action, the combined Second and Third Battalions of Merrill's Marauders were about to walk into trouble. On March 15, they'd started deep into the Kumon Range, following the eroded Tanai River gorge upstream. The plan was still general: the Marauders were to move south through the mountains and emerge from them some eighty miles south, near the Japanese headquarters city of Kamaing in the Mogaung Valley. They would inspect the area for roads, trails, and communications sites, and establish roadblocks that would stop Japanese supply from moving north to the fighting against the X Force, which was entering the Mogaung Valley farther north.

On March 18, the Marauders finally encountered the Detachment 101 leader Vincent Curl and his army of three hundred Kachins near their village of Janpan. And, as orders from Stilwell were still forthcoming concerning specific locations for the roadblocks, Merrill called a rest break the following day. Then, on March 19, the world inside north Burma turned magical. In their jungle village, the Kachins treated the Second and Third Battalions' complement of nearly two thousand Marauders to the heights of native hospitality. Water buffalo were slaughtered, butchered, and roasted over fires. Gongs were struck and native dances performed in costumes decorated with bearskins and feathers. Merrill was presented with his own freshly slaughtered goat, and as the Kachins' traditional rice beer flowed, the American medics treated any and all sick villagers. For a day and a night, it was possible to believe the horrors of north Burma had all been a bad dream.

But the following morning, their orders now in from Stilwell, life for the Marauders regained its misery, and the Marauders and a few Kachin guides left the village for battle once again. Merrill ordered Second Battalion and the "Khaki" Combat Team from Third Battalion to proceed south, reconnoiter the trails leading into Mogaung Valley, and block the Kamaing Road in the valley at the little town of Inkangahtawng. Third Battalion's "Orange" Combat Team would remain behind to await a resupply airdrop.

On March 23, the Inkangahtawng force, led by Colonel McGee, had arrived at their objective, and advance patrols were soon encountering Japanese resistance in the village. To lay their block across the Kamaing Road north of Inkangahtawng, McGee took Second Battalion across the Mogaung River and as close to Inkangahtawng as he could, advising the Khaki team to remain on the far side of the river and in the relative safety of the mountains to protect the rear. After trying to surround the two Japanese platoons in Inkangahtawng and being repulsed, McGee selected his spot for the roadblock and dug in.

The following morning, just past dawn, the Japanese attacked with a ferocity not seen in weeks. For the Second Battalion, everything was wrong. Their foxhole positions fronted a thick stand of tall grass, and as Japanese mortar barrages began to fall, the grass prevented the Marauders from seeing the enemy. Then, with no warning, no whistle blowing, and no screams of "Banzai!" on the initial charge, the first wave of Japanese soldiers rushed out of their grassy cover.

At twenty paces, the Marauder guns opened up, and the Japanese began to fall. Soon, the enemy was getting dangerously close to the American perimeter. One Japanese lieutenant, Charlton Ogburn, Jr., said: "Kept on coming, crying '*Banzai!*' and waving his sword, even after he had been nearly cut in two by the .45-caliber slugs of a Tommy gun. He fell with his head on the edge of the Tommy gunner's foxhole, his sword severed."

Captain Fred Lyons was crawling through the underbrush to a gun post "when I saw the first wave. Big Japanese marines, fully six feet tall, wearing yellowish khaki uniforms that seemed to envelop them like gunny sacks." He slid into a foxhole and started shooting. With each new wave of attack, Lyons could see the strained looks on the opposition's faces, expressions that turned to shock and surprise as the American machine guns opened up. "One guy's rifle flew forward like a spear as he fell. Another guy sank to the ground, hit in the stomach."

Just ahead of where Lyons was positioned, a Japanese soldier made it inside the Marauder perimeter, jumping into a foxhole already occupied by a Marauder private named Ryan. Ryan grabbed the attacker's rifle, and they began to wrestle for control of the weapon, straining and pulling to break each other's grip. In the foxholes surrounding Ryan, everyone watched, afraid to shoot for fear of hitting the American. Then Ryan gave the gun a twist and the Japanese soldier fell free, leaped up to get out of the foxhole, and was met by the bullets from a half-dozen American weapons, killing him instantly.

As the day progressed, the carnage began to mount. By the fourth wave of Japanese attack, bodies were piled so high that the next wave of Japanese attackers was having trouble charging the Marauder positions for the Japanese dead beneath their feet. In one place, Lyons counted Japanese bodies seven deep. During a break in the fighting, Lieutenant Cadmo—who operated a Browing Automatic Rifle—had to sneak out of his foxhole and kick dead Japanese soldiers out of the way to clear his range. Before the day was out, sixteen different attack waves threw themselves upon the Marauders.

Knowing his stores of ammunition were low, unit commander Colonel McGee chose to keep his losses confined to the two dead and twelve wounded. He ordered the evacuation of the Kamaing Road blockade. It was a wise decision, since at that same moment—streaming out of Kamaing's headquarters garrison to the south—two battalions of Japanese troops were streaking across the valley floor toward the Kumon Range, trying to cut off the Marauders and keep control of the valley floor while protecting Kamaing's eastern flank.

With the Japanese now bearing down on the Second Battalion and Khaki Combat Team, McGee pushed everyone back up the trail and into the mountains, where they bivouacked for the night near the little outpost of Ngagahtawng. The next morning, they were on the move again, their goal being the jungle village of Auche in the foothills of the Kumon Range. To cover their flank, where two large jungle trails off the Mogaung Valley converged, Lt. Colonel Beech of Third Battalion directed a detachment led by First Lieutenant Logan Weston to delay the Japanese from chasing the Marauders into the jungle by providing resistance near where the trails met. As Weston and his men slowed the eight hundred or so attacking Japanese, and as the majority of the Marauders made Auche, Japanese artillery began to pound the little village, driving the Second Battalion and Khaki Combat Team farther up the trail to the hilltop village of Nhpum Ga. And with a light machine-gun squad, led by Corporal Warren Ventura, now providing resistance, the men of Second Battalion and Khaki Combat Team hurried up the trail for Nhpum Ga, shells falling all around them as they moved.

At Nhpum Ga, McGee and his men were met by Merrill, who—hearing of eight hundred heavily armed Japanese attackers coming his way—decided to split his forces. Second Battalion would establish a dug-in perimeter at Nhpum Ga, at twenty-eight hundred feet elevation. Both combat teams from Third Battalion—a group that also included Merrill, Hunter, and the Kachins—would remove themselves up the valley five miles farther north, to a smaller hamlet called Hsamsingyang, where they would establish a rice-field airstrip for supply and the evacuation of wounded.

For the Marauders Second Battalion, it was the first time they would dig in for a static, defensive battle, an idea even Merrill acknowledged was dicey. The Marauders were an offensive unit, built for fast-moving skirmishes and feints. They had no tanks or heavy artillery to defend themselves, and other than their hilltop high ground, they had nowhere to hide. Against a better-armed Japanese force, how long could they defend their position?

As Second Battalion finished the trenching of their hilltop fortress—an area four hundred yards long and perhaps two hundred yards wide—word began filtering back from scouts that the Japanese were already maneuvering up the hillside and slowly encircling it.

The Japanese, in fact, had moved with remarkable speed. Within hours—and following a skirmish with a Marauder unit—the Japanese had taken control of the spring-fed water hold just behind the village, the sole source of water for all of Nhpum Ga.

By nightfall, Nhpum Ga's hilltop was completely surrounded. For the roughly eleven hundred Marauders stuck on that hilltop, there was no route of escape and, worse, no land-based means of getting supplies or water. Then, slowly but relentlessly, behind barrages of light "knee mortars" and 70- and 75-millimeter high-trajectory Howitzers, the Japanese began to scale Nhpum Ga's slopes. The Marauders were now forced to maintain their circular "wagon wheel" perimeter of trenches day and night. Rifle fire popped at any hour, as did jarring bursts from both Marauder and Japanese machine guns. But it was the constant mortar and artillery fire that began to wear at the Marauders' nerves and what was left of their morale. Explosions boomed endlessly.

"The sneaking, crawling Japs weren't so bad . . . eventually we could spot them," said Captain Fred Lyons. "But the mortar fire they were lobbing inside the wagon wheel was raising hob with our supplies and killing off animals and men."

By the third morning of the siege, though the Japanese were being kept at bay on the slopes of Nhpum Ga by the American positions, seventy-five mules had been killed by explosions and gunfire, and the animals lay rotting among the Marauder foxholes. In another two days, the number of dead mules had risen to 112, and the stench from the decomposing animals, the Marauders' inadequate sanitation, and the Japanese dead that now lay downhill of Nhpum Ga's perimeter was forcing some of the Marauders to vomit or dry-heave constantly.

With no water available, what few Kachins had been left behind at Nhpum Ga were instructing the Marauders to suck the moist joints from the hilltop's bamboo trees. Then, as bamboo inside the perimeter ran out, the Marauders began to drink stagnant water found in elephant tracks and pig and elephant wallows in the hilltop's mud. By day five, there was no water left at all. They would go another full day before five hundred gallons of water—in sausage-shaped plastic bottles—were individually parachuted onto the hilltop via air transport from Ledo.

And all the time, Japanese rifle and mortar fire took more men. Japanese snipers were now climbing trees downhill of Nhpum Ga's perimeter and, remaining hidden until they had a clear shot, they were popping off Marauders one by one. At one point, while running a communication line between foxholes, Fred Lyons learned precisely what being hunted is like. "I had gone out to lay a line of telephone wire when the puff of an explosive bullet kicked up the dirt a couple of yards from my feet," he remembered. "I flopped and looked around but could see nothing. Another puff kicked up the dirt. I wriggled and twisted, pulling my wire with me. Still another puff. Five times the sniper, concealed in a tree somewhere near the clearing, shot at me. And five times he missed."

Because of all the putrid dead men and animals, the Marauders had now given Nhpum Ga a new nickname: "Maggot Hill." But despite the new and jocular designation, events were, by turns, surreal and nightmarish. During one night, a groggy Japanese soldier wandered inside the American perimeter, obviously lost and looking for his old foxhole. He was shot through the head and left on the mud to rot. Another night, when three figures wandered into camp, they, too, were shot by Marauder sentries. Unfortunately, they were Americans returning from a reconnaissance expedition. One of them, Lieutenant Brendan Lynch, was mortally wounded and died two days later.

Said Marauder Joseph Ganlin of the siege:

Here's what I remember about Nhpum Ga: A thirteen-day blur. Nothing comes straight to mind. A dead Jap, six feet tall, laying in the mud in his strange yellow khaki uniform. I remember having nothing to drink. Thirsty all the time. Very little to eat, sometimes just two K ration biscuits for a whole day. The Japanese had longer bayonets than we did. Their bayonets were hooked with barbs on the end, too. And there was always shooting . . . and always explosions. The dead animals, stinking so much it would make your throat close or make you just plain throw up. And the maggots squirming on the bodies. I was obviously in a daze, because none of it seemed to bother me too much. By the time we got surrounded on Nhpum Ga, we had been in four or five major battles and at least thirty skirmishes, and I was dead on my feet. The only thing keeping me—all of us—going was that the Japanese wanted to kill us. They meant to kill all of us. We were stuck on that hilltop, and all we could do was keep going.

After a week, as ammunition began to run low, the Marauders once again made successful radio contact with Ledo—and, just as their first call for water had been, this new request was quickly answered. Help, in the form of ammunition, would soon be on its way. And, word had it, the first parachute drop was to be a planeload of very useful hand grenades. Unfortunately, as the drone of cargo-aircraft engines grew close and the boxes of ammunition slid from the plane's drop doors, the parachuted weapons drifted on the wind and fell wide of Nhpum Ga, ending up in the jungle surrounding the hilltop. Within hours, the Japanese were showering American-made grenades upon the Marauders.

On another drop, cooks in Ledo filled an entire transport plane with boxes of fried chicken after learning that the Marauders had been living on coffee and cigarettes for eight days. As the airplane flew over Nhpum Ga's hilltop, boxes of sweet-smelling chicken drifted to the muddy green earth beneath folds of white silk. The Marauders set up a mess area in the center of their hilltop bastion, and—leaving a skeleton crew of sentries along the perimeter—every man who could forgot his duties in the pursuit of fried chicken. "With the fighting underway only three hundred yards off," Fred Lyons said, "it was a strange sight to see a bunch of battle-worn GIs elbowing one another to be first in line for a leg or a breast." And yet, despite exhaustion and encircling Japanese attackers, the Americans were managing to hold their own.


OF ALL THE WEAPONS and supplies the Marauders at Nhpum Ga had at their disposal, none were proving more valuable than Second Battalion's Nisei interpreter, Sergent Roy Matsumoto. This son of Japanese-Americans—his grandfather had emigrated to California, from Hiroshima, Japan, around 1900—Matsumoto had been a Long Beach, California, grocery deliveryman before the war. Then, in 1941—at the age of twenty-eight—his bank accounts were seized and he was arrested and sent to a Japanese internment camp in Jerome, Arkansas (where he was incarcerated as an "enemy alien"). "Right after the war started," Matsumoto says, "we were rounded up and taken to a temporary camp at Santa Anita Racetrack in Los Angeles, then they sent us with all the Japanese from the Los Angeles area to Arkansas." In the fall of 1942, however, a recruiting officer arrived at the camp asking for Japanese-American Niseis to help the war effort, and Masumoto joined on.

"We went to Camp Savage in Minnesota," he recalls, "for military language school. Then we went to Camp Shelby Mississippi for basic training, and after returning to Camp Savage from basic, I was one of the members of the fourteen-man language team headed for Burma. We took a forty-day trip to Bombay, then we were shipped to Wingate's Chindit jungle warfare school." Since arriving in CBI, Matsumoto—a man incarcerated just two years earlier as a suspected "enemy alien"—had proven his patriotic worth several times.

Now, at Nhpum Ga, Matsumoto spent his nights running from foxhole to foxhole, then crawling forward into the underbrush and listening to the Japanese, who were coming so close their conversations were audible. One night, Matsumoto decided to crawl downhill, dangerously close to a Japanese foxhole, where two Imperial Army soldiers were talking.

"It was total dark, and they couldn't see me," he recalls. "And I crawled maybe fifteen yards away and I began to listen. They were just talking. Like all of the Eighteenth Division, they were from Kyushu Island. I'd learned that dialect when I was delivering vegetables back in California. I'd had several people from Kyushu on my route. They were talking about all the same things we talked about—what they were going to do when the war was over. They were saying how they missed their wives and about the kinds of chickens they were going to raise when they got home . . . I was so close, I could see the flicker of the stars in their eyes. It was very dark. Their eyes were one of the few things I could see well. That whole night was strange. It seemed to go on and on, you know? Even now, I couldn't tell you how long I was down there, listening."

After a long time lying still in the darkness, a Japanese commander crawled to the soldier's foxhole. He informed the soldiers that, at sunrise, there would be a full-frontal attack on the Americans. It would be against the Marauders' weakest part of the perimeter, where a steep cliff was flanked on both sides by a flatter incline. If the Japanese attacked on the inclines, the Marauders weren't going to be able to defend their outcrop position. "They had us," Matsumoto says. "They had us and they knew it. They were going to take that position in the morning. And, boy, they were ready to do it."

As the commander left the two soldiers, Matsumoto slipped slowly back from the foxhole, and—when a safe distance away—he stood and ran to inform Lieutenant Edward McLogan, whose platoon occupied the weak perimeter zone. McLogan withdrew his men, booby-trapped the foxholes, and quietly dug in a camouflaged wall of automatic weapons on a slope above their old position.

At dawn, with cries of "Banzai!" and "Die Joe! Die!" the Japanese attacked behind a wall of thrown hand grenades. As roughly forty-five Japanese rushed from the jungle—their khaki uniforms and wrap leggings dirty from the mud—they threw more grenades, bayoneted empty foxholes, and fired wildly up the hill. Then, when they were fifteen yards from the hidden Americans, sixty Marauder automatic weapons opened fire. The entire line of Japanese soldiers fell to the ground, dead. When a second wave swept forward from the jungle, they hit the dirt after growing confused by the empty foxholes and the piles of Japanese dead. It was then that Matsumoto began to scream: *"Tosugekinini! Tokkan! Susume! Susume! SUSUME!"* ("Prepare to advance! Advance. Charge! Charge! Charge!")

The second wave of Japanese rose to their feet, stared at one another, and began running up the hill, directly into a storm of American machine-gun and Browning Automatic Rifle fire. When the siege was over, fifty-four Japanese were dead, including two officers. Matsumoto added, "It's impossible to estimate how many of them we wounded." For his efforts, Roy Matsumoto, the former "enemy alien," would eventually be awarded the Legion of Merit.

AFTER A WEEK at Nhpum Ga, the days and nights of unquenched bloodletting oozed together. With killing as ferocious as anything going on in the Pacific's island-hopping campaign—only in a reversal of roles between the Americans and the Japanese—the Marauders defended their position as the Imperial Army pushed relentlessly closer. And all that drove the Marauders on was the hope that, true to radio calls, they would soon be getting reinforcements from Third Battalion. And the Marauders would also soon be getting a command change. In the early days of the siege at Nhpum Ga, General Merrill's heart condition—aggravated by the month and a half of hard living in the jungle—had left him so weak that Stilwell ordered him evacuated to India. For the forseeable future of Merrill's Marauders, Colonel Hunter was now in charge.

Finally, on the afternoon of April 4—and after what seemed like endless waiting—Third Battalion had worked down the valley from Hamsangyang, announcing their arrival at the siege with a barrage of recently supplied mortar and artillery shells, pounding the Japanese encirclement troops from behind with ferocious power. Knowing that the Japanese usually withdrew during shelling, Hunter had Third Battalion's men creep forward through the jungle as far as they could, then ordered all available mortar rounds and Howitzer shells dumped on the Japanese encirclement positions. As the Japanese pulled back, Hunter ordered the firing to stop, and he sent his men on a footrace to take the Japanese trenches and foxholes. The ruse worked, and the Americans of Third Battalion were two hundred yards closer to Nhpum Ga's summit.

Still, despite the Third Battalion's leap closer to Nhpum Ga, April 4 had not been a good day. On Nhpum Ga's hilltop, only seventy pack mules were still alive, the last stores of blood plasma were being used on the wounded, and at dawn the Japanese had taken a heavy machine-gun position using grenades. Word came by radio that First Battalion was now on a forced march down the Hukawng Valley and into the Mogaung Valley to double-encircle Nhpum Ga and drive off the Japanese—but they were still days away. And on the hilltop, the scene remained unchanged, with the ragged Americans barely hanging on. High in a tree, the body of a dead Marauder dangled like a horrific marionette: he'd had the misfortune to be too close to a five-hundred-pound bomb dropped on the Japanese by an American P-51 dive bomber, and the explosion had flung him into the branches. Everyone was sick, thirsty, unshaven, and exhausted. Because they'd been drinking the water from elephant wallows and footprints, nearly all the Marauders now had dysentery, and many had cut the seams from the seats of their trousers, so they could merely squat down to relieve themselves.

The darkly kaleidoscopic days and nights kept coming: explosions, mud, shooting, illness, malarial fevers, more explosions, hot sun, cold rain, and always an enemy creeping closer. Then, on April 7, Third Battalion radioed Nhpum Ga that they were within five hundred yards of the hilltop, but the intervening distance between was completely controlled by the Japanese, who were defending it bitterly, with rifle and mortar fire bristling nonstop.

Late that afternoon—after a seven-day march—a long line of First Battalion reinforcements became visible to the northwest, making their way down the trail from Hamsangyang. In the drawing darkness, the reinforcements began to fan out around the Japanese and Nhpum Ga. And as the fresher Allied soldiers began their double encirclement of Nhpum Ga's explosion-pocked hilltop, the Japanese—recognizing that they would be forced to fight front and rear battles against now-equal numbers—began slipping away into the jungle.

April 9, 1944, was Easter Sunday. By the time dawn had arrived, the Japanese presence at Nhpum Ga was giving in, with the retreating Japanese putting up only skirmishes. Pushing toward the hilltop village from Hamsangyang, Third Battalion and First Battalion encountered occasional sniper fire, but mostly they found, in the assessment of Charlton Ogburn, "dead Japs everywhere." The thirteen-day siege was finally over. As Hunter and his men widened their base perimeter, they began to assess the losses. The defense of Nhpum Ga had cost the Marauders 59 dead and 314 wounded. But on the slopes of Nhpum Ga, as mop-up parties moved through the jungle, they found upward of four hundred dead Japanese.

Colonel Hunter radioed Ledo: he wanted five hundred pounds of chloride of lime air-dropped in right away, to cover the decaying soldiers and lessen the stench. He also ordered his men to turn flamethrowers on the dead mules to kill the maggots. With the smell of burned flesh and hair filling the air, the interment of the dead soldiers and mules began. Each of the American casualties was buried in the center of Nhpum Ga, their dog tags fixed to headstone crosses of bamboo. As the burials continued, Hunter radioed headquarters for drops of new uniforms, water, and a ten-to-one supply of rations. He also ordered up cases of blood plasma and dysentery medicines.

Before long, crates of relief-giving goods were parachuting in from the skies. There were banquets. Men bathed. Occasionally a Japanese sniper or probing unit would push close to the Marauder positions, but Merrill's and Hunter's men were now so used to the harassment they slapped the enemy back like flies. The Americans were still sick with dysentery and malaria and Naga sores, but thanks to the food and the victory, they felt that their mission was a complete success. Back in India, they had been told by commanders in Wingate's Chindit divisions that their time in the field would be a *maximum* of ninety days. As they toted up their time in the field, they realized that their mission was now approaching that delightful number. The Marauders felt sure they were going home.

THEN AFTER SEVERAL DAYS of rest near Nhpum Ga, a horrible rumor began to circulate through the Marauder camps. The gossip was unthinkable, and no one wanted to believe it might be true: the Marauders couldn't be sent on to take Myitkyina.

All three battalions of Marauders were exhausted. They had fought well and bravely. They had bested the Japanese in some of the most torturous jungle on earth, and their ninety days were almost up. And anyway, they were already too far south. A jungle hike to attack "Mitch" would require twenty miles of backtracking between Jambu Bum and the Kumon Range, then a near-vertical eastward scramble over the peaks of the Kumon Range themselves.

Moods in the 5307th began to turn sour, however, when several high-ranking officers from Ledo flew in to check on the Marauders' physical condition. Then the men learned that Colonel Hunter had already detailed an advance party to survey a trail over the Kumon Range. They also learned that General Merrill would soon return, and that he was to be commanding a special force made up of the roughly fifteen hundred Marauders who remained, two Chinese regiments, and three hundred Kachin guerrillas. The Marauders' third mission was beginning to take shape.

Slowly intelligence about mission three began to leak out. It was to be called "End Run" and it was, in Stilwell's estimation, the killing stroke against Japanese forces in northern Burma. As Stilwell's X Force kept pushing General Tanaka's main Japanese Eighteenth Division south out of the Hukawng and Mogaung Valleys, they would be so preoccupied that they wouldn't reinforce Myitkyina. And if the X Force pushed hard enough, they might even draw some Japanese battalions away from "Mitch" to help what was perceived to be the main fighting for the last Japanese foothold in the Hukawng and Mogaung Valleys, the town of Kamaing. With the Japanese diverted by the Kamaing fighting, the Marauders and the other units would sweep in from the northwest, engage the Japanese for Myitkyina, and take it by force—beginning with the critical Japanese supply post at the airfield on the northwest edge of town.

Once Myitkyina was held by the Allies, Stilwell's thinking went, the Japanese would have no choice but a full retreat. And with the Japanese driven out, the mission's long-deferred primary goal—the reopening of the combined Ledo-Burma Road—could be undertaken as soon as the road-building engineers caught up.

Like it or not, the Marauders realized, they were headed for Myitkyina.

AMONG THE MARAUDERS, troop morale plummeted to an all-time low. Though now well fed, they remained weak, sick, and pushed-over-the-edge tired. Their numbers had been halved by fighting and jungle disease. And the usual lifeblood of any army unit—colors, insignia, and battlefield promotions—remained completely forgone.

To the Marauders, says Charlton Ogburn, Jr., even the mention of Stilwell's name became "a red flag to a bull." The Marauders were truly exhausted, and given the lack of concern being shown by Stilwell for their fighting spirit—he hadn't visited them since Shingbwiyang—they believed he was more concerned with the Chinese X Force than with his own Americans. Furthering this impression, when Colonel Hunter suggested to command that his officers be awarded oak-leaf clusters—to show successive decoration for exceptional work—Stilwell responded by telling Hunter that his men should "spend more time fighting and less time worrying about promotions." (Stilwell, faced with a fractious coalition command, liable to come apart at the slightest show of favoritism, understood precisely what he was doing. But it was a recognition that did not make his seeming indifference any easier for him to conscience. In fact, he felt awful about the Marauders, but he cared more for the success of the entire North Burma Campaign.)

On April 28, after almost three weeks of rest, the first Marauder units and their new Chinese and Kachin reinforcements set out for a long-unused trail through the peaks of the Kumon Range, with, in Ogburn's characterization, "that what-the-hell-did-you-expect-anyway spirit that served the 5307th in place of morale." Despite the Kachins' warning that such a large force could never crest Naura Hkyat, the sixty-one-hundred-foot pass along the mountain's spine, they went. At times they were forced to crawl on hands and knees up the steep slope. To Roy Matsumoto: "It was unbelievable. Sometimes you'd be there, hanging on the mountainside, your hands clutching a root or small tree, which was all that kept you from sliding down the mountain. We were climbing straight up, like mountain climbers. But we were carrying lots of weight and, well, we were exhausted. But, somehow, we kept going."

More steps had to be cut for the used-up mules, which continued slipping and falling, sometimes breaking their necks. Each time a mule died,

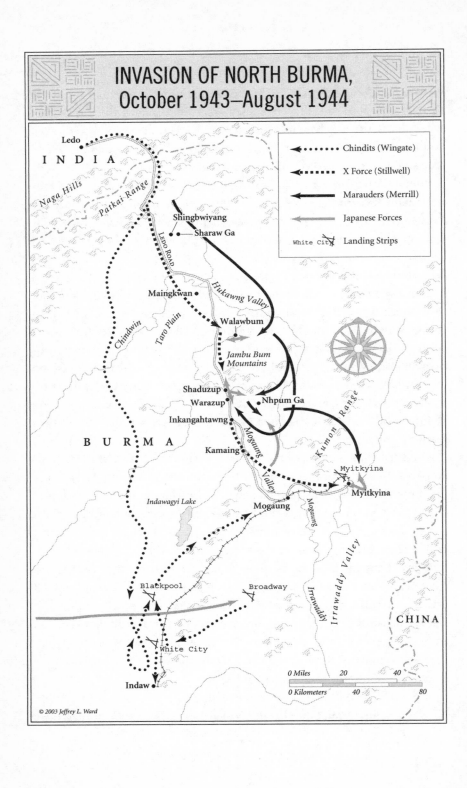

# INVASION OF NORTH BURMA,
## October 1943–August 1944

**Legend:**
- Chindits (Wingate)
- X Force (Stillwell)
- Marauders (Merrill)
- Japanese Forces
- White City ✕ Landing Strips

INDIA

Ledo

Naga Hills

Paikai Range

Ledo Road

Shingbwiyang
Sharaw Ga

Maingkwan

Hukawng Valley

Chindwin

Taro Plain

Walawbum

Jambu Bum
Mountains

Shaduzup
Warazup
Inkangahtawng

Nhpum Ga

Kumon Range

BURMA

Kamaing

Mogaung Valley

Myitkyina
Myitkyina

Indawagyi Lake

Mogaung

Mogaung

Blackpool

Broadway

Irrawaddy Valley

Irrawaddy

CHINA

White City

Indaw

0 Miles    20    40
0 Kilometers    40    80

© 2003 Jeffrey L. Ward

the unit would have to stop, redistribute the dead animal's load, and abandon all supplies that couldn't be repacked. In a single day, Third Battalion lost twenty mules and was forced to abandon more than four thousand pounds of equipment in the jungle. As the march progressed, discipline fell to zero. Men often wandered into bivouac camps hours late, and instead of boiling water to purify it—or dropping purifying halazone pills into the canteens they filled in rivers—some Marauders were simply swallowing the halazone and washing it down with untreated water.

Two days later, on May 1, after a few spitting drizzles, the skies began to rain steadily—and the near-vertical mud of the Kumon Range grew slippery as grease. "We were scarcely ever dry," Ogburn said of the march. "When the rain stopped and the sun came out, evaporation would begin. The land steamed. The combination of heat and moisture was smothering . . . For those weakened by disease, it was too much. For the first time, you began to pass men fallen out beside the trail."

For six days, the Marauders were virtually out of touch. And Stilwell, for all his belief in his American forces' superiority and hardiness, was now stewing, too. "Depression days, commander's worries," he wrote in his diary for May, 1, 1944." I start them off for Myitkyina, it rains, the resistance grows here [for the X Force]. Why didn't I use them on our front? Is the gap too big? Will they meet a reinforced garrison? Does it mean we'll fail on both sides, instead of only one? Can I get them out? Are the Japs being sucked toward Mogaung or . . . staying in Mitch? Etc., etc., and nothing can be done about it. The die is cast, and it's sink or swim. But the nervous wear and tear is terrible."

# Chapter 13

IN THE MESSY, sprawling, grand sweep of World War II, the spring of 1944 was a time pregnant with change. In Russia, Odessa and Sebastapol had been recaptured from the retreating Wehrmacht by Stalin's Red Army, while—all across southern England—Allied forces were preparing to storm the German-defended beaches of Normandy in Operation Overlord (a full-frontal attack virtually certain to have the words *blood-smeared* etched all over it).

In the Pacific, U.S. air raids off carriers at sea continued to pound isolated, Japanese-held islands like Truk, the Solomons, and—on a larger scale—New Guinea into ruin, but the Pacific island-hopping campaign toward Tokyo was still slow going. In Burma, Stilwell's Chinese X Force had yet to clear out the Hukawng and Mogaung Valleys, and the American soldiers of Merrill's Marauders were still stumbling through northern Burma's mountainous jungle with no clear end in sight.

And like the Marauders, for Orde Wingate's Chindits in Burma, the spring of 1944 was proving miserable. After landing at Broadway in early March, the Chindits had quickly fortified their forward base, then they began sending out attack columns. Mike Calvert's unit, called the Seventy-seventh Infantry Brigade, was the first off. And, after taking a few days to prepare, they went on foot to the southeast, into the dank, dark, primeval jungle of the Kaukkwe River Valley, one valley south and east of the Mogaung. Their mission's orders were straightforward: as they had done during the first Chindit raid, Calvert's men were to blow the Mandalay-Myitkyina Railway at its bridges and disrupt Japanese lines of supply and communication.

Even as they set out, Calvert's Seventy-seventh Infantry met with resistance, especially at a small cleared hill topped by a gilded pagoda not thirty miles southwest of Broadway. There, after a planning session in the deep jungle, the Chindits made a surprise charge from the thick forest, with the Japanese, in Calvert's words, "entering into the spirit of the thing," fixing their bayonets and charging back. "There, at the top of the hill, about fifty yards square, an extraordinary melee took place, everyone shooting, bayoneting, kicking at everyone else, rather like an officer's guest night."

Soon after, that same night, Calvert's men began blowing spans of the railway, and Calvert—staying put near his newly captured Pagoda Hill—decided to establish another Chindit base. This new stronghold, eight hundred yards wide by one thousand yards long, was ideal for his mobile army. There was ample water, a large field into which he could cut a series of airstrips, and, at its center, a series of small, wooded hills, each thirty to fifty feet tall, that would provide cover. As air drops of food and weapons began to rain down on this newest base, Calvert's men dubbed this new bastion "White City," for the pale parachute cloth that soon festooned the area's trees, and which the Chindits retrieved and used as shade against the hot tropical sun.

As Calvert set to fortifying White City, a second attack column, the Sixteenth British Infantry Brigade, led by Brigadier Bernard Fergusson—another hero of the first Chindit raid the year before—had pushed even farther southeast and set about disrupting the Japanese garrison at the railroad town of Indaw and its outlying village of Thetkegyin. According to Wingate's and Slim's plan, pummeling Indaw and Thetkegyin were crucial tactical maneuvers, since the Japanese were using the two towns—plus Indaw's rail station and two new airstrips—as staging areas for their attack on India. Using Chindits who had been flown in to Chowinghee and, in addition, a unit that had hiked south through the jungle all the way from Ledo, Fergusson began his attack on March 26 by blockading the main road leading west out of Indaw toward India. A few miles west of town, the Chindits spread out and dug foxholes over a well-vegetated, thousand-foot stretch following the road's northern shoulder. On the road's opposite side, they pegged an even longer strip of trip-wired hand grenades to the earth, intended to wound or kill any Japanese who tried to escape their ambush on foot. Then, at each end of the thousand-foot road-block, Fergusson positioned at least one flamethrower, which would be used to set the first and last troop-carrying trucks afire.

At 2:30 a.m., word came from sentries watching Indaw that a huge, thirty-plus convoy of trucks was headed for the Chindit snare. Nearly all of the vehicles were inside the trap when the flamethrowers sluiced their strings of fire across the road, turning several trucks to infernos. The Chindits opened fire on the trucks with machine guns and as many as six hundred dozing Japanese soldiers—startled by the attack—leaped from the backs of the trucks and, predictably, ran for the opposite edge of the road, where they began setting off the grenades. Inside the explosions, and with Chindit small-arms fire riddling the air, the Japanese began taking cover beneath their vehicles; the Chindits began killing them with hand grenades. Few Japanese managed to escape, and, at dawn, as the Chindits examined their spoils—there were hundreds of Japanese dead on the road—they were equally thrilled to find they'd also destroyed a payroll truck filled with money. The Chindits, amazingly, hadn't lost a single man. A few hours later, when a fresh force of Japanese out of Indaw counterattacked, six of Fergusson's men were killed before the Chindits could withdraw to the hilly jungle north of the road.

North of Indaw, the morning brought more fighting. There, Fergusson had sent several units of the "hiked in" Chindits along the fifteen-mile road north out of Indaw toward Thetkegyin, to probe for large encampments. After a few hours of walking up the road, the Chindits suddenly saw the buildings of Thetkegyin in the distance. As the Chindit signalman Philip Sharpe recalled:

> As we pressed on towards Thetkegyin there was an air of foreboding. All was quiet around us and as the tension increased, the only sounds were the hoofs of the mules as they scuffed the hard-baked track, and the odd nervous remark. The scrub [along the roadside] became more sparse, the sun became unbearably hot and our shirts were sodden with sweat . . . After two hours we halted in the scrub on the edge of an expanse of paddy . . . at the other side of the paddy we saw the huts of the village of Thetkegyin. Almost at once, sporadic firing broke out to our left and within minutes became a

fusillade of shots with long bursts, as machine-gun fire was exchanged with the Japs. A hail of bullets whistled fan-wise overhead, ricocheting off the trees. One mortar bomb exploded between our two signal mules and one was torn apart by the blast, the blood splattering all around us. Our wireless set was reduced to pieces of torn metal. Simultaneously, two yellow lorries pulled up with a cloud of dust no more than fifty yards away. How the Japs failed to see us was amazing, because we were not in solid jungle. They ran into the thickets behind us, presumably to encircle the rest of our column. I vividly remember that some had machine guns, and all were wearing white vests, jungle green slacks and soft PT (physical training) shoes. They were huge fellows, nothing like the Japanese we had expected.

The battle, too, would resemble nothing they'd anticipated. For several days, the Japanese troops at Thetkegyin—reinforced by more men streaming north from Indaw—would attempt encirclements of the Chindits, but the Chindits would slip eastward into the thicker jungle, regroup, and attack the Japanese again. Fergusson's Chindits, however, were overmatched, and every hour brought casualties. After two days of nonstop skirmishing, Fergusson ordered his men to withdraw and move north through the jungle. They would create another new fortress, to be called Aberdeen, north and west of White City.

BY THE TIME the successful drive to disrupt Indaw and Thetkegyin was finished, the Chindits had been in the jungle for three weeks. Malaria, parasites, and jungle fevers were beginning to take a toll. Added to this, on March 24, the Chindits were dealt a morale-shattering blow: Wingate was dead. During a flight to India after a troop-morale visit at Broadway, the Mitchell B-25 bomber Wingate had been riding in suddenly plunged into the Naga Hills west of Imphal, killing everyone aboard. The crash was so violent that only Wingate's battered Wolsley pith helmet and some letters from home survived intact; Wingate's body was charred beyond recognition.

At White City, Calvert was stunned. "Now he was dead," Calvert said of the moment. "We were still numb from the shock. We could not yet understand or appreciate the consequences. It was like going smoothly along in an aeroplane when the navigator comes in and says 'The pilot has died of heart failure. There is no copilot and none of us knows what to do.' "

The Chindits were rudderless. To take Wingate's place, General Slim tapped Major General Joe Lentaigne—one of Wingate's unit commanders— passing over Calvert because, in Slim's assessment, "Mad Mike" was too aggressive and erratic: too much like Wingate himself. Still, no matter who had been chosen to lead the Chindits, the new commander would always stand in Orde Wingate's shadow. Without Wingate, could the Chindits be Chindits? Would Lentaigne drive them to succeed? Or would they flounder—possibly with disastrous results?

There was only one way to know, and the time had come to find out. They had to push on.

AS APRIL 1944 ARRIVED, the Chindits continued their struggle north, snaking and fighting through a jungle that was thick with the enemy. Beyond disrupting Japanese planning, their goal was to meet with Stilwell's X Force along the Kamaing Road. Instead, every direction the Chindits moved, they found only bloody conflict. The Japanese were ambushing Chindit advance parties anytime they went out, and as the Japanese began to surround White City, command in India gave orders to evacuate the base and secure another glider-landing clearing in the jungle forty miles farther north. The new base, designated "Blackpool," was strategically perfect. It was situated in a narrow valley, and both the Mandalay-Myitkyina Railroad and the main road to north Burma from Mandalay ran through Blackpool's boundaries. If they could take and hold the base, the full flow of Japanese goods and troops would be cut off from the south.

But as the Chindits began to relocate, both the Japanese army and the early arrival of Burma's summer monsoon refused to cooperate. In the rain, the Chindits quickly secured Blackpool's perimeter, cutting off the main road from Mandalay and the rail line. But after the Chindits blockaded the valley, the Japanese and the weather parried their every step to further fortify Blackpool or broaden their attack. When an airstrip was carved into a Blackpool rice paddy, the Japanese moved in antiaircraft guns and blasted down any plane that attempted to fly on or off the base. When mule-carried artillery was ordered in by Lentaigne to defend Blackpool, the mules were slowed when they couldn't descend the muddy, three-thousand-foot mountain trails into the valley.

The jungle was also continuing to destroy the Chindits' health. Malaria and dysentery had now depleted the men's energy and—as a complication to the malaria—jaundice was setting in. "The whites of my eyes turned brown and I was passing what looked like strong tea," recalls Lieutenant Geoffrey Straight of the Chindit First Battalion. "I tried to eat, but everything placed to my mouth totally turned my stomach. The only item I could eat for a fortnight was the fruit bar in the breakfast rations."

Like the Marauders defending Nhpum Ga, the Chindits were an offensive force that was now being put in a defensive position. As the buildup inside Blackpool continued, Japanese patrols began to press increasingly against the base's perimeter. Each day brought heavier amounts of enemy artillery on the Chindit positions. Then, on May 19, after several weeks of preparation, the Japanese unleashed a huge field artillery bombardment on Blackpool, efficiently knocking out the Chindits' few cannon positions and taking casualties. Several Chindit units—including Lentaigne's Twenty-sixth column—were blown to bits.

As the day thundered on, Japanese aircraft started bombing the Chindit positions inside Blackpool with variations of "tree burst" barrages. But now, rather than firing 81-millimeter mortar rounds into the foliage above the Chindit billets, Japanese aircraft were flying low over the units and laying out strings of "parachute bombs" that drifted slowly to earth, exploding when their delicately set detonators nestled into the treetops or the muddy earth.

The siege for Blackpool would reach its climax on May 23. Following a day of bombing and shelling, the Japanese slammed into the eastern perimeter of the bastion's boundary at sunset, overrunning an artillery position and an antiaircraft emplacement. Through the night, Japanese reinforcements streamed inside the breach, and—accompanied by the constant crackle of small-arms fire—artillery rounds continued to fall on the Chindit positions on either side of the break. By dawn, a larger-than-expected Japanese force had taken control of the area, and they were working their way deeper inside Blackpool. When Chindit outer units began to radio that Japanese troops were also now massing on several ridges just outside Blackpool, calls from Chindit field command began for a tactical withdrawal.

But if the Chindit hilltop positions around Blackpool were now pulling back, at the remaining positions inside Blackpool's flat plain, the onslaught was growing overwhelming—and no easy route for escape presented itself. A Chindit senior medical officer, "Doc" Desmond Whyte, later recalled just how ferocious the last spasms of the night's counterattack had been: "In some sixty minutes, three hundred shells exploded within the block perimeter, wreaking havoc among men and animals. We dug ourselves out of the mud to rescue what we could [and found that] the jungle birds had burst into song after the din, a strange contrast . . . The main dressing station was becoming unmanageable with helpless wounded, some critical; and we blessed the inventor of tubunic morphine."

May 24 began with its sunrise obscured by monsoon rains. Sheets of water poured from the clouds and lightning ripped the skies. The roar of thunder accompanied by the din of shelling, and another call for the evacuation of Blackpool came in. Surrounded by the Japanese, Doc Whyte, his men, and all possible casualties were ordered to withdraw north from the valley floor by any means possible. Soon—with nineteen men laid out on stretchers and thirty dead having to be left behind in the trench that was functioning as Blackpool's infirmary and morgue—a line of stretcher bearers, medics, and walking wounded began toward a ridgeline to the north of Blackpool's clearing.

"We carried the remainder [of the patients with us], one helping another, up the muddy hill," Whyte recalled. "The shells were tearing men and animals apart . . . Enemy snipers had taken up positions on either side of the only track possible. As we stumbled and slithered upward, the blinded men tied in a line by lengths of cloth, my ear rang as a shot hit a tree beside me. Heavy monsoon rain was falling. I half spun round as a bullet went through my medical pack, scattering my string of casualties. We made the first ridge and somehow got over the top, awaiting the inevitable attack from the enemy. Why the Japanese failed to follow up and finish off the remainder of our force remains a mystery."

Despite troop losses, illness, and the abandonment of Blackpool, the Chindits kept struggling north toward Stilwell, Sun, and the X Force. But because of the wounded they were now carrying and the rainy mud of the season, the push north was agonizingly slow. For the Chindits, triage was replacing momentum. They were behind enemy lines and they were increasingly helpless.

———

IN MAY 1944, everywhere Joseph Stilwell looked he saw problems. The Marauders, now on their way to battle for Myitkyina, had all but disappeared into the Kumon Range. His X Force was stalled north of Kamaing, and though he kept ordering General Sun Li-jen and his troops to attack the Japanese stronghold, the Chinese wouldn't drive forward in sufficient numbers to force a Japanese withdrawal. And the Chindits had sustained so many casualties they were unable to distract the Japanese from the rear.

On an operational level, Stilwell's life was no more settled. The radio buzzed constantly with summonses from Mountbatten's headquarters in Ceylon and Chiang's residence in Chungking, directives that Stilwell deflected by ordering his trusty and able second in command, Dan Sultan, to attend to. Until the campaign for Myitkyina was over, Stilwell had decided, he was staying put. He was gaunt, pale, and, on many days, so bereft of physical energy all he was able to write in his diary was "sick." On the days when he felt strong enough to visit command posts in the X Force forward areas, the exertion would flatten him. "Fell up the hill into CP, exhausted . . . No wind, no legs . . . Felt like an old man when I staggered in," he wrote in his diary on May 8. He also began to sleep even less than his usual four or five hours a night, since anytime he fell into a deep sleep he now dreamed of frantically diving underwater in search of his drowned children. By day, he was afflicted with constant stomach cramps and abdominal pain. The only thing keeping him upright and moving, he wrote in his diary, was his mission, which he felt the soldiers under his command understood in a way officials in Washington, London, and Chungking never would.

When the CBI theater newspaper, called *Roundup*, published an analysis of the theater's activities thus far, it ended with this assessment of its commander: "Someday when the war is only a filthy memory, the whole story of Stilwell in Asia will be told, the epic of an unpretentious man who went forth sword in hand and slew the dragons of adversity in their dens."

The review, it is said, is one of the few bits of information during the North Burma Campaign that made Vinegar Joe smile.

FOR THE MARAUDERS, no matter what was happening to the X Force and the Chindits, their mission trudged blindly on. On April 28 and 30, with General Merrill having established a base at Naubum, the Third and First

Marauder Battalions moved out, followed behind on May 7 by Second Battalion, which was still patching its wounds. By May 3, Marauder First Battalion summited the Kumon Range at Naura Hkyat, finding that the hillsides on the mountain's far slopes were even steeper and more densely jungled than those they'd already come across. Their only relief, in fact, came from the jungle's uninhabitable remoteness, which meant there were no Japanese troops to fight. To Nisei Roy Matsumoto, "it was a long, long, hot and slow walk. Hot and wet. Sometimes, we'd be crawling on our hands and knees, grasping at roots to pull ourselves up with. Other times, on the downhill side, we'd be slipping and falling like jumping off a cliff."

On May 5, Third Battalion was first to reach the outskirts of the little Kachin village of Ritpong, which housed a Japanese garrison of about 150 troops, fifteen miles north of Myitkyina. As the men of Third Battalion (plus their new reinforcements from the Chinese Eighty-eighth Regiment) attacked, the Marauders were amazed—and momentarily fascinated: the Chinese called for the battle to start with blasts from a bugle. Still, the Chinese were fighting well, and Third Battalion commander Colonel Henry L. Kinnison decided to let the Chinese take the day, moving his own troops south of Ritpong to set up a jungle ambush site. When the fight was over, despite some Chinese casualties, all but four of Ritpong's 150 Japanese soldiers had been killed. Unfortunately, the clash likely also alerted the Japanese to enemy forces now on the eastern side of the Kumon Range and apparently headed for Myitkyina.

WITH RITPONG SECURED, Third Battalion of the Marauders now feinted away from the coming battle at Myitkyina. Under orders from Merrill, they marched due east through the jungle, where they engaged the Japanese for yet another garrison village called Tingkrukawng, appearing to be headed for the larger supply town of Nsopzup one more valley to the east. The battle for Tingkrukawng lasted three days, and during that time the Marauder's First and Second Battalions finished their climb over the Kumon Range and, working downhill, began to prepare their attack on Mytikyina.

But as all three battalions kept moving, along with the hunger and disease still wearing at them, a new and even more life-threatening illness began to present itself. Shortly after the fight at Ritpong, medics in several different units began seeing what they were calling the FUO, or "fever of unknown origin." Doctors would later discover that the illness, characterized by a high body temperature and lesions on the skin, was a deadly mite-borne disease—called brush typhus or mite typhus—that had probably been transported into the jungle by the Japanese. Before long, 149 Marauders in the End Run force had been stricken, and they were being evacuated from Ritpong to India by constant round-trips in a light, Stinson L-5 liaison aircraft that landed on an oss strip just south of the village, one of the few flat places under Marauder control.

Still, by May 15, the Marauders and their Chinese and Kachin counterparts were poised to the north and west of Myitkyina, ready to attack, and awaiting the operation's "start date" of May 17. On May 16, Merrill radioed to Stilwell: "Can stop this show till noon tomorrow, when die will be cast, if you think too much of a gamble. Personal opinion is that we have a fair chance and should try."

Stilwell radioed back, "Roll in and swing on 'em."

AT 10 A.M. ON MAY 17, the combined Merrill's Marauders attacked Myitkyina. In the words of the Army's official history, the charge was so smooth it looked like a "school demonstration, for though the Japanese knew Myitkyina was in danger, the actual assault was a complete surprise."

North of town, Battalion Three was still hurrying south from their latest battle at Tingkrukawng, while Colonel Hunter sent his First Battalion south of town, to overrun the city's main ferry terminal, halting all traffic on the Irrawaddy. According to plan, Hunter's Chinese reinforcements were to join with forward members of Battalion One to capture the rail line coming into Myitkyina from Mandalay and the west, and to seize the airfield west of town. Having spent the night bivouacked a few miles north of the railroad's tracks, which lay just across the road from the airstrip, when the call for attack went up, Captain Fred Lyons led his forward unit of the Second Battalion close to the action as well.

"I remember taking a patrol along the railroad line that ran into Myitkyina from Rangoon," Lyons said. "And by now my dysentery was so violent I was draining blood. My shoulders were worn raw from the pack straps, everyone was sick, so we set up our machine gun at the tracks, since we knew we'd find the Japanese patrolling the rail line to keep it open. A scout on the road ahead of us suddenly held his rifle high in the air. That meant 'Enemy sighted.' Then he started moving the rifle vigorously up and down. That meant 'Enemy in force.' "

The scout bugged out to safety, while Lyons's patrol crouched in a clump of brush. Lyons was so sick and tired that he'd become indifferent to the battle's outcome. "At least if I died," he later recalled, "the war would be over."

Then marching along the railroad's service road four abreast, Lyons and his patrol saw a battalion of perhaps one thousand Japanese troops nearing the airfield. "They had no idea we were there. The gunner crouched low and tightened down. The gun spoke. And the Japanese flopped down everywhere, dozens of them, the rest of the column spewing from its formation and running into the bush."

The skirmish for Myitkyina's airfield was under way. And as successive waves of Marauders from Battalion One and the 150th Chinese Regiment began pouring onto the airfield from other positions, with perhaps two hundred Japanese dead in the initial ambush, Fred Lyons's patrol realized it had to escape quickly—or be killed by a much larger enemy army that, at that very moment, was regrouping. They gathered their machine guns and slipped into the jungle, sometimes staggering, sometimes running, often dragging each other through the swamps and muck. After an hour of sweating and running so hard they were vomiting, Lyons and his team finally lost the Japanese. "I was so sick I didn't care whether the Japs broke through or not," Lyons said. "All I wanted was unconsciousness."

As the Marauders and Chinese swept across the Myitkyina airstrip, Colonel Hunter watched awestruck. For the first time, the Marauders were not making an attack in thick jungle, and the entire advance was visible. With incredible speed and skill, the Marauders advanced on critical positions across the airfield, the Chinese, with their disproportionately long Lee-Enfield .303 rifles and fixed bayonets visibly distinct from the Marauders, with their Tommy guns and carbines. As geysers of Japanese mortar round explosions fell blessedly long and wide of their marks, the Marauders kept pushing across the airfield. By ten-thirty, Colonel Hunter radioed to Stilwell that they were "in the ring," meaning they were on the airfield proper. With the Marauder advance, the Japanese defense of the field grew even weaker and more sporadic, as the capture of the ferry terminal cut off reinforcements from the large Japanese encampment on the river's far shore.

By three-thirty that afternoon, Hunter was pleased to radio Stilwell again. This time, he sent the coded transmission of "Merchant of Venice," which meant the airfield was secure and transport planes could begin landing. Within hours, aircraft loaded with antiaircraft units and Chinese X Force troops (but without the supplies Hunter had requested) began landing at Myitkyina.

Stilwell was ecstatic. If all went according to plan, Myitkyina would soon be the first Japanese stronghold in Asia to be recaptured by Allied forces. It was also an objective he'd been warned, again and again, that couldn't be accomplished before the brunt of the summer monsoon hit in mid-June. In his diary for May 17, he wrote that a stream of cargo planes was now flying into Myitkyina day and night. Then, in capital letters: WILL THIS BURN UP THE LIMEYS.

As if he'd predicted it, Churchill sent an immediate message to Mountbatten demanding an explanation of how "the Americans by brilliant feat of arms have landed us in Myitkyina." Mountbatten, who was far more concerned with his own defense of Imphal and Kohima against Japanese attacks, hadn't even been informed Myitkyina was to be attacked.

By May 19, whole regiments of X Force soldiers were now camping along the Myitkyina airstrip's edges. Also at the airfield, Lt. Colonel Gordon Seagrave had established a patchwork open-air hospital, and Hunter had spent much of the day and previous night working out the best way to overrun the seven hundred-person city and its thousands of Japanese occupiers—and he had two good reasons to be cautious.

Two days before, on May 17, on the heels of the airfield's occupation, Hunter had sent in two battalions of new Chinese X Force fighters (from the 150th Regiment, which had just entered Burma) to attack downtown Myitkyina. Unfortunately—in the excitement—they took the wrong road, became confused, and began to fire upon one another. In one scenario, a few Japanese intelligence agents had been hiding in trees as the Chinese approached. Once the two Chinese battalions were on opposite sides of them, the Japanese fired at both units, prompting the Chinese to fire back and eventually engage each other. In another version, the two Chinese battalions became separated, and getting jittery after not finding any enemies, they mistakenly started shooting at the first troops they encountered. The next day, May 18, Hunter had sent two more Chinese battalions from the

150th Regiment into the city again, only to see their blunder repeated. Once again, the Chinese battalions engaged each other. In two days, the Chinese 150th had sustained 671 casualties at their own hands. Hunter was now anxious about taking the initiative, especially since he technically had no orders beyond the capture of the Myitkyina airfield.

In the intervening two days, Myitkyina's thousands of Japanese defenders dug in, creating World War I–style earthwork trenches across the city and on the river's far shore. When the Marauders finally began their attack, they carried with them little artillery, no armor, and pitifully weak air support due to the cloudy monsoon skies. By now, 80 percent of the Marauders were diagnosed by Colonel Seagrave as having dysentery, and one man, Lt. Samuel Wilson, was sent to India as purportedly the "sickest man in World War II." He was diagnosed with—and eventually recovered from—simultaneous cases of mite typhus, amoebic dysentery, malaria, infected jungle sores, nervous exhaustion, and starvation-related wasting.

"We made surgical tables out of cots and stretchers, which we called litters," said one of Seagrave's nurses, a private from West Virginia named Mitchell Opas. "And Seagrave went from station to station, patching men up or declaring them dead. I remember we'd work thirty-six hours at a stretch, using lights at night, then fall asleep for four hours, and work another thirty-six-hour stretch. More than a month would pass like that. And I can remember thinking: the fighting must be terrible if this many dead and wounded are coming out from our end."

As Merrill's Second and Third Battalions grew exhausted, Marauder First Battalion threw themselves against the entrenched Japanese. Away from the fighting for Myitkyina, a combat team from Marauder Third Battalion—working without any supplies of food—took the village of Charpate, five miles to Myitkyina's northwest. The Allies now held the land to Myitkyina's west, south, and northwest. But to the city's north and east the Japanese were still able to cross the Irrawaddy and enter the city. In the wet, slick, hot conditions brought on by the monsoon, the fight for Myitkyina had become a stalemate.

During the first few days of June, Stilwell took full command and control of the Chindits (as had been planned for some time), as well as the Chinese and American troops deployed in the Northern Combat Area Command of Burma. Word also filtered to the Northern Kachin Levies to begin their push south along the Irrawaddy from the battle line at

Sumprabum, eighty miles north of Myitkyina, in a bid to close off the city's northern boundary.

With typical Kachin élan, the units began to ambush their way south, attacking the Japanese and losing few of their own since they engaged the enemy only in skirmishes they were certain of winning. They were a scruffy, jungle-tried group. Behind them, they led pigs to eat on ropes (plus their untethered mascot, a black pig named Porky), while, on their shoulders pet parrots perched and fluttered. And as they marched, they hummed and sang their own version of a going-to-battle song, improvising native Jingpaw lyrics to the tune of "As the Casissons Go Rolling Along": "Shall we fight / Shall we run / It is all too difficult . . . as the Levies go rolling along. We just passed a pretty girl / Why don't we just stay with her . . . as the Levies go rolling along . . ."

From across the river, on its Japanese-controlled eastern shore, other Kachin Levies were now moving south, too. Almost daily, gunfire could be heard from across the Irrawaddy. After each engagement, some of which lasted several hours, the corresponding Kachin unit would eventually radio back to its British leader, Colonel Ford: "All OK now." Then, several hours after each skirmish was over, a swimmer would invariably materialize from across the river, carrying with him a bag filled with Japanese ears as proof of the Kachins' success.

The wall of irregular forces began to press down on Myitkyina out of the north, further closing a ring around the Japanese, who were now hoping just to survive. One day the Kachin Levies' unit leader, Major Ian Fellowes-Gordon, watched in amazement as perhaps one hundred Japanese troops crept past the Kachin Levies' radio headquarters about ten miles north of Myitkyina, making no attempt to engage the enemy and clearly hoping to be overlooked. The Kachins declined to oblige them, streaking into the jungle ahead of the Japanese and killing them in an ambush. Exhausted from the jungle, and away from the direct fighting at Myitkyina, the enemy had obviously given up.

"Japanese morale," Fellowes-Gordon surmised, "had gone at last."

ALONG THE STREETS of Myitkyina, however, that realization was still weeks away. Day and night, a buildup for crushing the Japanese continued. Bulldozers cut three more airfields in the Allied-controlled territory around the city, to accommodate the now-constant flow of C-46s and C-47s to the battlefront. On each incoming trip, the aircraft would be filled with fresh Chinese troops and American advisers, food and ammunition, radios, medical supplies, and construction equipment.

By June, the Marauders were being removed from service for medical reasons ("Galahad is just shot," Stilwell wrote in his diary on May 30). The newcomers sought out veterans to learn the best ways of fighting the Japanese and of living through each new, miserable, and steaming-hot afternoon. Men worked shirtless in the rain and heat, which, many days in June, streaked past 100 degrees at the original Myitkyina airstrip.

On every trip back to India, each aircraft was filled with Chinese, American, and Kachin wounded. For the Marauders, at the medical recall's peak, they were now being flown to infirmaries in India at a rate of 150 a day. At the moment when Fred Lyons was to "call it a trip" and be evacuated under orders for dysentery and malaria, he remembered leaving with a sense of pride and trepidation for the newly arriving troops. "They were green, brave as hell, thrown in because the battle for Myitkyina was reaching the crucial stage, and we needed men—any kind of men. The newcomers grasped at every chance to talk with the Marauders, seeking advice even as we were being loaded into the transports."

To shore up his force, Stilwell had given orders that all available and able-bodied men in the theater were to be transported to Myitkyina. Other reinforcements, flown in from Calcutta, had to be given weapons training by Colonel Hunter himself once they'd arrived at Myitkyina. Beyond the Marauders who remained and the Chinese forces already on hand—some of whom were more battle hardened than others—the new Allied reinforcements called to Myitkyina included two battalions of American engineers off the Ledo Road (MPs, truck drivers, laundry operators, and mess workers), only a few of whom had fired a rifle since basic training.

Stilwell was anxious about his new soldiers, and with every passing day—as the buildup in troops and goods around Myitkyina continued—he fretted more and visited the city with increasing frequency. He had become a man with one thing on his mind, and the suspense of taking Myitkyina had rendered him uneasy in epic proportions.

"Imagination again," he wrote in an undated addition to his diary. "I often dream of going down into holes to pull the kids out, or looking for them frantically underwater. I think of situations . . . quite needlessly . . . that turn my guts to water."

BUT IF PROSPECTS WERE troubling at Myitkyina, Allied hopes in other portions of Burma were brightening. On May 11, the first thirty-two thousand of Chiang Kai-shek's 115,000-man Y Force had crossed the Salween River on rubber and bamboo rafts, headed for Burma. Now called the Chinese Expeditionary Force (or CEF), they leapt the raging, whirlpool-laden Salween at two places in a single day, then they began to climb from the river's rocky, thousand-foot gorge and began inching into the cloud-covered, ten-thousand-foot Himalayan peaks beyond.

Their goal was the ancient Chinese city of Lungling, along the Burma Road, which had been occupied by the Japanese, who'd invaded out of Burma in 1942. To attack Lungling, however, they'd first have to bypass thousands of Japanese troops entrenched atop the fortresslike summit of Sungshan (Pine Mountain), an interconnected series of more than twenty ridges, each roughly sixty-eight hundred feet tall and overlooking the Burma Road's Salween River crossing. Sungshan's steep, rocky, and largely unvegetated face had received the nickname "The Eastern Gibraltar." And on May 11, the CEF began to climb the slopes of Sungshan, retaking that portion of the Burma Road from the Japanese, but halting their climb in a containment position that left Sungshan's big battle in the future.

Traveling with the CEF was another of Stilwell's favorite American commanders and aides, Brigadier General Frank Dorn. Along with Merrill, Dorn had been with Stilwell since before the "walk out" out of Burma in 1942. "They've done well at last," Dorn wrote to Stilwell in a May 11 report. "There was even enthusiasm. . . . I have never seen such a cheerful bunch of men." As he jeeped down the Burma Road, past Sungshan and toward Lungling in a chilly pouring rain—dodging pack horses, pack cattle, mules, and transport bearers—Dorn reported that the CEF troops appeared to be moving in one endless column. "The whole mob started yelling, '*Ting-how*' (The Best!), 'Hello, OK,' and other Americanized expressions which have become passwords of the CEF."


AS THE Y FORCE BEGAN to successfully engage the Japanese in China, the X Force seemed to awaken in the Mogaung Valley as well. After weeks of goading by Stilwell, the Chinese Thirty-eighth Division under General Sun Li-jen began moving again. At dawn on the morning of May 19, General

Sun suddenly said to his American liaison officer, "We go to take Kamaing now." And, with impressive speed, he got his division together and proceeded to attack Kamaing frontally. Artillery barrages fell on the outskirts of the city, followed by incursions by armored tanks. Aerial bombing runs on Kamaing devastated the Japanese supply dumps, then proceeded to destroy their ammunition depots as well.

As Chinese tank units secured the northern edge of the city, General Sun began sending in infantry platoons, which found the Japanese doing little to defend their now-smoldering bastion. Tanaka's troops were in tatters. Thanks to the Chindits cutting off their rail support from the south, each Japanese soldier in Kamaing was living on a handful of rice a day, plus whatever roots and leaves he could find. Just like every other army in Burma—be they British, American, Indian, or Chinese—the Japanese Eighteenth was merely clinging to life and fighting with whatever weapons they could find and whenever they could summon the strength. The men of Tanaka's Eighteenth Division were trying to conserve their ammunition for one last, valiant stroke against the enemy.

In Kamaing, even as the X Force was overwhelming them, Tanaka's starving troops were fortifying their spirit with hope and prayer. They knew their leader, the great General Shinichi Tanaka—unbeatable vanquisher of Singapore, Malaya, and all of south Asia—must have a brilliant plan.

# Chapter 14

JUNE 1944 ARRIVED with a question mark attached to every Allied push in CBI—and the CBI theater itself was starting to fracture under the strain.

In CBI, the "Americans used to say you needed a crystal ball and a copy of *Alice in Wonderland* to understand it," wrote Theodore White, *Time* magazine's China correspondent, about the Burma war effort:

No Hollywood producer would dare film the mad, unhappy grotesquerie of the CBI. It had everything—majarajas, dancing girls, warlords, headhunters, jungles, deserts, racketeers, secret agents . . . American pilots strafed enemy elephants from P-40s. The Chinese Gestapo ferreted out beautiful enemy spies in their own headquarters and Japanese agents knifed an American intelligence officer in the streets of Calcutta. Chinese warlords introduced American army officers to the delights of the opium pipe; American engineers doctored sick work elephants with opium and paid native laborers with opium, too. Leopards and tigers killed American soldiers, and GIs hunted them down with Garands. Birds built their nests in the exhaust vents of B-17s in India while China howled for air power.

It was craziness. And all of it—the grimly bloody slugfest for Burma; the Ledo-Burma Road; the Flying Tigers; the Hump airlift; the exploits of

Chennault's Fourteenth Air Force; the tortured path of the lend-lease goods to the airfields of Kunming; and the heroics of the Long-Range Penetration forces—all of it, somehow, continued to issue from the Allied effort to keep China free and in the war. With each new day, the Allies in CBI kept staggering forward through the same chaotic mire they'd been trapped in since World War II's beginning. And now, as the summer of 1944 arrived—bringing with it the monsoon—CBI promised to grow even more muddy and impossible.

AT MYITKYINA, Colonel Hunter and his Marauders were now used up and being evacuated. Even worse, Myitkyina was still held by a minimum of thirty-five hundred Japanese troops, all of whom were dug in against new and largely untested Chinese and American reinforcements from India. Then, on June 3, Stilwell's field commander at Myitkyina, General Hayden Boatner, radioed more bad news to Stilwell's headquarters in Shaduzup. On that single day, 320 Chinese troops had been lost and—owing to monsoon rains so heavy soldiers could barely see their hands in front of their faces—the airfields were closed and the attack had completely stopped. The assault on Myitkyina was literally standing still.

In the Hukawng Valley, the X Force was still bashing at the Japanese stronghold of Kamaing ("That should have been a killing," Stilwell wrote in his diary). And though they chewed deeper into the Japanese Eighteenth daily—pushing the battle line forward with artillery and tanks followed by troops—they could not break Tanaka and his men. Complicating matters, the X Force couldn't turn up the Kamaing Road toward Mogaung and Myitkyina to assist the Marauder reinforcements until the Japanese in Kamaing were destroyed. Yet, hard as Stilwell pushed his Chinese Generals Sun and Liao, the X Force couldn't finish the job.

Meanwhile, in China, the Y Force had become bogged down, too. After containing Songshan and attacking Lungling with gusto, the Chinese Expeditionary Force had been confused and repelled by the same style of wily counterattacks that the Japanese had used at Myitkyina, and—again like Myitkyina—the highest-altitude combat zone on earth had degenerated into a World War I–style battle of attrition. The Chinese didn't relent, however, and despite huge losses to both forces, the Y Force eventually took the city on June 10. Now they had to turn their attention to the Japanese garrison city of Tengchung, forty miles to Lungling's north, and to the long, impregnable, and still-Japanese-controlled ridge of Sungshan, which still imperiled the Burma Road and its Salween River crossing.

Finally, in Burma south of Myitkyina and Kamaing, the rangy and fast-moving Chindits still remained too weak to distract the Japanese from the rear. Only one Chindit unit, the Morris Force—which was patrolling the east bank of the Irrawaddy River south of Mytikyina—remained on the move.

After two years of planning and training, the assault on Burma had crumbled into a mud-caked, bloody, rain-soaked stalemate.


ON JUNE 4, the day after Stilwell was informed about the stalled Myitkyina campaign, Vinegar Joe was summoned immediately to Chungking for what was billed to be a highest-level meeting on the North Burma Campaign's fate. Upon his arrival at Chiang's residence on June 5, however, Stilwell was met by a smiling Chiang Kai-shek and a grumbling Claire Lee Chennault. Chiang let Chennault direct the meeting, and the commander of the Fourteenth Air Force began a litany of accusations aimed at Stilwell. Chennault's forward airfields were being overrun by the Japanese, Chennault said, and Stilwell, CBI, and SEAC weren't doing enough to defend them. Second, the Fourteenth Air Force needed more fuel. What few aircraft Chennault had, he pointed out, weren't as effective as they could be; they were spending too much time sitting on the ground.

Stilwell listened to Chennalt's full presentation. Then he hopped the first transport plane he could find back to Shaduzup. Of the meeting, Stilwell wrote in his diary: "As expected, chiseling gasoline for the Fourteenth Air Force. All he wants is the world and nothing in return. . . . Peanut much surprised over north Burma success."


BACK AT SHADUZUP, Stilwell returned to the business of driving the Japanese from North Burma. Readdressing his problems at Kamaing and Myitkyina, he was immediately disheartened to learn that, as of June 9, Chinese casualties totaling 1,867 had been evacuated from Mytikyina. His troops were being mowed down by the bunkered-in Japanese, and owing to the heavy rains, few new transport aircraft were arriving with fresh fighters. Because of the pressure—and a growing pain in his abdomen, which medics said might be related to his stomach, or to his liver and the jaundice—Stilwell was now gaunt, pale, and weak. On afternoons when he felt strong enough to visit Myitkyina or the forward command posts of the X Force, the exertion would sometimes devastate him, sending him to his tent for the rest of the day.

Stewing in his tent on such a day in the weeks before his June 4 call to Chungking, Stilwell had decided he needed to break the Japanese stand-offs. If the X Force could finally destroy the Japanese at Kamaing, the Chi-nese forces would be freed to fight at Myitkyina. The question remained: How? Consulting his maps, Stilwell saw that between Kamaing and My-itkyina, the Kamaing Road stretched like a flattened "u" oriented roughly east to west. The X Force occupied the road's western end at Kamaing, while the Chinese and Americans balasted up the road's eastern terminus at Myitkyina. In between, there stood seventy miles of Kamaing Road. And at its center was the Japanese garrison town of Mogaung, which was sup-plying soldiers and goods to the battles on either side. To break the Japan-ese, Stilwell decided to smash the road at its center, pounding on Japanese reinforcements in Mogaung. There was only one hitch. He'd need battle-tuned troops to do it.

After consulting Allied force deployments around north Burma, Stilwell had only one real choice for his attack on Mogaung, and it was the re-maining Chindits. All of his other units were already actively fighting or—in the case of the V Force and the Levies and Detachment 101—too small and irregular for the job. Since Lentaigne's men had been forced to aban-don Blackpool on May 24, they had struggled north through the jungle—carrying casualties by stretcher and on their backs—and established camps encircling the narrow, twenty-mile-long impoundment called Indawgyi Lake. With the lake under Chindit control, Sunderland Flying Boat sea-planes had started landing on the water to evacuate the dead and wounded at the pace of hundreds of men per day. With the arrival of each new plane, the still-healthy men—who had taken to calling themselves "The Chindit Navy"—paddled out to the aircraft in native dugouts filled with dead and wounded.

Stilwell decided to set Wingate's Circus back into action. He directed the thirteen-hundred-man Morris Force north up the Irrawaddy River, to assist Merrill's troops at Myitkyina, and ordered the Chindits' best unit,

Mike Calvert's Seventy-seventh Infantry, to leave the area around Indawgyi Lake and push fifteen miles northeast. They were to attack and destroy the Japanese occupying the hilltop town of Mogaung, snapping the Kamaing Road in two and isolating the combat zones at Myitkyina and Kamaing. On June 3, the same day Hayden Boatner radioed Stilwell that the Myitkyina attack was stopped, Brigadier Calvert stood atop a twelve-hundred-foot ridge overlooking Mogaung's grid of rain-sodden streets, which waited two miles in the distance to his north.

The fifteen-mile trip to the hills outside Mogaung had been a rough one. Just the day before—after encountering several Japanese units unexpectedly—Calvert's Seventy-seventh Brigade had lost five dead and twenty-six wounded to rolling skirmishes with the enemy. Now, with roughly eight hundred men remaining of his original twelve hundred— and estimating that fifteen hundred enemy troops were probably stationed in Mogaung—Calvert made an emergency call for extra Chindit fighters and Kachins, plucking them from the stalled units at Indawgyi Lake. Then he began planning how to flatten Mogaung's hilltop fortress.

AS AN OBJECTIVE, Mogaung proved a difficult town to attack. To the north and west of its grid of hilltop streets, a bend in the monsoon-filled Mogaung River hemmed in the city's low, woodsmoke-hung huts and two-story buildings. To the east of town, a pair of flooded creeks spread out across the landscape, turning the area's rice paddies and farm fields to thick mud. The only way to successfully attack Mogaung, Calvert understood, was across some relatively dry fields and paddies south of town. Which, of course, was precisely what the Japanese would expect and be prepared for.

Calvert decided to throw off the enemy's defense. While he kept a larger, six-hundred-man portion of his army—the South Staffordshire battalion and his Gurkha Rifles—in position to invade Mogaung directly from the south, his initial attack would come from the southeast. There, a road crossed a damaged bridge over one of the two flooded creeks—the thirty-foot-wide Wettauk Chaung—at an outlying village called Pinhmi before continuing into Mogaung. He would start his campaign on Mogaung at Pinhmi and the Wettauk Chaung.

To subdue Pinhmi, Calvert sent several hundred men from his healthiest unit, the Lancashire Fusiliers, into the village, taking it and two hundred Japanese casualties with very light fighting in three days. Aside from capturing twenty large dumps of ammunition and about fifteen trucks, the fusiliers discovered that the village was primarily a large hospital site for Japanese wounded in fighting in Kamaing and Myitkyina. Unfortunately, many of the injured Japanese were still battling from their beds: in one case, the first fusilier through the door of the first infirmary was shot in the head and killed, necessitating a clearing of the ward with a volley of Chindit hand grenades. At other medical stations, the Chindits arrived to find dead Japanese troops who'd gathered around one of their own grenades and detonated it. One Japanese soldier taken prisoner choked himself by eating his blanket. Still the capture of the town went quickly. Three days later, with Pinhmi secured, the fusiliers were free to move to the bridgehead over the Wettauk Chaung and wait for their next orders. As they waited, the unit's Kachins continued their jungle intelligence work, scouring the rain forests for enemy troops and returning nightly with bags full of Japanese ears, for which Calvert (in violation of Stilwell's orders) paid one Indian rupee for each right-side specimen.

At the Pinhmi Bridge, Calvert and his men expected a Japanese defensive force to be dug in and waiting on Wettauk Chaung's far side. But once they arrived near the bridge, the enemy's presence, troop number, and even existence were difficult to prove, since the bridge embankment on the far shore was concealed by a tapestry of marsh grass and scrubby trees. It was time for a gamble. And at 6 p.m. on June 8, Brigadier Calvert arrived at the bridge and decided to test its defense.

In the summer evening, the Chindits laid a stripe of mortar rounds up the damaged span and along the creek's far side. As the volley continued, the faces of the fusiliers at the bridge grew stony. Though the heavy mortar fire was dislodging no Japanese from the jungle on the river's far shore, this did not mean with certainty that there were no Japanese present. The Pinhmi Bridge could be a monumental trap. As shows of reassurance, the fusiliers began pressing their hands into each other's faces and saying, "Buck up. Here we go. Buck up." Then they fixed their bayonets and, on Calvert's order, charged onto the bridge.

It was mayhem. The Japanese gunners on the river's far side waited until the lead fusiliers were halfway across the bridge before firing, and curtains of Chindit soldiers began to fall. A few of the fusiliers continued, crawling on their bellies along the bridge's surface, trying to push far enough forward to throw hand grenades into the enemy pillboxes, but the Japanese fire was too heavy. Bullets from Japanese rifles and machine guns were spattering everywhere across the bridge and its approach ramp. For several minutes the scene was chaos. Smoke and the sound of gunfire consumed the bridge. Then, when he'd decided the Chindits' progress was completely stopped and could go no farther, a fusilier company commander—Major David Montieth—sounded an order for withdrawal. As the Chindits began to pull back, leaving themselves again in the open, casualties piled up. Before the thirty-minute engagement was over, at least one hundred of the fusiliers had been killed or wounded.

Later that night, visiting the casualties in Pinhmi, Major Montieth vowed that he would figure out how to get across the bridge. The following morning, June 9, as Montieth returned to the bridgehead to reconnoiter for the next attack, he was shot dead by a sniper hiding on the creek's far shore.

Calvert knew he'd made a mistake—and he set about fixing it. Before dawn the following morning, June 10, he sent a company of Gurkhas, led by Lieutenant (and acting Captain) Michael Allmand, to ford the creek one bend downstream from the Japanese positions. Then Calvert faked another Chindit buildup at the bridgehead, distracting the Japanese. An hour later, the Gurkhas set upon the bunkered-in enemy from behind with rifle fire and grenades, but the attack was repelled and the Gurkhas had to retreat into the jungle. They redoubled their efforts, this time advancing on the Japanese position from the downstream flank, slogging close to the bunker through waist-deep mud, dense reeds, and the nutrient-black water of the Wettauk Chaung. After a nervy period of shooting and advancing, shooting and advancing, with each movement covered by explosions from Gurkha hand grenades, the assault succeeded. When the Gurkhas finally took the bridge position, they found thirty-five dead Japanese.

The bridge was now open, but the delay had been costly: 130 of Calvert's men had been lost, and in the intervening two days the Japanese had moved two more battalions into Mogaung from Myitkyina, giving the town a defensive force, Calvert estimated, of four battalions, or perhaps three thousand to four thousand men. Mogaung was going to be a bloodbath. Only one question still hung in the air: Which of the two opposing armies would spill more blood?

As the fusiliers began making their way from Pinhmi toward Mogaung, perhaps a mile to the west along the Pinhmi Road, the Japanese put up a ferocious defense. For three more days, the fusiliers and a battalion of Calvert's South Staffords were pinned down as they tried to advance up the road toward Mogaung from the southeast.

To the south of Mogaung, and still awaiting the signal for a full assault on the city, the larger Chindit force was also getting jittery. Japanese raiding parties had started probing the hills south of the city. The Gurkhas and Kachins killed at least twenty of the enemy during such encounters. To make matters worse, a new South Staffordshire company commander, Major Archie Wavell—son of Viceroy (and general) Archibald Wavell of India—had been shot in the wrist by a Japanese sniper, shattering his radius and ulna bones and necessitating the amputation of his hand, an event that Calvert was certain the viceroy would hold against him.

Calvert's units kept the pressure on Mogaung. Often they crawled up the Pinhmi Road toward Mogaung, but the fortified Japanese defense positions and snipers were keeping them away. Sixty more men were killed or wounded and Calvert comforted himself and his men by announcing (with Wingate-ian illogic) that, "When you think you are beaten, the other chap is probably worse, so have another go."

Calvert then received a radio transmission from Lentaigne: "Unless Archie Wavell is evacuated immediately, you will be dismissed from commanding your brigade." Viceroy Wavell had, obviously, been advised of his son's condition and wanted him back in India. Calvert tried desperately to get the young Wavell aboard every incoming light aircraft that landed at Pinhmi's waterlogged airstrip—where they were retrieving the Chindit dead and wounded—but the younger Wavell wouldn't budge. Understanding that many of the Chindits were in far more critical condition than he was, Wavell obstinately refused to leave the battlefront, no matter how forcefully Calvert ordered his evacuation. Finally, after sixty-some of the two hundred Chindit casualties had been airlifted out, Calvert was able to drive Wavell aboard the plane and out of his life.

Day and night, the Japanese continued defending Mogaung with everything they had. Chindit numbers were plummeting. On June 13, three of Calvert's battalion commanders stood in front of Mad Mike with a grim assessment. To both the southeast and the south, the Chindits were still four hundred to six hundred yards away from Mogaung, and the Japanese were extremely well positioned to defend the city. Of the eight-hundred-some Chindits who had started the campaign on Pinhmi and Mogaung, perhaps 550 remained, and nearly all of the Chindits still fighting were suffering from malaria, trench foot, Naga sores, and exhaustion.

Calvert knew his commanders were right. The following day he sent one of his officers, Captain Andrews of the Burma Rifles, west of Mogaung and across the Mogaung River toward Stilwell's base at Shaduzup. Andrews's orders were simple: he was not to return without at least one Chinese Regiment of five hundred to six hundred men. In the meantime, Calvert's Lancashire Fusiliers were to halt their push up the Pinhmi Road and take a breather, while his other two still-active units—the Gurkha Rifles and the South Staffords—were to begin moving slowly toward the outskirts of Mogaung from the south, an approach that triggered Japanese artillery and mortar fire that fell nonstop around them.

On June 18, Captain Andrews arrived back at Calvert's shelter, announcing that, just across the Mogaung River and west of the city, he had with him the First Battalion of the Chinese 114th Regiment—about twelve hundred men. Standing with Andrews, however, was an American lieutenant colonel (an "adviser" whose name now appears to be lost to history). Calvert sized up the reason for the American's presence perfectly: he was a "baby-sitter" sent by Stilwell, to make sure that Calvert and his men were fighting. The American kept spitting on the dirt floor of Calvert's shelter, and the Chindit commander took a fast and sturdy dislike to him. The lieutenant colonel was, Calvert later recalled, "A type, I suppose, which each country throws up at times. He had very little knowledge of the army or fighting, but was a great blusterer who would sit in my shelter spitting all over it to show that he was tough, calling the Chinese cowards, calling on us to attack, and saying that he represented General Stilwell and the United States and the Statue of Liberty and one or two other things." (Eventually, after the American colonel blew his nose on the floor of Calvert's shelter, Mad Mike is said to have taken the American to an exposed position near the Mogaung River—in direct line of fire from several Japanese sniper positions—to discuss tactics. Once in sight of the sniper nests, Calvert hung back near his vehicle and encouraged the American to step away from the car for a better view. Much to Mad Mike's displeasure, none of the snipers shot the colonel.)

As the Chinese reinforcements began spreading out, setting up artillery emplacements to the southwest and south of Mogaung, Calvert and the rest of his units waited. He now had a force approaching the size of the Japanese in Mogaung, and he was ready to assault the city.

On June 21, one of Calvert's night patrols returned to his shelter with unbelievable news: the rail bridge into Mogaung from Mandalay was unguarded. The following morning, Calvert ordered a probing attack of the bridge, which, as had happened at Pinhmi Bridge, was repelled by well-camouflaged and dug-in Japanese defenders, who held their fire until the last moment. Eleven Chindits were killed and sixteen more were wounded.

Then, on the evening of June 22, radio reports arrived at Calvert's shelter. The Chinese were now well arrayed around Mogaung. They were ready to start the siege. The night was a rare, clear one, and to ensure the attack's success Stilwell granted Calvert one of the largest airborne bombing raids in the theater thus far. In the darkness of June 22, more than seventy bombing sorties were carried out by the Tenth Air Force from India, and they dropped both blast and delayed-fuse bombs, which continued to blow up even after the aircraft had departed. Then, between 3 a.m. and 3:15 a.m., a barrage of no less than one thousand Chindit mortar rounds fell on Japanese defensive positions from the Chindits' forward locations south of Mogaung. As the mortar attack was ending, several hundred members of the South Staffordshires—weighed down by extra ammunition and hand grenades—began crossing the four hundred yards of rice fields south of Mogaung in an attempt to enter the town, which was ringed by Japanese pillbox fortifications of poured concrete.

The Japanese responded with rifle and mortar fire of their own, but the South Staffords were moving too quickly and the explosions fell behind them. By dawn, Chindit flamethrowers were cooking Japanese defenders alive inside their bunkers. "You could hear the screams and smell the burnt bodies," recalled South Staffordshire platoon commander Tom O'Reilly. "However the lad who was using the flamethrower was hit and was on fire himself and was running around in circles screaming. There was no hope of saving him, so he had to be shot."

Throughout the day, all three Chindit inits, ably assisted by the battle-hardened Chinese, drove deeper into Mogaung. The South Staffords encountered Japanese bunkers under virtually every house and building, and they systematically cleared them with flamethrowers. The most protected of the Japanese positions, a stronghold dug in beneath a large house with metal grills covering the windows to repel grenades, became engulfed by fire from several Staffordshire flamethrowers simultaneously. Inside, more than twenty Japanese soldiers were roasted alive.

Slowly the Chindits were overwhelming their opposition. As the Staffords pushed on, the Gurkha Rifles captured the railway bridge, losing one of their most respected leaders in the advance, acting Captain Michael Allmand, who had led the Gurkhas in overruning the Japanese bunker back at Pinhmi Bridge. He had again been attacking Japanese bridge defenders—this time at the Mogaung River—when he charged a machine-gun nest and was shot and wounded. He died a few hours later, dealing a fierce blow to Chindit morale.

As darkness fell, Calvert advanced with his command personnel into Mogaung, where they spent an uncomfortable night pinned down at the edge of town by enemy fire. The following morning, the Lancashire Fusiliers moved into Mogaung from the southwest and the Chinese, who had been ordered to take the town's rail station between Pinhmi and Mogaung, succeeded in driving out the large Japanese unit holding it.

The defense of Mogaung was beginning to crack, but the Japanese fought gamely on through June 24, occupying smaller and smaller zones inside the town. Then on the night of June 24, while Japanese mortar rounds and bullets continued to devil the Chindits and Chinese, Calvert's rearguard heard a BBC news report: Chinese-American forces were said to have captured Mogaung. When Calvert was told of the inaccurate news report, he grew livid. He quickly tracked down the propaganda's source: the American colonel, who, despite knowing the battle was still pitched, had radioed his erroneous update to Stilwell. To fix the mistake, Calvert wasted no time in radioing Stilwell's headquarters in Shaduzup: "The Chinese forces having taken Mogaung, Seventy-seven Brigade is proceeding to take umbrage."

If every one of Stilwell's commanders was as stupid as the American colonel now in Mogaung, Calvert joked, all of Shaduzup was probably searching its maps for the village of Umbrage.

The Japanese, however, must have been listening to the BBC news as well, because they took the hint. On the morning of June 25, as Calvert's men and the Chinese again began to probe and press farther into Mogaung, they discovered that the town's surviving defenders had, in fact, moved out. By noon, with some help from American P-51 Mustang fighters whose five-hundred-pound bombs demolished a few bunkers still holding enemy troops, Mogaung was under Allied possession.

The Japanese were gone. The Kamaing Road had been cut in two.

WITH MOGAUNG SECURELY in hand, Stilwell wasted no time in ordering the Chindits forward. On June 25, the day Mogaung fell—and just as he'd had done to Merrill's Marauders shortly after Nhpum Ga—Vinegar Joe issued new orders for Calvert and his men. They were to attack and overrun the Japanese-controlled railroad village of Hopin, southwest of Mogaung. From there, the Chindits could push hard directly north and penetrate the Japanese Eighteenth from behind at Kamaing—meeting up with the X Force and taking down Tanaka's Eighteenth Division for keeps.

Calvert, however, had other ideas. At Mogaung, he had lost 255 dead and another 521 wounded. He was down to a quarter of his original force, and those not officially out of battle were wrestling with minor wounds and barely survivable levels of illness and exhaustion. Calvert's Seventy-seventh Brigade, which had once been the Chindits' most proud and feisty column—of Gurkha Rifles, King's Liverpool Regiment troops, Lancashire Fusiliers, and South Staffordshires—was now down to a "last fit three hundred." They had also been out in the field for four months, far longer than the ninety-day battlefield limit promised during training back in India. Calvert decided that he and his Seventy-seventh Brigade were going home—or were at least entitled to some rest and reinforcement.

So on the evening of June 25, as Stilwell's radioed orders came through to attack Hopin, Calvert radioed back. He refused the directive, claiming he didn't have the manpower to succeed.

"Send one company," Stilwell responded over the airwaves.

"If I counted every rifleman who could stand, I could hardly *muster* a company," was Calvert's return message. "I have only three hundred men all told. Do you want me to form the Kings Royal Staffordshire Gurkha Fusiliers?"

Instead, as a punishment for Calvert's insubordination, Stilwell changed his mind. Calvert and his men were to proceed straight to Myitkyina and enter the fight there. Calvert, who freely admitted to a "phobia" about Myitkyina (a larger-scale and more deadly version of the Mogaung fight he'd just concluded), chose a different and even more obstinate path of action.

Instead of attacking the Japanese somewhere, he ordered his column's radios turned off, then he pushed northwest up the road from Mogaung directly into Kamaing. The Chindits and on-loan Chinese would join the Chinese X Force there. Calvert had decided that he and his men were going to be evacuated.

The trip was brutal. Following two and a half months of rain, the dirt road to Kamaing was now a strip of shin-deep mud the consistency of oatmeal. The Chindits were so exhausted that the twenty-five-mile walk took more than a week. Two of Calvert's men simply fell down and died along the way. And as the first of Seventy-seventh Brigade's troops began to arrive in Kamaing, after several days' silence, Stilwell ordered the insubordinate Michael Calvert to appear in front of him in Shaduzup—immediately.

Mad Mike was jeeped to Stilwell's headquarters. It appeared that he was headed for a dressing down.


AFTER A NIGHT blessedly spent on a tented cot near Stilwell's command post, Calvert was—the following morning—led directly into the general's tent. Inside he found Stilwell seated behind a table and between General Boatner and Stilwell's eldest son, Lt. Colonel Joseph Stilwell. To everyone, the scene looked like a court-martial. Calvert politely shook the three Americans' hands, then he was offered a seat at the table opposite Stilwell.

Stilwell initiated the conversation. "Well, Calvert," he said, "I have been waiting to meet you for a long time."

"I have been waiting to meet you, too, sir."

Stilwell nodded. "You send some very strong signals."

"You should see the ones my brigade major *won't* let me send," Calvert responded.

Stilwell, whose wrinkled and patrician face had been stony, began to turn up the corners of his mouth. Then he chuckled. In the next moment, he was roaring with laughter. He bent over in hilarity, slapping his knees and the backs of the officers sitting beside him. "I have the same trouble," he finally managed to say, "with my own staff when I draft signals back to Washington."

Calvert had chosen precisely the right thing to say. With the meeting's tension broken, Calvert began telling Stilwell of the Chindits' sacrifices. He talked of how they'd been flown into Broadway since Piccadilly was closed. He recalled how they'd kept a chart of Stilwell's progress down the Hukawng Valley, eagerly anticipating a meeting with the X Force, but then abandoned the chart because the X Force was moving so slowly. How, trapped in the jungle without protection and with Japanese artillery falling almost constantly around them, they had been fighting their way north for four months—virtually unsupplied and unsupported—until they were slowed by the need to carry their mounting casualties with them. And how, at Blackpool, battalion commanders had wept at the destruction of their men. Unlike Merrill's Marauders, the Chindits had been given little regular army support until Mogaung. Instead, they had spent four months hopscotching from makeshift jungle camp to camp, always deep inside enemy territory. Only at Mogaung, where American aircraft and Chinese reinforcements had helped smash the Japanese, had there been any real help for the Chindits. It was actually a wonder, Calvert said, that the Chindits hadn't sustained *more* losses.

"Is this true?" Stilwell kept asking as Calvert told of the nonstop sieges at White City and Blackpool. "Why wasn't I told?"


INSTEAD OF HAVING his court-martial written on the table separating him from Stilwell, Mike Calvert was awarded the Silver Star on the spot—as were all four of his unit commanders. As a reward for their valor, all remaining Chindits were to be evacuated—that is, once the Chindit columns still encircling Indawgyi Lake moved north and kept the Kamaing Road closed until the battle for Kamaing was finished. As Calvert himself was flown out to the airfields of Assam, he looked down to see the long, straight, glistening line of the monsoon-flooded Ledo Road shimmering like a bright thread through the surrounding jungle.


AS WORD OF Stilwell's awarding of medals and evacuation orders spread, it was the Americans—especially the few equally exhausted Merrill's Marauders still fighting—who grew angry. While the Chindits awaited their flights to India, the British and Americans at Shaduzup mixed in friendly camaraderie; mainly because, beyond the Japanese, the Americans now believed their next-most-hated enemy in Burma was their own commander. Stilwell had kept the Marauders on the field for longer than Wingate's promised ninety days, since the success of the north Burma campaign meant more than their rest and ease. As their commander, it was a decision he'd had to make alone, and he was suffering a commander's pain for it.

One night, as a Chindit captain named Fred Freeman was in his pre-evacuation bivouac near Stilwell's headquarters, an American officer—just in from the fighting at Myitkyina—invited Freeman for a dinner followed by a movie at the camp's mess. Freeman, who hadn't had a warm meal in months, gladly accepted, and as they sat in the canteen tent—enjoying a banquet of real beef and potatoes and vegetables—a bottle of Haig Whiskey was produced. When the Scotch was poured, the American turned to Freeman and said, "Captain, I want to ask you a straight question and I want a straight answer. Tell me: What is your frank opinion of General Stilwell?"

Freeman considered the question for a long minute: Did the Americans love their commander . . . or hate him? Was he a hero to them the way Wingate was to the Chindits? Or was he the butt of every derisive joke? After all, Stilwell had been the only Allied commander in CBI and SEAC who'd unswervingly done what he'd promised.

Still, Freeman didn't want to lie, and he felt Stilwell was being unnecessarily brutal to his men. "I imagine," Freeman finally answered, "he has good qualities that have been concealed from us in the Chindits."

"Well," replied the American, "if you want to know our opinion of him, we think he's a lump of crap!"

# Chapter 15

ON JUNE 29, after forty days of nonstop pressure on the Japanese Eighteenth Division at Kamaing, General Shinichi Tanaka
had no choice. Chinese artillery, tanks, and troops were tearing
deeper into the town with each hour. And the supply road to Mogaung
had now been cut by the Chindits and the Chinese. After a brave defense
of the Hukawng and Mogaung Valleys, Tanaka was losing troops to the
X Force by a ten-to-one margin. His army was out of everything; Tanaka's
men had been living primarily on rice and scavenged roots and leaves, and
they no longer possessed the ammunition or energy to mount a sufficient
defense. With no choice left to him, Tanaka was compelled to order a full
retreat from north Burma.

In the streets of Kamaing, Tanaka's soldiers (troops in their twenties
who were so broken they stood hunched over like old men) began withdrawing into the jungle to the west and south. Of his original six thousand
soldiers, Tanaka could now count fewer than three thousand. They joined
with the roughly two thousand soldiers from Mogaung and Myitkyina
who'd been shipped to the Hukawng Valley to assist Tanaka's defense, and
together they began a journey on foot and by truck toward the Japanese
stronghold of Mandalay, 150 miles to the south.

In some places, scores of Japanese sick were forced to start impromptu
jungle infirmaries, where hundreds of men too sick to carry on would sim-

ply lie down in forest clearings, or spread out beneath trees near roadsides so they could beg passing comrades for food or water. In other places, men who had died from self-inflicted gunshots lay in the roadside weeds. Sometimes, when a man was too weak or sick to recover, he was, in the recollection of Japanese Staff Sergeant Yasumasa Nishiji, "Given a grenade and persuaded, without words, to sort himself out." Other times, Nishiji recalls, "Soldiers took their lives in pairs. They embraced, placing the grenade between them. We called it a double suicide."

For the Japanese in Burma, the collapse had begun.

YET IF STILWELL WAS feeling imminent victory in northern Burma, as portions of his X Force were now turning east down the Kamaing Road toward Myitkyina, his own career tumbled once again into jeopardy. Owing to his refusals to leave north Burma and his single-mindedness about the north Burma campaign, many commanders in the region—including Chiang Kai-shek and with the exception of the patient William Slim—were now overtly or tacitly lobbying George Marshall and President Roosevelt for Stilwell's recall. In India, Frank Merrill—again laid up with heart problems—was getting regular visits from Mountbatten, where the SEAC commander had started suggesting that Stilwell's second in command, General Daniel Sultan, or the Americans' chief of planning for SEAC, General Albert Wedemeyer, should become Vinegar Joe's replacement. "Good God—to be ousted in favor of Wedemeyer—" Stilwell wrote on June 20, "that would be a disgrace."

Stilwell, however, remained unconcerned with these latest rumors of his demise. Instead, he concentrated all of his energies on finally smashing the entrenched Japanese at Myitkyina. The Japanese were encircled on three sides—to the north, west, and south—by an army made up of any unit Stilwell could muster. Yet the Japanese, even as they were backed against the swollen Irrawaddy River to their east, refused to surrender the city. On the broad river's far shore, units of Kachin Levies continued to harass the large Japanese encampments in the towns of Maingna, Mi Na, and Wangmaw, while aerial bombing runs by the Tenth Air Force decimated supply depots and buildings on both sides of the river. Still, the Japanese refused to give in. They were fighting with virtually no supplies and living on a quarter bowl of rice a day, yet somehow they continued to defend the city.

Every day in June and into July, through mud and rain, Myitkyina was consumed by combat and artillery fire. Recalled Mitchell Opas, a member of Seagrave's medical staff:

During the summer siege of Myitkyina, we worked a minimum of eighteen hours a day, seven days a week. Oftentimes we worked in thirty-six-hour stretches. And the casualties just kept coming. We'd get one day's men patched up and ready to be evacuated, grab a few hours sleep, and the casualties would start pouring in again at daybreak. Seagrave was a very religious man—he'd been a missionary in Burma before the war—and every day he'd remind us that God was on our side. But, well, standing in surgery eighteen hours a day, I was less inclined to think God was around much at all. During the summer of 1944, I don't recall ever seeing daylight. Instead, every day, I saw only the inside of an operating theater, where I leaned over muddy soliders who'd been shot or blown up. Every day during that summer I went into that operating theater in darkness and left it in darkness. The fighting at Myitkyina never seemed to end.

STILWELL WASN'T going to back down. Though he was losing 130 men a day to sickness and casualties at Myitkyina, he kept pushing. Through a few captured POWs, he knew the Japanese were cut off from outside help and supply, and he had gotten reports that Japanese medical officers had started floating their dead and wounded down the Irrawaddy in rafts to evacuate them.

By mid-July, the few Japanese taken alive as prisoners from Myitkyina were informing Allied interrogators that the thirty-five hundred Japanese forces at Myitkyina had suffered 790 dead and 1,180 wounded, but that the Imperial Army—led by their Major General Genzu Mizukami—would never give up. They had been ordered by Imperial Japanese Command to fight to the last man. In terms of combat, Myitkyina had become as viciously concentrated as any battle in World War II: comparable to the U.S. Marines' costly and famed conquest of Tarawa in the Pacific Island Campaign, which had taken place nine months earlier.

"Rain, rain, mud, mud, mud, typhus, malaria, dysentery, exhaustion, rotting feet, body sores," Stilwell wrote home to Win. "If we are badly off, what about the Japs with little medical help and their supplies shut off?

This has been a knock-down-and-drag-out affair . . . I feel guilty about Mitch but we'll get it in due time."

Across the river from the battle at Myitkyina, the Japanese forces were finally starting to give up. It was now the end of July, and they had been fighting nonstop since May 17. They were starving—many hadn't eaten in several days—and what few fighting troops remained were either exhausted or were wounded but still able soldiers who'd been ordered back into combat. Under such horrific conditions, Japanese soldiers began to desert Myitkyina, either by floating themselves down the Irrawaddy or by crossing the eight-hundred-foot-wide river and disappearing into the jungles east of the far shore. Noting the dwindling Japanese troop numbers, the Americans and Kachins decided not to let them escape. As July came to an end, two Detachment 101 units were hunting Japanese deserters, lying in wait along the Irrawaddy twenty miles downstream of Myitkyina and combing the jungles east of the river a safe distance from the dying Japanese encampment. Between the two OSS groups, killing one man at a time, they had soon tracked down and eliminated five hundred to six hundred Japanese deserters. As July 1944 came to an end, Myitkyina's commander, Major General Mizukami, knew the defense of his last stronghold in north Burma would soon be over and that his forces would surely be destroyed.

At dawn on August 1, after a valiant fight, Mizukami acted as any honorable Bushido warrior would. He washed and dressed in his cleanest uniform, walked off to a tree, and sat down facing northeast toward Japan.

From his dispatch case, he pulled out a piece of notepaper and a pen, and wrote his final orders: "The survivors of the Myitkyina garrison are ordered to proceed south."

Then he placed the order beneath a small stone in front of him, knelt down—still facing northeast—and leaned his chest against a small tree trunk: ensuring that he would die falling honorably forward instead of back. Across the river, Mizukami could hear the booms and chatter of Allied hand grenades and rifle fire coming ever closer. In the rising light, the muddy and swollen Irrawaddy slid gently past as it had for thousands of years.

Then Mizukami unsnapped the holster to his service pistol, switched off its safety, and cocked the weapon.

For a long minute he prayed for forgiveness to the emperor and the people of Japan. Then he lifted his pistol, pushed its barrel tightly against his skull, and pulled the trigger. The Japanese defense of Myitkyina was officially over.

THREE DAYS LATER, on August 4, 1944, Joseph W. Stilwell's polyglot Myit-kyina Assault Force drove the last Japanese holdouts into the Irrawaddy River from the streets and buildings of Myitkyina. Finally, at a teak forest called Kyun Bin Ta—along the Irrawaddy south of town—three remaining Japanese soldiers who'd been holding off hundreds of Chinese and Americans from trenches, slipped into the river and began to swim downstream. The imperial Japanese Army had been smashed out of northern Burma.

Against impossible odds and operational cross-purposes from every quarter, Joseph W. Stilwell and his armies had succeeded. In his diary for the day, Stilwell wrote simply: "Myitkyina—over at last. Thank God. Not a worry in the world this morning. For five minutes anyway."

# Chapter 16

IF ONE LEADER in World War II was as impressed by Orde Wingate's Chindits as Winston Churchill had been, it was Lt. General Reyna Mutaguchi: the thick-bodied, black-eyed, bullet-headed commander of the Japanese Fifteenth Army in Burma. Mutaguchi had been a troop commander during Japan's early China campaigns and had been present for the fall of Peking. As his imperial army occupied increasingly large chunks of China, Mutaguchji openly despised the Chinese for their inability to defend themselves, and his hatred grew stronger with every Chinese defeat. When not berating the Chinese, he spent part of every day's energies actively ridiculing the British, whose defenses his army had crushed in a week at Singapore.

Then, in the spring of 1943 and following Wingate's successful, if costly, initial Long-Range Penetration mission into Burma, Mutaguchi decided to finally act on his anti-British impulses. If the pathetic British could cross central Burma's impenetrable jungles and mountains on foot from India, he reasoned, then his disciplined and well-commanded Imperial Japanese forces could accomplish far more headed in the opposite direction.

It was a plan he'd carried in the front of his mind for more than a year. In fact, back when Japan had slashed into Burma and occupied it in mid-1942, there had been a subsequent plan—called Operation 21—that proposed to honor the Imperial Japanese momentum and invade India along

two routes without pause. The first, up the Hukawng Valley and into Assam, would have destroyed the still-faltering early days of the Hump airlift.
The second and larger thrust—the truly killing blow—would come after
the Japanese crossed the seven-thousand-foot Chin Hills of central Burma
and overran the towns of Imphal and Kohima, home to east India's dis-
combobulated British and Indian armies.

Mutaguchi was confident and ready. He had even taken a preparatory
step that mirrored the successful invasion of Burma (where Colonel Keiji
Suzuki had tapped into the Burmese army's willingness to overthrow the
colonial British). For the past year, a Japanese officer—Major Fukiwara
Iwaichi—had been training forty thousand to forty-five thousand members of the Indian National Army who'd claimed sympathy to the Japanese
after being captured in Malaya in late 1941 and early '42. The Indians—
soon led by the radical Indian nationalist Subas Chandra Bose—had decided that an India ruled by the Japanese surely could be no worse than
one run by the colonial British.

But in July 1942, Operation 21 was scrubbed. As final details of the invasion plan had been ironed out, Imperial Japanese Command in Tokyo
changed its mind. They decided against the invasion; troops and supplies
were stretched to the limit. Eighteen months had now passed and by December 1943—encouraged as Gandhi's "Quit India" program continued to
excite the Indian populace and undermine British control—Mutaguchi
decided that Operation 21's hour was finally at hand.

Despite supply privations that still plagued the Imperial Army in
Burma, Mutaguchi and his superior Hideki Tojo—now the Japanese prime
minister, supreme general, and minister of war—were in agreement about
the invasion. Stilwell's Chinese troops out of India and Chiang's armies in
China could probably be held at bay in northern Burma, but General
Slim's armies in India were likely to soon begin their own invasion into
Burma. British forces were already massing in Arakan to the south, appar-
ently to reprise early 1943's unsuccessful advance down the peninsula toward Akyab Island. This time, if they were successful in capturing Akyab,
they'd most certainly invade Rangoon. Mutaguchi also believed that, after
Wingate's limited overland success in 1943, a much larger British and Indian irregular army might soon invade Burma along Wingate's old routes.
Therefore, for the Japanese, a preemptive invasion and the occupation of
India would destroy the last true impediment between Japan and its control of all Asia.

As word came to Mutaguchi that Stilwell's army was now forcefully invading the Hukawng Valley, Mutaguchi decided against his own push up the Hukawng. There was only one certain place left for the Japanese to smash their invasion into India. First, Mutaguchi would force the British to commit their reserves with a fierce, feinting attack on Britain's forces on the Arakan Peninsula. Then, with the Brits distracted, Mutaguchi's Fifteenth Army would attack the headquarters city of Imphal with three full infantry divisions—the Thirty-first, Thirty-third, and Fifteenth—along a broad front at the central Burma-India border. He also believed that, were his troops to move fast enough, the disorganized British would be forced into their only tactical option: a complete withdrawal from northeast India, which would likely leave behind a good deal of provisions for the coming rainy season. It was a plan, Mutaguchi believed, that could not fail.

REMARKABLY, DURING THIS SAME PERIOD, the British General William Slim had envisioned Mutaguchi's entire tactical plan. And after considering his options, Slim decided to play directly into Mutaguchi's program. He would, however, increase his odds for succeeding by drawing the Japanese even closer to him.

Slim, recalling his difficulties providing communications and supply to the Chindits during their first raid, figured not to put up resistance against the invading enemy. Instead, he withdrew his two most forward armies—the Seventeenth and Twentieth Indian Divisions—from India's vertical and mountainous tangle of border with Burma. Then he concentrated the rest of his troops and weapons on the broad Imphal plain: a flat dish of a valley twenty by forty miles wide—and fifty full miles inside India from the Burmese border.

To destroy the Japanese, Slim would force *them* to overextend their lines of communication and supply. He understood this meant sacrificing some precious Burmese borderland and, at first, none of his officers agreed to his plan without argument. But as he viewed it, this "drawing in" of the Japanese was the sole sure way to smash their forces to bits, which would give Slim's Fourteenth Army an easier time during the coming reinvasion of Burma.

For both sides, the issue of where to fight for the future of India had been settled. Two armies—each thirty thousand to forty thousand men strong—would go head-to-head around Imphal, and the winner would take all. The broad Imphal plain was to become a killing field.

MUTAGUCHI RECEIVED his orders to invade India, an offensive called U-Go, on January 7, 1944. By early February, Mutaguchi had chosen his Fifty-fifth Division for the diversionary sideshow on the Arakan Peninsula. The Arakan feint was an invasion he called Ha-Go. And to accomplish it, roughly ten thousand imperial troops would attack portions of British XV Corps (the Indian Seventh Division and Fifth Division), which would keep the British from their own advance toward Akyab Island and, ultimately, Rangoon.

On the Arakan Peninsula, Mutaguchi's plan was to first attack and surround the more exposed Seventh Division, as it lay on the eastern side of the steep Mayu Mountains and closer to his armies. From there, once the Seventh Division was destroyed or disabled, his troops could cross the mountains and attack and envelope the Fifth Division. His hope was that these two attacks—were they executed quickly and ferociously enough— would also draw some of Slim's forces south to help with the defense, weakening British strength around Imphal, where the real battle was to be waged.

Just after dawn on February 6, 1944, a small British signal company— which had been placed on a hillside for better radio reception—was quietly overrun and destroyed by the initial thrust of Japanese. As the Japanese began to inspect the radio they'd captured, they looked into the valley to their south and, through a lifting morning fog, were amazed to see endless rows of British tents and tanks across the landscape in the distance. Somehow, the two hundred men of the Japanese Fifty-fifth Division's Second Battalion had maneuvered into a perfect high-ground position above the Indian Seventh Division headquarters: at a place called Sinzweya. Then the fog descended again and obscured their view.

As the Japanese began to spread themselves across the mountainside for better reconnaissance, they saw that between themselves and Sinzweya there stood a small hillock called Launggyaung, which was topped with several more tents and even a few tanks.

Time was of the essence, since the British would soon discover something amiss at their hillside radio post. And because there were no other fighting units immediately available (much of the Fifty-fifth Division was

either cutting off roads connecting the peninsula to the mainland or following too far behind), the two hundred men of Second Battalion would
have to take on the hilltop encampment themselves.

Their leader, Captain Midorigawa, split his battalion into two equal
groups and got them in positions to attack Launggyaung. Then, at about
11 a.m., they charged. Amazingly, Midorigawa's two hundred Japanese
infantrymen took the British position without a fight. Despite the imposing presence of the tanks, Launggyaung was populated by clerks and
typists—soldiers not accustomed to combat—and many of the British and
Indian soldiers, rather than mounting a defense, stood from their desks
and file cabinets and escaped toward Sinzweya, two miles downvalley to
the south.

Captain Midorigawa and his Japanese troops were thrilled. After more
than a year of patient waiting and slow starvation, the Imperial Army now
had its first victory in the Ha-Go / U-Go invasion. And that evening, as a
portion of Midorigawa's men raised a Japanese flag on what they were now
calling "Flag Hill," others in the unit discovered a cache of British food and
liquor in a supply tent. As darkness fell on February 6, 1944, the Imperial
Japanese forces at Launggyaung ate heartily of the captured food, then
they lifted their glasses in a toast to victory.

That night's celebration, however, would prove the apex of Japan's invasion of India.


THE FOLLOWING MORNING, on February 7, the Japanese Ha-Go invasion
began its next stage as more than one hundred Japanese Zeros initiated the
full-scale attack on Sinzweya. During the entire day, Japanese fighter aircraft again and again swept and strafed Sinzweya's open valley and tents
and tanks, firing off long strings of bullets as two full battalions of the
Japanese Fifty-fifth Infantry Division—more than two thousand of the division's nearly ten thousand troops—massed on the mountainsides above
Sinzweya, awaiting their signal to attack.

As a defensive encampment, Sinzweya had both assets and liabilities. At
about twelve hundred yards square, it was a large and treeless area of
dried-up rice paddies ringed by low hills and mountains, making visibility
to all the surrounding hillsides a defensive plus. A small hill at Sinzweya's
center—the focal point of the valley—functioned as the Indian Seventh
Division's ammunition dump. Another small but conspicuous hill on the

east side of Sinzweya's valley was the camp's artillery depot. Also in Sinzweya's valley—beyond the lines of tents that functioned as barracks—was a hospital, a field-dressing station, several administrative areas for all of the XV Corps (both Fifth and Seventh Divisions), several motor pools, and a number of mess tents and supply magazines. Owing to the openness of the area, all of these places were easily visible and accessible from the others, which could prove a defensive plus, since defenders could see any enemies that made it to the valley floor. It was as if the Seventh Division was occupying the flat bottom of a box. In fact, in order to shorten the name for XV Corps Administrative Headquarters, everyone had taken to calling it the "Admin Box."

With the morning's first strafing attack—and after the loss of Laung-gyaung a day earlier—the British Brigadier General Geoffrey Adams (commander of both the Seventh and Fifth Divisions), knew an attack was imminent. To defend the Admin Box, he sent out an early radio call. All five of Seventh Division's outlying brigades and weapons were to return to the Admin Box at once. If the Japanese were going to attack, Adams had decided, they would have to defeat the bristling steel of a full British-Indian division in a 100 percent defensive posture. Once all of his brigades and weapons were accounted for and arrayed around the valley, Evans called a short meeting at his headquarters. The only battle order he had, Adams told his commanders, was short and specific: "Your job is to stay put and keep the Japanese out."

By nightfall of February 7—after a full day of Japanese aerial attack—bullet pocks and dead mules littered Sinzweya. Then, under cover of darkness and with lightning speed, the Japanese began their assault on the Admin Box. To the Japanese, the attack was going to be *ento jinchi sakusen* ("the cylinder position operation"), meaning Japanese munitions and troops were to pour down off the mountainsides and onto Sinzweya's exposed valley's floor like water through a funnel. As planned, Japanese mortar fire began to rain down on the Admin Box from hillsides all around the base. Inside this horrible situation, the entrapped British and Indians sat tight, trying to discern the precise locations of the Japanese troop and artillery positions. Adams decided the majority of the Japanese were on the east side of the Admin Box, and he ordered the Seventh Division's motorized tanks and 75-millimeter artillery to begin pounding back against the Japanese position. To shift the battle from artillery to troops, Adams sent out a battalion of British West Yorks, who, in a night raid beyond the base perimeter, began to drive the Japanese guns off the hills east of Sinzweya.

What Adams didn't realize, though, was that Sinzweya's funnel was open for a complete 360 degrees. And with much of the British firepower and strategic thinking momentarily directed eastward, Adams and his men neglected other areas of Sinzweya's perimeter. Suddenly, from the west, Adams and his command team heard the popping bursts of small-caliber Japanese rifle fire coming behind them. It was about then that Adams heard someone shout: "Good God, they've gotten into the hospital!"

The situation was even worse. Not only had the Japanese somehow battled their way inside the infirmary—which stood just three hundred yards from the Admin Box's Staff Headquarters—they'd already established a defensive zone around it. The hospital had been weakly guarded (by only about twenty West Yorks and a complement of walking wounded) and the building had been overrun before anyone could put up a defense. Inside, the Japanese were interrogating their prisoners, binding some of them by their hands and feet, and bayoneting others in their beds. The infirmary's Indian medical officer, Lieutenant Basu, was questioned by a Japanese commander who demanded all of the hospital's quinine, morphine, and antitetanus serum, while other Japanese soldiers destroyed anything they couldn't use.

Through the night, and because of the indiscriminate nature of artillery, Brigadier Adams held his fire upon the hospital. The following morning, however, as the Japanese began dragging prisoners outdoors and machine-gunning them in plain view of the British, Adams began to reconsider. A group of twenty British soldiers were led out behind the building; the Japanese told them it was time to "come and get treatment." As the prisoners were led into a dry creekbed just behind hospital, the Japanese troops sprayed machine gun volleys at them until all of the British had fallen. But three soldiers—including Lieutenant Basu—somehow evaded injury. To save their lives, Basu and his fellow survivors "went doggo," falling as if they'd been shot, then—when the Japanese weren't looking— placing their hands out, into the blood of their compatriots and friends, and smearing their own faces and bodies with it to appear mortally wounded. For several hours, the three lay still in the pile of corpses, waiting for an unguarded moment. Eventually they slipped away to freedom.

On the morning of February 9, thirty-six hours into the siege and after

Adams decided that all of the British and Indian troops inside the hospital had been executed, the British brought artillery and tank fire down upon the building. With the barrage over, a unit of West Yorks with bayonets entered the infirmary to finish the Japanese, but they found many of the building's invaders had abandoned it. When the hospital was taken back, the British found the bodies of thirty-one British and Indian soldiers and four doctors inside.

It was as close as the Japanese would ever come to victory in Sinzweya. For the next thirteen days, the Indian Seventh Division would defend the Admin Box against daily onslaughts. And Mutaguchi's Fifty-fifth Infantry would eventually be out-gunned. The Indian Seventh Division had a full complement of weapons and tanks, while the Japanese—who were outfitted to move quickly—had only eight small cannons and Howitzers and were forced to attack mostly with rifles and light machine guns.

Slowly—with stores of better supplies playing their parts—the British began to pound their artillery against the Japanese, gaining the upper hand in the battle for the Admin Box. Luck played a part, as well. On the evening of February 11, 1944, a West Yorks sentry named Maloney stood alone at base perimeter on the Admin Box's south side, where his orders were to defend a dry and steep-banked creek bed that snaked out of the mountains. Sometime after dark, he suddenly spotted two enemy soldiers working their way along the creek bed toward his position. When the Japanese got in easy range, Maloney killed both with a quick burst from his rifle. The following night, Maloney spotted a larger collection of Japanese coming down the creek from exactly the same direction. This time, Maloney was not only ready, he had brought several other men with him. When the Japanese get close, more than forty were ambushed and killed by machine-gun fire and hand grenades.

The Indian Seventh Division's luck would continue. One of the Japanese dead who'd fought hardest—he'd actually scrambled up the creek bank to attack one of Maloney's men with a sword—was carrying a tactical map. It turned out that the bend in the creek where Maloney had set up his watch was a rendezvous point, and each night thereafter dozens more Japanese soldiers wandered into Maloney's death trap. Soon, 110 enemy combatants had been dispatched at the spot, without the loss of a single Seventh Division soldier.

The days passed, and the Japanese assaults on the Admin Box continued

fiercely and relentlessly. Close-contact injuries—mostly by bullet wound-
ings and bayonetings—caused the majority of casualties on both sides. It
was a favorite tactic of the Fifty-fifth Division's field commander, Lt. General Shozo Sakurai, to attack in darkness. On February 14 and 16, at
precisely 10:20 p.m., Sakurai sent waves of Japanese soldiers against the
concertina wire of the Admin Box from one hillside or another. Because of
Seventh Division's defensive posture, however, the Japanese screams of
"Banzai!" were always quickly drowned out by the explosions of tank shells
and bursts of machine-gun and rifle fire. On both nights, after only thirty-
five minutes, the shooting would stop and the night air would fill with the
agonized screams of wounded Japanese. Then, as the oscillating flashes
from British star shells lit up the dark sky like fireworks, the British would
witness hundreds of imperial soldiers writhing on the ground in their
khaki uniforms or dangling in the perimeter wire bleeding to death.

Still, the Admin Box was so full of vehicles, mules, men, storage magazines, and equipment that it was often difficult for a Japanese soldier *not* to
find a target anytime he fired toward Sinzweya. Soon the base hospital was
again filled with British and Indian casualties, and the two surgeons
there—unshaven and exhausted—worked nonstop in thirty-six-hour shifts,
their aprons dripping with blood.

After a week inside the Admin Box, supplies began to run low. Adams
and his men began to worry about the amounts of artillery shells and ammunition they had, as well as how many provisions they retained to feed
the troops. Anxiety was heightened one night when an attack wave of
seventy-five Japanese Zero fighters laid down such fearsome strafing lines
that several fires were ignited on Ammunition Hill, detonating some explosives there—including several heavy artillery shells, which streaked
crazily through the night sky.

Night after night, despite using up their stores of ammunition, the artillery and tanks controlled by Seventh Division were slowly tearing down
the Japanese. During the days, Seventh Division's tanks roamed the base
perimeter, firing at any jungle activity they saw; at night, Adams positioned them at pressure points in the jungled hillsides, treating them like
mobile bunkers. One night, at the southern end of the Admin Box, a full
Japanese battalion—865 men—tried to infiltrate the Admin Box from a
mountain designated on British maps as Hill 315. But as the raiding force
pushed down the mountainside toward base perimeter, it was machine-

gun and artillery fire from a line of tanks that drove them back. After subsequent waves of attackers were repulsed, Sakurai sent several units of
suicide fighters to destroy the tanks. None ever got close.

On some days, the British would take the fight to the Japanese, usually
with Seventh Division's tanks leading strategic charges. When ten tanks
from the Twenty-fifth Dragoons were ordered to take back a hill at the
north of the Admin Box called C Company Hill, they began their assault
by firing long-range, 75-millimeter high-explosive shells against the entrenched Japanese, tearing the surrounding jungle to shreds and exposing
the enemy positions. As the tanks drew closer—followed by several detachments of West York infantrymen—the tank gunners switched artillery
from high-explosive shells to solid shot, which pummeled the enemy and
better assured that their own men would not be wounded by friendly explosions. When the tanks were finally opposite the Japanese entrench-
ments at point-blank range—still firing solid shot shells and with their
machine guns roaring—the mechanized assault halted and, from behind,
the West Yorks stepped in with bayonets to finish the job.

C Company Hill was back under British control.


AFTER THIRTEEN DAYS of siege in and around the Admin Box, the Japanese Fifty-fifth Infantry Division above Sinzweya had been decimated by
the steady and better-equipped British defenders—and the Imperial
Japanese losses were truly staggering. Four days into the battle, on February 11, General Sakurai had 2,190 men on the hillsides surrounding
Sinzweya, all of them confident and ready to attack. Ten days later, on February 21, only four hundred Japanese troops remained.

The next day, on February 22, Sakurai decided to make a final valiant
assault on Sinzweya: he ordered a second "open cylinder" attack, an all-out
charge on the British positions in the valley below. Shortly after the order
went out, however, the attack was suddenly postponed. As his battalions
began reporting to Sakurai in advance of the assault, it became apparent
that there were no artillery projectiles left, and—owing to illness and
injuries—the Fifty-fifth Infantry could muster only a total of about
one hundred soldiers for their charge.

Two days later, Sakurai terminated Sinzweya operations and ordered a
systematic withdrawal from the hillsides around the Admin Box. Under-

supplied and without field artillery or antitank weapons, the Japanese had gambled that their usual brand of streaking attack and tactical encirclement would overwhelm the British. Japan had miscalculated.

THE JAPANESE WITHDRAWAL at Sinzweya became a valiant touchstone for the British and likely stands as the turning point for the war in Burma. At the Admin Box, "British and Indian soliders had proved themselves, man for man, the masters of the best the Japanese could bring against them," wrote William Slim. "It was a victory, a victory about which there could be no argument, and its effect . . . was immense."

Just as the Chindits, the X Force, and Merrill's Marauders were finding out almost simultaneously, the regular British army now understood that the Japanese could not only be beaten, they could be pounded until they shattered. It was a lesson Slim and his men would need to remember, since the biggest battle of the war in Burma was now approaching India like a thunderhead from the east. Just across India's border with Burma, an invasion force of forty thousand Japanese soldiers was now staged and ready to attack.

DESPITE THE CARNAGE of the Admin Box, the fight for Sinzweya had never been anything more than a Japanese diversion from Mutaguchi's larger plan: the invasion and defeat of the British-Indian army on the Imphal plain. And in early March 1944, just two weeks after the withdrawal from Sinzweya, the Japanese began their attack in earnest.

Employing the same windy rhetoric that all Japanese commanders used to inspire their men, Mutaguchi issued these U-Go orders to his troops: "The army has now reached the state of invincibility, and the day when the Rising Sun shall proclaim our victory in India is not far off. When we strike we must reach our objectives with the speed of wildfire, despite all the obstacles of the river, mountain, and labyrinthine jungle . . . We must sweep aside the paltry opposition we encounter and add luster to army tradition by achieving a victory of annihilation."

WITH THOSE LOFTY PRONOUNCEMENTS, U-Go was underway. On March 8, a Gurkha patrol from Slim's Fourteenth Army spotted two thousand Japanese troops moving west through the jungle near the towns of Mulabem and Tiddum. But while the Gurkhas quickly reported their findings to headquarters, no one inside Slim's army believed two thousand Japanese troops presented much danger. Slim knew that far more Japanese would be coming and he bided his time, waiting for the enemy to get beyond their range of supply and communications.

Then, on March 13, Slim and his troops could no longer wave off the Japanese presence. A large invasion force was now materializing out of the jungle and they were attempting to block the Tiddum Road south of Slim's headquarters in Imphal. On that day, close to midnight, a withdrawal order finally went out to the Seventeenth Indian Division to return to Imphal, but it was too late. The Japanese had managed to block the Tiddum Road at Tongzang—110 miles south of Imphal—isolating the Seventeenth Division and the Twentieth Division to their south. Over the next week, at two more places along the road, the Japanese slid between the Seventeenth and Twentieth Indian Divisions. To General Slim, the British and Indian forces and the Japanese were now set up and visible in alternating layers along the Tiddum Road, like a 110-mile slice of "Neapolitan ice" that extended all the way to the Burmese border. Because of the Tiddum Road's snaking, switchback construction up and down the hills of the Manipur River Valley—where its now-bricked surface made the three-thousand-foot, forty-hairpin-curve "Chocolate Staircase" at least navigable—roadblocks and ambushes could be expected anywhere. So rather than order his two divisions trapped along the road to move, General Slim decided to keep his forces stationary for the time being, air-dropping in extra troops, ammunition, and food for them as needed.

By March 19, the U-Go invasion seemed, from all outward appearances, to be going Mutaguchi's way. Despite the Indian Seventeenth Division having thirteen thousand soldiers—including several detachments of Gurkha guerrillas adept at jungle fighting—they could not displace the Japanese Thirty-third Division astride the Tiddum Road around the town of Tongzang. Using artillery and flanking movements, the soldiers of the Seventeenth Division fought wisely and gamely, but the Japanese—despite having been there only a few days—were well spread out. And the Japanese weren't staying put. Even as they defended Tongzang against the charges of the Seventeenth Indian Division, several detachments of Japanese troops were moving north along the road toward British Fourteenth

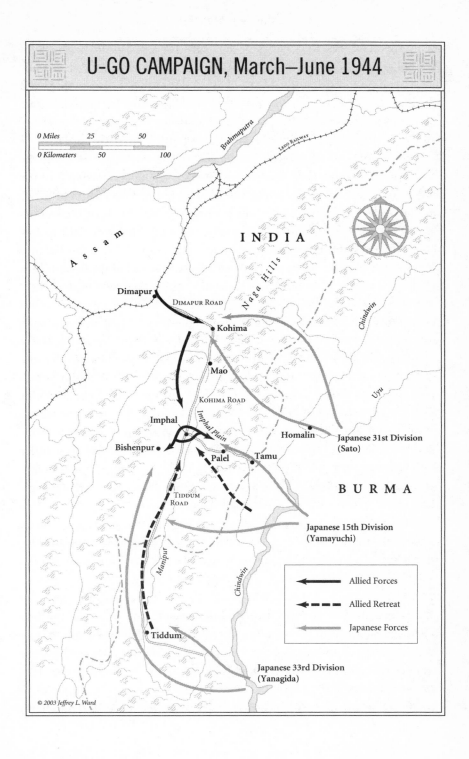

# U-GO CAMPAIGN, March–June 1944

0 Miles 25 50
0 Kilometers 50 100

Brahmaputra

LEDO RAILWAY

A s s a m

I N D I A

Naga Hills

Chindwin

Dimapur

DIMAPUR ROAD

Kohima

Mao

KOHIMA ROAD

Ujyu

Imphal Plain

Imphal

Homalin

Japanese 31st Division
(Sato)

Bishenpur

Palel

Tamu

TIDDUM ROAD

B U R M A

Manipur

Japanese 15th Division
(Yamayuchi)

Chindwin

Allied Forces

Allied Retreat

Japanese Forces

Tiddum

Japanese 33rd Division
(Yanagida)

© 2003 Jeffrey L. Ward

Army Headquarters. In a matter of days they were within thirty-six miles of Imphal.

General Slim, however, stuck to his plan. He ordered his troops along the Tiddum Road to carry on with their assaults on the Japanese, supplying and reinforcing both the Seventeenth and the Twentieth Indian Division with air drops from the Royal Air Force and U.S. Army C-47s. With Stilwell's approval, reinforcing troops and supplies were diverted from bases in Assam, and after two years of Hump flying, the airborne crews had become supernaturally proficient: they could parachute provisions for an entire eight-hundred-man battalion inside a one-hundred-yard circle almost 100 percent of the time, and could off-load four tons of cargo from a landed C-47 in minutes.

With the fighting along the Tiddum Road south of Imphal at a slow burn—and now with some idea of the numbers and character of the forces he was up against—Slim began to more seriously piece together his defense of Imphal. Following approvals from Mountbatten and Stilwell, Slim began airlifting the battle-tuned "Ball of Fire" Fifth Indian Division to Imphal from the Arakan Peninsula. A month before, Fifth Division was the unit that evaded the feinting attack from Japan's Fifty-fifth Infantry, owing to the pitched battle for the Admin Box. And in just eleven days, Fifth Division's twelve thousand troops—plus artillery, mules, jeeps, ammunition, and logistics and support units—was flown in by troop transport to help with the defense of Imphal. Just as Adams's forces had done at the Admin Box, General Slim and his Fourteenth Army began compressing themselves down into a tightly protected perimeter, presenting a steely defense that would prove difficult to break into constituent pieces. They were growing ready.

Now all that remained was for time, supply problems, and distance to start taking their tolls on the Japanese invaders.


IN TRUTH, the job of defending the Imphal plain and the roads leading north and south from it was monumental. While Imphal itself was defensible, the roads leading out of it were difficult to keep open, bounded as they were by steep mountains draped in thick jungle that obscured the size, armaments, and position of enemy forces.

To the north, the road stretched eighty miles from Imphal to a second—and far smaller—British base in the town of Kohima. Forty-five miles northwest of Kohima, and along the same twisty mountain track, stood the critical rail junction in the city of Dimapur. If the road to Dimapur was severed, cutting off Kohima and Imphal from rail supply, the entire British and Indian army in east India—perhaps sixty thousand men—would have to be supplied by air, an impossible task.

To the south of Imphal, the Tiddum Road was now completely blocked by the Japanese at three places. First, a Japanese central column had come straight up the road toward Tiddum out of Burma from the south. Second, a Japanese left column had swung wide of the road to the west and emerged from the jungle onto the road about ten miles north of Tongzang, taking the town and blocking the Indian retreat. Finally, a third battalion had driven north through the mountains east of the Manipur River Valley, emerging from the jungle along the Tiddum Road at Milepost 109 and Tongzang, with its large British-Indian supply of food and ammunition. When the supply dump fell on March 18, the Japanese inventoried its contents and giddily reported to Mutaguchi that enough food, ammunition, and artillery had been seized to run Lt. General Motozo Yanagida's southernmost Thirty-third Division for two months.

The British Seventeenth and Twentieth Divisions south of Imphal were now fully trapped, and Slim stuck to his larger plan: he ordered both armies to continue their attacks on the roadblocks, but not to move too appreciably north back toward Imphal. After all, the British and Indians could do little to reopen the Tiddum Road until Mutaguchi revealed the rest of his plans. Eventually, Slim reminded himself, with ample supplies air-dropped to his men as the Japanese continued to fire and eat what little ammunition and food they'd carried in, the Tiddum Road blockades could be broken easily and the Japanese repelled.

Throughout March 1944, Mutaguchi's larger plans remained obscure. In the latter part of the month, as the Indian Fiftieth Parachute Brigade repelled the leading edge of the Japanese invaders in the village of Sangshank northeast of Imphal (resulting in 850 Japanese casualties), Mutaguchi's Thirty-first Division armies stayed out of sight. They massed beneath the mountainous jungle canopy east of Imphal and Kohima. In response, Slim had no option but to wait until Mutaguchi showed his full scheme. But as a final reinforcement, aside from airlifting the Indian Fifth Division north out of Arakan to help with his defense of Imphal, in early April Slim brought the British XXXIII Corps to east India to help defend the corridor between the towns of Kohima and Dimapur.

With the addition of the Indian Fifth Division and the XXXIII Corps, the British possessed superior manpower and weaponry against the Japanese. Mutaguchi, who had expected his fast-moving and lightly outfitted armies to battle only three divisions, was now facing nearly five. And he was also leaning on one tenet of his invasion perhaps a bit too heavily. He still expected his invasion of India to require only three weeks.

To provision his troops and help carry their equipment, Mutaguchi had supplied his forces with meat on the hoof—in the form of thousands of cattle and oxen. But as Mutaguchi's troops and livestock kept hacking and stumbling their way through the mountainous, steaming jungles toward Imphal and Kohima, things began to turn bad. By April, the cattle started to die of disease and exhaustion, since they were used to pulling carts on roads, not carrying heavy loads over mountains.

"The cattle could not climb the steep, rocky paths, which even we soldiers found hard," said Manabu Wada, a senior private transportation soldier with Mutaguchi's Thirty-first Division. "Our cattle and horses fell down the mountainside, taking our provisions with them; the slopes were so steep we couldn't go down to retrieve anything."

Compounding the army's hunger, with the exception of the food depot at Tongzang, most enemy provisions still remained under British control. It was time for Mutaguchi to conquer east India; otherwise his men would begin to starve.


ON THE NIGHT of April 5, 1944, the Japanese Thirty-first Division, nearly twenty thousand men commanded by Lt. General Kotuku Sato, attacked Kohima first. For the British, who had mostly concentrated their forces in Imphal, only thirty-eight hundred troops were on hand to defend the city, and the majority of these defensive forces were state policemen, convalescents, and rear-echelon troops. Only fifteen hundred of the garrison, fewer than half, were trained infantry and riflemen. Compounding their problems, the Kohima garrison had no barbed wire to create a cordon around the city. As the Japanese encirclement began, the Kohima troops were forced to tighten their base perimeters in short order. Then, after the single water pipe that supplied the troops was severed by the invaders, Japanese sharpshooters began to hit the steel water tanks at the Kohima garrison. Within hours, the British in Kohima had only the water in their canteens to sustain them for the coming days.

As fighting increased, some units from the Indian 161st Brigade—a portion of the "Ball of Fire" Indian Fifth Division—attempted to reinforce Kohima by pushing down from the northeast, but they were driven back by Sato's troops, who had already surrounded the city. Like an anaconda crushing its prey until it can no longer breathe, Sato's men continued to push constantly against the British perimeter with rifles and mortar fire, and by the afternoon of April 6—for a second time in twenty-four hours—the Kohima defensive force had to contract its perimeter.

For Sato and his Thirty-first Division, with Kohima cut off by his troops after only a day of invasion, there was now an exceptional opportunity. With the British off-balance, the time was right to strike forty-six miles northwest of Kohima and take the railhead at Dimapur. Once the rail yard was captured, severing the flow of supplies and ammunition to Slim and his East Indian forces, the Brits and Indians would begin to weaken daily and the Japanese would be a giant bound closer to success. Mutaguchi agreed with Sato's attack plans, but when he advised his superior—General Masakazu Kawabe—of this next critical step, Kawabe, an inflexible and stately old-school warrior in charge of all Japanese forces in Burma, staunchly disagreed. He believed capture of the Dimapur rail junction was "not within the strategic objectives," and ordered Mutaguchi and Sato to stand down on Dimapur and remain in position around Kohima.

In the end, the aborted attack on Dimapur may rank as the greatest missed opportunity in Japan's invasion of India. With the Dimapur railhead left open—allowing the flow of weapons, soldiers, and supplies to continue for Kohima and Imphal—the potential for the overwhelming Japanese invasion of India was lost. And possibly the successful Japanese invasion of India was lost as well.

EVEN WITHOUT THE ATTACK on Dimapur, though, the early weeks of April 1944 brought the British and Indian forces at Kohima mounting trouble. After only two days and under constant Japanese pressure, thirty-eight hundred British and Indians were trapped inside Kohima in a triangular zone that measured only four hundred to five hundred yards to a side. But if surrounded, the British-Indian forces weren't backing down. Over the next week, with the Kohima defenders surviving on little food and less than a pint of water a day, the British and Indians began a gutsy, all-out defensive that ranks among the most valorous of World War II.

Day after day, the Japanese were capturing the high ground along a ridgeline overlooking Kohima's small downtown. After the Japanese captured the field supply depot on one hilltop overlooking the British perimeter, they began using the field bakery's huts and enormous iron ovens as cover, firing weapons and throwing grenades on the defenders, then slamming shut the oven doors before the British could retaliate. To displace the Japanese, a young munitions officer cobbled together "pole charges"— twenty-five pounds of explosive packed in empty ammunition boxes and delivered inside the warehouses on long bamboo poles—which had devastating effects, literally blasting the Japanese to pieces.

Then, on April 7, the British decided that it was time to take back the field supply depot and Supply Hill, as that stretch of the ridge was known. As the Royal West Kents attacked the field supply depot's hilltop under fierce automatic weapons fire and showers of grenades, Lance Corporal John Harmon began an almost superhuman two days of heroics. In the attack's initial charge, Harmon noticed two machine guns working against the West Kents from a small nest on the attack's flank. Using his teeth to pull two grenade pins, he walked toward the enemy position just outside the machine guns' swing, lobbed the grenades into the nest, and—after the explosion—jumped down into the enemy position and finished the job with his bayonet. Then he lifted one of the machine guns above his head and began screaming to his battle company in fierce triumph.

Inspired by Harmon, the Royal West Kents' entire D Company began shouting and, in unison, charged the field supply depot. Using their rifle butts, hands, bayonets, and knives for weapons, they recaptured the depot, driving out or killing the entire Japanese unit that had been occupying the building. With the depot retaken, Harmon discovered that several Japanese still appeared to be locked inside the bakery's ovens. He rushed out, gathered up an armload of grenades, and hurried back inside to drop one grenade into each of the ten ovens' smokestacks. After the explosions, Harmon pried open each oven door and, among the dead, he found two enemy soldiers still alive. Harmon lifted them both and—once again to the mad cheers of his Royal West Kents—dragged them back across the base perimeter as POWs.

The following morning, April 8, after a night of nonstop (and quite accurate) shelling and probing ground attacks by the Japanese, Harmon's D Company was ordered to attack yet another machine-gun position, this one on a knobby hillside at another edge of the British perimeter. After instructing his Bren gunner to lay stripes of overlapping covering fire onto the machine-gun post, which sat at the edge of a trench, Harmon again walked calmly toward the Japanese. He killed the two forward gunners in the trench with his rifle, then fixed his bayonet and charged the machine-gun emplacement, jumping into the trench and killing all three of the weapons operators. With the position taken—just as he'd done the day before—Harmon celebrated by leaping out of the trench, raising the heavy gun above his head, and bellowing in victory.

The British cheered him on until, to their growing horror, they watched as Harmon began to stroll—never hurrying—back down the hill amid growing enemy rifle and machine-gun fire. They shouted at Harmon to run, but he kept walking. To cover him, the Royal West Kents fired against all visible enemy positions, but halfway back to the British lines Harmon was hit in the spine and mortally wounded by a sniper. As he was dying, and after a group of West Kent medics rushed out and dragged him back to the trench, Harmon, his cool still not broken, used his last breaths to inspire his comrades. "I got the lot," he said. "It was worth it."

ON THE NIGHT of April 8, the strangest battle of the entire Kohima engagement began. On a once-elegant tennis court sited on a strategically important rise above a bungalow formerly occupied by the local British deputy commissioner, several units of Japanese soldiers attacked a British detachment there in an attempt to take the court as a lookout.

With each new wave of Japanese fighters, the British troops behind sandbags on the court's far baseline repelled the invaders with rifles and hand grenades. All night long, the Japanese tried to establish their tennis-court beachhead on the opposite baseline. Bullets and grenades flew across the midcourt net. Like an epic Wimbledon, the battle for the tennis court raged through the night and into the next morning and afternoon. Finally, after an entire day of nonstop skirmishing and explosions, the British managed to pin down the attacking Japanese, encircling and destroying them. At Kohima, tennis remained in British hands.

BUT CASUALTIES FOR both sides were rising disconcertingly. The Kohima garrison was now fighting primarily out of trenches, their medical staffs working to stitch up the wounded twenty-four hours a day. Then, on April 13, the medical inspection building itself took two direct hits from Japanese artillery, killing four of the already small surgical and treatment team.

By April 15th, after eleven days of constant attacks and defensive reconfigurations, the Japanese appeared to finally have the British at checkmate. After a long struggle, a critical ridge above Kohima's triangular perimeter was finally taken by Sato's men.

For the British, it was a last straw. Two days earlier, after more than a week without adequate food, water, and ammunition, British and American cargo planes had braved the ground fire of twenty thousand Japanese troops—flying down the narrow Kohima Valley from the north—and air-dropped supplies to the Kohima defenders. Unfortunately, the food, bullets, and extra mortars and mortar rounds missed their mark; they were carried on a breeze directly to the Japanese. The only Allied parachutes that fell within the Kohima defense perimeter, in fact, were artillery shells intended for the Indian 161st Brigade, still trapped two and a half miles northwest of the city. Consequently, inside Kohima, the few shells the British and Indian defenders had received weren't even the right caliber for their artillery pieces. Soon the Japanese were shelling the British and Indians with British-made weapons and, between barrages, they taunted the Kohima garrison across the no-man's-land, shouting to the British that their air-dropped rations were of especially high quality.

To the surrounded troops of the Kohima garrison, the end seemed near. On the morning of April 18, thirteen days into the siege, Kohima's defenders were readying to make a hand-to-hand stand for their base with bayonets drawn. Amazingly, on that same morning, Indian troops from the 161st managed to break through the Japanese encirclement and stream into Kohima, relieving the Kohima defenders with fresh men and weapons.

Two days later, the break in the Japanese ring around Kohima was secure enough that the sick, wounded, and dead from the battle could be evacuated, with the defensive force strengthened by a brigade from the Indian Second Division. In the thirteen days of siege for Kohima, more than six hundred British and Indian soldiers had been killed, and the scene awaiting the reinforcements was nothing short of horrific. Severed limbs lay among the jagged, leafless tree stumps along with blood-soaked boots, decay-bloated dead, and the red, blue, green, and white fabric of parachutes. "The ground everywhere was ploughed up with shell fire," wrote Major John Nettlefield, "and human remains lay rotting as the battle raged over them. Flies swarmed everywhere and multiplied with incredible speed. Men retched as they dug in. The stink hung in the air and permeated one's clothes and hair."

The gore and desperation of the scene, however, weren't just being experienced by Kohima's defenders. On the other side of the battle line, the Japanese had been dying, too, and they were being ground down. "We complained bitterly to one another about the incompetence of our generals," said Manabu Wada, the transport senior private with Sato's Thirty-first Division:

In mid-April . . . [we] had no rations left. The British had burned all their food and supply depots so that not even a grain of rice or a round of ammunition was left for us . . . Our three weeks' rations were exhausted . . . The enemy's heavy and medium artillery opened up on us as a prelude to their infantry attacks. For our part, we were limited to reply with just a few shells a day, while the British shells rained down on us in the hundreds and thousands in great barrages . . . We watched as enemy reinforcements arrived by truck with more and more ammunition to be thrown immediately against us. It was only at about three o'clock in the afternoon when they [the British] took their tea break, as we could see through our telescopes, that we had a respite from the shells, but we could not use our rifles on them because the range was too great.

And the battle remained far from over. On the evening of April 18, just hours after the Indian replacements had broken through, another pitched battle for the tennis court was under way. And despite the happy prospects of Indian reinforcements and extra weapons, the Japanese still had Kohima surrounded—and they remained heavily dug in at several of the most prominent points overlooking the city.

But slowly, with lungs that took in the scent of rotting corpses with each breath, the British and Indians began to widen their perimeter, even as sunset barrages of Japanese mortar fire and artillery continued to fall. Day after day passed and, finally, as more British and Indian men and weapons poured into the city—including a full brigade from the Indian Second Division—the balance of the battle began to shift.

In a patient and able uphill campaign, the British and Indians recaptured a vital command center on Kohima ridge. And with a toehold once again on higher ground, they began disrupting Japanese attacks and driving the Japanese from other positions along the ridge. Like a bolt-cutter going after the soft gold of a wedding ring, the British, Indians, and Gurkhas inside the Japanese encirclement began to split the weakened enemy forces into pieces, first dividing the Japanese troops along an east-west axis, then quartering them with a north-south break. They would have to fight Sato's troops bunker by bunker, hilltop by hilltop, but by the beginning of June, the Japanese were showing clear signs of exhaustion.

"It was not surprising that in the middle of May the British found it possible to recapture Kohima Ridge from us," recalled Manabu Wada. "Our losses had been dreadful. Our soldiers fought bravely, but they had no rations, no rifle or machine-gun ammunition, no artillery shells for the guns to fire. And above all, had no support from the rear echelons . . . At the beginning of the operation the regiment was thirty-eight hundred strong . . . [now] we were reduced to just a few hundred."

THOUGH THE BATTLE for Kohima was turning toward Allied victory, the British and Indian punch-ups for the Tiddum Road and the Imphal plain remained white-hot. Along the Tiddum Road, on March 21 and 22, the British and Indians had reengaged the Japanese for control of Tongzang's supply depot near Milepost 109. Assisted by several waves of British bomber aircraft, the town and its supply post were back in Allied hands by March 25—and what the British mop-up crews found at Tongzang was both enlightening and gruesome.

First, by the gluttonous consumption of food—which lay strewn everywhere like garbage—it was obvious that the Japanese were starving. Second, the Brits found the bodies of two Indian soldiers; each had been stripped naked and hung by the neck in the town's center. Once they were dead, the two Indians had obviously become bayonet dummies. Despite the horrors of Tongzang, the British and Indians now believed they could prevail against Yanagida's Thirty-third Division along the Tiddum Road south of Imphal. William Slim's "drawing out" of the Japanese into India was working. And thanks to superior manpower, waves of bomber aircraft, and vast reserves of air-dropped supplies and weapons, the British and Indian forces were staying strong as the Japanese were beginning to wither.

The fight for Imphal and Kohima, where two thirty-thousand- to forty-thousand-man armies now squared off against one another, became the region's focus. Cut off from all supply since the Japanese had severed the road to Kohima at the end of March, Slim had been constantly resupplied by airlift. Since April 18, British and American planes brought more than nineteen thousand tons of supplies and twelve thousand more troops to the Imphal plain. It seemed that every man and morsel of rice would be needed by Slim's forces, as Mutaguchi, his Japanese Fifteenth Infantry Division, and its commander, Lt. General Masafumi Yamauchi, were now attacking Imphal with every bit of force their troops could muster.

Like the invasion of Burma two years early, the Japanese "March on Delhi" was staged as a series of steps, with no forward motion made until the area most recently taken was secured and fortified. In the hills above Imphal, Yamauchi's Fifteenth Infantry would invade and conquer an area, reinforce it with sandbags and concrete pillboxes, and then drive forward again with an almost suicidal energy. When the British and Indians could get close enough to counter these new bunkers with pole charges, the Japanese didn't run. Instead, confronting their own certain deaths, they continued firing on the enemies until the charge detonated and ripped them to bits.

The Japanese were absolutely unafraid for their individual salvation—and few outwardly feared death. Every Imperial Japanese soldier understood that medals and awards were given only for successful campaigns and service to the emperor; none was ever awarded for valor on the battlefield. Each soldier functioned as a small piece of the whole; without his best efforts, the entire platoon, regiment, battalion, or division could suffer humiliation. He also knew that, while he was away, his parents, siblings, and family members were not allowed to do, say, or write anything in a letter to the soldiers that might make them hesitate to offer up their lives for the emperor. That is how the attack-minded Imperial Japanese soldiers had been programmed to think. In order to get the formalities of dying on the battlefield out of the way, in fact, many Japanese troops, especially the Bushido-trained officers, held funerals for themselves *before* departing Japan for combat.

Said Susumu Miyashita, an infantry soldier in the Imperial Army:

At the time leading up to the war, everything was kind of insane in Japan. At first, only a small contingent of people wanted the war, which, if you will look at our history, remains an extraordinary event. We are a peaceful people. But as the war went on and grew in scope, an insane nationalism took hold, and people who weren't at first supportive of the war began to be dragged inside this insanity. Most of us weren't Bushido, but the practices of it and the pressure to go and fight honorably began to work its way into our consciousness. Once you had been drafted and were inside that culture, it was everywhere and you forgot the outside world. Those beliefs infected you until you, too, thought with all your being that it was more honorable to die than to be taken as a prisoner . . . That the greatest honor you could do for your family, your country, and your emperor was to die advancing the Japanese cause in Asia. Almost to a man, we were willing to die. We considered that fate far better than to live on and not succeed in our objectives to conquer Asia.

Even William Slim—who bore the brunt of the Japanese warriors' fanaticism—was impressed by his enemy's bravery. "The strength of the Japanese army lay," he later wrote in his memoirs, "in the spirit of the individual Japanese soldier. He fought and marched till he died. If five hundred Japanese were ordered to hold a position, we had to kill four hundred and ninety-five before it was ours—and then the last five killed themselves."

Soon, at Imphal, Kohima, and all across CBI, stories were being told about Japanese suicides when a soldier—perhaps too sick or wounded to avoid capture—would endeavor to take his life rather than remain as a prisoner. Some Imperial Army POWs slashed their own throats with the lids from ration cans. Others drank kerosene. Still others would try to hang themselves or would smash their heads against plaster buildings or rocks until their skulls were pulped. Others threw themselves off stair landings or balconies.

Still, at Imphal, Kohima, and along the Tiddum Road, the confident genius behind William Slim's initial "drawing out" of the Japanese was starting to exert itself. Isolated from their limited supplies in Burma by tall mountains and one hundred miles of jungle, the Imperial Japanese were becoming weakened and addled. Still, they fought on. Despite British tank units and aerial bombings and pole charges—not to mention the ever-widening front of British and Indian infantries starting to drive them back—the Japanese kept attacking with all the ferocity they could summon.

Even as they were being killed at a rate of four or five to one, every Japanese soldier fought to his death. During one battlefield cleanup along the Tiddum Road, after some Japanese chose to fake death and one by one ambushed a detachment of Gurkhas collecting corpses for burial, the Gurkhas started to take their own precautionary steps. Pulling out their long and razor-sharp knives, called *kurkris*, which hung on their belts, the Gurkhas ensured all subsequent enemy troops were dead by slashing their throats before grabbing up a supposed casualty. When a passing British officer saw a Gurkha about to cut the throat of a still-living Japanese soldier who—until that moment—had feigned death, the officer stopped the killing with an off-the-cuff order: "You mustn't do that, Jim," he said.

Hearing the command, the Gurkha turned to the officer somewhat disappointedly, held back his blade, and—with a pained expression draped across his face—responded, "But, sahib, we can't bury him *alive?*"

BY LATE MAY 1944, the Japanese had eaten all their livestock and used up most of their ammunition. There was hopeful talk throughout the Japanese invasion force—from the Tiddum Road in the south to Kohima in the north—that a full withdrawal order to Burma would soon be issued. General Mutaguchi, however, refused to quit. When Yamauchi and Yanagida, his commanders of the Fifteenth and Thirty-third Divisions—along the Tiddum Road and in Imphal—sent messages to Mutaguchi that they had no food or weapons, Mutaguchi ordered the fighting to continue at all costs. Then he finished the order with this directive: "Continue in the task until all of your ammunition is expended. If your hands are broken, fight with your feet. If your hands and feet are broken, use your teeth. If there is no breath left in your body, fight with your spirit. Lack of weapons is no excuse for defeat."


WHEN MUTAGUCHI RADIOED those orders out, however, his betrayal had already been set into motion. On May 13, General Sato—the attacker of Kohima—had been the first to request permission to remove his forces from combat. In the past six weeks, after having come so close to crushing the Kohima garrison, he had now lost three thousand dead and four thousand wounded and the British and Indians were now taking back much of Kohima Ridge as the British XXIII Corps was beginning to press on his troops from the Dimapur sector. Sato's army had nothing to eat, little ammunition to fire, and with his troops either vitally damaged or exhausted, he sought to retreat toward the Burmese border, where he could more easily get provisions and first aid.

Upon hearing the request, Mutaguchi denied it. When Sato requested a tactical withdrawal from Kohima for the second time, Mutaguchi again refused. Sato grew furious and began to rant. "This is shameful," he shouted to his staff. "Mutaguchi should apologize for his own failure to the dead soldiers and the Japanese people. He should not try to put the blame on his subordinates."

Still, despite his anger, Sato stood by his orders—even though the fight for Kohima had become hopeless. Off and on for two more weeks, Sato's men tried to keep the encirclement of Kohima together, but the defensive pressure was simply becoming too great. When Sato requested air-dropped provisions from the Japanese air force in Burma, he was denied. When he requested drops a second time, he added this note of desperation: "Since leaving the Chindwin, we have not received one bullet from you, nor a grain of rice." Again, no planes or airdrops of supplies arrived.

On May 25, Sato informed Mutaguchi that he and his men were withdrawing from Kohima. This time, the message was not a request but a terse statement. "My division's rations are now exhausted," he radioed in. "We have completely used up ammunition for mountain artillery and heavy infantry weapons. The division will therefore withdraw from Kohima by 1st June at the latest and move to a point where it can receive supplies."

Mutaguchi responded with a statement of his own: "Withdraw and I will court-martial you," he radioed back.

Sato, receiving the message, signaled he'd had enough. "Do what you please," he radioed back. "I will bring you down with me."

Sato had crossed the Bushido code. And he knew his actions, while sparing his troops, would have dire consequences for him personally.

Mutaguchi, with Sato now missing somewhere east of Kohima, grew frenzied and distraught. "He has lost the battle for me!" he shouted. And hoping to somehow reverse Sato's plan, Mutaguchi sent his chief of staff, Major General Kunomura, to find Sato and order him back to his encirclement of Kohima. When Kunomura found Sato on May 27 and quoted orders to him—as well as reminding him of the consequences for insubordination—Sato screamed back: "The army has failed to send me supplies and ammunition since the operation began! This failure released me from any obligation to obey the order! And in any case it would be impossible to comply!"

When Kunomura again reminded Sato of his perilous place inside the imperial army, Sato told his superior that he no longer cared about Mutaguchi. Instead he offered that he, Sato, would show Imperial Headquarters "how stupid Mutaguchi has been!" As a preemptive gesture, he radioed off one last message, this one to Imperial Army Command in Rangoon: "The tactical ability of the Fifteenth Army staff lies below that of cadets." And at midnight on May 31, Sato ordered the withdrawal of his troops from Kohima. He ended his message by commanding that all of his army's radios be turned off.

AS JUNE 1944 ARRIVED, the arguing between Japanese generals in India had become pointless. Due to lack of food and ammunition, the fortythousand-man Japanese invasion army that had set out to conquer India four months before was disintegrating. Soldiers were living on diets of leeches, slugs, tree buds, and boiled grasses. One regiment, which had at one time been four thousand men strong, now numbered a hungry and exhausted 460 troops; only half of these survivors were still capable of steadying a rifle enough to fire it accurately.

As with Sato a few weeks before, Mutaguchi was now entertaining requests for withdrawal from Lieutenant General Yanagida along the Tid-

dum Road and Lieutenant General Yamauchi at Imphal. After four months
on the battlefield, Mutaguchi was realizing that his proposed three-week
invasion of India was a complete and humiliating failure. He sacked
Yanagida and Yamauchi for their weakness and radioed off a request for
the withdrawal of all three divisions to General Kawabe, the Imperial
Army's Burma area army commander in Rangoon. But Kawabe, just as
Mutaguchi had done to his own generals, refused. Instead, Burma Area
Command ordered Mutaguchi to continue the invasion.

Mutaguchi had few troops, little ammunition, and no fighting spirit left
in his men. Making matters worse, on June 22, the Fifth Indian Division—
proud and ready defenders of Kohima and the Arakan Peninsula before
that—reopened the road between Kohima and Imphal, allowing men,
tanks, artillery, ammunition, and supplies to move freely between the two
battle zones.

With this reconnection of General Slim's forces, the Japanese could expect only larger engagements by the British and Indians. On July 7, in despair for his men and the slaughter that awaited them, Mutaguchi took his
leave to a hilltop overlooking Imphal and chanted a Shinto prayer for help.
And, remarkably, the next day, July 8, five full months after Mutaguchi's diversionary troops on the Arakan Peninsula had fired the initial shots in the
"March on Delhi," the Japanese were given orders to begin their withdrawal from India back into Burma.

A Japanese news correspondent who had been traveling with Mutaguchi's forces characterized the retreat this way: "In the end we had no
ammunition, no clothes, no food, no guns. The men were barefoot and
ragged, and threw away everything except canes to help them walk. Their
eyes blazed in their lean bodies. All they had to keep them going was grass
and water. And there were jungles, great mountains, and flooded rivers
barring their way."

As he withdrew from the mountains above Kohima, using a walking
stick to support his weight, Senior Private Manabu Wada of the Thirty-
first Division described the walk vividly: "Our path to safety lay beyond
these mountains covered in dense jungle . . . The bodies of our comrades
who had struggled along the track before us lay all around, rainsodden and
giving off the stench of decomposition. The bones of some bodies were exposed. Even with the support of our sticks, we fell amongst the corpses
again and again as we stumbled on rocks and tree roots . . . and attempted

one more step, one more step. Thousands and thousands of maggots crept out of the bodies . . . I cannot forget the sight of one corpse lying in a pool of knee-high water; all its flesh and blood had been dissolved by the maggots and the water, so that now it was no more than a bleached uniform."

Once across the Chindwin—back safely in Japanese-occupied Burma— the remaining Japanese would attempt to regroup and mend, but the task would be near impossible. At Imphal and Kohima—and along the Tiddum Road—Mutaguchi had lost thirty thousand dead and thousands wounded. When asked by a correspondent how he felt about the defeat, Mutaguchi could only respond: "I have killed thousands of my men."

With the retreat, Mutaguchi was recalled from command and sent to Singapore in disgrace. Sato, too, was removed from his post during the retreat and was handed a sword by Colonel Shumei Kinoshita of Mutaguchi's staff. The implication was simple: he was to commit *seppuku*, disemboweling himself to restore his honor in the eyes of Imperial Command. When Sato refused to take his own life, he was brought up for court-martial. As Sato was readied to argue his case, however, doctors declared that his mental health was so destroyed by his ordeal that he was not fit to stand trial.

FOR GENERAL WILLIAM SLIM's British and Indian forces, the successful defense of Imphal, Kohima, and the Tiddum Road released them into a fighting fury. While Slim's army had lost fifteen thousand men in the defense, as the Japanese pulled away from India and back into Burma, the remaining British-Indian forces chased them through the jungle like hounds after scattering hares.

The British and Indians dogging the Japanese now entered a world strewn with Imperial Japanese casualties. Along the jungle trails leading toward Burma, corpses littered the earth. Japanese hospitals and field aid stations were sometimes filled to the ceilings with the now-bloated bodies of men who had been wounded in battle, and were then shot in their beds by comrades sparing them the disgrace of becoming prisoners of war.

At the formerly Japanese-occupied village of Mao, halfway up the road connecting Imphal and Kohima, British troops found a snatch of graffiti left behind on a house's wall by the fleeing enemy. In the angular letters of a nameless, English-speaking Japanese soldier, the message was both concise and menacing.

It read: BRITISH—TOO MANY GUNS, TANKS AND TROOPS. JAPANESE GOING, BUT BACK IN SIX MONTHS.

The writer could not have been more wrong.

# Chapter 17

FOR JOSEPH W. STILWELL, early autumn of 1944 must have seemed his sweetest season. After more than two years of arguing, training, being back-stabbed, caterwauling, scrapping, suffering, battling, bickering, and bullying, his Allied forces had finally conformed to his wishes—and he had succeeded mightily. With Allied victories down the Hukawng and Mogaung Valleys, at Myitkyina, and at Imphal and Kohima, the Japanese in Burma were now being destroyed, and his much-fretted-over Ledo Road was pushing its way toward a connection with the Burma Road out of China.

In just fifteen months, Brigadier General Lewis Pick's army engineers on the Ledo Road had moved 13.5 million cubic yards of earth (or 14,850,000,000 pounds, for anyone counting). It was enough soil, in the estimation of *New York Times* reporter Tillman Durdin, to have created a solid dirt wall three feet wide and ten feet tall between New York and San Francisco. Nearly every foot of the road had been cut through thick jungle, and much of it also crossed over steep mountains or through overgrown swamps. The Ledo Road's seven hundred bridges leapt across ten major rivers and 155 secondary streams, many of which rose forty-five feet during the summer monsoon. To make sure the road wouldn't wash out or flood under anything less than diluvian circumstances, General Pick also ordered an average of thirteen drainage culverts per mile beneath the narrow roadbed. Were those culverts laid end to end, they would have formed a single pipe 105 miles long.

By autumn 1944, the road was progressing past Myitkyina and south toward the port city of Bhamo on the Irrawaddy River, following behind the Mars Task Force (a new American unit in the image of the Marauders) and the X Force, who continued pushing Burma's Japanese occupiers further south. Now, if the Japanese along the road inside China could be dislodged, the Burma Road would soon be reopened—and it would run all the way from India to Kunming.

On October 1, 1944, at the town of Loglai along the road, the 858th Engineer Aviation Battalion celebrated its first year of service overseas. The road's primary maintainers since their arrival to the theater in January 1944, the men of the 858th were, as already mentioned, the only African-American unit in the entire Pacific region. But like many aspects of CBI's multicultural-multiracial melting pot, the skin color of the troops made less difference on the ground in Burma than it did back in the United States. As proof of this, every day the 858th's road troops worked alongside Gurkhas, white mechanized troops, and tribal Kachin, Wa, Shan, Lisu, and Naga laborers. At night, while all road workers took meals at their own camps, they often viewed new Hollywood movies together afterward, films that had yet to be released even in the United States. On other nights, parties and dances would be held, with the 858th's own swing orchestra—The Biggest Little Band in the Hump—providing the music. On one occasion, in fact, a show by The Biggest Little Band was even broadcast from their base in Burma to the United States by radio hookup.

Now, capping their first-year festivities—which included a church service and the awarding of a Bronze Star to Staff Sergeant Lambkins by Lt. Colonel Russell G. White—the night once again resounded with the boogie-woogie stomp of The Biggest Little Band in the Hump. The Allies were driving the Japanese from Burma. And premature as it was, the celebrating felt good.


ALONG THE BURMA ROAD in China, the Chinese Y Force had also finally made good. After retaking Lungling from the Japanese in June, the Y Force—or Chinese Expeditionary Force—had split into two phalanxes. The first had moved forty miles to the north, to the mountain-encircled city of Tengchung. There, the Chinese Fifty-sixth Division took on its mirror-image Japanese Fifty-sixth Division, which had been occupying the area for almost two years. The other phalanx had wasted little time in attacking the Japanese positions atop Sungshan's Eastern Gibraltar, about fifteen miles northwest of Lungling. It was time to drive the Japanese off the mountain.

No matter how you approached Sungshan, however, long before you could engage the fifteen hundred to two thousand Japanese entrenched along its twenty-six miles of ridgeline, you had to clamber up twelve hundred feet of nearly perpendicular slope studded with scrubby, stunted pines. Using bombing support from the Fourteenth Air Force—plus 75- and 150-millimeter Howitzers and 76-millimeter artillery emplaced on a nearby mountain—the Y Force began "softening" the Japanese positions for an attack.

Then, in early August, the Chinese began to climb the mountain's flanks from both the east and west sides. Thanks to very effective artillery ranging, the Chinese slowly scaled the mountain as their artillery pounded the soil sometimes twenty-five to forty feet up the hillside ahead of them. Using flamethrowers and moving from pillbox to pillbox, the Chinese—at great cost to their troops—began to overtake the sides of Sungshan as Japanese counterattacks came slower and slower. General Dorn and his fellow American advisers soon surmised that the Japanese were out—or running out—of ammunition, which proved to be true. When air drops from the Japanese fell on the mountaintop, high winds blew several of the shipments into Chinese hands. Still, the Japanese on Sungshan were not ready to give up.

Surrounded on all sides—effectively penned on Sungshan's narrow ridgeline—the Japanese made the Chinese come to them in their trenches. According to Sergeant Horace Green, who was a member of Dorn's American liaison team, the Chinese spent much of the next week pinned down on the mountainside within forty feet of the summit. Above them, the Japanese were tossing grenades and mortar rounds and homemade bombs on the exposed positions below, but the Chinese kept moving upward. By now, according to Sergeant Green, there had been so many Y Force casualties that its cooks and muleskinners were fighting as infantry. When one Chinese regimental commander found he had less than a full company to attack the summit, by way of raising morale he shouted: "From here on, every man killed will be buried in a coffin!"

By mid-August 1944, the Chinese had gotten atop the mountain. A month of hand-grenade battles and hand-to-hand fighting then raged in the revetments and trenches. Before the fighting was over sixty-two different pairs of Chinese-Japanese soldiers would be found dead in each other's grasp. Over the next two weeks, as the Chinese pushed relentlessly along the mountaintop positions, the Japanese began to recognize their situation. Once again, they started to shoot their own wounded, murdering them before they could be taken prisoner. Below the summit and in the trenches, the death toll was rising so quickly that thousands of dead from both armies—and clad in Chinese or Japanese khaki—lay rotting, almost indistinguishable on the mountainside.

For the Japanese, the end at Sungshan came when—inside a huge, four-story bunker atop the mountain—they chose to make a stand to the last man. Over nine days, the Chinese dug two twenty-two-foot tunnels into the mountain's stone beneath the bunker and, packing both tunnels with a total of six thousand pounds of explosives, blasted it—and the top of Sungshan—to dust. That was August 20, 1944. Forty-two Japanese troops inside the bunker were never found. Five other imperial soldiers somehow survived, and none would cooperate with their Allied captors.

In the battle for Sungshan, the Chinese had lost 7,675 men, the Japanese roughly 1,500. In the combined battles for Lungling and Sungshan, however, the casualty numbers were astronomical. The Chinese suffered 37,133 dead, the Japanese 13,620.

HEARING NEWS OF VICTORY at Sungshan, Stilwell radioed a message to Dorn: "Congratulations to the Iron Man on the reduction of Sungshan. Make it colossal and heartfelt and all that stuff, but do not refer to the seven thousand men who paid for it. Now, if you can knock off Tengchung, most of your worries will be over."

REMARKABLY, TENGCHUNG FELL four days later. It ended a fifty-one-day siege that had started when the Chinese Fifty-sixth Division had arrived on the edges of the city only to see the Japanese Fifty-sixth Division either withdraw out of the valley or retreat inside Tengchung's ancient walled city.

Tengchung had been old even when Marco Polo was said to have visited in the thirteenth century. The core town inside its walled citadel—where jade and precious goods had been traded since medieval times—could house twenty thousand people. Even getting a shot at the Japanese inside the citadel proved a problem. The walls of Tengchung's ancient city were thirty-five to forty feet high and as much as sixty feet thick at the base and eight feet thick along their tops.

For a period of time, the Chinese Fifty-sixth Division pounded Tengchung—inside the walls and out—from the mountainsides in the distance, using mortars and field artillery and waiting for the Japanese to begin to starve. After several weeks of barrages, though, when the "starve them out" plan appeared to be taking longer than expected, the Chinese decided to make a frontal attack, driving off the few Japanese holdouts not inside the citadel's walls. Then they began unsuccessfully to scale the ancient city's ramparts with ladders, usually being repelled by Japanese sentries. The key to Tengchong's destruction was finally Chennault's Fourteenth Air Force bombers, which not only smashed most everything inside the city walls—destroying it to save it—but bashed huge holes in the imposing fortress itself. With the ancient city's ramparts now broken, the Chinese—spraying streams of gasoline ahead of them and igniting it with flamethrowers—took the old city by burning off any Japanese defenders near the breaks in the walls.

As Li Shi Fu, an infantryman with the Chinese Fifty-sixth remembered: "A lot of Chinese infantrymen had died trying to scale the walls of the old city with ladders and other objects. We suffered a lot of dead. But once the walls were smashed and we could fight our way inside, the Japanese began to pull out quickly. Between the bombing and the flamethrowers, there was lots of fire, which is a symbol of rebirth in China. From the mountains all around this city—for thirty-five miles in any direction—you could see the city in flames."

As the Chinese fought their way deeper inside the old city's now smoking ruin, what they found was beyond imagining. As Li Shi Fu recalled:

There was an area for comfort women [Japanese-imported prostitutes], and the women had all committed suicide with pistols. In other areas of the old city, we'd sometimes find Japanese troops still shooting at us. By now, with our greater numbers, we'd quickly surround them and kill them. When we'd overtake the enemy position, we'd find the Japanese had chained these sol-

diers to the earth. They'd have put a chained shackle around the man's ankle, then they'd attached the other end of the chain to a spike that had been
driven into a boulder or the stone foundation of a building. There would be
a few cans of rations nearby for these soldiers to eat, and each man had been
given a little bit of ammunition. But each time we came upon these chained
men, we were amazed! *Amazed!* Chained to the battlefield! What kind of an
enemy had we been fighting?

BEYOND THE VICTORIES on the battlefield in Burma and China, the autumn of 1944 was satisfying to Joseph Stilwell for even yet another reason.
On August 1, with his successful North Burma Campaign nearly finished,
Stilwell had been awarded his fourth general's star. It was a rank that, at the
time, was shared by only four other full generals: Marshall, MacArthur,
Eisenhower, and Arnold. Still, on August 2, when Stilwell had first heard of
the promotion, though he was pleased with the honor, he downplayed it in
his diary. To him, it felt much like the awarding of his third star: "Just the
same as before, no thrill."

More interesting to Stilwell was the way his assertions about Chiang
and Chennault were finally proving true. Beginning in April 1944, the
Japanese had stepped up a broad offensive across east China, which Chiang and Chennault seemed incapable of stopping. As part of the operation
called *Ichi-Go* (literally "Number one") and employing fifteen full divisions and another five independent brigades, the Japanese army had
started driving relentlessly into central China from the north and east,
threatening to capture the full nation for the Japanese emperor. With each
new and thundering step in this Japanese advance, Chiang's Chinese Nationalist Army—which he'd assured the Allies were ready for battle—
seemed to evaporate: Japanese units of five hundred troops were literally
chasing off full Chinese divisions numbering in the thousands. Chiang,
still afraid to outfit armies under his own flag for fear of mutiny, was providing his troops nothing to fight with. It was a continuation of the recipe
Stilwell had been warning about for years.

After crossing the Yangtze River in central China, the Japanese pushed
on for the city of Changsha, the area of China that held most of Chennault's forward air bases—and from which the Fourteenth Air Force had
been badgering Japanese troops and shipping since 1942. Changsha had

come under Japanese attack three times since the Japanese initially invaded China in 1938, and with each engagement, the tricky and resourceful Chinese General Hsueh Yeuh had repulsed the invaders. It was a brio triple performance that had earned Hsueh Yeuh the nickname "The Tiger of Changsha" and his forces the handle the Iron Army.

Readying for the next onslaught, Hsueh arrayed his troops around the city, then placed his artillery on a mountain with a dominating view of the streets below. His plan was simple: he would allow the Japanese infantry close to Changsha, then he'd begin pounding them with heavy shell fire and allow his network of infantry to isolate stunned pockets of Imperial soldiers to engage and destroy them.

Unfortunately, not long before the attack began, Hsueh was ordered one hundred miles farther south, to prepare the next city, Hengyang, for the Japanese attack that was eventually expected there. Not planning to be away from Changsha for long, Hsueh left no one to coordinate Changsha's defense in his absence. When the Chinese commander of artillery requested infantry protection for his weapons—which the invading Japanese were certain to target first—he was refused.

Late on June 17, the Japanese attacked the artillery site and, taking advantage of the miscue, captured the mountainside emplacement. Then they began to move on the unsupported Chinese infantry below. The city collapsed in hours. By dusk on June 18, Changsha was in Japanese hands.

A few days later, when the adjutant commander of the Iron Army of Changsha was asked for an explanation, he claimed to U.S. liaison officers that the Japanese had used artillery shells and aerial bombs filled with poison gas, which had forced Changsha's immediate evacuation. Unknown to the adjutant, however, an American sergeant had been in Changsha on the morning of June 18 and he was telling a different story. The sergeant said that, on the morning of the attack, he awoke to find that the entire Chinese army had evacuated the city overnight. There had been no gas; there had not even been fighting.


FROM CHANGSHA, just as the Chinese expected, the Japanese next moved on for Hengyang, where—according to Chiang's spokespeople in Chungking—the Nationalist army would mount a huge and bitter counteroffensive. Stilwell, believing that any weapons he'd divert to this battle would be lost "to bandits," was cajoled nonetheless into authorizing a shipment of twelve thousand tons of guns and ammunition to be delivered via the Hump to Hsueh and his men at Hengyang. Once the weapons arrived in Kunming, however, they never surfaced in Hengyang, likely due—once again—to Chiang's preference not to arm his most effective generals, lest they turn on him.

Still, despite a lack of ammunition to fight with, there was to be a historic defense by Chinese nationalist forces at Hengyang. To document this great battle, the American journalist Theodore H. White journeyed to the city. But what he discovered there were not several Chinese Nationalist divisions slavering for a fight; instead he found two underequipped regiments—a few hundred men—who appeared to know they'd been ordered to their deaths. In their support, Chennault's Fourteenth Air Force put up a savage and cagey air defense—strafing Japanese supply convoys and bombing bridges just ahead of the invaders—but the Japanese kept coming and the Chinese were no equal to them.

"The men walked quietly, with the curious bitterness of Chinese soldiers who expected nothing but disaster at the end of the trip," White wrote of the Chinese troop movements toward Hengyang. "They were wiry and brown but thin; their guns were old, their yellow-and-brown uniforms threadbare. Each carried two grenades tucked in his belt; about the neck of each was a long blue stocking inflated like a roll of bologna with dry rice kernels, the Chinese soldier's only field rations. Their feet were broken and puffed above their straw sandals; their heads were covered with birds' nests of leaves woven together to give shade from the sun and supposedly to supply camouflage. The sweat rolled from them; the dust rose about them, the heat clutched the entire country, and the giddy, glistening waves rose from the rice paddies."

At the battlefront, the troops were supported by only two small artillery pieces—ancient 75-millimeter cannons from World War I—from which they had a total munitions supply of only two hundred shells. Chennault, in an effort to assist General Hsueh's ground troops, offered to turn over one thousand tons of his own weaponry, though that exchange would only take place were the munitions not to pass through the central government. In his first and only indictment of Chiang Kai-shek, who had been Chennault's primary supporter in the war, Old Leatherface acknowledged that, "I would not be interested in turning this over to the minister of war, because the chances are great that it would never reach Hsueh Yeuh."

The great defense of Hengyang never happened. The city quickly fell to the Japanese. With twelve thousand tons of weaponry missing, having never arrived for use by General Hsueh, Chiang's manipulations of lend-lease equipment were now fully exposed to the Allied Chiefs, and President Roosevelt especially was tired of the generalissimo's vacillations and false claims.

Roosevelt decided it was time to tie some strings to all new lend-lease deliveries earmarked for China. Moreover, to keep this scenario from happening again, he and George Marshall began to make back-channel suggestions to Chiang Kai-shek's foreign minister that it was time for Stilwell—the only general in SEAC and CBI in an offensive (rather than defensive) posture—to assume more control of the theater.

The threat of Stilwell commanding still more of Nationalist China's armies presented an unthinkable situation to the generalissimo, who understood his future lay not in merely overcoming the Japanese, but also, once the war was over, taking up the fight against Mao Tse-tung's Chinese Communist Army and Militia. While the several million Japanese troops already in China remained a real and lethal problem, Mao's Communists were far more fearsome: their regular army had now swelled to three million men, and its fattening rolls of conscripts showed no signs of diminishing. Because of the troops the Communists had amassed, the Americans had taken the equally unthinkable step of enjoining them to Chiang's Kuomintang Nationalist Army, to fight the Japanese invaders for the greater good of China.

Even if the Japanese could be routed from China, it was becoming increasingly obvious that a liberated China would soon have two governments, and be divided into Nationalist and Communist areas. Chiang also recognized that if he chose not to partner with the Communists to defeat the Japanese in China, war against Mao's army stood waiting in the wings as soon as the Japanese departed.

No matter where he chose to look, Chiang Kai-shek was exposed and in trouble.

————

BUT IT WASN'T ONLY Chiang whose fortunes were dimming on the Asian continent. The support once so generously provided to Claire Lee Chennault by President Roosevelt over the past few years was now eclipsed, too. As the *Ichi-Go* campaign slashed deeper into China, Chennault's air bases were coming under ferocious pressure, wih the most forward of them being preemptively destroyed by Old Leatherface's own men.

To keep the airfields and weapons out of Japanese hands, the Fourteenth Air Force was now bombing its own runways, blowing ammunition stores, and burning down air base buildings rather than see them fall to the Japanese. Chennault's claim of winning the war in China with airpower and subsequently placing all of Japan under attack by January 1944 was not only many months overdue, it had become fully visible as messianic hot air.

When Roosevelt and General Marshall asked Stilwell for his assessment of the Fourteenth Air Force's situation, Vinegar Joe was happy to oblige. "Chennault has assured the generalissimo that airpower is the answer," Stilwell wrote. "He has told him that if the Fourteenth AF is supported, he can effectively prevent a Jap invasion. Now he's realized it can't be done, and he is trying to prepare an out for himself by claiming that with *a little more*, which we won't give him, he can still do it. He tries to duck the consequences of having sold the wrong bill of goods, and put the blame on those who pointed out the danger long ago and tried to apply the remedy."

As soon as Stilwell's analysis had been written and sent, Chennault heard about it and, against direct orders from Stilwell, submitted his own view of the situation. With Chennault's letter to the president, the long smoldering bitterness between Stilwell and Chennault finally exploded. Through radio messages and written requests, Stilwell demanded that Chennault be "relieved of command at once." Chennault had nowhere to hide, but he did have one bit of armor left: his own celebrity. And after consideration by several members inside the War Department in Washington, the Americans decided that—because his early days with the Flying Tigers had made him a hero—General Chennault needed to remain in command for a time longer.

Stilwell was not happy about the decision, but shortly he would have other, more important concerns to fill his days.

SEVERAL MONTHS EARLIER, on July 6, 1944, as Stilwell's Chinese and American troops were fighting for Myitkyina and Chiang's army under General Hsueh were preparing their "historic counterattack" in Hengyang, President Franklin Roosevelt sent an official dispatch to Chiang Kai-shek.

The president informed the generalissimo that he believed "the future of all Asia is at stake." He also reminded Chiang that, while "fully aware of your feelings regarding General Stilwell, nevertheless . . . I know of no other man who has the ability, the force and the determination to offset the disaster which now threatens China and our over-all plans for the conquest of Japan. I am promoting Stilwell to the rank of full general and I recommend for your most urgent consideration that you recall him from Burma and place him directly under you in command of all Chinese and American forces and that you charge him with full responsibility and authority for the coordination and direction of the operations required to stem the tide of the enemy's advances."

Almost as a postscript, Roosevelt then added this final, blunt-instrument bludgeoning of Chiang and Chennault's military strategy in China. "Please have in mind," Roosevelt penned, "that it has clearly been demonstrated in Italy, in France, and in the Pacific that airpower alone cannot stop a determined enemy."

Roosevelt's message was as unsparing as it was straightforward. Stilwell, the planet's newest four-star general, was to become the boss of all Chinese forces in China and Burma. Were this suggestion not heeded, Roosevelt left the spectrum of repercussions wide open. And none of them—especially a suspension of lend-lease shipments or full American disengagement—stood as appealing choices to the Chinese Nationalist leader. With his letter of July 6, President Roosevelt had busted Generalissimo Chiang Kai-shek to the rank of "Peanut."

WHILE CHIANG'S IMMEDIATE RESPONSE to the letter remains unknown, he must have understood its implications. If his demands weren't heeded, Roosevelt—the most ardent fan of Nationalist China in World War II—seemed prepared to let Chiang's government wither in the face of the Japanese invaders and, later, the Communist Chinese forces certain to follow.

In response, Chiang had his foreign minister, T. V. Soong, telegraph the American emissary Harry Hopkins with this message: "Today a fateful decision is again being made in Washington. The War Department wants to force General Stilwell down his [Chiang Kai-shek's] throat . . . I personally assure you without qualification that on this point the generalissimo will not and cannot yield."

With Stilwell having finally exposed Chennault, the moment for his face-off with Chiang had arrived.

FOR THE NEXT SIX WEEKS, Chiang remained silent on the subject of President Roosevelt's July 6 letter. Ultimately, however, it would not be Roosevelt who forced Chiang's response. That job would go to the Imperial Japanese Army in China.

On August 26, 1944, a force of more than six thousand Japanese troops moved east out of Burma up Burma Road, where they attacked the Y Force at Lungling in southwest China. Under enormous pressure, portions of Chiang's army fell back and relinquished part of the city; some of the Y Force units retreated as far as the Salween River. Though the Japanese had no intention of attacking up the Burma Road deeper into southwest China, Chiang nonetheless began to fear an enemy drive on Kunming and its Hump airfields.

During high-level planning meetings in Chungking during the second week in September, the generalissimo requested that Stilwell rush his Chinese X Force and American Mars Task Force into China from just south of Myitkyina, where they could attack the Japanese from the rear. Stilwell refused: his men were exhausted, he claimed, and they had yet to clear the route of the Ledo Road south from Myitkyina, where it was to attach with the Burma Road at the Chinese border. Following Stilwell's refusal for troop support, Chiang threatened to withdraw his Y Force from the Burma Road entirely, setting them up instead in a defensive posture around Kunming. Chiang then said that he would, from this moment on, keep the Y Force in place along the Burma Road near Lungling only if he was free to control the flow of lend-lease equipment himself.

Chiang's bluff made Vinegar Joe furious. "He will not listen to reason," Stilwell wrote to George Marshall, "merely repeating a lot of cockeyed conceptions of his own invention. He imagines he can get behind the Salween and there wait in safety for the U.S. to finish the war."

In his diary, for September 8, Stilwell as usual cut to the heart of the matter: "The G-mo *must* control lend-lease. . . . What a nerve. That's what the G-mo is after—just a blank check. Now we come to the show-down."

ON SEPTEMBER 16, General Marshall passed Stilwell's impressions on to President Roosevelt and, for the president, they proved the last straw. Within days, Roosevelt sent Stilwell a directive that he was to "deliver personally" to Chiang. The letter—which Stilwell characterized as "a hot fire-cracker," with "a firecracker in every sentence"—informed Chiang that if the Y Force was withdrawn from fighting, Chiang must "be prepared to accept the consequences and assume the personal responsibility" for all results. Roosevelt then added that if Chiang didn't immediately reinforce his armies across the Salween and toward Lungling—and if he didn't grant Stilwell full command of all nationalist Chinese forces in both Burma and China—there would be "catastrophic consequences."

For Stilwell and Chiang, the moment of collision was at hand. On September 19, 1944, when Stilwell arrived with Roosevelt's letter at Chiang's private residence in Chungking, he was first met by Major General Patrick W. Hurley, the tall, fiery, and politically astute American emissary Roosevelt had dispatched two months earlier to try to "adjust" the tension between Chiang and Vinegar Joe.

Stilwell hustled Hurley into a conference room and showed him the president's letter. Hurley, sensing disaster, suggested that perhaps, as emissary, he should read the note to Chiang and attempt to temper its language. Stilwell disagreed, arguing the letter needed no paraphrasing and that, second, he had been ordered by the president to deliver it by hand.

A few minutes later, when Stilwell and Hurley entered Chiang's private chambers—and after the rite of tea service had been completed—Stilwell handed President Roosevelt's letter to a translator for reading aloud. Because there were other Chinese officials in the room—including T. V. Soong—Hurley stepped in and moved to salvage the generalissimo's pride by instructing a translator to redact the letter in Chinese characters. When the translation was complete, Stilwell took up the Chinese version and folded it.

With smug satisfaction, "I handed this bundle of paprika to the Peanut and then sank back with a sigh," Stilwell wrote in his diary. "The harpoon hit the little bugger right in the solar plexus and went right through him."

Chiang read the translated letter with no sign of embarrassment or emotion. He then looked at Stilwell and said only, "I understand."

For Stilwell, after nearly three years of "bickering and dickering," his victory over Chiang was complete. At long last, he had humiliated the generalissimo, making Chiang Kai-shek lose face in front of his own subordinates, an act that stands as the highest form of insult in China.

"What!" Stilwell ended his diary entry for September 19, 1944. "No teapots? No, just a calm silence. I got out promptly and came home. Pretty sight crossing the river: lights all on in Chungking."


AFTER HE HAD SETTLED into his Chungking headquarters, Stilwell sent a long, effusive, and embarassingly gloating letter off to Win. In it, aside from congratulating himself on his personal victory, he even penned a rhyme in the adolescent doggerel he'd once reserved for Joe Stilwell alone:

> I've waited long for vengeance—
> At last I've had my chance.
> I've looked the Peanut in the eye
> And kicked him in the pants.
>
> The old harpoon was ready
> With aim and timing true,
> I sank it to the handle
> And stung him through and through.
>
> The little bastard shivered,
> And lost his power of speech,
> His face turned green and quivered
> As he struggled not to screech.

For all my weary battle,
For all my hours of woe,
At last I've had my innings
And laid the Peanut low.

I know I've still to suffer,
And run a weary race,
But oh! The blessed pleasure!
I've wrecked the Peanut's face.

DESPITE HIS PERCEIVED VICTORY, Stilwell's problems with Chiang and China were far from over. In fact, the coming weeks would prove more toxic to Joseph W. Stilwell than to any other leader inside CBI or SEAC.

On September 23, word came to Hurley and Stilwell that, after a long and persnickety negotiation with the Americans, the three-million-man Chinese Communist force under Mao Tse-tung was prepared to join the fight for China against the Japanese. There were, however, several provisos. To insulate the two Chinese armies from one another—not to mention keeping apart the two opposing governments now claiming the same nation—the Communist forces would be restricted to fighting in the lands north of the Yellow River (where Mao's troops would be provided only enough lend-lease equipment to supply five divisions). This would leave the larger, and expansive, remainder of China to be defended by the Nationalists and all other Allied fighters they could muster. The restricted lend-lease equipment accorded Mao's troops would also help disabuse Chiang of the idea that the Americans were now arming the Chinese Communists against his Kuomintang Nationalists.

Hurley, for one, was ecstatic with the news of the Communist engagement. "This will knock the persimmons off the trees!" he shouted. Then he prepared to inform the generalissimo.

When Hurley presented Chiang with the glad news about Mao's Communist army, he was met with a shock. Suddenly, Chiang didn't seem to care about the Communists joining his fight to liberate China. The primary thing Chiang wanted, he said, was for President Roosevelt to know that Stilwell was being refused command of the Chinese Nationalist Army.

Stilwell was, in Chiang's estimation, "unfitted for the vast and complex duties which the new plan will entail." Then, second and even more important, Chiang said he wanted Stilwell relieved of all duties inside CBI and SEAC: effective immediately.

Hurley was stunned.

In the four days since Chiang had received President Roosevelt's letter—and after extensive discussions with T. V. Soong—Chiang had concluded that the Americans would not let China languish. No matter what Roosevelt implied, Chiang had decided, the president and the American people would continue sending lend-lease goods and weapons to China. The letter, in the generalissimo's estimation, was merely American bullying. The United States, in fact, had already drawn up a vital support program for China's postwar reconstruction; it was an agreement they could not back down from, since legally binding contracts had been fully negotiated and signed.

Generalissimo Chiang Kai-shek had decided to call the president's bluff, and Vinegar Joe Stilwell's command now dangled in the balance.

FINALLY, AFTER DOZENS of rejected requests for Stilwell's recall in the past two and a half years, Joseph W. Stilwell was now being left to twist in the wind. Despite succeeding at everything he'd attempted— the "walk out" of Burma, the creation of the Ledo Road, the clearing of Japanese forces from north Burma, the soon-to-be-reopened Burma Road, the training of the Chinese troops, and the Hump airlift—it appeared that "the old Deckhand" was finally in real peril of being recalled.

Following Chiang's refusal to grant Stilwell full control of the Chinese Nationalist Army, there came a three-week period of American negotiation with Chiang and T. V. Soong, but the generalissimo refused to budge. Major General Hurley, Secretary of War Henry Stimson, Chinese Ambassador Clarence Gauss, and even George Marshall himself all tried to broker an agreement that kept Stilwell on, but Chiang was adamant and would accept no compromises. The Americans offered that Stilwell could issue orders to the Chinese forces through a Chinese military intermediary, but Chiang said no. They suggested that Stilwell stay on, but a new official would control China's allocations of lend-lease; the generalissimo declined. They offered that Stilwell only command the X and Y Forces and the reopening of the Burma Road—and that he not command the Communists, as that conflict of interest might prove fatal to Chiang's regime. But it was too late. Chiang and his officers rejected every Stilwell-based command that was floated. They indicated that they might consider another American to take control of the Chinese armies inside China, but not—and never—Stilwell.

Joseph W. Stilwell had to go.

BY OCTOBER 1944, despite his string of impossible victories, Stilwell had few supporters in CBI, SEAC, or even in Washington. Only his one true ally in the region, William Slim, expressed continued support and appreciation for Vinegar Joe. Back at the end of July, Stilwell had even succeeded in aggravating the genial and generous Admiral Mountbatten. On July 30, at Mountbatten's behest, Stilwell the deputy SEAC commander (or "Sad Sack" as he called the title) traveled from north Burma—where the Myitkyina battle was finally going over—to sit in for a week at SEAC Headquarters on a hilltop estate in Kandy, Ceylon, while Mountbatten traveled.

Stilwell was looking forward to the visit and a well-deserved rest. But he remained his usual, no-frills soldier, which provided an obvious counterpoint to Mountbatten's perfectionistic self-promotion.

For a year, Stilwell had stood by as Mountbatten read and redrafted all public relations messages about himself, and had suffered silently during each of Mountbatten's visits to Stilwell's troops—where printed orders sent in advance described every stop's choreography. At each troop visit, for instance, Mountbatten preordered that the soldiers were to sit on the ground with their backs to the sun, so the men could see their commander in full light and without glare in their eyes. Then, with an air of "spontaneous vitality," the SEAC chief would drive up in a jeep, vault out, and jump atop a wooden packing crate that had been carefully positioned in advance. Once on his impromptu dais, the SEAC "supremo" would then deliver "an absolutely first-class and apparently impromptu speech. Simple, direct, and genuinely inspiring. The men loved it."

Stilwell, however, had grown tired of Mountbatten's show. (Though, in truth, Stilwell the Yankee blueblood also took great pains in managing his image as a straight-talking, rough-and-ready ground soldier.) When Stilwell arrived by air transport at Kandy, he was wearing not the formal and pressed uniform of the SEAC deputy, but his own unadorned battle fatigues. As usual, Stilwell's clothes were devoid of all general's stars, insignias, medals, and ribbons, which often left Vinegar Joe, in William Slim's assessment, looking "like a duck hunter." After being met at the "Kandy Kids" airfield by Mountbatten's black Cadillac—which was festooned with official pennants—Stilwell took a look at the car, shook his head, and said: "Get me a jeep." Then he stowed his bags in the Cadillac and drove himself up the mountain toward Kandy and headquarters, his left leg hanging out of the jeep as it followed the state car to Mountbatten's residence at the king's pavilion.

For a week, Stilwell sat in on SEAC meetings and took meals at Mountbatten's table. ("I've got to quit eating with Louis," he wrote. "I actually *like* those rum cocktails.") More often at Kandy, Stilwell made a point of being bored by the crisp and on-date international newspapers flown in from around the world, the leather club chairs, the platoons of barefoot servants, the grand library, and the constant motion of a staff of three thousand, which—much to Stilwell's displeasure—included numerous British female officers. (The women's staff at Kandy actually included a young American OSS worker named Julia McWilliams, who would later marry and become famous as television's "The French Chef," Julia Child.)

Stilwell, though, never was comfortable at SEAC HQ: "Something wrong with Headquarters at Kandy . . ." he later wrote in his diary. "I always felt half asleep."

While visiting Ceylon, Stilwell made no secret of his indifference at every afternoon's full-dress meeting, where long-range staff planning and the tiresome bookkeeping of rear-echelon logistics left him blank. To spice up the days, as he was effectively the military governor of Burma, Stilwell took devilish pleasure in loudly contemplating orders designed to upset the country's former colonizers, such as "freeing the Kachins, etc."

When Stilwell's week at Kandy was over, the returned Mountbatten, too, was likely relieved. He hosted Stilwell to a final farewell lunch, then sent him off for what was to prove the last time.

FROM SEPTEMBER 23 TO October 19, negotiating over the fate of Joseph W. Stilwell and CBI continued in Chungking and in Washington. Chiang had assented—with conditions—to Mao's Communist army and militias joining the fight for China, but he would not allow Stilwell anywhere near any command in free China.

In Washington, it became clear that, with the war for Burma nearly won—and the Ledo Road well on its way to reconnecting with the Burma Road—Stilwell had become expendable. The command change needed to come quickly, as a defense of free China from Japan's *Ichi-Go* offensive was becoming more crucial by the day. The Japanese Eleventh Army's thrust from the north had passed through Hengyang and was now aimed at the cities of Kweilin and Liuchow. If the Japanese weren't slowed or stopped soon, all of eastern China would be cut off by a twelve-hundred-mile line that extended from Mongolia in the north to the border with Indochina in the south. China would soon be cut in two.

By the second week in October, the Sino-American agreement on the fate of Stilwell and his theater of operations was starting to clarify. Stilwell and CBI—it had been decided—were over. Stilwell was to be recalled. At the same time, the China-Burma-India theater of operations was also to be dissolved and reconstituted into two new theaters. The first, India-Burma, was to be commanded by Stilwell's capable chief of staff, the American General Daniel Sultan. The region's second theater would be China, with the American General Albert C. Wedemeyer taking command of all American forces there and becoming Chiang's new chief of staff. (Taking Stilwell's SEAC duties would be Stilwell's supply second in command, Lt. General Raymond A. Wheeler.)

Stilwell had been sanguine about Sultan in India and Burma since he'd first heard of the plan in June. After all, Sultan had effectively run the theater for months while Stilwell bashed his way down the Hukawng Valley to Myitkyina. Instead, it was Wedemeyer's appointment that infuriated Stilwell. Vinegar Joe felt that the forty-six-year-old SEAC planner "thinks well of himself," which ranked as perhaps the ultimate Stilwell criticism of character.

With Wedemeyer's ascent, Stilwell recalled his diary entry of three months earlier. On June 22, he had written: "Good God—to be ousted in favor of Wedemeyer—that would be a disgrace." It now had a prophetic ring.

On October 19, George Marshall warned Stilwell by advance radio message that he was to be recalled to Washington immediately. "THE AX

FALLS," is how Stilwell began the day's terse and surprisingly unembittered entry.

Stilwell remained in Chungking for two more days. He visited with his commanders and favored journalists, especially Theodore White of *Time* magazine and Brooks Atkinson of *The New York Times*; he called on Madame Sun Yat-sen, and wrote fond, formal farewell notes to General Auchinleck and General Slim in India.

Finally, at 5 p.m. on October 20 he went to see Chiang Kai-shek. Once Stilwell's recall had been made official, Chiang had offered him the "Special Grand Cordon of the Blue Sky and White Sun" (the highest Chinese decoration possible for foreigners), but Stilwell had curtly refused. Now, over a ceremonial cup of tea, Stilwell and Chiang said polite good-byes. Stilwell asked the generalissimo to remember that all he had done had been for the good of China. Then he bade the "Gi-mo" farewell—saluting him while speaking the slogan, "*Tsui hou sheng li*" ("For the final victory")—and left.

Shortly after noon on a cold and cloudy October 21, 1944, General Joseph W. Stilwell packed his possessions in his field bags, rolled up his maps, and called for a car to Chungking's airfield. Waiting for him at the field were Patrick Hurley (who would soon be named ambassador to China, as Gauss was resigning in solidarity with Stilwell) and T. V. Soong. As they stood on the airfield's flatness saying farewells in an icy wind, Hurley acknowledged to Stilwell that he, as emissary, had "bitched it up." Stilwell did not disagree. For Stilwell, he had already chuckled about being "Hurleyed out of China" and of having become a "fugitive from the Chiang gang."

Then, as Stilwell was finishing the good-byes, a Chinese touring car rolled down the runway toward the small group, and General Ho Ying-ch'in—the Chinese secretary of war and a sometime Stilwell supporter—drove up to say good-bye as well.

At 2:30 p.m. on October 21, 1944, Joseph W. Stilwell climbed the stairs to an American transport plane headed for Kunming. As the aircraft's captain revved the engines, Stilwell stood in the plane's doorway and looked out at the dark and roiling sky of Chungking one last time. "What are we waiting for?" he finally asked. Then he shut the hatch.

Before departing from CBI, Stilwell made three days of farewell stops at Kunming: at Y Force Headquarters at Paoshan, China; at Myitkyina; and at

Ramgarh. He did not, interestingly, visit SEAC Headquarters at Kandy in Ceylon.

On October 24, the Old Deckhand finally arrived in Delhi for a last visit. Then, two days later, Vinegar Joe Stilwell climbed aboard one more air transport and—after thirty-two months of constant fighting in pursuit of the impossible—he departed India for the long trip to Washington. "Shoved off—" he wrote, "last day in CBI."

# Chapter 18

▦▦ WITH JOE STILWELL and CBI now officially in the past, all illu-
▦▦ sions that the war for Burma and China had been simplified
▦▦ would quickly prove precisely that: illusions.

The Japanese in Burma were still fighting and dying for their emperor—and to defeat them, the Allies would have to hunt them down and
kill them town by town, trench by trench, and man by man. In the north,
General Sultan's combined X Force and Mars Task Force kept after the
still-retreating remnants of Japan's Myitkyina fighters, driving them south
down the Irrawaddy River Valley. In east India and western Burma,
William Slim's Fourteenth Army kept the pressure on, too, but through
much of the end of 1944, all Slim's men found were enemy dead.

The Japanese were evacuating India and western Burma with all possible haste, leaving behind only skeletal sentry forces to slow the British and
Indians with moving skirmishes. Japan and its Supreme General Kawabe
were in tactical retreat, their new plan being to set up a defensive perimeter as impervious as a stone wall along the north-south trace of the Irrawaddy River. Starting at Lashio in the north and extending to Mandalay
on the river farther south, the Japanese line of defense would eventually
move overland and away from the river to Rangoon on the sea. And as the
Japanese withdrew, the British were forced to clean up their enemy's mess,
most often burying the dead left behind instead of fighting them.

"It was always a disappointment in the Burma campaign to enter a town that had been a name on a map and a goal for which men fought and died," Slim wrote. "There was for the victors none of the thrill of marching through streets which, even if battered, were those of a great, perhaps historic, city—a Paris or a Rome. There were no liberated crowds to greet the troops. Instead, my soldiers walked warily, alert for booby traps and snipers . . . A few frightened Burmans, clad in rags, might peer at them and even wave a shy welcome, but at the best it was not a very inspiring business."

Instead of battle, the British-Indian troops were forced to deal with war's horrible aftermath on the India-Burma border. In the Burmese town of Tamu, just across the border from India, Slim's Second Division entered the town without a fight. As they occupied it, what Slim's men found, and smelled, were grisly reminders of how destitute the retreating Japanese in Burma had become. At Tamu, more than 550 Japanese casualties lay unburied in the streets, their decaying bodies emaciated—or bloated with rotten gas—and their uniforms in tatters. Scouts for the Second Division often found groups of corpses lying around the bases of Tamu's stone Buddhas, whose placid expressions and unmoving eyes stared indifferently past the decayed men at their feet. In other places—often at infirmaries or small, open-air field hospitals—the British would find Japanese wounded on cots and stretchers, all of them shot through the head by comrades who had no means of evacuating them and didn't want to leave them as potential prisoners. The Japanese in Burma were tired, hungry, on the run, and—most of all—desperate.

At its height, the Imperial Japanese Army had possessed eighty-five thousand troops in Burma. Following Stilwell's Hukawng Valley campaign, the slugfest for the Admin Box, and the battles at Imphal, Kohima, and along the Tiddum Road, only twenty thousand to thirty thousand Japanese troops remained. And quite obviously, undersupply and disease were taking their toll on what Japanese soldiers were still standing.

Now, all William Slim had to do was find and engage the Japanese in Burma—and do it before they could reinforce their new line of defense. "Our problem, therefore," Slim later wrote, "was to get as many divisions and as much armour as possible, and as quickly as possible, into the Shwebo Plain [in central Burma], and there fight an army battle."

———

IN CHINA, in the weeks following Stilwell's departure, Japan's *Ichi-Go* offensive had gained an apocalyptically fearsome momentum. Through September and October 1944—amid the distracting Stilwell contretemps— the Fourteenth Air Force continued losing its most forward air bases to the fast-moving Japanese Eleventh Army out of the north, as Stilwell had predicted. And having taken Hengyang and Chuanhsien, the Eleventh Army was now directing its force toward the city of Kweilin. Unfortunately for the Allies, the suburbs of Kweilin were home to one of Chennault's largest air bases, and Chennault was bellowing about the vulnerability of his Liangtang Airfield (not to mention the peril to his base at Liuchow, one hundred miles farther south) to anyone who'd listen.

In late October 1944, when the newly installed General Wedemeyer finally voiced concerns to Chiang about the defense of Kweilin and Liuchow, the generalissimo "assured" him that the Chinese army could hold the Kweilin for "at least two months."

Wedemeyer was a highly educated and elegantly tall man. He had a thick and rich head of silvering black hair, the aquiline facial features of a movie star, and a self-assurance that verged on monomania (his autobiography is titled *Wedemeyer Reports!*). Priding himself on his insight and affability, he planned to use "honey instead of vinegar" in relations with Chiang and—as a gentlemanly start to that—he'd already locked away all files and communications pertaining to Stilwell and Chiang, vowing not to read them until the war was over. But for all his smarts, looks, and top-drawer character, Wedemeyer still had a flaw: he'd chosen to take Chiang Kai-shek at his word.

On November 10, Kweilin fell to the Japanese in a day. With the threat of invaders on their doorstep, Kweilin's hundreds of thousands of citizens had by then evacuated the city by packed rail cars, in boats, and on foot. Meanwhile, Chennault's men abandoned and demolished all 550 buildings on their air base, taking every gallon of gas and every piece of equipment they could carry with them before blowing up or burning what remained.

Left to defend the city were Chiang's demoralized and starving Chinese Nationalist forces. One army unit at Kweilin—fourteen thousand men strong—had only two thousand usable rifles, and little ammunition to fire from them. "The scattered reserves that had been rushed from other fronts [to Kweilin]," wrote Theodore White, "were spread in disorganization over an area of five hundred miles; some were tired, others untried, all leaderless. Some had old Chinese guns; some had Russian guns, others prewar Japanese artillery. No one had enough ammunition."

In a city now evacuated—and with free food and drink abandoned in restaurants and shops across the city—the Chinese chose to nourish themselves instead of prepare for Kweilin's defense. And as one of the prettiest and liveliest cities in China, there seemed endless provisions for the Chinese to sample. When Theodore White left the city just ahead of the Japanese invaders, "The last five soldiers I saw at the northern gate," he wrote, "had seventeen bottles of wine that they were finishing with great good cheer as they waited for the enemy."

DAYS AFTER KWEILIN'S FALL, the city of Liuchow—one hundred miles south of Kweilin—fell to the Japanese Eleventh Army as well, which then united with Japanese invasion troops out of the east and Indochina. China was cut in two.

By mid-November 1944, the Japanese had not only closed eastern China, they had put together a nearly sixty-thousand-man army of invaders. And this entire combined force seemed to be aiming itself toward Chungking, Chiang's wartime capital.

As outwardly cordial as the relationship between Chiang and his new American chief of staff appeared, behind the scenes Wedemeyer—who was trying to turn the Chinese army into an effective fighting force—was soon being driven mad. "If only the Chinese will cooperate!" he complained in reports to George Marshall and the War Department. According to Wedemeyer, Chiang and his advisers were "impotent and confounded," while the Chinese army commanders were fossilized by "political intrigues and false pride."

At the War Department, Marshall could only wax nostalgic. At least Stilwell had silently struggled to remedy China's problems without calling constantly for aid.

IN 1944, THROUGHOUT EAST CHINA the only Allied force doing any good was an OSS unit of about fifteen Americans officers and enlisted men. Led by Major Frank Gleason—a twenty-five-year-old, red-haired Pennsylvanian—they were tearing down everything on the highways between Liuchow and points west; blowing bridges and razing towns to deprive the Japanese of all possible spoils.

At Tushan, 150 miles west of Liuchow, Gleason again heard what he'd believed to be an apocryphal story. The Chinese army, a local told him, had huge stores of weapons hidden just outside of town. When Gleason investigated, what he found staggered him. Three huge ammunition dumps, each with twenty to thirty warehouses, were arrayed around the city. In total, there were fifty thousand tons of ammunition, more than fifty new artillery pieces, tens of thousands of artillery shells, weapons of every type, and—best of all for Gleason—twenty tons of dynamite. And now, with the Chinese army in shreds and the crisis in east China so close they didn't have time to distribute this monster cache, Gleason was forced to blow it all up.

By four that afternoon, the weapons stores were gone—exploded into uselessness. As Gleason and his men left town headed farther west, the first scout parties of the Japanese were entering Tushan from the east. Finding the city in near-total destruction, the Japanese scouts sent word of the devastation back to the main invasion force, which called off their larger-scale movement to Tushan. The Japanese advance teams then stayed in Tushan for several days before abandoning it and withdrawing to rejoin their larger force.

With their east China campaign finished, Prime Minister Tojo's Japanese Eleventh Army was momentarily sated. It was time for the Japanese in east China to take a well-deserved rest.

THOUGH EASTERN CHINA REMAINED firmly inside Japanese control, by late 1944, the momentum had gone to the side of the Allies in Burma and southwest China. The North Burma Campaign, coupled with William Slim's charge out of India, had retaken and secured fifty thousand square miles of Burma, and a battle line 450 miles long stretched from the rail yards of India to Burma's central plains.

Chasing the Japanese Fifteenth Army, William Slim was already planning for a massive battle of the Shwebo Plain. On the broad and level area west of the Irrawaddy, a battle would leave the weakened Japanese exposed to the British and Indians, who possessed far superior numbers of troops, aircraft, and artillery. But Slim's plan was not to be. By September 1944, the

Fifteenth Army's mustachioed General Kawabe—with his defeat at Imphal and Kohima—had been replaced by Lt. General Heitaro Kimura, a seasoned tactician and artillery leader fresh from headquarters in Tokyo. Kimura had wisely decided to retreat beyond the Irrawaddy, where he could create the rock-solid defensive wall on the river's eastern shore.

The implication to Slim was obvious. While he could certainly attack and take Mandalay, which sits on the river's western shore, units from his Fourteenth Army was going to have to cross the river to engage the Japanese. And Slim knew that his army's crossing of the river—no matter where it occurred—would be heavily opposed. The crossing of any river while under fire, in fact, remains one of the most difficult challenges any army can face. And the thousand-foot-wide Irrawaddy wasn't simply another river, it was an obstacle all its own.

FARTHER NORTH IN BURMA, General Dan Sultan's combined X Force and Mars Task Force had succeeded beyond expectations. They had united the Ledo Road and the Burma Road, starting the trip by leaping across the Irrawaddy south of Myitkyina on the world's longest pontoon bridge—at 1,180 feet—that had been floated in place by General Pick's engineers. They had driven the Japanese out of north Burma, and their battlefield time had toughened them into a force of fearsome competence. The X Force, once skinny and sickly, now seemed to radiate health and military vigor.

"Stilwell's divisions," wrote Theodore White, "were tough and good, and they knew it. They had flesh on their biceps, meat on their bodies. They handled modern American instruments of war with familiar confidence. They were more than sure of themselves; they were arrogant. They slugged Americans, British, Burmese, anyone who got in their way. They held up trains at the point of tommy guns. They were the best troops China had ever had, and they bristled with pride as they approached the last objective separating them from their country."

The X Force was finally going to set foot back in China. Having cleared north Burma of the Japanese—and with William Slim's Fourteenth Army hemming in the Japanese farther south in Burma—the X Force had new orders. Sultan and his men were to chase the Japanese up the Burma Road into China, link up with the Y Force on the frontier, and crush all Japanese troops still closing the Burma Road.

# Chapter 19

WITH THE ALLIES NOW on total offensive in Burma and China, the air war became a powerful supplement to ground troops still battling a determined (if systemically undersupplied) Imperial Japanese Army.

By the end of 1944, while the Flying Tigers, the Hump pilots, and Chennault's hot-handed Fourteenth Air Force had gotten most of CBI's airborne glory during World War II, it was the Tenth Air Force out of India that was now doing the heaviest damage to the enemy. And that destruction was now coming with punishing regularity. During one three-month stretch of 1944, the Tenth flew more than eighty-five hundred sorties over the Japanese in Burma and India, dropping more than 3.7 million pounds of bombs. During the fighting at Myitkyina alone, the combined air forces dropped 754 tons of bombs on the entrenched Japanese, 20 percent more explosives than were expended during the same period by the infantry's artillery there.

Besides troop carrier squadrons and Hump crews, which by late 1944 were ferrying men and supplies around the theater with stunning speed, the bomber wings of the Tenth Air Force were dealing daily, crushing blows to the Japanese. The Tenth would hit and run on railroads, airfields, communications areas, supply bases, and—perhaps most of all—bridges. One bomber squadron inside the Tenth—the 490th—destroyed eight bridges in seven days and perfected a technique invented in Europe called "skip bombing": the explosives would be released as the aircraft was in a shallow dive over rivers, allowing the bombs to land on their bellies, skip forward into bridge abutments, and explode. Another unit, the Seventh Bomb Group, was the glutton of the aerial world. By steel-strapping 250-pound bombs to the 500-pound ones actually affixed to their bomb-bay racks, they could pack twelve thousand pounds of bombs into a B-24 designed to carry just 8,800 pounds.

One of these Seventh Bomb Group crews, T-333 (designated with a "T," as they had been put together at Tonopah Army Air Field in Nevada), would become famous for something else as well. They would bomb shut the bridge on the river Kwae.

ASSEMBLED FROM ACROSS the United States, T-333 was made up of ten men with hometowns as disparate as Cascade, Montana; Belton, Texas; Minneapolis, Minnesota; Greenwood, Mississippi; and Rochester, New York. Their ages ranged from eighteen to twenty-seven, with the median falling just below twenty-two. And their pilot was among the youngest of the group: a twenty-year-old kid named Charles F. Linamen.

"Curly," as Linamen was nicknamed, was a big, bluff, second lieutenant with a broad face, a by-the-book style, and a self-described "touch for flying airplanes." Never interested in school, he'd dropped out in eleventh grade and soon found his way into the army. At first Linamen was trained to be an aircraft mechanic. But after passing a qualifying test, a physical exam, and a review board, he was granted admission to the Air Cadets in 1942, graduating in 1943. Then, after several months of training in Nevada, T-333 was shipped off to Hamilton Field outside of San Francisco to collect an aircraft to ferry to CBI: a spanking-new B-24 Liberator. They also got their orders for the long trip overseas and, in August 1944, after touching down in Gander, Newfoundland, on the Azore Islands off Spain, Marrakech, Tunis, Cairo, Iran, Karachi, and Pandeveswar, they finally reached their home airfield at Madhaiganj, northwest of Calcutta.

No matter where Chuck Linamen trained or traveled, however, one thing remained constant: he was from Warren, Ohio. And anytime he walked up to a water fountain and looked down—in North Africa or India or Nevada—he was staring at the name of his own hometown in embossed words around the water fountain's steel drain. "And right down where the drain was, where the water runs out, it said 'Halsey W. Taylor,' on the top of the drain and on the bottom it said 'Warren, Ohio.' At any water fountain on earth, it sometimes seemed, the second I looked down I was home."

As 1944 became 1945, after several months of Hump airlift duty, Linamen and his crew were ordered back to Madhaiganj. They were to assist with the new Allied push, including both the attack on Burma and the drive to reopen the Burma Road into China. And according to Linamen, none of T-333's men regretted the change in orders. "The Hump was tough and dangerous duty. What people today think is an impossibly rough flight? If you were flying the Hump, you'd call that smooth. There were always thunderstorms: first there was an updraft, then a downdraft, and the winds could hit almost three hundred miles an hour. And there was hail inside the tops of those storms, too. I've seen aircraft landed with holes the size of grapefruits in their skin from hailstones. So, yeah, in a way, I was happy to stop flying gas to China and get to combat bombing at lower altitudes."

Linamen and his crew were also happy to escape the difficulties of China, a nation that—despite the Hump supplies streaming in—was on pitifully short rations. "Even as they were finally getting the better of the Japanese," said T-333's trim and precise bombardier, Bill Henderson, "everyone could see that graft and corruption had destroyed the country's soul. It was terrible. *Terrible.* One morning a tiny, elderly Chinese woman—who wore leggings wrapped so tight they emphasized her tiny wrapped feet—picked through our garbage barrel. She was searching for food. She wanted nutrition of any kind. We watched as she ran her fingers around the inside of an empty sardine can, which somebody must have gotten in a care package from the States. Then she sucked on her fingers to get any of the sardine oil that might still be in the can. All I could think was: that's what starvation looks like. She was starving."

AT MADHAIGANJ, T-333's first orders were to bomb the Burma-Siam Railroad into disruption. And for their initial trip, Linamen's unit was assigned an old "D Model" B-24, whose nose art read *Pecker Red.* In CBI—and later in the India theater—due to the scarcity of aircraft, B-24 crews were generally issued a different plane each morning alongside their flight schedules and orders, which allowed ground crews to match each plane's personality to the job at hand. Aircraft with newer or more efficient engines—giving them the capability to fly longer trips—would be assigned to crews bombing distant targets in Burma or Singapore. Aircraft whose bomb bays had been customized for specific types of weapons—the oddly shaped iron of fragmentation "banana bombs," or five-hundred- or one-thousand-pound bombs—would be used on runs where their specific qualities could be best employed.

At first, everyone wanted to fly the newest, shiniest, best performing B-24s at Madhaiganj, the ones with messages and phone numbers from the factory's rivet girls still penned on struts near the tail-gunner's turret. But after a little time in combat, everyone's lust for the newest planes changed. "It turned out you wanted the oldest ship you could get," Linamen said. "Every time the Japanese saw a new ship or new configuration in the air, they'd shoot at it first because it was something new and, presumably, it was more dangerous."

Between January and April 1945, T-333 flew fifty-two bombing missions out of Madhaiganj, but for most of the men—Chuck Linamen in particular—one of these missions stood out. "It was April 1945, and by this time there'd been two operational bridges over the Meiklong—which is also called the Kwae Yai—for some time. One was the old wooden bridge and the other was the new steel bridge brought in by the Japanese. Anyway, headquarters decided it was time to take both of those bridges down for good."

The two bridges were about one hundred yards apart over the Kwae Yai, and as they stretched hundreds of yards across the largest river in the region, they were the most vulnerable spots to damage the railroad. Understanding this, the Japanese had also lined the bridgeheads heavily with antiaircraft weapons. Still, no matter the deterrents, Seventh Bomb Group tacticians believed that if both bridges could be taken out, all supplies traveling the rail line would have to be brought to the eastern shore of the Kwae Yai by train, offloaded, placed onto barges, and floated to the western shore of the river before rail transport could be continued. As supplies began to accumulate on both shores of the river, Seventh Bomb Group planners felt these stockpiles, too, would become vulnerable to air strikes. For the Seventh Bomb Group, the two bridges had become fixations. Since roughly October 1944—after the end of the monsoon—several successful missions had damaged both bridges. But in every instance, the bridges were quickly repaired.

Finally, after six months of regular bombing, on April 2, 1945, Chuck Linamen climbed aboard a B-24 to be copilot for his systems operations officer, John Sims, the mission's pilot. Kanchanaburi and the Kwae Yai were a long way from Madhaiganj, but after a seven-hour flight, Linamen watched as Sims piloted his aircraft perfectly over the steel bridge, gave the signal for bomb drops, and sent two steel spans of the new bridge into the river. For the Japanese, there was no more steel to replace the bridge spans. The steel bridge on the River Kwae was officially closed.

THE FOLLOWING MORNING, on April 3, 1945, it was T-333's turn. Just past midnight, T-333 and several other flight crews assembled in the briefing room for their orders. They were to take off at 2:30 a.m. instead of the usual few minutes before dawn, and their 9 a.m. target was the wooden bridge over the Kwae. When the routing and the target were once again announced, a collective groan went up in the briefing room. The target was seven to eight hours distant, and even with the new auto-pilot devices and enlarged bomb-bay fuel tanks, the round-trip was a long one: a fourteen- to sixteen-hour day that, unfortunately, was to start shortly—at two-thirty in the morning—and might not end until seven or eight that night.

Worse than the long hours was the obvious danger. With the steel bridge out, the Japanese would focus all of their defenses on the wooden bridge, making it a more difficult target to bomb. So the operations office had assigned another squadron of B-24s to roll in as "flack supressors" ahead of the "bridge busters." They were to fly to the target ten or fifteen minutes in front of T-333 and its formation, drop antipersonnel shrapnel bombs on the area's antiaircraft gun emplacements, and move out.

For this run, the B-24 that T-333 had been issued was so new that it had yet to have a name or portrait painted on its nose. It also had newer, far more sophisticated radar aboard, and its belly was painted black—not the usual green camouflage or the silvery sky-blue—which meant it was intended for "night recon" and mapping.

For six and a half hours, all went smoothly. Flying slowly to conserve fuel and not alert the enemy, they crossed India and Burma, and entered

Thai airspace near Three Pagodas pass. Right on schedule, as T-333 and its formation began to make the turn over its IP—the "Initial Point" where a bombing formation started its run—it was 8:59 a.m.

But as Linamen and his formation began to make their turn on the target, the flack-suppression aircraft were nowhere to be found. Worse still, there was no smoke or dust clouding the air near the bridge, meaning the defensive positions around the bridge hadn't been hit. There were also no aircraft visible in the skies other than Linamen's formation. T-333 and its fellow bombers had been stood up.

"The choice was mine," Linamen said. "Did we go ahead and bomb? Or not? So my copilot, Brad Hamblett, looked over at me and said: 'What are we gonna do?' And I said, 'We don't have the fuel to fool around and wait here . . . we're going."

With his usual announcement—"Crew, this is pilot: Get set. We're going."—Curly Linamen began the first of three bombing runs on the bridge. And as they approached the target, Linamen—as he always did—turned over control of the aircraft to his bombardier through the autopilot, so Bill Henderson could line up the target in the crosshairs of his bombsight. In the distance, the wooden bridge looked impossibly thin, but Henderson—a compact, steady man with a nervous smile—stayed calm. As the B-24 approached its target, Henderson completed his precomputation, factoring in the airspeed, distance, and wind. Then, at the precise moment the bridge moved through his sight's crosshairs, he tripped his bombing lever.

Though two one-thousand-pound bombs were supposed to fall from the B-24's belly, only one appeared. As it fell, Henderson was gripped with anticipation and frustration. He checked his intervalometer, the device that told him how many bombs were loaded and falling, and—unfortunately—it was correct. Only one one-thousand-pound bomb had been dropped.

But what a shot it was. It was falling beautifully . . . down, down, down, becoming smaller and smaller as it plummeted. Finally, with an in-unison sigh from every crew member who had a vantage, the one-thousand-pound bomb hit the bridge squarely: precisely at its center and between the two rails. Seconds later, it exploded, taking out two wooden spans.

The wooden bridge over the Kwae Yai was down.

Henderson released control of the B-24 back to Linamen, who quickly flew it back to the IP to make the second of his three runs. As Linamen made the long turn over the jungle south of the bridge, Henderson cranked another one-thousand-pound bomb into place above the open bomb-bay doors. Then it was time for the next pass. Once again, Henderson took control of the B-24. This second time, over the target, both bombs were delivered, but they fell slightly off-course, hitting about ten feet to the south (or left) of the bridge. Knowing they probably had only one more pass before the antiaircraft guns would fix their altitude and begin pouring flack on them, Henderson cranked all three remaining one-thousand-pound bombs into the ready position.

As the B-24 began to make its final pass, Linamen and Henderson heard their aircraft's gunners reporting flack bursts very close to the aircraft. They kept flying, moving closer and closer to the target. At the moment of the drop, Henderson noticed that, in his bombsight, the bridge had drifted a little to the right in his crosshairs. All three bombs slid from beneath the aircraft, plummeting down and forward toward the bridge's thin shape. As they grew closer to the already broken span, though, it became obvious that these bombs, too, were going to fall wide of the target.

Henderson paused to snap a photo—which today he admits was "a foolish mistake"—before turning control of the B-24 back to Linamen. After the picture had been taken, Henderson switched over the autopilot. "Pilot from bombardier," he said. "OK to turn."

With Henderson's message, Linamen retook the B-24 and immediately dropped the right wing into a banking turn, bringing the left wing to near vertical. At that same moment, a blizzard of flack battered the aircraft and the entire plane lurched crazily backward and down. They had been hit and the entire crew understood that they had been hit badly.

The B-24 went into an uncontrolled turn, then it began to spin. Inside the cockpit, the instrument panel had broken free of its mount and was bouncing up and down in a blur. Copilot Brad Hamblett tried to steady it with his hands so he could check the gauges. But even as Hamblett was trying to make sense of them, the B-24—all 110-foot wingspan and 64-foot length—was spiraling downward. Linamen was calling Hamblett for help with the controls. Hamblett dropped the instrument panel and pitched in. He used both feet in an attempt to depress the aircraft's right rudder pedal, but the rudder wasn't budging.

Everything inside the B-24 was shuddering and vibrating, and above the din of the engines came the noise of shearing metal as the plane's struts and spars strained to stay together. They had virtually no right rudder control—they couldn't turn the B-24 to the right at all—and there was absolutely no aileron purchase. Finally, Hamblett and Linamen managed to get the B-24's nose up and steer it out of the spin into a stall (the only way out of the spiral, since there weren't enough flight-control surfaces to turn the B-24 right and out of the spin). Then—ever so slowly—the ungainly B-24 went up and over itself in a wing-over roll, coming out to the left and pointed roughly northwest toward India.

Somehow—with as much luck as skill—they'd pulled it off. They were not only still airborne, they were headed for home. Now, with the engines on emergency power and the pilots taking turns standing on the rudder pedal in exhausting five-minute stretches, they were flying toward safety. The B-24 was listing and jerking. Its right wing was tilted ten to fifteen degrees down—and they were losing altitude and airspeed—but they were still airborne. And they were beating it for Madhaiganj.

As crew T-333 flew west, toward the Andaman Sea, perhaps sixty miles in the distance, the question now on everyone's mind was: Just how far can we go? The aircraft was making 175 or 180 knots per hour, and by manipulating the trim tabs and rudders, it seemed to be flying OK. If there was enough fuel to make it across the Andaman Sea, over southern Burma, and to Akyab Island, they could at least bail out over friendly territory and let the aircraft crash into the Bay of Bengal.

Then, somewhat strangely—and almost in unison—the crew began to evaluate the equipment aboard the aircraft. All of it, every bit, was new. The entire aircraft was new. It was too valuable to lose. In the next few minutes, the crew came to one horrible and collective conclusion. No matter where they were forced to set it down, they were going to have to land this B-24. They couldn't let it crash.

As they flew toward the sea, now visible in the distance, crewmen began discussing their options on the internal communications channel. Nobody wanted to bail out over Burma; and, just as important, nobody wanted to sacrifice the plane. Instead, they could fly over the Andaman Sea, keeping well south of the antiaircraft guns in Rangoon, and turn up the beach along the Arakan Peninsula toward Akyab Island and, beyond that, the British airfield at a place called Cox's Bazaar in southeast India. The question of whether they could get that far drifted unspoken in the air.

The last of the jungle passed beneath them, and they began their flight's long leg across the Andaman Sea. With each minute, the crew grew more apprehensive about their chances of landing the disabled aircraft, even as the plane's engines—which were still running flat out on emergency power—began to show signs of overheating. Finally, two hours along, the Arakan Peninsula came into view in the distance. As T-333's aircraft made landfall once again, now over friendly territory, Curly announced that he and Brad were going to pilot the B-24 as far as they could. Then, he said, when they couldn't keep it in the air any longer, they were going to land it on the beach somewhere between Akyab Island and Cox's Bazaar. Anyone who preferred to bail out, they suggested, was free to do so over the beach shortly before the landing, and a search-and-rescue team would be dispatched to find them immediately.

For a long minute, the aircraft's internal communications channel was silent. Nobody piped up to jump. Then Curly Linamen's voice was back over the headsets. "I am getting ready to start descent."

The drone of the engines dropped and from over the com channel came a response—one nobody aboard has ever admitted to. "We're all going with you . . ." the voice said. "What the hell are you waiting for?"

Linamen ordered the crew to move all loose equipment to the back of the aircraft, making it as tail-heavy as possible. Then he continued lowering the B-24's airspeed as the crew braced for a crash. Linamen dropped the landing gear. For a long minute, the crew held its breath as Linamen and Hamblett brought the B-24 within yards of the sand. At the last second, the B-24 rose slightly—the two pilots avoided a small sand dune—then, in the next moment there was a shudder, a large *whump*, and the B-24 began to skid, its struts and landing gear vibrating madly. They were down—and Linamen and Hamblett shut off the engines and fought to keep the plane from spinning. In the next second, the entire aircraft jerked, halted, and stopped as completely as if they had hit an impenetrable obstacle. The crew slammed against bulkhead walls. Linamen and Hamblett smacked against their seat harnesses.

The B-24's nose wheel had stuck in a patch of soft sand and sheared off, tipping the aircraft forward and dropping the B-24's nose to the beach; the plane stopped with a violent jolt accompanied by the deafening shriek of more shearing metal. Then there was only silence. Somewhat miraculously, the men of T-333 had survived.

Another second later, as everyone realized the aircraft was down and stopped, they all hurried for the forward escape hatch, climbed out of it, and hustled down off the crashed B-24's nose turret, which was partly buried in the sand. With the crash over, the crew now feared a fire and explosion.

The B-24's propellers were still spinning, and as he hurried down the aircraft's nose to the beach, Bill Henderson stepped on the nose turret's Plexiglas, fell through it, and cut his leg deeply on the shattered plastic. He extricated himself and kept going. The crew ran to a safe distance up the beach, then they turned to look at their smashed airplane.

The B-24 that had just bombed the bridge on the river Kwae was ruined: its wheel struts were bent or broken, its fuselage tilted forward at a seventy-degree angle, and its nose buried in the sand.

Then, as they waited to be retrieved by the British out of Cox's Bazaar, the men of T-333 looked down the shoreline behind their wrecked aircraft, and grew even more flabbergasted. From touchdown to a complete stop, the B-24's entire crash had taken only one hundred yards of beach.

# Chapter 20

THERE WAS a good reason the Japanese never reconstructed the Kwae bridges. By early 1945 in Burma and southwest China, events on the ground were no less one-sided than they were in the air. For the Japanese, supplies had stopped flowing and the armies were growing destitute. Even worse, owing to the work of the tenth Air Force, the situation for both supply and withdrawal was poised to deteriorate still further.

"We were already tired and hungry," said Infantry soldier Susumu Miyashita. "We had no food and little shelter. We slept exposed on the earth. We were used up. We had no muscles left in our legs. We were skeletons in dirty and torn uniforms. We had broken boots and not much ammunition. Birds pecked at the unburied dead along roadsides. And the British were now coming for us."

Three years earlier, Miyashita said, the Japanese Imperial Army had been invincible. Now, in Burma, they were in complete—and perplexing—collapse. And mixed with hunger and confusion, the humiliation of that loss drove many soldiers, including Miyashita, to consider suicide.

"We had conquered south Asia in six months," Miyashita said. "And now we had nothing, and the British were coming, and they were very strong. *Very* strong. There was nothing to do but keep going. I was sick with malaria. I had been sick for some time. Several times already, I had considered suicide. I thought, if I hold a hand grenade to my chest and pull the pin, the suffering will be over. In one act, I can end it. But I couldn't do it. I was just alive enough to desire to keep going."

ON THE ARAKAN PENINSULA in Burma's southwest, the British and Indians were now retaking land from the Japanese with great leaps toward Rangoon. In central Burma, William Slim's forces had crossed the Shwebo plain, and were now arrayed near the Irrawaddy at several spots. For a time, they monitored the Japanese, watching as they tried to reinforce defenses on the river's far shore. In China, General Wedemeyer had flown two X Force divisions to Kunming in preparation to repel the Japanese Eleventh Army coming from the now conquered east, but the attack never materialized. The Japanese Eleventh, exhausted and under-provisioned, had invaded too far ahead of their supply lines. Due to a lack of food and weapons, the Japanese campaign for east China had also been forced to halt.

At the same time, in the north and east of China, the Chinese Communists had started ripping into the Japanese occupation forces and, often as not, they were shredding them. While Chiang Kai-shek and the Kuomintang stuck with their time-honored route to American favor and goods (diplomacy and propaganda), Mao Tse-tung had chosen to prove Chinese Communist value to the United States on the battlefield. Mao believed the best way to win over the Americans—which would earn him more weapons and support—was to wage unstoppable war. Mao's even larger goal was, by war's end, to have the Chinese Communists controlling China's now-occupied seacoast from Shanghai to Tientsin. If the Communist forces could accomplish this, all American commanders coming ashore in China would be greeted by the Communists, obviously a tactical and supply advantage during reconstruction. Also, were civil war against the Kuomintang to break out after the Japanese threat was repelled, the Communists would possess the same harbor-control stranglehold over the Kuomintang that the Japanese had been exercising for the past seven years.

In late 1944, Mao had also relocated his best field commander, Huang Chen—the flashy, ruddy-faced defender of the Communist's blockade line in the north—to lead his armies attacking the Japanese in northern Hunan Province, the original home of Chinese Communism. Already Huang was

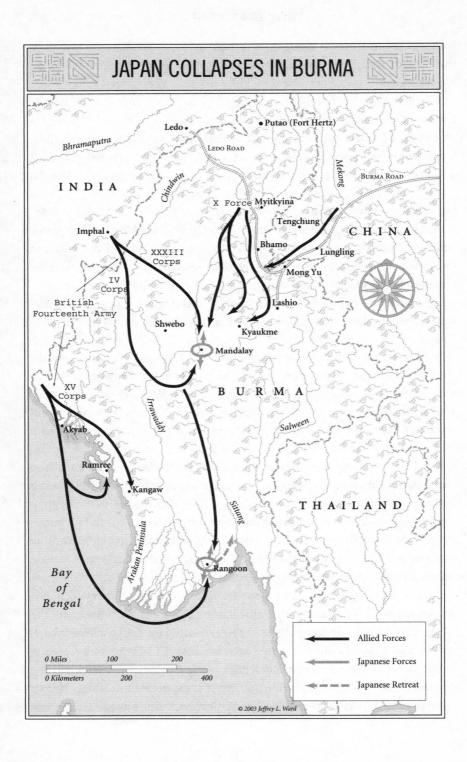

# JAPAN COLLAPSES IN BURMA

Bhramaputra

Ledo

Putao (Fort Hertz)

LEDO ROAD

Mekong

BURMA ROAD

I N D I A

Chindwin

X Force  Myitkyina

C H I N A

Tengchung

Imphal

Bhamo

Lungling

XXXIII
Corps

Mong Yu

IV
Corps

Lashio

British
Fourteenth Army

Shwebo

Kyaukme

Mandalay

XV
Corps

B U R M A

Irrawaddy

Salween

Akyab

Ramree

Kangaw

Arakan Peninsula

Sittang

T H A I L A N D

Bay
of
Bengal

Rangoon

| | Allied Forces |
| | Japanese Forces |
| | Japanese Retreat |

0 Miles    100    200

0 Kilometers    200    400

© 2003 Jeffrey L. Ward

bashing his way through Japanese occupiers toward Pingkiang and Chang-sha, two of the cities conquered the previous autumn by the Japanese Eleventh Army.

The introduction of three million fresh and well-supplied Chinese Communists was not simply turning the tide of war in China. In succes-sive steps, Mao Tse-tung now intended to break the backs of both the Japanese *and* the Kuomintang.


JANUARY 27, 1945, would prove the war in Burma's crowning day for the Allies. By then, William Slim's Fourteenth Army had control of Shwebo and the Shwebo plain west of the Irrawaddy, and—in what would prove a top-drawer example of Slim's tactical genius—he was set to entrap General Kimura's forces in central Burma.

By January 1945 in north and central Burma, the retreating Japanese were down to a single bastion west of the Irrawaddy: the port city of Man-dalay, halfway up Burma's keystone shape. At Mandalay's center, the square mile of its former imperial palace (renamed Fort Dufferin by the colonial British) was encircled by a wall twenty-six feet high and thirty feet thick, making it a perfect place for a fortress stand. But rather than pound against the walls of Fort Dufferin, Slim had chosen another tack. He had received intelligence that the Japanese Fifteenth and Thirty-third Divisions weren't headed for Mandalay, but for the town of Meiktila, ninety miles east of the Irrawaddy and the same distance south of Mandalay. If Slim could trick Kimura into thinking he was going to jump the Irrawaddy at Shwebo—as well as attack Mandalay from there—he might be able to get a fast-moving invasion force across the river farther south before Kimura fortified Meiktila with troops and weapons. If he could outrace the Japa-nese to Meiktila, he could cut them off in central Burma and trap them between two of his largest armies.

Slim's plan was now set: the twenty-two-thousand-man XXXIII Corps—which had done such a fine job along the Dimapur Sector in the battle for Kohima—would get into place for an attack against Mandalay and at a crossing of the river nearby. Meanwhile, a dummy IV Corps Headquarters (home to the Fifth and Seventh Indian Division), would be established north of Shwebo, which would send and receive faked messages from field units supposedly farther north, promoting the illusion that the IV Corps was crossing the Irrawaddy somewhere north of Shwebo.

In truth, Slim had ordered the IV Corps into radio silence and had them cross the Irrawaddy south of Mandalay and nearer Meiktila. Once across the river, the IV Corps was to race for the supply dumps at Meiktila and destroy them. This would leave Kimura cut off from supply, and with the British XXXIII Corps to his north and the IV Corps to his south, Kimura would have no choice but surrender.

On January 27 of 1945, Slim's plan was already well on its way toward working. Kimura had massed his armies along the shore north of Shwebo, even removing some of the units fighting Sultan's X Force and Mars Task Force on the Chinese frontier to help. In the meantime, the IV Corps had already vaulted the Irrawaddy and were making their way to Meiktila.


BUT THAT WASN'T THE ALLIES' FINEST MOMENT on January 27. Farther south, down on the Arakan Peninsula, an amphibious attack on the city of Kangaw had also turned the Allies' way. After a ferocious bombardment as the Allies had been coming ashore on January 22, and after five days of surging attacks and counterattacks that rivaled those at Kohima and Imphal in ferocity and carnage, the Allies had managed to block the highway leading south out of the Arakan Peninsula. They had severed the Japanese escape route to Rangoon, and the Japanese were now scattering into the forest to the highway's north in total disarray.

According to infantryman Susumu Miyashita,

There was no order to our withdrawal anymore. The jungle and our physical condition was killing us as much as the British and Indians were. By now, four of every five men dying in the withdrawal were dying of starvation and disease. Malaria was killing us, too. There was no more discipline. There was no one giving orders. We were in the jungle, and everyone was now on their own. During the battle for Kangaw, I had been shot twice: once through the shoulder and once through the knee. And every day, as I limped and crawled southeast toward Thailand and freedom, I would search for a vehicle with gasoline in it. If I could find one, I would siphon a bit of gas out of its tank with a long cane and use the gasoline to clean my wounds. Otherwise, the maggots would grow huge. Gasoline was the only thing available that I could find to kill the maggots. My life, every day, had become a struggle to stay alive.

While a few stalwart Japanese units would continue to contest the British and Indians for the road until February 11, the Allied blockade held. The undersupplied and retreating Japanese on the Arakan were driven into the unrelenting torment of Burma's densest and most miserable jungle.

JANUARY 27, 1945, WAS a day of celebration for the Allies in south Asia for yet another reason. During the past three weeks, contingents of General Sultan's X Force and Mars Task Force had driven up the Burma Road toward China—killing the retreating Japanese at a six-to-one ratio—and they now were almost to the border.

Meanwhile, in the opposite direction, the Y Force had pushed down the road out of China to the south and west, driving the Japanese from the towns of Mangshi and Zhefang without heavy fighting. Following the Burma Road and clearing enemy troops from it in a broad front, they worked down the Black Mountain Grade off the Tibetan Plateau and toward lowland Burma. Between September 1944 and January 1945, the Japanese at Lungling, Tengchung, and Sungshan had lost 19,620 dead. And despite the far-larger losses of the Chinese Y Force—37,133 dead—the momentum had swung to the Chinese and Americans, who now had the remaining Japanese along the Burma Road firmly in a pincer.

On January 27, 1945, following a line of American-made tanks up the road, the X Force rolled toward the final Japanese-occupied town along the Burma Road: the *atap* and wood-shelter village of Pinghai. As it had been doing since defeating the Japanese at Myitkyina, the X Force came in with its armor showing and its cannons blazing. For the first wave of attack, X Force tanks pounded the landscape ahead of the troops with 75-millimeter cannons. Nothing seemed to elude the X Force tank guns: houses were demolished, groves of banana trees were reduced to smoldering pickets, and tent shelters were vaporized. Behind the tanks, the infantry then moved in off the surrounding ridges at a crouching run, their machine guns spraying every clump of brush or likely Japanese hideout for kills.

But as the infantry units disappeared into the village, a strange and completely alien event began to unfold. Nothing happened. Instead of the rattling of semiautomatic rifles, there came only silence. At a few of the abandoned and still-standing shelters, the Chinese went to the kitchens, pulled out greenish sticks of sugarcane, and started munching. The Japanese, apparently, had pulled out. China lay only an hour ahead, and there was no longer an enemy blocking the way home.

Still chewing their sugarcane, the Chinese continued up the road, which bisected a valley tufted by rice paddies. Then, at a fork in the road just ahead—perhaps a mile up the road in the distance—X Force scouts spotted a knot of ragged troops in blue and gray uniforms. The Chinese, now itching to kill any Japanese fighters they could find, deployed across the rice paddies, flanking the road fork and cutting off the enemy's escape. Then, just before the order to fire was given, the American liaison officer with the X Force—Brigadier General George Sliney—pieced together the situation, ran to the battle line, and began marching up and down in front of the X Force fighters ordering them not to shoot. At one point, Sliney even threw himself down in front of a machine gunner who had already opened fire. The blue and gray uniforms, Sliney knew, were those of the Y Force.

Hurrying ahead on foot, Sliney walked toward the Y Force deployment. As he did, the Chinese soldiers at the road's fork recognized the American uniform. Like long-lost friends, the Y Force Chinese started running toward the general and his khaki-clad X Force troops behind. Everyone was cheering and throwing his fists in the air. As the American tanks rolled up the road, the Y Force continued shaking hands and laughing and shouting *Ting hao!* (The Best!) to every American face they encountered.

The troops out of China looked terrible. They were hungry, tired, and dirty. Their uniforms were torn, their faces were drawn, and many were wearing shoes made of woven grass. Their weapons were old and worn, with some of them dating from World War I. Conversely, the X Force Chinese out of Burma—in their neat khaki uniforms and sturdy leather boots—were well fed and well muscled and carried shiny new weapons. Much as the Japanese had two years earlier, the X Force now looked invincible. And as the two armies met along the road, the Y Force soldiers couldn't believe the goods at the X Force's disposal. They had troop carrier trucks and artillery on new carriages—and they had tanks, which were virtually unknown in China. Having never witnessed such armored beasts before, a few of the Y Force fighters even reached out and tentatively touched the warm steel of the elephant-like vehicles.

And there, at a clump of five American tanks at a crossroads on the Burma-China border, the Burma Road was reopened.

# Chapter 21

ON JANUARY 12, 1945, World War II's first overland-vehicle convoy from India to China fired up its engines and, with a slow and jerky rumble, began to organize along the road leading northwest out of Ledo, in northeast India. The goal of "Pick's First Convoy," as it was known, sat far in the distance, eleven hundred miles away. To get there, the convoy would cross jungled mountains in India and north Burma, swampy lowlands in the Hukawng Valley, the broad Irrawaddy River, the ten-thousand-foot peaks of the Tibetan Plateau, and the raging Salween and Mekong rivers. Then, still working to the northeast, they hoped to reach the supply warehouses of Kunming, China. The trip was slated to take roughly two weeks.

The convoy numbered 113 vehicles: jeeps, ambulances, GMC 6 × 6 cargo trucks, and Chrysler weapons carriers. As it assembled that first morning—just as had happened with everything else in CBI—getting organized took longer than anticipated. By early afternoon, though, following a long wait at "Mile O" in Ledo, the three-starred jeep of General Daniel I. Sultan rolled up the road—past the convoy's long snake of olive-drab steel, green canvas, and black rubber—before finally stopping at the convoy's head. By order of Sultan and Pick, there were no news correspondents, magazine photographers, or newsreel cameramen present. The news outfits would meet the convoy as it rolled toward Myitkyina, 287 miles and three days in the future. What was happening now, the start of the First Convoy, was to be strictly army, intended purely for the troops who'd fought and sweated and chiseled the road to completion.

When Sultan's jeep finally arrived at the convoy's lead truck, it stopped and the general hopped out. His manner and look resembled a sturdy, uniform-clad version of the actor Edward G. Robinson. With a snappy salute, General Louis Pick—his service cap tilted rakishly to the right and his wooden shepherd's crook momentarily in his left hand—met Sultan. The two shook hands.

"Sir," Pick said, "the Ledo Road, lifeline to China, is open. I have the first convoy formed and ready. I would like your permission to take it through to China."

Sultan smiled. "Congratulations, General Pick," he said. "You have done a splendid job. I am confident this is the first of many convoys to go along this road to our Chinese allies."

And after another quick salute, Pick turned and shouted, "Line 'em up, Mullet!" to his caravan's commander, Colonel DeWitt T. Mullet. Mullet waved the first vehicles ahead and engines that had been idling for an hour began to rev. At the head of the column, two military police in white helmet liners and gloves led the first truck up the road out of Ledo headed for Kunming. The convoy's lead truck jerked and moved out. Pinned to both sides of the canvas Conestoga-style roof over the lead truck's bed, banners read: FIRST CONVOY LEDO ROAD. PICK'S PIKE—LIFELINE TO CHINA. Beneath that canvas roof of the first convoy truck, however, was not the lend-lease freight all of the other trucks were carrying. Instead, under this canvas and concealed by zipper-closing flaps, sat a manned antiaircraft gun capable of making 360-degree swivels. Japanese fighter aircraft were not going to get Pick's First Convoy.

This line of trucks was going all the way to Kunming.


THE FIRST CONVOY ROLLED OUT of Ledo, passing gas stations and army warehouses and clanging across the steel Bailey bridge at Jairanpur. A few miles ahead, in the town of Nampong, the convoy crossed a second bridge, the one known as the Hellgate: last stop before the border with Burma. Then, two miles later, they began to make the long, snaking climb toward Pangsau Pass and Burma, where, just two years earlier, the first American bulldozer had crunched into the jungle, uprooting trees and tearing away the forest's soft loam.

Like a miles-long snake, the convoy kept rolling. Following the road's hairpins, they crossed the mountaintop, then began to descend the opposite side of Pangsau, whose name in Jingpaw means "strangers coming." Finally they were in Burma. And once over the pass's 3,737-foot summit, the road crossed a grassy tended area and began to descend. As the road slithered into that first Burmese valley, it became a narrow trace that eased through a jungle so thick the vegetation seemed to lean threateningly in on the vehicles from both shoulders. When the midwinter sun began to set, General Pick ordered buckets of oil lit along the road at all potential trouble spots as a warning to drivers.

The trucks passed through the native village of Namlit, its thatched stilt houses and bare-breasted Naga women amazing the GIs and Chinese soldiers who drove and rode in the troop carriers. Despite having been billeted sixty miles away, in a place where modernized Nagas were another part of the scenery, they had never seen nonacculturated tribals. Then, as the evening grew crisp and cool, the first trucks from the convoy rolled down off the last of the Patkai Range foothills and into the Hukawng Valley. Five miles ahead was where they would stop for the night. They would bivouac at Mile 109, which, fittingly, was the site of Stilwell's first field headquarters in Burma: the little village of Shingbwiyang.

That night they ate at an engineers' mess and were served a fine meal of beef and potatoes by troops from the 858th Aviation Engineers. Then, with the *burrrrr* of cicadas rolling out of the jungle to lull them to sleep, the men of Pick's First Convoy slung their hammocks between trucks and bedded down.

ON THE MORNING OF January 13, 1945, after packing their hammocks and reloading their trucks, General Pick's First Convoy moved out of Shingbwiyang and into the Hukawng Valley.

Away from the rumpled Patkai hills, the once-meandering roadbed now stretched south down the valley as straight as if drawn with a ruler. As the convoy rolled on, with its Chinese and American troops aboard, it passed more members of the 858th Aviation Engineers doing roadside maintenance. It passed Indian laborers from Ledo, as well as Nagas—with their enormous silver earrings and brilliantly red loincloths—plus groups of

Kachins in their black and green plaid sarongs, which they called *longyis*.

Bouncing farther south down the valley, the caravan troops began to see signs that, not too long ago, war had been waged here. They passed blackened, burned-out Allied and Japanese tanks and, in the river courses and thickets of jungle, Japanese troop-carrying vehicles that had been shot to pieces and then towed out of the way by road-construction crews.

They motored past shiny, American-looking service stations, which, in recent months, had been plunked into place every twenty miles along the roadside. They passed airstrips every twenty or thirty miles, too, which had been cut into the dirt parallel to the road. They crossed the Tarung River on a pontoon bridge, then crossed the Tanai River by fording it at low water. They passed through the riverside towns of Maingkwan and Walawbum, where Frank Merrill's Marauders and Stilwell's X Force had turned the tide of the North Burma Campaign. Then they rumbled over the bridge of the Numpyek River, at almost the same place the Marauders had withstood the first "tree-burst" artillery counterattack in March 1944.

Finally, having traveled 179 miles since Ledo, the First Convoy rolled into Shaduzup. Here, Pick and Mullet had already decided, the group would spend its second night on the road.

THE FOLLOWING MORNING, wrapped in a heavy fog, Pick's First Convoy moved past the mountains of Jambu Bum and the Kumon Range, both of which were obscured in the mist, and as they continued, the air's dense moisture began to turn the layers of Ledo Road dust now covering the convoy's trucks into a thick, pasty mud. They passed Inkangahtawng and Kamaing, once home to the proud and seemingly invincible Japanese Eighteenth Division.

By midmorning, the fog had burned off as the convoy passed Mogaung and dropped into the Irrawaddy Valley. In the now-bright morning, the truck and jeep drivers began to spot the silhouettes of small, liaison aircraft moving through the sky above them. Inside each plane, photographers and cameramen from the Army Signal Corps were documenting the convoy's progress.

Then, about ten miles from Myitkyina, at a fork in the road called Pick's Triangle (where one road went south toward Bhamo and the other east toward Myitkyina), the First Convoy was met by what seemed a battalion of war correspondents and photographers. The vehicles stopped so their crews could be interviewed and photographed, and the GIs and Chinese aboard smiled for photos and granted interviews to what turned out to be more than forty world news outlets. General Pick, walking around the photo op with his crooked "Pilgrim Stick," made a memorably adventurous looking leader.

Then, after an hour, the soldiers climbed back into their vehicles and, turning east, headed for a special bivouac area set aside for them in the battle-shattered streets and buildings of Myitkyina.

They were now roughly one quarter of the way to Kunming. Since starting out three days ago, they'd traveled 287 miles.

FOR BOTH THEATERS of war in south Asia, the closing year of World War II would prove no less chaotic than the opening year had been.

In the new China theater, General Wedemeyer, true to his predictions, was enjoying an outwardly cordial relationship with Chiang. He built a corps of bright young American officers and—through a series of programs and strategic plans—proceeded to upgrade the Nationalist Chinese Army in short order. By early 1945, he'd brought in nutritionists and logicians and weapons-training experts. He'd also started chairing three-times-weekly meetings between the Americans and the Chinese, conferences designed to promote openness and trust. And because the two fronts in southeast and southwest China were relatively quiet—both sides were too exhausted and in short supply to fight—Wedemeyer was able to convince Chiang to retool what he was now calling "the New Army" with better weapons and supplies.

But beyond Wedemeyer's persuasive ways, Chiang had a second—and even more compelling—reason for reconstituting his troops. In northern and eastern China, just as they had been doing since November 1944, Mao Tse-tung's Chinese Communist Army was proving a fearsome war machine. They seemed to be attacking the Japanese everywhere at once, often overrunning them like a prairie fire. By spring—as Chiang's generals began their own series of offensives against the Japanese at Chihkiang—it had become obvious that once China defeated its outside invader, a civil war for its soul was all but certain.

In Burma and India, General Sultan's X Force and General Slim's Fourteenth Army continued to grind down the Japanese. Using his pincer move on Meiktila, Slim managed to entrap the Japanese Fifteenth Army, and they crumbled and began running—largely on foot—through the jungles for Thailand as fast as their exhausted bodies could carry them.

At Mandalay in March of 1945, the Japanese were still poised to make their stand inside the imperial palace of Fort Dufferin. Encircled by a moat 225 feet wide and fortified by twenty-five-foot walls, the fort was sure to be, in Slim's estimation "a very formidable object to a lightly equipped army in a hurry." But Slim, always the self-possessed pragmatist, knew that patience and positioning would tilt the battle in his favor.

First he decided to take "the great rock" of Mandalay Hill just to the west of Fort Dufferin. An immense chunk of tawny stone that rose 774 feet above the fort, the hill was also studded with gilded pagodas and temples. Slim recognized that Pagoda Hill, as he called it, was the high-ground vantage he'd need to win the battle. And to clear the hill of enemy troops, he sent in several detachments of Gurkhas, who painstakingly drove out snipers nested in each of its temples and pagodas. Three days later, after pitched combat and mortar explosions, the hill was in British hands. From there, Slim and his men could look down inside the walled square mile of Fort Dufferin, whose ramparts and moats now began to remind Slim of "an immense edition of the toy fortress I used to play with as a boy."

For days, Slim ordered RAF and Tenth Air Force bombers—plus short- and medium-range artillery—to smash at Fort Dufferin's walls, but the effort had little effect. When five-hundred-pound aerial bombs proved insufficient, Slim ordered two-thousand-pound versions "skip bombed" across the moat and into the walls. After a week of nonstop bombardment and shelling, finally, a few breaches were opening. Then, for four nights in a row, British, Gurkha, and Indian assault teams tried to cross the fort's moat in rafts, only to be repelled each time. Slim had had enough. He ordered another round of heavy bombing and shelling, and on March 20, as the assault teams were readying to go again, six Burmese soldiers exited the fort waving white flags.

Fort Dufferin had been abandoned. Under cover of night, the Japanese had escaped through drainpipes that ran to the Irrawaddy from beneath the moat. Mandalay had fallen.

NOW ALL THAT REMAINED for William Slim was a footrace to Rangoon, which the general hoped to retake before the monsoons began. Rangoon, that final glittering prize in Burma, lay three hundred miles to the south of the British Fourteenth Army, and Slim estimated that his army would have to cover ten miles a day to reach and take it ahead of the summer rains. He also understood his troops would certainly meet regular Japanese resistance along the way.

To help drive back the Japanese en route, Slim decided to make his thrust armored and mechanized. But Slim also knew his tank units were tired; they had been struggling since the war's start, owing mostly to outmoded equipment. With his tank battalions, Slim knew he had a morale problem. To impress upon his armored units just how valuable they were to this operation, he personally traveled to all of his tank commanders and implored them to keep every tank they had operational and moving until they reached and retook Rangoon. Once Rangoon had been fought for and secured, he joked, the tank commanders were free to push their tanks off Rangoon's docks into the sea.

Even as his mechanized forces clattered toward Rangoon, the Japanese were abandoning Burma, with thousands of troops now trying to cross the Sittang River near the same bomb-shattered bridge where, a little more than three years earlier, they had invaded. The men were exhausted, and many—trying to swim across the wide river—simply drowned.

Said infantryman Susumu Miyashita:

The Sittang River crossing was the cruelest event of the whole war. Every man was sick to the point of dying. Of the 16,575 men in my original division, only 4,492 survived. About one thousand were killed in actual fighting. The other eleven thousand died during the withdrawal. I remember standing on the shore of the Sittang River with many other men. I wasn't strong enough to swim across the river. Then some men made a raft of bamboo. But I was afraid that if I floated across on that I might fall off and drown. Eventually, some of us found a traditional Burmese boat and floated across, and as we were crossing I watched as the bamboo raft I'd decided not to cross the river on grew too overloaded with soldiers and sank. The men on that raft all drowned. Before it was over, ten thousand Japanese troops would drown, though the British claim they only ever recovered six hundred bodies. After all that had happened in Burma, the tragedy of the Sittang was still the worst of it. In the greatest sense, it was a tragedy.

———

AT MYITKYINA ON JANUARY 15, 1945, General Pick's First Convoy was forced to wait, since the combined X and Y Forces had not yet cleared the road ahead. And they would not, in fact, get it cleared and secured for two more weeks. At Myitkyina, Pick and his men would just have to "sit tight and sweat it out."

To keep the men occupied, Pick had provided for special service musical shows, where—with the exception of two brave Red Cross volunteers, Judy Asti and Audrey Edwards—all the roles, male and female, were played by Red Cross men in drag. Pick also made sure that, nightly, all the convoy members and correspondents were given large and well-provisioned banquets.

But the waiting was slowly eating at morale. Dozens of times a day, the correspondents—now eager to get going so they could post their stories with bylines from "along the Burma Road"—were hectoring Lt. Colonel Don Thompson, public relations officer for General Sultan. Thompson finally grew so tired of the constant "when are we going to shove off?" queries that, in order to buy himself some time, he claimed he'd issue a press release shortly that would lay out all relevant information. After enjoying a blissfully quiet period without correspondents' harassment, he issued this totally unusable statement—in parody of Gertrude Stein—to the correspondents: "What are mountains? Mountains. What is mud? Mud. A convoy is a convoy is a pain in the neck."

But at Myitkyina, the pain in the neck was just beginning, since it now looked as if a competing convoy would reach Kunming out of Burma first. The previous August and September, members of the Mars Task Force and engineering units led by the American Colonel Robert Seedlock had bushwhacked east of Myitkyina to explore an alternative, and possibly shorter, route to Kunming. Called the Tengchung Cutoff, it was the old Marco Polo Trail from Myitkyina over the mountains to the ancient walled city of Tengchung, which had recently been liberated by the Chinese Fifty-sixth Division. The nine-day Seedlock Expedition had been a success, discovering not only a shorter route, but an easier one.

On January 20, 1945, while General Pick and Colonel Thompson continued to sit in Myitkyina, the Tengchung Cutoff caravan—initiated at Myitkyina, overseen by Lieutenant Hugh A. Pock, and composed of a tow truck and two American 6 × 6 cargo trucks—rolled across the Chinese border. Two days later, on January 22, Pock's convoy was in Kunming—

and Pick and Thompson were furious. Thompson and Pick now resorted to splitting hairs, arguing that the official First Convoy would still be "Pick over Pock," since the Tengchung convoy hadn't traveled the Ledo Road, didn't exclusively follow the Burma Road in China, and was carrying no lend-lease provisions. Like so much in CBI over the past four years, even the theater's crowning event—the First Convoy and reopening of the Burma Road—had degenerated into petty farce.

Finally, on January 23, 1945, after a wait of eight days, the Ledo Road and Burma Road were deemed sufficiently cleared of Japanese forces for Pick's First Convoy once again to move out. They crossed the Irrawaddy on the 1,180-foot pontoon bridge, then continued south without incident down the broad Irrawaddy Valley. Just before dark, General Pick and his caravan made the city of Bhamo, their next planned bivouac spot, 369 miles from Ledo. To celebrate, the convoy dined on heated K rations before making camp by stringing their jungle hammocks between trucks.

BUT THE CONVOY'S eighty-miles-a-day speed of January 23 would be short-lived, since January 24 had, from the start, been scheduled as among the trip's shortest legs. From Bhamo, as had been planned, it would make a forty-mile run along the road as it snaked torturously over a Himalayan spur, ending the day in the town of Namkham.

Laid out along the Ruili River, Namkham and the river had long been considered Burma's historical border with southwest China. And since the Japanese had only been expelled from Namkham a week before, Generals Pick and Sultan had hoped to use it as a staging ground in case, up ahead, the Japanese were still planning to attack the convoy.

As they filed down the narrow gravel into Namkham, the American and Chinese soldiers, for the first time, witnessed the recent aftermath of battle. Most every structure in town was smashed, bullet slashed, and now lay on the ground, smoldering. The Golden Eye Buddhist Monastery, once an elaborately constructed compound with teak arches and golden pagodas, was a smoking ruin. Inside the Golden Eye's walls, gilded statues of Buddha and those of minor deities lay toppled amid the shattered walls and roof tiles. Those statues still standing were missing heads and plaster arms and hands. At the few habitable structures in town, groups of bored-looking GIs sat reading magazines on porches, tossing out half-hearted waves to their compatriots in the convoy. As a triumphant entrance, Namkham was as depressing as hellos get.

THE DEPRESSION WAS to grow worse. The caravan's next leg was another short jump, this time a thirty-mile run to the northeast, to the town of Mong Yu on Burma's border with China.

Mong Yu was where the Ledo Road met the Burma Road, leaving Burma behind for the Chinese town of Wanding in Yunnan Province. Unfortunately, since they expected convoys to soon start rolling down the road toward Kunming, the Japanese had set up heavy artillery on a mountaintop overlooking Wanding and Mong Yu, and they had been shelling the road—with terrifying accuracy—for days. So for three more days, the First Convoy was forced to sit and wait as members of the combined X and Y Forces used American tanks, artillery, and infantry encirclement to push the Japanese hilltop position back.

Then, on the morning of January 28, 1945, sixteen days after leaving Ledo, General Lewis Pick rolled up to the Burma-China border crossing, which had been draped with red banners for the occasion. He stepped from his jeep and, raising a pair of scissors offered to him, cut a ceremonial tape separating Burma and China.

Just to Pick's right, next to the banners at the border, a large sign with two arrows painted on it was staked to roadside earth. One arrow pointed behind Pick, to where the convoy had already been. Beneath it were the words,

LEDO ROAD

LEDO 478 MILES

The other arrow, pointing ahead of Pick's jeep toward China read:

BURMA ROAD

KUNMING 566 MILES

Also on hand for the event was the brassiest of the Allied brass: T. V. Soong and Generals Sultan and Chennault (who would soon quit his command of the Fourteenth Air Force), and Howard Davidson from the Tenth

Air Force. Even Generals Sun Li-jen and Wei Li-huang—commander of the Chinese Salween Force—were on hand. And though Stilwell had been gone from the theater now for three months, he, too, was very much there in spirit.

Shortly after the tape had been cut, General Dan Sultan stood on a dais and read a congratulatory message to the group from Vinegar Joe, lauding all those present and missing on their efforts to complete the road. "I take off my hat," he said, "to the men who fought for it and built it."

UNFORTUNATELY, THE SUBTEXT of Stilwell's congratulatory message at Wanding was lost on no one. Time had caught up with the Ledo-Burma Road and the valiant efforts of the men who'd fought for it and built it. Beneath the celebration, every man at Wanding knew that, since about the time of Stilwell's departure from CBI, the overland approach to Japan had become unnecessary.

The Allied chiefs had opted to attack Japan from the Pacific islands and not from China. This line of thinking made the fight to "keep China in the war" almost pointless. The war on Japan would now be fought from the sky, by planes off Pacific Ocean islands. Already, American troops were fighting for the Ryukyu Islands, which would place Allied bombers well within striking distance of the Japanese mainland.

Despite the sweat and toil of creating the Ledo-Burma Road, despite the blood spilled on the soil of Burma, India, and China to support the road, the Burma Road had become obsolete even as it was being opened. The war had evolved past an overland supply route from India to China. Time had simply run out.

AFTER THE WANDING CEREMONY and with all haste, Pick's First Convoy moved on, climbing the Black Mountain Grade to the top of the Tibetan Plateau in search of Kunming, still 566 miles away. For an entire week the column of trucks and jeeps kept rolling from dawn to dusk, twisting and turning along a now-cobbled roadbed that often seemed to hang dangerously on the mountainsides.

Once atop the Tibetan Plateau, the long line of trucks and jeeps passed Zhefang and, just a bit farther up the road, the ruins of Lungling. They passed the former Japanese revetments atop the ridgeline of Sungshan, with its vantage over the Salween River. The convoy then followed the road as it dropped down the ridge in a series of long switchbacks, leapt the Salween along a newly repaired suspension bridge, and started up the other side. Once back atop the Tibetan Plateau, the convoy traversed the famously windy stretch of open valley near Dali, moving between mountains of pinkish-black granite whose jagged edges whistled nonstop from icy, night-and-day gales.

THEN, ON FEBRUARY 4, 1945, a full twenty-four days and eleven hundred miles after leaving Ledo, General Lewis Pick's First Convoy found itself contemplating one more ceremonial strip of ribbon blocking the road.

This one spanned the cobbled pavement at the Western Gate to the city of Kunming. They had officially arrived. Pick's First Convoy had gotten to Kunming twelve days behind the Tengchong Cutoff "convoy," and fourteen days behind a Navy jeep driven from Ledo by two Americans from the Sino-American Co-Operative Organization—which had bested everybody. But now, with Pick's journey completed, the official First Convoy had finished the trip. The Ledo-Burma Road was open.

At Kunming's West Gate, the honorable Lung Yun, governor of Yunnan Province, welcomed Pick and his caravan. "This is a happy occasion for China," he said. "The arrival of the convoy marks the opening of the great new highway, just named the Stilwell Road."

As if to make it official, Lung quoted a directive from Chiang Kai-shek. "We have broken the siege of China," Chiang proclaimed in his message. "Let me name this road after General Joseph Stilwell, in memory of his distinctive contribution and of the signal part which the Allied and Chinese forces under his direction played in the Burma campaign and the building of the road."

Following Lung's renaming of the road, General Pick made a short speech. In it, he honored "the engineers who toiled and bled and fought to carve the road through the jungles and swamps and across mountains to the Burma Road." Then, as Pick finished his statement, he nodded to Lung, who reached up and—using a scissors—snipped the ribbon closing the West Gate.

General Pick's First Convoy was now free to enter Kunming.

BACK IN THE UNITED STATES, just as he was preparing to make a statement on the occasion of the road's opening to *The Army Hour* radio program, Joseph W. Stilwell learned of the road's name change. Rather than being pleased or angry at the news of the Stilwell Road, however, Stilwell—who now sat in a radio studio looking drawn in his baggy wool army officer's suit-jacket and tie—seemed indifferent.

"I wonder who put him up to that?" was all he ever wondered aloud about Chiang's gift.

Then, just as he had done with his message when Pick's Convoy had crossed into China at Wanding, Stilwell went on the radio and praised the men—the infantry, the engineers, the laborers, the truck crews, the quartermasters, the medics, the Hump pilots, the pursuit and bomber pilots, and the air crews—who had not only created the road, but who'd worked to keep China in the war while the road was being built.

FOLLOWING THE OPENING of the Burma Road, World War II would continue bloodily on for nearly seven more months. And before it was over, Joseph W. Stilwell—tired, emaciated, and with skin as flat gray as the thatch of hair on his head—would find himself back in command of the U.S. Army.

In June 1945, Stilwell visited Douglas MacArthur's troubled command in the Philippines and advised the War Department about it. He then was given command of the Tenth Army fighting for Okinawa after its commander, General Simon Bolivar Buckner, was killed by artillery fire there.

A month earlier, on May 8, the war in Europe had finally come to an end with Germany's unconditional surrender. And now, in June 1945, many of the still-active Allied units from Europe were already being ordered east, to arrive in China or the Pacific islands to help finish the throat-cutting war in the Pacific. Stilwell, understanding the weight of his new post and the influence of the coming influx of troops to Asia, realized that—due to his proximity to Japan and Korea—his command would likely be the one to go ashore first in both Korea and Japan.

After the nightmare of Burma and Chiang Kai-shek, Stilwell was again riding high. Despite a now-constant deep fatigue, Stilwell's knowledge that he once again had a critical command seemed a final, satisfying cap to his often frustrating career. Stilwell remained Marshall's favorite field general. And in Okinawa, just like in CBI, Stilwell again had an impossibly big job ahead.

Since April 1945, the Tenth Army had owned the unpleasant duty of wresting Okinawa away from the occupying Japanese, who despite having been softened by a months-long bombing campaign, were fighting to the last man and bullet. Once on Okinawa, the Tenth Army—which included his old prewar unit, the Seventh Division out of Fort Ord—began ripping at the Japanese, who slammed back with every weapon at their disposal. Within weeks, whole patches of the sixty-mile-long island were pocked with explosion craters and blackened with ash.

Every day, the Americans pushed farther inland on the island's steep, volcanic ridges, encircling platoons or flushing the enemy from graveyards and networks of caves with flamethrowers. Often they were pinned down in enemy ambushes and crossfire. The mortar wars and muddy ground fighting were grueling. By the time Okinawa fell, twelve thousand Americans were dead and thirty-six thousand more had been wounded. The Japanese, though, had fared far worse. More than one hundred thousand Imperial Japanese soldiers were killed in the fighting for Okinawa, while another eight thousand were taken prisoner.

On June 23, 1945, Joseph W. Stilwell took command of the Tenth Army and while mopping up on Okinawa, also began planning a twenty-four-hour-a-day, seven-day-a-week "whipping into shape" of his forces, which he was convinced would soon go ashore on Japanese soil. Like many of his subordinates, Stilwell understood that, while the fighting for Okinawa had been brutal and bloody, the battle for actual Japanese real estate was going to be more horrible than could be imagined. He knew of the kamikazes. He knew that, in recent weeks, the Japanese had started wearing vests wired with explosives and, appearing to surrender, had walked close to Allied platoons and detonated themselves. Stilwell knew that the war for Japan would be uglier than any fighting the world had ever seen. "I have got to be an SOB or risk disaster," he wrote in his diary.

Stilwell's training for the invasion of Japan, however, would never reach fruition. On August 3, 1945, Stilwell received his orders, code-named Blacklist. He and the sixty-thousand-man Tenth Army were to invade Korea and sever Japan's peninsular link to the Asian mainland. Supporting the Tenth Army, Stilwell was pleased to see, he would also be getting one corps of roughly thirty thousand Canadians, one of thirty thousand Australians, and a full 13,700-man division of Indian infantry taken from SEAC. "Mountbatten has to give up units for this operation!" he wrote in his notebook. "Life is funny."

But life had always been funny for Joseph W. Stilwell, too. On August 6, 1945, the first atomic bomb was dropped on Japan. And with that blast and the one to follow three days later, World War II would finally come to an end, which Stilwell, like everyone else on earth, welcomed.

At the moment when World War II officially ended, Joseph W. Stilwell stood on the deck of the USS *Missouri* in Tokyo Bay. He was the ranking American army officer aboard ship, and alongside General Douglas MacArthur, who officiated for the Allies, and a deck full of Allied commanders, he watched as six Japanese military and governmental leaders signed a document called the "Japanese Instrument of Surrender."

World War II was finally, officially, and irrevocably over.

Joe Stilwell could go home.


WITH HIS TENTH ARMY DISSOLVED (other less-tested units would be assigned to occupy Japan), Joseph W. Stilwell was immediately "promoted" to Washington to serve as president of the War Equipment Board, which assessed what to do with the world of lend-lease equipment now spread across the globe. Of the posting, Stilwell commented, "I am eminently suited to something else and would just as lief sit on a tack."

By January 1946—no doubt with some lobbying by George Marshall—Stilwell had been reassigned. He was now to command the Western Defense Command at the Presidio in San Francisco, just inside the Golden Gate Bridge and only a few hours from the house he'd built more than a decade before—and had hardly ever occupied—in Carmel. During this time, Stilwell continued to advise on the coming war between the Kuomintang and the Chinese Communists, on affairs in Japan, and on the weapons board, which hosted him twice as an observer for atomic tests on Bikini in the Marshall Islands in July 1946. When Stilwell returned home from his trip to the Marshalls, his wife could see more than ever before that he'd undergone a profound physical collapse.

Though he had been thin and heavily lined for years, he now seemed to have shrunk. His clothes no longer fit—he was swimming in them—and he often suffered spells of dizziness, chills, and bouts of exhaustion so profound that he would fall asleep in a chair no matter what he and Win were doing. Finally, after being home for weeks, Stilwell consulted a doctor, who informed him of "something suspicious in my liver."

The next day, as if to stick the diagnosis up his doctor's nose, Stilwell went out and walked for miles along the California coast.

It would be his last walk. On September 28, 1946, Joseph W. Stilwell was admitted to Letterman General Hospital for tests. A week later, on October 3, he underwent exploratory abdominal surgery, which uncovered advanced metastatic cancer in his stomach, liver, and trunk. He had been fighting his condition for years. He was in no pain, which confounded the doctors, but the prognosis was grim. The time had come for Vinegar Joe Stilwell—the ultimate survivor—to get his affairs in order.

He had seen combat in the Philippine Campaign of 1904 and two world wars. Along the way, he had raised a family, predicted the rise of Japan as a world power, foreseen the taking of east China by Japan, and presaged the collapse of Chiang Kai-shek's Kuomintang government due to corruption. He had earned the respect of the men he commanded, had weathered the humiliation of a recall, and—at Okinawa—had risen again to one of the highest commands on earth.

Ironically, it wasn't this phoenixlike rebirth that Stilwell prized most. Instead, it was a private moment he'd had on Okinawa, shortly after taking control of the Tenth Army. He'd been riding in a jeep when an American soldier, detailed with several others in clearing out a hole near the roadside, looked up at the passing vehicle and shouted, in an obviously pleased voice: "Hey guys, Joe's back!"

NOW FACING his own death, Stilwell typically refused to just "lay down and take it" as he'd so often said. Instead, he wanted to attain just one more goal. Though he'd earned four general's stars, the Distinguished Service Cross, the Distinguished Service Medal, and the Legion of Merit among others of the military's top distinctions, there had been one medal he'd coveted and not been awarded.

The one decoration that had eluded Stilwell was the simple and lowly

Combat Infantryman Badge: an elegant but spare uniform pin reserved for infantry soldiers who have, while under battlefield fire, proven themselves to their command and their country.

Now, forty-six years after he'd first set foot on West Point's soil as a cadet, that single, simple award—plus his family gathered around him in Carmel—was all Stilwell seemed to want in the world. It was a strange yet perfectly Stilwellian desire. And the secretary of war's office granted it without batting an eye.

On October 11, 1946, in a bedside ceremony, a sleeping Joseph W. Stilwell was awarded his Combat Infantryman Badge. The following day, October 12, 1946, Stilwell stirred in his own bed, woke briefly, and asked his nurse, "Say, isn't this Saturday?" Then he rolled back onto his side and drifted off to sleep for the last time, his newest medal still on a bedside table. A little after noon that day, Joseph W. Stilwell was declared dead.

For the record, October 12, 1946, was a Saturday.

Stilwell was right.

# Epilogue

AND THEN, the road is behind me.

On a morning in December of 2002, I find myself under a gray-sky drizzle along the six-lane Dongfeng Donglu, the largest east-west boulevard in Kunming, China, population 3.5 million. Skyscrapers rise all around, blocking out the twelve-thousand-foot peaks in the distance. Busy citizens hurry off to work, their trousers pressed and their windbreakers zipped tight. Above the tire-on-rain hiss of the street's busy traffic, the only noise is a constant ringing of mobile phones.

None of the Old Soldiers would recognize today's Kunming. Somehow, I barely recognize it myself. Since the first time I visited, many weeks after meeting Sunglasses at his border station in Jairanpur in 2001, I have traveled the road twice again to gather its stories. During each transit, the ways of the old have been steamrolled by the impossible-to-stop new. In Kunming, the landscape changes as fast as the concrete can dry. Farther up the road toward India, the changes are more subtle. At Myitkyina, lightbulbs have replaced candles and kerosene lamps. In the Mogaung Valley, growling trucks slowly supplant the creaking wooden wheels of bullock carts. And eleven hundred miles off in Ledo, the wood-stoked mud ovens in restaurants are now run by propane-gas jets.

Bone-tired and dripping, I reflect on my trips from northeast India to

Kunming filled with blood-sucking leeches, mud, frustration, friendship, sweat, laughs, bugs, and often-demanding living conditions.

Back in 2001, shortly after leaving Sunglasses and his roadblock at Jairanpur—and still determined to see the whole road—I finally managed by nerve, guile, and some good old jungle bushwhacking to catch a glimpse of the concrete slab at Pangsau Pass.

Then, by flying from northeast India to Yangon (the former Rangoon) via Calcutta and Bangkok, I started north toward Pangsau's border three times. Along the way, I took airplanes, cars, trucks, elephants, and a 1943 Willys Jeep left over from the war toward my goal. In Myanmar, I interviewed hundreds of people—including many Kachin and Naga tribal natives—who not only were present for the creation of the road, but who participated in the blood-spattered fighting that allowed for its completion.

One night in the shanty village of Shingbwiyang, I stood awestruck as an armada of colorful, candle-illuminated balloons—each more than six feet tall—were launched from a park near Stilwell's old asphalt airstrip; then they drifted into the starry darkness above the Patkai Range's black bulk. In Tanai—the former Walawbum—I shared breezeless, airless accommodations with bedbugs, and was then kept awake all night by bats fluttering through my room until dawn. At Myitkyina, I spent days with Michael Rosner, son of the recently deceased Denis Rosner, the Anglo-Burmese captain of the Kachin Levies, and enjoyed many meals with the glad-hearted Kachin leader and famed Levie conscript, Ah-Gu-Di.

Then it was on to Bhamo and China, the most exhausting leg of the trip, since the road—which had degenerated in Myanmar to a mere footpath between Shingbwiyang and Pangsau—now remained wide enough for the passage of vehicles but was so potholed and washed-out that each day's driving was a vertebrae-shattering ordeal.

In China, following the old cobblestone Burma Road from Wanding to Kunming, I passed the totally rebuilt cities of Mangshi and Lungling, toured the trench lines of the Eastern Gibraltar at Sungshan, and stared out my car's window as we climbed atop the gorgeous, windy, high-altitude landscape of the Tibetan Plateau. There, as in James Hilton's *Lost Horizon*, mountainsides of tiered green rice paddies tapered toward the peaks, like stairs to eternal paradise.

Once again in Kunming, my thoughts flip through the fading mental snapshots of the road's snaking length. The iridescent green of a wild peacock perched high in a rain forest tree outside Shaduzup. The eighteen-foot cobra that shot across the road's mud in front of me near Jairanpur, moving jerkily, as if on puppeteer's strings. The evening spent overlooking the breadth of the Irrawaddy at Myitkyina, where gilded pagodas glinted at me from atop jungled ridgelines, their reflections caught in the flat river's surface. Then, twelve hours later, emerging from sleep to find that heavy rains upstream had raised the eight-hundred-foot-wide river by a full fifteen feet, and now hundreds of downed trees were hurtling past in the flood. "Keep watching," my guide said. "If we are lucky, we'll see baby tigers clinging to the floating treetops."

And the people: miners and missionaries, soldiers and students, farmers, shopkeepers, and government officials. All of them—every one of them—still using the road every day, linking this moment with the life-stained and now largely forgotten trace of mud, cracked pavement, and smoothly worn cobblestones that was once Stilwell's obsession. The road isn't only history; it is very much alive.

Standing in the rain, wet to the skin and at the ragged end, I break into a smile, just as I did back on Sunglasses's porch in Jairanpur at this story's beginning. Because no matter what the Old Soldiers say, the road is still there.

# Notes

A book like this one is impossible to write alone. Most every sentence in it is imbued with historical fact of one sort or another, and each of these facts is then shaded and shaped by related events. Because of this—and my deep interest in rendering these details and their colorations accurately—beyond the books cited in these notes, I've enlisted the help and advice of several individuals to assist in placing all of these components in context.

Primarily I want to thank David Quaid and Bob Passanisi, historian emeritus and current historian of the Merrill's Marauders (and actual Marauders themselves!), as well as Chung Cheh, General Sun Li-jen's adopted son, and Richard Ming-Tong Young (General Stilwell's aide-de-camp during during World War II), who was at Vinegar Joe's side from February 1942 until August 1945. Finally, I'd like to thank two Chinese World War II historians: Ge Shuya in Kunming and Li Zhi Cai at the Baoshan Museum of History in Baoshan. All of these people either generously combed my manuscript for stray characterizations and errors, or helped me guide the proper facts into order.

A thank-you larger than I can accurately express goes to these six people. This said, any factual errors in this manuscript remain mine alone.

Regarding my research citations: in the interest of conserving space I have not included most references to General Joseph W. Stilwell's diary entries, as they can be looked up for the day in question (generally included in my text) by consulting their edited and book-length version, *The Stilwell Papers* (William Sloane Associates, New York, 1948). Regarding the personnel records of Stilwell's career, they are available in Stilwell's "201 File." All 201 Files are available through the U.S. Adjutant General's Office in Washington.

For the large-scale narrative of events in the China and the China-Burma-India theater during World War II—such as dates or the movements and designations of troops, etc.— I refer readers to the green-bound series *U.S. Army in World War II*. The three volumes dealing with CBI are all authored by Charles F. Romanus and Riley Sunderland and are titled

*United States Army in World War II: Stilwell's Mission to China* (Washington, D.C.: Office of the Chief of Military History, Department of the Army, 1953).

*United States Army in World War II: Stilwell's Command Problems* (Washington, D.C.: Office of the Chief of Military History, Department of the Army, 1956).

*United States Army in World War II: Time Runs Out in CBI* (Washington, D.C.: Office of the Chief of Military History, Department of the Army, 1959).

These histories are accurate and lucid big-picture recountings of events during the war and they infuse every page of this book, though—in a few specific cases—I refer to them in the notes, as their gravitas is required.

Also important to the narrative has been the five-volume *Stilwell's Personal Files 1942-1945*, by Joseph W. Stilwell, Charles F. Romanus, and Riley Sunderland (Baltimore: Scholarly Resources, 1976).

Regarding all other information in this text, I've included either the date of the author's interview, the periodical and its publication date, or listed the book citation by author and page number (and title and publication date, if the cited author has more than one book listed), so readers can find the fact's original or previous usage.

## Prologue

5 ratio of combat casualties to sick evacuees: Moser, Don, *China Burma India* (Alexandria, VA: Time-Life Books, 1978), pg. 136.

6 dog-Latin: The Stilwell Papers, jacket copy.

## Chapter 1

13 114 people: Tuchman, Barbara W., *Stilwell and the American Experience in China* (New York: MacMillan, 1970), pg. 295; Moser, pg. 31.

13 Stilwell as nearly blind: Foreword by Winifred Stilwell, *The Stilwell Papers*, pg. x.

15 Radio message: From a photo of the original message taken by the Army Signal Corps, May 6, 1942. Also can be seen in Tuchman, photo insert three.

15 Smashed radio: Dorn, Frank, *Walkout: With Stilwell in Burma* (New York: Thomas Y. Crowell, 1971), pg. 159. A note: Dorn's book claims that he drafted the final message out of Burma during the Stilwell walk out. The text of this message, however, differs greatly from others' accounts and was signed by Dorn and not by Stilwell. Therefore, I cite Stilwell's final message—complete with a photo from the Signal Corps cited above—in my manuscript.

15 "Dr. Cigarette": Interview with Seagrave nurse Daw Aye Nunt, at Myitkyina 11/25/02 and 11/26/02.

16 "By the time we get out of here . . .": Tuchman, pg. 296.

16 105 steps per minute: Tuchman, pg. 296.

16 Events of "walk out of Burma," including condition of Than Shwe and Merrill: Seagrave, Gordon, S., *Burma Surgeon* (New York: W.W. Norton, 1943), pp. 243–277.

17 Stilwell general family history: John Easterbrook, Stilwell's grandson. See also Tuchman pp. 9–300.

17 "at 5 feet, 7 ¾ inches—was technically too short": This erroneous fact, while taken from Tuchman, pg. 12—with her citation of Samuel T. Hubbard's *Memoirs of a Staff Officer* (New York: Cardinal, 1959)—is rendered false by published 1900 requirements for cadet application to West Point, which are available through the historian's office at the academy.

18  1905 war-game maneuvers: Efficiency Reports. National Archives, Regional Group 94, Adjutant General's Office File # 530007.

19  "very interesting day": Tuchman, pg. 52 from Stilwell letters.

19  "a damned waffle-tail clerk": Tuchman, pg. 53 from Stilwell letters.

19  "Sitting, just sitting": Tuchman, pg. 57 from Stilwell letters.

20  "There will never be a work of history . . .": Tuchman, pg. 140 from Stilwell notebooks.

20  "a genius for instruction" and "qualified for any command . . .": "George Marshall Efficiency Report on Stilwell," July 1929–June 1930, Stilwell 201 File.

21  "Third Army War Games in Louisiana": *The New York Times*, (5/7/40) and (5/26/40), *Newsweek*, (05/13/40). "History of the Third Army," Study No. 17, Historical Section, Army General Files. Also Tuchman, pp. 208–209.

21  U.S. Army ranking in world: "World Almanac, 1938" pg. 706.

23–24  description of creation of Burma Road: Tan, Pei-Ying, *The Building of the Burma Road* (New York: McGraw-Hill, 1945), pp. 1–182.

25  Rape of Nanking and three hundred thousand Chinese dead: Chang, Iris, *The Rape of Nanking* (New York: Penguin, 1997), pp. 81–104.

25  "*hakko ichiu*": Interviews with All-Burma Veterans Association of Japan delegates, Atsumi Oda and Sesumu Miyashita. In Okayama, Japan, 2/14/01 and 2/15/01.

29  "the most-impossible job": Moser, pg. 36.

30–31  Stilwell's route to India: Stilwell, *The Stilwell Papers*, pp. 39–43.

31–32  fall of the Sittang Bridge: Khan, Bashir Ahmed, Khan Papers (Lahore, Pakistan); Allen, Louis, *Burma: The Longest War 1941–45* (London: J. M. Dent, 1984), pp. 3–4 and 36–44.

34  impressions of fallen Rangoon: Allen, pp. 44–45. Also inverview with Burmese-Chinese eyewitness Jameson Koe, 1/27/01 to 1/30/01.

34  George Rodger impressions: Allen, pg. 44.

35  Japanese roadblocks: Slim, Field Marshall Viscount William J., *Defeat into Victory: Battling Japan in Burma and India, 1942–1945* (New York: Cooper Square Press, 2000), pp. 29, 33, 109, 113.

36  "The country . . .": Slim, pg. 51.

36  British army water and rations problems: Slim, pp. 70–71; Moser pg. 25.

36  "There's no trace of it . . .": Tuchman, pg. 288.

37  Kyaukse meeting scene: Tuchman, pp. 289–290.

38  "The clearing was littered . . .": Tyson, Geoffrey, *Forgotten Frontier* (London: W. H. Targett, 1945), pg. 79.

38–39  Haynes and Scott with Stilwell: Scott, Robert L., Jr., *God Is My Co-Pilot* (New York: Scribner, 1943), pp. 104–105.

39  "Effect evacuation": Tuchman, pg. 292.

39  "Burn the damn thing . . . Burn the son-of-a-bitch": Dorn, pp. 118–119.

40  "I had you all line up here . . .": Dorn, pg. 170.

40  "Jeez! Even his old *hat* . . .": Dorn, pg. 171.

41  "a lot of cigarettes": Seagrave, pg. 256.

41  Tim Sharpe description: Dorn, pg. 209; Seagrave, pp. 260–261; Tuchman, pg. 297.

42  "Not a one . . .": Moser, pg. 33.

42–44  conditions of British evacuation of Burma: Slim, pp. 100–110.

44  "a relic of a blade . . .": Slim, pg. 108.

## Chapter 2

Most of the information not specific to the stories of Atsumi Oda or Ah-Gu-Di in this chapter is available in the *United States Army in World War II* histories. Other sources are acknowledged by page.

Beyond that, all other information in this chapter comes from interviews conducted with Mr. Oda in Okayama, Japan, 2/14/01 and 2/15/01; or Ah-Gu-Di in Myitkyina, 2/1/01 to 2/3/01; 05/16/02 and 5/17/02; 11/25/02 and 11/26/02.

50  135 different linguistic groups . . . sixty-seven different languages . . .: National Museum, Yangon, Myanmar.

51  "drive the Japs back to Bangkok . . .": Fellowes-Gordon, Ian, *Amiable Assassins: The Story of the Kachin Guerrillas of North Burma* (London: Robert Hale, Ltd., 1957), pg. 12.

52  Gamble and Leach and their entrance at Fort Hertz: Fellowes-Gordon, pg. 12. A note: I have taken pains to find out the first names of Gamble and Leach, but, sadly, have been frustrated. Neither the British army nor the Australian army is forthcoming with records of them, and interviews with several Northern Kachin Levies who served under both men (as well as Colonel Ford, who replaced Gamble) didn't turn up their given names, either. If anyone knows and can verify the first names of these men, please contact this book's publisher and I will reflect the changes in future editions.

52  five hundred men strong: Fellowes-Gordon, pg. 15.

## Chapter 3

56  "Normally, planning precedes . . .": Romanus and Sutherland, *Stilwell's Command Problems*, pg. 10.

57  "a 478-mile, all-weather track of gravel, thirty feet wide and four inches thick . . .": Chaphekar, S. G., *A Brief Study of the Burma Campaign, 1943–1945* (Calcutta: Maharashtra Militarisation Board, 1955), pp. 99–100. This is the generally accepted description of the road, though in Romanus and Sunderland, *Stilwell's Command Problems* (pg. 141), another assessment has the road surface as "about ten inches thick on the average and from twenty to twenty-eight feet wide." While included in the war's official army history, this statement seems inaccurate to the author, who has traveled the road's length on three occasions.

57  "mountainous terrain, canyon sections . . .": Romanus and Sutherland, *Stilwell's Mission to China*, pp. 306–307.

57  require seven hundred bridges: *Ex-CBI Roundup*, a magazine published monthly except August and September (Whittier, Calif., 1946–present). This citation: "Another Look at the Burma-Ledo Road," by Nels Brueckl, April 1992.

58  "an immense, laborious task . . .": Churchill, Winston S., *The Second World War: Volume Five, Closing the Ring* (New York: Houghton Mifflin, 1951), pg. 560.

60 munching a porcupine . . . : Moser, pg. 62.

60 The Allies "could not choose a worse place . . .": Churchill, pg. 560.

60 "We argued that the enormous expenditure . . .": Churchill, pg. 561.

## Chapter 4

61 Robert E. Lee: Chennault, Claire Lee, *Way of a Fighter* (New York: G. P. Putnam's Sons, 1949), pg. 3.

62 the Chinese boasted five hundred planes: Chennault, pg. 59; Moser, pp. 57–59.

62 a salary of $600 to $750 a month: Chennault, pg. 103; Boyington, Gregory "Pappy," *Baa Baa Black Sheep* (New York: Bantam Books, 1958, 1987), pg. 4; Moser pg. 72.

63 On the open radio frequency: Chennault, pg. 129.

64 1,465 rounds of ammunition: courtesy Curtiss.

65 One booze-soaked evening in Rangoon: This story has several permutations and has been said to have occurred out of both Rangoon and Kunming, though those close to the story—who wish to remain anonymous—claim that the "first bombing of Hanoi" originated out of Rangoon. References to it exist in Moser, pg. 60, and in Smith, Robert M., *With Chennault in China: A Flying Tiger's Diary* (Tab Books, 1984). Smith's version is believed to be apocryphal.

65 "unprincipled bandits": Chennault, pg. 174; Moser, pg. 61.

## Chapter 5

67 "CBI command . . .": White, Theodore H. and Jacoby, Annalee, *Thunder Out of China* (New York: William Sloane Associates, 1946), pg. 145.

68 The first Air Transport Command "Hump flight" was a reconnaissance mission by Capt. Charles L. (Chuck) Sharp on December 23, 1941. Flying a C-47 (or DC-3) from an airfield at Dinjan in India's State of Assam, to Kunming, Sharp ferried sixteen troops from India to China over the Himalayas.

68 Capable of carrying nearly eight tons: courtesy of Curtiss Aviation. Also specifications reprinted in Donald, David (editor), *American War Planes of World War Two* (New York: Barnes and Noble/Aerospace Publishing, 1995), pg. 63.

69 Charles F. Linamen, interviews 6/2/00 and 6/3/00; also 9/14/01 and 9/15/01.

71 Chiang's three demands: Romanus and Sunderland, *Stilwell's Mission to China*, pg. 172; Stilwell (White note), *The Stilwell Papers*, pg. 118; Tuchman, pg. 312.

72 statistics regarding Chinese troops freezing to death: Tuchman, pg. 327.

72 Chinese army was flourishing at Ramgarh: Stilwell, *The Stilwell Papers* (White note), pg. 137; Tuchman, pg. 326.

72 Chinese characterized by Slim as "magnificent": Slim, pg. 144.

72 lack of supplies: "Burma Victory" film, Army Signal Corps, 1944.

72–73 Stilwell using a shoelace as a chin strap: Tuchman, pg. 343.

74 "This is the most dreary": Stilwell, *The Stilwell Papers*, pg. 126.

74–75 Stilwell and Byroade exchange: Tuchman, pg. 336, from interview with Byroade; verified by John Easterbrook.

75 Stilwell's order to Chennault to speak his mind: Chennault, pg. 212.

75 Chennault report to Willkie: Chennault, pp. 212–216.

77   Thanksgiving letter to Mrs. Stilwell: Stilwell, *The Stilwell Papers*, pp. 171–172.

78   particulars of Arakan invasion: Allen, pp. 95–113; Slim, pp. 147–167.

79   "fantastically bad" situation on Arakan front: Slim, pp. 156–159.

79   "spilt milk": Slim, pg. 160.

## Chapter 6

For the bulk of the overview material concerning Orde Wingate, two sources are invaluable. First, the Wingate Files at the Imperial War Museum in London (designated WPEL/IWM "early life" files; WPA/IWM "Abyssinia" files; and WPC/IWM "Chindit" files) are of inestimable help. Also critical to my understanding of Wingate was the fine biography *Fire in the Night: Wingate of Burma, Ethiopia, and Zion* by John Bierman and Colin Smith (New York: Random House, 1999). In deference to these two vast stores of information, I cite them separately and together as sources in their entirety. Beyond these two sources, I will include other citations that added valuably to the understanding of Wingate.

92   "A constant stream of orders . . .": Stibbe, Philip, *Return via Rangoon* (London: Barnsley/Leo Cooper, 1995), pg. 25.

92   "Everyone is taught to be doctor minded": Chinnery, Philip D., *March or Die: The Story of Wingate's Chindits* (London: Airlife Publishing, 1997), pg. 30.

92   descriptions of Chindit foraging: Chinnery, pg. 29.

93   calling him Tarzan: Bierman and Smith, pg. 265.

93   "Brigadier Bela Lugosi": Moser, pg. 96.

93   Eccles. 9:10 Revised Standard Version.

93   "big enough to deliver blows . . .": Chinnery, pg. 20.

94   single-file columns they called "snakes": Mike Calvert interview, BBC, 1997.

95   Calvert description: Bierman and Smith, pg. 244.

96   Conron incident: Chinnery, pg. 38.

96   Bromhead ambush: Chinnery, pp. 38–42.

97   blew the forty-foot rail bridge . . . and Calvert's birthday: Chinnery pp. 44–45.

98–99   Calvert abandoning troops: Chinnery, pg. 71.

100   "The mountains between us and our goal . . .": Bierman and Smith, pp. 286.

100   "could never have known what hit them": Bierman and Smith, pg. 287.

101   Fergusson radio message and response: Bierman and Smith, pg. 286.

102   Calvert's good-bye: Chinnery, pg. 70.

103   Calvert and doors: BBC interview, 1997.

104   interview with Gum-Jaw-Naw, at Myitkyina 2/1/01 to 2/3/01; 05/16/02.

104–105   Wingate's monologue and Jeffries's response: Interviews with Gum-Jaw-Naw, at Myitkyina 2/1/01 and 2/3/01; Bierman and Smith, pp. 299–301.

105   Dominic Neill: Bierman and Smith, pp. 306–307.

106   "Whatever the actual facts . . .": Slim, pg. 163.

106   Wingate's return to England: Bierman and Smith, pp. 313–322.

107   "a tiger of a man . . .": Mary Churchill interview, Bierman and Smith, pg. 314.

108   "After a long struggle . . .": Tuchman, pg. 385.

## Chapter 7

111 eight hundred thousand tons of supplies abandoned in Rangoon: Kinvig, Clifford, *River Kwai Railway* (London: Brassey's, 1992; 1998), pg. 23.

111 Japan lost sixty-seven ships: Kinvig, pg. 23.

111 Imperial Japanese Command rescinded its initial eighteen-month plan: Adams, pg. 57.

112 railroad route: Kinvig, pp. 40–46; Remnick, Gerald: *Death's Railway* (Glencannon Press, Palo Alto, CA: 2002), pg. 63; Adams, pg. 56; *Ex-CBI Roundup* ("Building the Death Railway," by David Fogarty, January 1985).

113 Japanese ripping up redundant rails: Kinvig, pp. 50–51.

113 an eighteen-mile stretch between Tokyo and Yokohama: Kinvig, pg. 45.

113 Japanese pamphlet: Tsuji, M., *Singapore—the Japanese Version* (New York: Mayflower Dell, 1966) pg. 246; Kinvig, pg. 35.

114 sixteen thousand Allied prisoners . . .: Remnick, pg. 64.

114 professional "beer tasters,": *Ex-CBI Roundup* ("Railroad to Death's Door," by Boyd Sinclair, April 1979).

115 an eventual sixty thousand POW laborers: Kinvig, pg. 35; Adams, pg. 57.

115 Geoffrey Pharoah Adams's recollections of POW treatment and transport: Adams, pp. 54–61.

117 description of housing at Tamarkan: Kinvig, pp. 54–55; Remnick, pp. 64–65.

117 *tenko, kumis, han,* and *Hancho*: Kinvig, pg. 65.

117 description of bridges to be built: Kinvig, pg. 71; Adams, pg. 57.

118 "light sick": *Ex-CBI Roundup* ("Railroad to Death's Door," by Boyd Sinclair, April 1979).

118–119 Lieutenant Bridge incident: Adams, pg. 58.

119 descriptions of bridge building: Adams, pp. 55–64.

119 cholera outbreaks: Kinvig, pp. 130–137.

121 flood destroying the wooden bridge: Adams, pg. 63.

121 descriptions of punishments: Kinvig, pp. 65, 67, 142, 145, 147, 210.

122 "Pom" escape story: Adams, pp. 60–61.

123 "*atap* staring": Apthorpe (unpublished; Imperial War Museum, file DPS 4/2); Kinvig, 148–149.

123–124 Kaneshiro and Okamoto description: Adams, pg. 60.

124–126 Adams at work on the steel bridge and Lieutenant Fuji: Adams, pp. 64–78.

## Chapter 8

127 Project 7-A: *Ex-CBI Roundup* ("Project 7 on the Hump," March 1982).

128 Ray Dahl interview with author, via telephone 01/26/02 and 06/14/02.

128 aspic and Becty à L'Anglaise: from reproduced dinner menu for April 26, 1945, from Firpo's Restaurant. Reprinted in *Ex-CBI Roundup* (February 1988).

128 "Coolies go around with $50 bills": Stilwell, *The Stilwell Papers*, pg. 51; Tuchman, pg. 261.

129 "When I saw the American establishment at Chabua . . .": Sevareid, Eric, *Not So Wild a Dream* (New York: Atheneum, 1976), pg. 247.

129 Hump crews betting: Moser, pg. 84.

130 "There's your mess": Tuchman, pg. 365.

130–131 Ray Dahl interview via telephone with author, 1/26/02 and 6/14/02.

130 Hump cargoes of money, severed trucks, and a grand piano: John Easterbrook, 2/24/03.

131–142 Events surrounding the crash and rescue of Hump aircraft and its crew: Sevareid, pp. 250–301.

135 All full names and hometowns of the "bail-out" crew and support troops were taken from *Ex-CBI Roundup* ("Our Good Friends the Head Hunters," by Eric Sevareid, October 1986, reprinted from *Reader's Digest*).

## Chapter 9

144 Mountbatten is "a good egg": Stilwell, *The Stilwell Papers*, pg. 230.

145 "Stop the wisecracks . . .": Moser, pg. 100.

145 "Dear George . . .": Tuchman, pg. 390.

145 "some less impossible task . . .": Tuchman, pg. 391.

146 "I have told him the truth . . .": Tuchman, pg. 394.

146 Stilwell and Mountbatten arrive in Chungking: Tuchman, pp. 394–395; Moser, pg. 100.

148 Stilwell on Chennault: Tuchman, pg. 385.

148 The Deckhand: Stilwell, *The Stilwell Papers*, pp. 219, 235, 256.

149 Slim and Stilwell comic exchange: Moser, pg. 119.

149 Ledo Road: Ogburn, Charlton, Jr., *The Marauders* (New York: Harper & Brothers, 1956), pg. 79; *Ex-CBI Roundup* ("Another Look at the Burma-Ledo Road," by Nels Brueckl, April 1992).

150 "the Chocolate Staircase": Slim, pg. 362.

151 "We have to go in through a rat hole . . .": Tuchman, pg. 416; Moser, pg. 119.

152 Nevin Wetzel recollections: *Ex-CBI Roundup* ("Return to Burma," by Nevin Wetzel, July 1979).

154 Sun Li-jen fears: Tuchman, pg. 420.

155 Stilwell's entropy and "Gus" quote: Tuchman, pg. 421.

155 "full of beans . . .": Stilwell, *The Stilwell Papers*, pg. 275.

155 "Progress is slow . . .": Stilwell, *The Stilwell Papers*, pg. 277.

## Chapter 10

The material contained in these pages came from Peers, William R., and Brelis, Dean, *Behind the Burma Road: The Story of America's Most Successful Guerrilla Force* (Atlantic Monthly Press, 1963), pp. 25–132, or from the army's green-bound official World War II histories cited at the beginning of the Notes.

164 Boatner's orders: Fletcher, James S., *Secret War in Burma* (James Fletcher, 1997), pg. 30.

165ff Except where otherwise indicated, the material contained in these pages came from Ogburn or from the army's green-bound official World War II histories cited at the beginning of the Notes.

165 Galahad as unconventional: Tuchman, pg. 433; Moser, pp. 122–123.

166 All Fred Lyons statements: *Ex-CBI Roundup* ("Here's What Really Happened," by Fred Lyons, as told to Paul Wilder, April 1969; July 1991).

167 All Joseph Ganlin statements from author interview in Milford, Massachusetts, on 6/3/00 and 6/4/00.

167 "hard-hitting American unit": Tuchman, pg. 433.

167 "Aw to *hell* with this . . .": Tuchman, pg. 433.

168 "Tree roots . . .": *Ex-CBI Roundup* ("Here's What Really Happened," by Fred Lyons, as told to Paul Wilder, April 1969; July 1991).

171 "*FRANK MERRILL IS IN WALAWBUM . . .*": Stilwell, *The Stilwell Papers*, pg. 282.

171 Fred Lyons "could feel the muscles . . .": Ogburn, pg. 116.

172–173 All Roy Matsumoto battlefield impressions and quotations from author interviews, via telephone on 10/14/02 and 10/15/02.

174 "Toboggan slide rustle": Ogburn, pg. 119.

175 "Stricken figures in a ballet": Ogburn, pg. 129.

175 "Eleanor eats . . .": David Quaid interview, 4/17/03.

176 Marauder casualty list: Ogburn, pg. 134.

## Chapter 11

178 interview with Atsumi Oda, in Okayama, Japan, 2/14/01 and 2/15/01.

179 four tons of supplies and weaponry: Kennedy, David M., *Freedom from Fear: The American People in Depression and War, 1929–1945* (New York: Oxford University Press, 1999), pg. 668.

179ff Except where otherwise indicated, the material contained in these pages came from Ogburn, or from the army's green-bound official World War II history.

## Chapter 12

185 Stilwell to Chungking: Tuchman, pg. 441.

186 Y Force movements: Stilwell, *The Stilwell Papers*, pg. 287; Tuchman, pp. 443–444.

186–187 Wingate's typhoid: Bierman and Smith, pp. 328–332.

187 blocking of Piccadilly and Chindit insertion into Burma: Slim, pp. 258–265; Calvert, pp. 21–31; Bierman and Smith, pp. 349–360.

189–190 Vincent Curl and the Marauders at Janpan: Ogburn, pp. 191–192.

190–192 McGee and the ill-fated Kamaing Road blockade at Inkangatawng: David Quaid interview, 4/17/03; Ogburn, pp. 193–194; Tuchman, pg. 442.

192 eight hundred heavily armed Japanese attackers: Ogburn, pg. 195.

192 Hsamsingyang and events surrounding evacuation: Ogburn, pp. 199–201.

192 Marauders in defensive posture as dicey: Romanus and Sutherland, *Stilwell's Command Problems*, pp. 188–191.

193–199  Siege at Nhpum Ga: Ogburn, pp. 190–221; Romanus and Sutherland, *Stilwell's Command Problems*, pp. 188–191; Tuchman, pg. 442.

193  dead mule tally: Ogburn, pg. 201.

194  Brendan Lynch friendly fire accident: Ogburn, pg. 202.

195  Roy Matsumoto history, author interviews via telephone on 10/14/02 and 10/15/02; Ogburn, pp. 204–206.

195–197  All Roy Matsumoto battlefield impressions and quotations from author interviews, via telephone on 10/14/02 and 10/15/02.

197  Marauder command change: Romanus and Sutherland, *Stilwell's Command Problems*, pg. 189; Tuchman, pg. 441; Ogburn, pg. 200. A note: Facts about the Merrill evacuation differ. Ogburn claims, possibly correctly, that Merrill suffered another heart attack early in the Nhpum Ga fighting. Romanus and Tuchman say he was ordered out of Burma by Stilwell and had a heart attack later. As Romanus is author of the army's "official" history, I stand with him unless verifiable facts can prove otherwise.

198  April 4 had not been a good day: Ogburn, pp. 210–211.

198  a dead Marauder dangled like a horrific marionette: Ogburn, pg. 211.

199  "dead Japs everywhere": Ogburn, pg. 216.

199  Nhpum Ga casualty reports: Ogburn, pg. 218; Romanus and Sutherland, *Stilwell's Command Problems*, pg. 191.

199–200  horrible rumor: Ogburn, pg. 220.

200  Moods turning sour . . . high-ranking officers: Ogburn, pp. 220–221.

200  "End Run" for Myitkyina: Tuchman, pp. 444–446; Romanus and Sutherland, *Stilwell's Command Problems*, pp. 204–211.

201  "a red flag to a bull": Ogburn, pg. 279.

201  oak-leaf clusters: Ogburn, pg. 227.

201  "spend more time fighting and less time worrying about promotions": Ogburn, pg. 227; Moser, pg. 127.

201  Naura Hkyat: Ogburn, pg. 231.

201  Roy Matsumoto impression and quote from author interview, via telephone 10/15/02.

203  Battalion Three lost twenty mules and abandoned four thousand pounds of equipment: Ogburn, pg. 231.

203  misuse of halazone pills: Ogburn, pg. 226.

203  "We were scarcely ever dry . . .": Ogburn, pg. 230.

## Chapter 13

204  dank, dark, primeval jungle: Calvert, Michael, *Prisoners of Hope* (London: Leo Cooper, 1996), pg. 47.

205  "entering into the spirit of the thing . . .": Calvert, pg. 50.

205  Account of White City setup: Calvert, pp. 52–55; Chinnery, pp. 127–130.

205–206  Fergusson's roadblock at Indaw at Thetkegyin: Chinnery, pp. 139–159.

206–207  Philip Sharpe recollections: Chinnery, pp. 151–152.

207  account of Wingate crash scene: Slim, pp. 268–269; Moser, pg. 116.

207  "Now he was dead . . .": Calvert, pg. 90.

208  Slim's command choice and questions: Slim, pp. 269–270; Allen, pp. 348–349.

208  Description of Blackpool: Calvert, pp. 158–173; Chinnery, pp. 193–194.

208  Japanese antiaircraft guns at Blackpool: Calvert, pg. 160; Chinnery, pg. 194.

209  "The whites of my eyes turned brown . . .": Chinnery, pg. 195.

209  Bombardment at Blackpool: Calvert, pp. 159–160; Chinnery, pg. 197; Slim, pg. 277.

209  "parachute bombs": Chinnery, pg. 196.

210  Desmond Whyte testimony: Chinnery, pp. 199–201.

211  Stilwell sleep and nightmares: Stilwell, *The Stilwell Papers*, pg. 299.

211  *Roundup* assessment: Tuchman, pg. 440.

212  Roy Matsumoto on Naura Hkyat: author interviews, via telephone 10/15/02.

212  Chinese bugle blast: Ogburn, pg. 235.

212–213  "fever of unknown origin": Ogburn, pp. 232, 235, 252, 258, 267.

213  Merrill/Stilwell radio messages re: Myitkyina: Moser, pg. 129.

213–214  May 17 and Fred Lyons: *Ex-CBI Roundup* ("Here's What Really Happened," by Fred Lyons, as told to Paul Wilder, April 1969; July 1991); Ogburn, pp. 243–244.

214–215  scene at Myitkyina airfield: Ogburn, pg. 244.

215  Churchill radio to Mountbatten: Tuchman, pg. 448; Moser, pg. 129.

215  Chinese friendly fire at Myitkyina: Ogburn, pg. 247; Stilwell, *The Stilwell Papers*, pg. 297; Tuchman, pg. 449.

216  Samuel Wilson and illness: Ogburn, pg. 255.

216  Mitchell Opas impressions and quotes are from an author interview, in Milford, Massachusetts, 6/3/00.

217  Porky the mascot: Fellowes-Gordon, pg. 63.

217  Levies Jingpaw lyrics: Fellowes-Gordon, pg. 81.

217  "All OK now": Fellowes-Gordon, pg. 77.

217  One hundred Japanese troops crept past and "Japanese morale . . .": Fellowes-Gordon, pg. 110.

218  Galahad replacements: Romanus and Sunderland, *Stilwell's Command Problems*, pg. 241; Tuchman, pp. 450–451.

218  "Imagination again . . .": Stilwell, *The Stilwell Papers*, pg. 299.

219  Y Force campaign: Tuchman, pp. 452–453.

219  Description of Sungshan: author visit, 12/3/03.

219  Dorn's message to Stilwell: Tuchman, pp. 452–453.

220  "We go to take Kamaing now": Romanus and Sunderland, *Stilwell's Command Problems*, pg. 215; Stilwell, *The Stilwell Papers*, pg. 297; Tuchman, pg. 453.

## Chapter 14

221   "Americans used to say . . .": White and Jacoby, pg. 145.

222   320 Chinese troops had been lost . . . the attack had completely stopped: Stilwell, *The Stilwell Papers*, pg. 301.

223   Morris Force: Calvert, pg. 228; Chinnery, pp. 182–187.

223   Chiang summons Stilwell to Chungking for meeting: Stilwell, *The Stilwell Papers*, pg. 302; Tuchman, pg. 451.

224   Sunderland Flying Boat seaplanes: Slim, pg. 278.

225   June 3, Mike Calvert on a twelve-hundred-foot ridge: Calvert, pg. 185; Chinnery, pg. 210.

225   Calvert's Seventy-seventh Brigade had lost five dead and twenty-six wounded: Calvert, pg. 182; Chinnery, pg. 210.

225–226   Plan of attack at Mogaung: Calvert, pp. 187–189; Chinnery, pg. 210.

226   taking of Pinhmi: Calvert, pp. 194–197.

226   fusilier shot in head at infirmary: Calvert, pg. 195.

226   Japanese detonating their hand grenades: Calvert, pg. 195.

226   Japanese soldier chokes himself with blanket: Calvert, pg. 196.

226   Calvert ear purchases: Calvert, pg. 195.

226–227   Pinhmi bridge events: Calvert, pp. 201–204; Chinnery, pg. 211; Allen, pg. 370.

228   Kachins against Japanese south of Mogaung: Calvert, pg. 205.

228   "When you think you are beaten . . .": Chinnery, pg. 212.

228   Archie Wavell amputation events: Calvert, pp. 206, 208–209; Chinnery, pp. 212–213.

228–229   Calvert commanders confront Calvert: Calvert, pg. 206; Allen, pg. 371.

229   Calvert dispatches Andrews; Andrews's return: Calvert, pp. 215–220; Chinnery, pg. 214.

229   events surrounding American colonel "baby-sitter": Calvert, pg. 226, Chinnery, pg. 214.

230   Mogaung Rail bridge mistake: Calvert, pg. 227.

230   seventy bombing sorties: Calvert, pg. 227; Chinnery, pg. 215.

230–231   attack on Mogaung: Calvert, pp. 227–240; Chinnery, pp. 214–219.

230   Tom O'Reilly quote: Chinnery, pp. 215–216.

231   Michael Allmand's death: Calvert, pp. 232–233; Chinnery, pp. 215–216.

231   BBC news report and fallout: Calvert, pg. 238; Chinnery, pg. 218.

231   taking umbrage: Chinnery, pg. 218; Allen, pg. 374.

232   Chindit casualty figures at Mogaung: Calvert, pg. 243.

232–234   Calvert/Stilwell radio exchanges and potential court-martial: Calvert, pp. 243–251; Chinnery, pp. 219–220.

235   Fred Freeman story: Chinnery, pp. 219–220.

## Chapter 15

236  Particulars of Japanese retreat: Romanus and Sunderland, *Stilwell's Command Problems*, pp. 218–220; Tuchman, pg. 453.

237  "Given a grenade . . ." quote by Nishiji: Tamayama, Kaquo and John Nunneley, *Tales by Japanese Soldiers* (London: Cassell, 1992), pg. 202.

237  calls for Stilwell removal: Stilwell, *The Stilwell Papers*, pg. 305; Tuchman, pg. 465.

237  a quarter bowl of rice a day: Stilwell, *The Stilwell Papers*, pg. 308.

238  Mitchell Opas impressions and quotes from an author interview, in Milford, Massachusetts, 6/3/00.

238  Japanese situation at Myitkyina: Romanus and Sunderland, *Stilwell's Command Problems*, pp. 252–256; Allen, pp. 381–385; Tuchman, pg. 484; Moser, pg. 133.

238  "Rain, rain, mud, mud, mud . . .": Stilwell, *The Stilwell Papers*, pg. 308.

239–240  Mizukami suicide: Allen, pp. 384; Moser, pg. 133.

240  Kyun Bin Ta last soldiers: author interview with Ah-Gu-Di, at Myitkyina, 11/26/02.

240  "Myitkyina—over at last . . .": Stilwell, *The Stilwell Papers*, pg. 311.

## Chapter 16

241  Mutaguchi's physical description and plan: Romanus and Sunderland, *Stilwell's Command Problems*, pp. 165, 195–198; Slim, pg. 290; Allen, pp. 150–170; Tuchman, pg. 438.

241–242  Operation 21: Allen, p. 150.

243  William Slim's plan to draw out the Japanese: Slim, pp. 298–299.

244  Mutaguchi receives orders: Allen, pg. 167.

244  Mutaguchi's Arakan feint: Allen, pg. 170.

246–251  Siege for the "Admin Box": Slim, pp. 234–244; Allen, pp. 170–190.

251  "British and Indian soldiers had proved themselves . . .": Slim, pp. 246–247.

251  Mutaguchi's windy rhetoric: Moser, pg. 148.

251–252  Slim's defensive preparations in India: Slim, pp. 285–296; Allen, pp. 191–193.

252  "Neapolitan ice": Slim, pg. 301.

252–255  Tongzang and the blockage of the Tiddum Road: Slim, pg. 298; Allen, pp. 195–206.

255  Slim's airlifts to Imphal: Slim, pp. 306–307.

255–256  Sangshank battle: Slim, pg. 300; Allen, pp. 212–227.

256  Manabu Wada characterization and quote: Tamayama, pg. 175.

256  thirty-eight hundred troops: Allen, pg. 234; Rooney, pg. 73.

256–257  Japanese sever Kohima water: Slim, pg. 316; Allen, pg. 235.

257  Sato advises Dimapur strike: Romanus and Sunderland, *Stilwell's Command Problems*, pg. 174; Moser, pg. 150.

257–258  triangular zone: Allen, pg. 235.

258  conditions inside Kohima perimeter: Allen, pp. 234–236: Rooney, David, *Burma Victory: Imphal and Kohima, March 1944 to May 1945* (London: Cassell & Co, 1992), pp. 77–78; Moser, pg. 151.

258 "pole charges": Allen, pg. 235; Rooney, pg. 77.

258–259 Lance Corporal John Harmon heroics: Allen, pp. 235–236; Rooney, pp. 77–78.

259–260 battle for tennis court: Allen, pg. 237; Rooney, pg. 79; Moser, pg. 151.

260 Kohima air drop: Rooney, pg. 81.

260–261 British last stand at Kohima: Allen, pp. 237–238; Rooney, pp. 81, 84.

261 Nettlefield quote: Moser, pg. 152.

261 "We complained bitterly . . .": Tamayama, pg. 175.

262 battle for Kohima shifts to British favor: Slim, pp. 320–324; Allen, pp. 266–275; Rooney, pp. 86–101.

262 "It was not surprising . . .": Tamayama, pg. 176.

262–263 battle for Tongzang: Allen, pg. 241; Rooney, pg. 38; Grant, pp. 72–80.

264 "At the time . . .": Author interview with Susumu Miyashita in Okayama, Japan, 2/14/01 and 2/15/01.

264 "The Strength of the Japanese army . . .": Slim, pg. 538.

264–265 battle for Imphal: Slim, pp. 318–346; Allen, pp. 246–260; Rooney, pp. 141–180.

265 "But sahib . . .": Slim, pg. 336.

265–266 "Continue in the task . . .": Moser, pg. 156.

266–267 relations between Sato and Mutaguchi: Allen, pp. 287–293; Rooney, pp. 98–100, 103–105; Moser, pp. 156–157.

267 Mutaguchi entertains requests for withdrawal: Allen, pp. 280–281, 296, 297–298, 299.

268 Mutaguchi requests withdrawal: Allen, pp. 307–308, 310–313; Rooney, pg. 180.

268 "In the end we had no ammunition . . .": Moser, pg. 157.

268 "Our path to safety . . .": Tamayama, pp. 177–178.

269 "I have killed thousands of my men": Moser, pg. 157.

270 graffiti at Mao: Moser, pg. 157.

## Chapter 17

271 13.5 million cubic yards of earth: *The New York Times Magazine* ("General Pick of Pick's Pike," by Tillman Durdin, Feburary 11, 1945); Ogburn, pg. 79.

271 pounds of earth moved: author interview with Luck Stone Quarries at Shadwell, VA, 4/14/03.

271 Seven hundred bridges and other facts: *National Geographic* ("Stilwell Road—Land Link to China," by Nelson G. Tayman, Bridge Engineer with the Army Engineers, June 1945); *Ex-CBI Roundup* ("Another Look at the Burma-Ledo Road," by Nels Brueckl, April 1992).

272 858th Engineer Aviation Battalion history: *History of the 858th Engineer Aviation Battalion* (unpublished), National Archives, Suitland Branch, Suitland, Maryland; *National Geographic* ("Stilwell Road—Land Link to China," by Nelson G. Tayman, Bridge Engineer with the Army Engineers, June 1945).

273–274 Sungshan: Romanus and Sunderland, *Stilwell's Command Problems*, pp. 354–360, 394–398; Tuchman, pp. 452–453.

274  sixty-two different pairs of Chinese-Japanese soldiers: from plaque at Sungshan, author visit 12/4/03.

274–276  Tengchung fighting: Romanus and Sunderland, *Stilwell's Command Problems*, pp. 390–395; author visit 12/4/02 and 12/5/02.

275–276  Li Shi Fu, author interview at Tengchong, 12/4/02.

277  Hsueh and the collapse at Changsha: White, pp. 70, 181–183; Tuchman, pg. 454.

278  Stilwell losing twelve thousand tons of guns and ammunition for Hengyang defense: Tuchman, pp. 472–473.

278  "The men walked quietly . . .": White and Jacoby, pp. 187–188.

278  Chennault offers one thousand tons of his own weapons, with conditions: Tuchman, pg. 472.

279  Roosevelt wants an enhanced role for Stilwell in China: Tuchman, pp. 480–481.

279  Chiang and the Chinese Communists: Tuchman, pp. 475–479; White and Jacoby, pp. 199–213.

280  Fourteenth Air Force bases coming under attack: Tuchman, pp. 480, 488.

280  "Chennault has assured the generalissimo . . .": Tuchman, pp. 458–459.

281  "the future of all Asia is at stake . . .": Tuchman, pg. 470.

282  "Today a fateful decision . . .": Tuchman, pg. 471.

283  "a hot firecracker . . .": Stilwell, *The Stilwell Papers*, pg. 333.

283  Stilwell, Hurley, and delivery of Roosevelt's letter to Chiang: Tuchman, pp. 493–494.

284  "What! No teapots? . . .": Tuchman, pg. 494; Stilwell, *The Stilwell Papers*, pg. 353.

284  "I've waited long for vengeance . . .": Stilwell, *The Stilwell Papers*, pg. 334.

285  "This will knock the persimmons off the trees!": Tuchman, pg. 495.

286  negotiations for Stilwell to remain in China: Tuchman, pp. 496–500.

287  Mountbatten choreography: Tuchman, pg. 436.

287  of "spontaneous vitality," "an absolutely first-class and apparently impromptu speech . . .": "The men loved it": Tuchman, pg. 436.

288  Stilwell's arrival at Kandy, Ceylon: Tuchman, pg. 473.

288  "like a duck hunter": Slim, pg. 254.

288  "Kandy Kids": Tuchman, pg. 473.

288  "I've got to quit eating with Louis . . .": Tuchman, pg. 473.

288  "Something wrong with Headquarters . . .": Tuchman, pg. 474.

288  "freeing the Kachins, etc.": Tuchman, pg. 475.

289  Japanese aimed at Kweilin and Liuchow: White, pg. 194.

289  "Thinks well of himself . . .": Tuchman, pg. 429.

289–290  "THE AX FALLS": Stilwell, *The Stilwell Papers*, pg. 345.

290–291  Stilwell's last days in CBI: Stilwell, *The Stilwell Papers*, pp. 345–349; Tuchman, pp. 502–504; White, pg. 225.

## Chapter 18

293   "It was always a disappointment . . .": Slim, pg. 366.

293   Scene at Tamu: Slim, pg. 366.

293   Twenty thousand to thirty thousand Japanese troops remained: Slim, pg. 378.

293   "Our problem . . .": Slim, pg. 380.

294   Chennault worries on Liangtang: Chennault, pg. 326.

294   Generalissimo assurance on Kweilin: Wedemeyer, Albert C., *Wedemeyer Reports!* (New York: Henry Holt, 1958) pg. 290; Moser, pg. 188.

294   Wedemeyer files all Stilwell/Chiang correspondence away: Wedemeyer, pg. 305.

294   "honey instead of vinegar": Wedemeyer, pg. 301.

294   Kweilin falls: White and Jacoby, pp. 190–194.

294   "The scattered reserves . . .": White and Jacoby, pg. 190.

294-295   Last days of Kweilin: White and Jacoby, pp. 190–193; Chennault, pp. 306–307; Moser, pp. 170–177.

295   "The last five soldiers . . .": White and Jacoby, pg. 191.

295   "If only the Chinese will cooperate!" and "political intrigues and false pride": Tuchman, pg. 517; Romanus and Sunderland, *Time Runs Out in CBI*, pp. 52, 165.

295-296   Frank Gleason episodes: White and Jacoby, 195–196.

296   fifty thousand square miles of Burma: White and Jacoby, pg. 259.

296   Slim's plan of attack for Shwebo: Slim, pp. 373–375; Moser, pp. 191–192.

297   "Stilwell's divisions . . .": White and Jacoby, pg. 259.

## Chapter 19

298   eighty-five hundred sorties: Moser, pg. 155.

298   754 tons of bombs . . . 20 percent more explosives: Romanus and Sunderland, *Stilwell's Command Problems*, pg. 251.

298-299   eight bridges in seven days: Moser, pg. 155.

299   Seventh Bomb Group as bomber gluttons: Henderson, William, *From CBI to the Kwai* (Leon Junction, TX: O & B Publishers, 1991), pg. 4.

299   hometowns and ages of T-333 crew: Henderson, pg. iv.

299-300   Chuck Linamen quotes, from author interviews 6/2/00 and 6/3/00 in Milford, Massachusetts; also 9/14/01 and 9/15/01 in Houston.

300   Bill Henderson quotes, from author interview, 9/14/01 in Houston, plus Henderson, pg. 47.

302   collective groan on April 3, 1945: Henderson, pg. 69.

302   "flack supressors" and "bridge busters": Henderson, pg. 70.

302   "night recon" B-24: Henderson, pg. 69.

303   "The choice was mine . . .": Chuck Linamen quote, from author interview, 6/2/00 in Milford, Massachusetts.

303   the target looked impossibly thin: Henderson, pg. 72.

303   bombing of wooden Kwae bridge: Henderson, pp. 71–73.

304  B-24 in spiral with Hamblett: Henderson, pg. 73.

304–305  Hamblett recollections: Henderson, pg. 73.

305–307  B-24 crash: Henderson, pp. 74–77.

## Chapter 20

308  "We were already tired and hungry . . .": author interview with Susumu Miyashita, in Okayama, Japan, 2/14/01 and 2/15/01.

309  Slim's forces monitoring the Japanese: Slim, pg. 408.

309  two X Force divisions flown to Kunming: Wedemeyer, pg. 290.

309–311  Situation with Chinese Communists: White and Jacoby, pp. 257–258.

309–311  Huang Chen and Communist victories in central China: White and Jacoby, pg. 258.

311  Fort Dufferin description: Allen, pg. 407.

311–312  Meiktila attack: Slim, pg. 412; Allen, pg. 398.

312  Kimura troop movements: Slim, pp. 408–409.

312  attack on Kangaw: Slim, pp. 460–461.

312  "There was no order to our withdrawal . . .": author interview with Sesumu Miyashita, in Okayama, Japan, 2/14/01 and 2/15/01.

313  Chinese/Japanese casualties between September 1944 and January of 1945: notes made by author at Lungling, China, 12/3/02. Also interview with Li Zhi Cai, director of Baoshan Museum of History, at Baoshan, Yunnan, China on 12/6/02.

313  attack on Pinghai: White and Jacoby, 259–260.

314–315  X and Y Force meeting: White and Jacoby, pg. 260; Moser, pp. 190–191.

## Chapter 21

Where not specifically cited, all information in this chapter is taken from Romanus and Sunderland, *Time Runs Out in CBI*, or from *Ex-CBI Roundup* ("The First Ledo Road Convoy," by William Boyd Sinclair, June 1989; "The First Ledo Road Convoy Ends," by William Boyd Sinclair, July 1989).

320  Wedemeyer's relations with Chiang: Wedemeyer, pg. 305.

320  Wedemeyer programs building trust: Wedemeyer, pp. 296–297; Moser, pg. 188.

320  Chinese Communists moving like a prairie fire: White and Jacoby, pg. 262.

321  "a very formidable object . . .": Slim, pg. 469.

321  taking of Mandalay hill: Slim, pp. 468–470; Moser, pg. 160.

321  "an immense edition of the toy fortress . . .": Slim, pg. 469.

321  assault on Fort Dufferin: Slim, pp. 421, 423.

321  Fort Dufferin surrender: Slim, pg. 423.

322  Slim visits tank units and jokes: Moser, pg. 192.

322  "The Sittang River crossing . . .": author interview with Sesumu Miyashita in Okayama, Japan, 2/14/01 and 2/15/01.

323  Judy Asti and Audrey Edwards: "With the American Red Cross on the Burma Road" (unpublished manuscript) by Judy Asti and Audrey Edwards.

323  Tengchong cutoff: *Ex-CBI Roundup* ("The Burma Road Engineers," by Robert F. Seedlock, July 1983).

328  "I wonder who put him up to that?": Tuchman, pg. 511.

329  By the time Okinawa fell: Tuchman, pg. 518.

329  "I have got to be an SOB or risk disaster": Tuchman, pg. 520.

330  "I am eminently suited . . .": Tuchman, pg. 523.

330  Stilwell's profound physical collapse: Tuchman, pg. 528.

331  dizziness, chills, and bouts of exhaustion: Tuchman, pg. 528.

331  "something suspicious in my liver": Tuchman, pg. 528.

331  Letterman General Hospital: Tuchman, pg. 528.

331  October 3 surgery: Tuchman, pg. 528.

331  confounding the doctors: Tuchman, pg. 528.

331  "Hey guys, Joe's back!": Tuchman, pg. 520.

332  desires and is awarded the Combat Infantry Badge: Tuchman, pg. 528.

332  "Say, isn't this Saturday?": Tuchman, pg. 528.

## Selected Books and Diaries Not Included in Notes

"A" Company, 9th Battalion, Royal Sussex Regiment. *Myitkyina to Mandalay: A Diary of the North Burma Campaign, 1944–1945.* Unpublished diary, London: Imperial War Museum.

Ankers, Leslie. *The Ledo Road.* Tulsa: University of Oklahoma Press, 1965.

Belden, Jack. *Retreat with Stilwell.* New York: Alfred A. Knopf, 1943.

Brett-James, Anthony. *Ball of Fire.* London: Gale & Polden, 1951.

Briscoe, D. A. "Peter," ed. *The Friendly Firm Remembers: Stories by the Members of the 194 Squadron RAF.* Victoria, B.C.: Windrush, 2000.

Callahan, Raymond. *Burma 1942–1945.* London: Davis Poynter, 1978.

Central Office of Information, prepared for South East Asian Command. *The Campaign in Burma.* London: His Majesty's Stationery Office, 1946.

Donald, David, ed. *American War Planes of World War Two* (Barnes and Noble/Aerospace Publishing, 1995).

Fergusson, Bernard. *Beyond the Chindwin.* New York: Collins, 1945.

Hunter, Charles N. *Galahad.* New York: The Naylor Company, 1963.

Li, Zhi Cai, ed. *The Expeditionary Army in China: Warfare in West Yunnan.* Baoshan: Yunnan Arts Press, 1999.

Smith, R. Harris. *OSS: The Secret History of America's First Central Intelligence Agency.* New York: Delta, 1972.

Spencer, Otha C. *Flying the Hump: Memories of an Air War.* Fort Worth: Texas A&M University Press, 1994.

Tsuji, M. *Singapore—the Japanese Version.* New York: Mayflower Dell, 1966.

United States of America War Office. *Merrill's Marauders.* U.S. War Department, 1944.

# Acknowledgments

First and foremost, I thank my wife, Janet, for her love, patience, and countless acts of kindness during the three years I've worked on this book. No matter if I am halfway around the world or in the next room, she remains the calm center of my life's sometimes wildly spinning wheel.

I also need to thank my children, James and Anna, who assented to their father's being an absentee parent off and on for nearly a year so I could complete the trio of expeditions this book required. I love you. Thanks for letting me back in.

Finally, one more burst of love and gratitude to my parents, Jim and Joan Webster in Chicago, who—for a lifetime now—have given me their strength. For that tireless marathon, I've dedicated this book to them.

In the United States, I thank Oliver Payne, Bill Douthat, Bernard Ohanian, and Bill Allen at *National Geographic* for generously sponsoring the third "Burma Road Expedition" and for helping me sort out that trip's welter of adventures and experiences upon my return. I also want to thank Steve Perrine and Dave Zinczenko at *Men's Health*, who kept the freelance assignments flowing during the writing of the book. Thanks also to Kathleen Burke, Don Moser, Jim Doherty, Beth Py-Lieberman, Jack Wiley, and Carey Winfrey at *Smithsonian* magazine, for all the support and work you've passed my way.

Hearty handshakes all around to the CBI Veterans Association, the Hump Pilots Association, and the Merrill's Marauders Association, for directing me to the people and stories worth telling. Of this wide-ranging group, I especially thank CBI radio engineer Ed Pollard (and his lovely bride, Stella), who served as emissary to these people and organizations, and Chuck Linamen, Mitch Opas, Roy Matsumoto, Bill Henderson, Ray Dahl, Scottie David, Andy Anderson, Joe Schoop, Ed Kennedy, Jim Fletcher, Joseph Ganlin, Jerry Haslip, Joseph Giordano, Frank Norton, Vincent Mocari, Leo Godbout, Ledo Road shovel operator George Erban, Joseph Davis, Ruby Davis, Wendall Phillips, Warren Jones, Orville Strassberg, Earl Cullum, and Boyd Sinclair.

In Charlottesville, nods to neighbors Grice and Ellie Whiteley, Ed and Suzanne Chitwood, and Donald and Anne McCaig for all their support.

At the National Archives in Washington and Maryland, I give kudos to Joe Giordano and Melissa Templeman for their terrific direction through the archives' vast resources. Likewise to Heather Wagner at the Hoover Library Archives at Stanford University.


In London, I want to thank Noel Gallagher; Richard Golland and Roderick Suddaby at the Imperial War Museum's accommodating Dome Reading Room; Alan Wakefield, David Bell and Emma Crocker at the Imperial War Museum's Archive; the Burma Star Association; the Chindit Society; the lads of the 194 Squadron RAF; the good people at 22 Jermyn Street (for providing a room); George Morley (for providing eats); Liam Gallagher, Alan White, Andrew Bell, and Gem Archer.


For travel in India, thanks to John Edwards of TigerMountain Travel in New Delhi, plus Jim Bever at the U.S. Embassy in Delhi, E. P. Teki at the Indian Embassy in Washington, and Sanjoy Changkakati and everyone at the Hotel Bhramaputra Ashok in Guwhati. In Arunachal Pradesh and Assam, big blessings on Bora Ete, Tabom Bam, Ozing Dai, Mhonchan Lotha, Ranjit Barooah, the entire Namshum family in Lohit (thanks again for the fishing gear!), and Rohinso Krisikro at Wakro.


In Myanmar, gratitude greater than the largest of golden *zedis* goes to U Hi'ton Hla (Tony) of Wildbird Tours in Yangon, the only man on earth capable of gaining me permission to visit Pangsau Pass. Also in Yangon, my thanks for hospitality go to

Jameson and Lynn Koe, Colonel Ye Htut, Htilar Sitthu, and to all the folks at my home away from home, Seasons Hotel. In Myitkyina and along the road, I must thank Shar Khan (King of the Burma Road), Ah-Gu-Di, Gum-Jaw-Na, the staff at the Paradise Restaurant and the Sumpra Hotel, Enrico Lum Khong, Ismael Khan, Mary Rosner, Michael Rosner, and Captain Kaung San Oo of the State Peace and Development Council, Sagaing Division. Also thanks to U Aung Ko and U Tin Win (at the Myanmar Embassy in Washington), who helped smooth my trips.

In Myanmar, my biggest thanks are reserved for U Thein Aung, better known as Jiro, who served as my guide, interpreter, friend, commiserator, and adviser on all three expeditions. May we visit again soon, my brother.

In China, thanks to Zhu Jing Jang in Beijing, Ge Shuya in Kunming, Guo Jing at the Yunnan Museum, and Li Zhi Cai of the Baoshan Museum of History.

In Japan, thanks to Atsumi Oda and Susumu Miyashita in Okayama, and to Denny Petite and Kei Honda in Tokyo. Also in Tokyo, huge applauding thanks to Naoko Hatayama of the Japan Foreign Press Center for her tireless work on my behalf, and also to Miss Haneda at the FPC.

In Paris and in cyberspace, I also need to say a quick "appreciate it" to Elizabeth Austin Asch, plus thank you to my sister, Susan, in Chicago, and my brother, John, in Sheboygan and Hong Kong for all their help and support.

And at last, gi-normous words of appreciation to those associated with the actual making of this book. First to Mark Jenkins, who graciously dropped the idea into my lap—and I owe you one. Second, to my agent Kristine Dahl at ICM in New York, who arranged everything. And, finally, to my editor, John Glusman, at Farrar, Straus and Giroux, who patiently supported this book—and its sometimes jungle-besotted author—until there existed this thing you now hold in your hands. Let's do it again. Thanks also to Aodaoin O'Floinn at FSG.

# Index